THE FLIGHT
OF THE CENTURY

CHARLES LINDBERGH & THE RISE
OF AMERICAN AVIATION

THOMAS KESSNER

OXFORD

UNIVERSITY PRESS

2010

OXFORD
UNIVERSITY PRESS

Oxford University Press, Inc., publishes works that further
Oxford University's objective of excellence
in research, scholarship, and education.

Oxford   New York
Auckland   Cape Town   Dar es Salaam   Hong Kong   Karachi
Kuala Lumpur   Madrid   Melbourne   Mexico City   Nairobi
New Delhi   Shanghai   Taipei   Toronto

With offices in
Argentina   Austria   Brazil   Chile   Czech Republic   France   Greece
Guatemala   Hungary   Italy   Japan   Poland   Portugal   Singapore
South Korea   Switzerland   Thailand   Turkey   Ukraine   Vietnam

Copyright © 2010 by Thomas Kessner

Published by Oxford University Press, Inc.
198 Madison Avenue, New York, New York 10016

www.oup.com

Oxford is a registered trademark of Oxford University Press

Library of Congress Cataloging-in-Publication Data
Kessner, Thomas.
The flight of the century : Charles Lindbergh
and the rise of American aviation / Thomas Kessner.
p.   cm. — (Pivotal moments in American history)
Includes bibliographical references and index.
ISBN 978-0-19-532019-0
1. Lindbergh, Charles A. (Charles Augustus), 1902–1974.
2. Air pilots—United States—Biography.
3. Aeronautics—United States—History—20th century.
I. Title.
TL540.L5K385 2010
629.130092—dc22
[B]   2010006082

1 3 5 7 9 8 6 4 2
Printed in the United States of America
on acid-free paper

B'EZRAS HASHEM

FOR RACHEL

"Colonel Lindbergh has displaced everything. . . . He fills all our thought. He has displaced politics. . . . [H]e has lifted us into the upper air that is his home. . . . We are all better men and women because of this exhibition in this flight of our young friend. Our boys and girls have before them a stirring, inspiring vision of real manhood. What a wonderful thing it is to live in a time when science and character join hands to lift up humanity with a vision of its own dignity."

Charles Evans Hughes,
New York Times,
June 15, 1927

CONTENTS

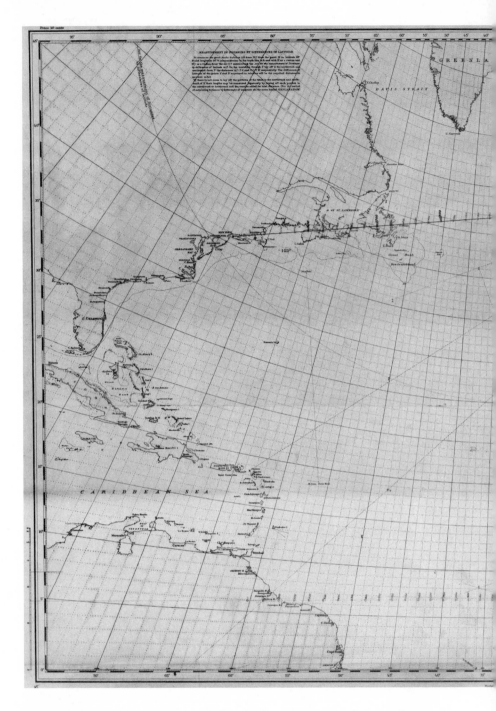

Lindbergh's handwritten annotation reads "Used in laying out great circle course for New York to Paris flight. San Diego Calif., 1927 C.A.L." *From the American Geographical Society Library, University of Wisconsin–Milwaukee Libraries.*

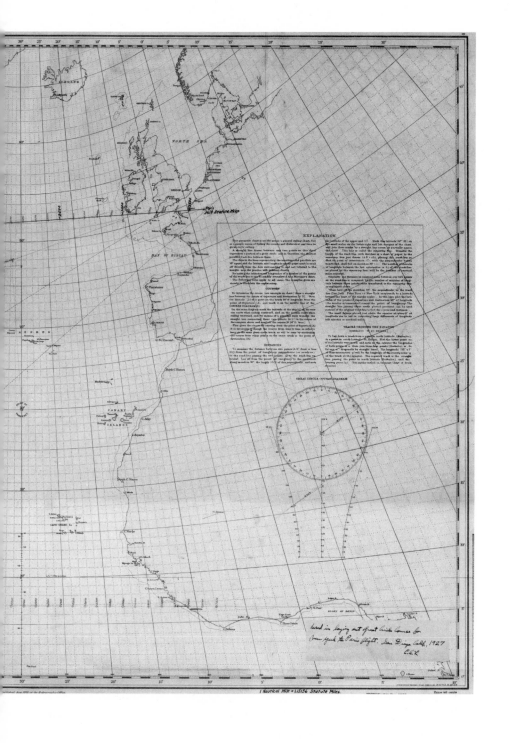

Used in laying out Great Circle Course for New York to Paris flight. San Diego Calif., 1927

C.A.L.

EDITOR'S NOTE

CERTAIN DAYS ARE INDELIBLY etched in our memories. Most readers of these words will recall with wrenching clarity where they were and what they were doing when they learned of the terrorist attacks of September 11, 2001. Those who are old enough will remember with similar sharp-edged horror the assassination of President John F. Kennedy on November 22, 1963. Dwindling numbers will recall the wild celebrations that broke out on V-J Day, August 15, 1945, or the shocking news of the Japanese attack on Pearl Harbor on "the date that will live in infamy," December 7, 1941.

Few are left, however, who can remember May 21, 1927. At 10:22 p.m. that evening, a clean-cut, boyish, twenty-five-year-old midwesterner landed his single-engine monoplane, *The Spirit of St. Louis*, at Le Bourget Aerodrome near Paris after a thirty-three-hour nonstop flight alone across the Atlantic Ocean from New York. A hundred thousand Parisians trampled down fences, bowled over security guards, and swarmed onto the tarmac to lift the "Lone Eagle," Charles A. Lindbergh, above their heads and pass him along—threatening bodily harm in their joyful eagerness to touch the hero who had done what many had tried but no one before him had accomplished. The news of Lindbergh's flight flashed around the world via cable, radio, and print media. He became an instant global celebrity whose fame lasted not for fifteen minutes but for years. No individual and no single event in history so thoroughly captured the imagination of millions. "From this day at this place," announced France's air minister, "will date a new era in world history." Richard Byrd, famous in his own right for his pioneering flight to the North Pole and a contender with Lindbergh in the race for a nonstop transatlantic flight, generously praised Lindbergh for having achieved "one of the greatest individual feats in all history."

The story of Lindbergh and his flight of the century has been told by many authors, including Lindbergh himself, but none has told it better than Thomas Kessner in the pages that follow. Though we know how the saga of Lindbergh's thirty-three tense hours in the air comes out, Kessner's gripping narrative will keep a reader at the edge of his or her seat. But this book is much more than a chronicle of the famous flight, more than a biography of Lindbergh, more than a profound meditation on the triumphs and tragedies of Lindbergh's life, though it is all of these. Above all it is an incisive and highly readable exposition of the theme expressed by the subtitle: the rise of American aviation.

Before 1927, aeronautics in the United States lagged behind European nations, especially France. Orville and Wilbur Wright had made the first successful flights in 1903, but the demands of war and anticipated future wars caused Europeans to forge ahead in flight during the 1910s and 1920s. Although the U.S. Post Office inaugurated airmail service, in which Lindbergh won his initial spurs, plans for commercial air transport were more advanced in Europe than in the United States. The excitement generated by Lindbergh's flight changed everything. Almost overnight, scores of American cities built new or improved existing airports; new airlines were incorporated; and investors poured money into all aspects of airplane design, manufacturing, and operations.

Lindbergh became an active leader in these ventures. His fame and flying skills made him a superb advocate for American aeronautics. He flew endless hours over North and South America, Europe, and Africa—with his wife Anne Morrow Lindbergh as copilot—mapping flight routes and establishing crucial navigation aids. Lindbergh helped launch or develop several airlines, including Pan Am and TWA. American aviation leapfrogged over the European leaders, and though the Great Depression cramped progress for a time, Lindbergh's pioneering achievements endured as one of the most important factors in the evolution of American aeronautics.

Lindbergh also launched—unwittingly and unwillingly—another modern phenomenon: celebrity culture. A loner who cherished privacy, he was unprepared for the unparalleled attention he attracted. Journalists dogged his footsteps. The kidnapping and murder of his first child, the sensational trial of the alleged kidnapper, the tabloid reporters and paparazzi photographers who continued to threaten the safety of his family all drove him to move abroad from 1935 to 1939. The Lone Eagle espoused isolationism and expressed admiration for the order and efficiency of Nazi Germany. Like other heroes, Lindbergh had a tragic flaw— a lack of empathy. Kessner deals sensitively but straightforwardly with this facet of the flyer's complex character.

In any event Lindbergh's contributions were never really in doubt. "He had advanced American commercial aviation to international leadership," writes Kessner, "changing forever the interplay of time, distance, trade, travel, big business, diplomacy, and defense." Although he lived to the age of seventy-two, Lindbergh's major contribution to America—and the world—came in his twenties, and in particular on that spring evening in Paris in May 1927.

James M. McPherson

INTRODUCTION

ON A RAINY FRIDAY MORNING, May 20, 1927, Charles A. Lindbergh, a twenty-five-year-old air mail pilot from Minnesota, with limited flying experience, fired up his small single-engine monoplane and took off for Paris from New York's Roosevelt Field on Long Island. Constructed in a mere sixty days by a little-known San Diego aircraft company, the *Spirit of St. Louis* was so simple in design that some referred to it as flying fuel tank. Stripped of every extra ounce, the plane carried five sandwiches, a couple of canteens of water and its six-foot-two pilot scrunched into the tiny cockpit. With his forward vision entirely blocked by a huge fuel tank, Lindbergh relied on a bank of primitive instruments and a set of home made navigation plans to take him on a journey no one had ever completed before. Half a dozen men—in the most advanced multiple-engine planes, equipped with state-of-the-art guidance and communications systems—had previously attempted this flight and perished.[1]

He had no radio and flew alone across a thirty-six-hundred-mile course, in his modest silver vehicle of wood, cloth, and metal. Much of the flight was over uncharted ocean. Battered by sleet storms and hazards he had not even imagined, he tested the limits of human endurance, staying awake for close to sixty hours straight, the last thirty-three hours alone with his machine in the air. The sheer terror, of knowing that any let-up meant certain death kept him awake, but only barely. During the twenty-second hour of his flight, he found himself surrounded in the cabin by shapeshifting phantoms that resembled humans but had no substance. These strangely familiar forms revealed to him secrets of the heavens but none remained with him after the flight. As suddenly as they came aboard his cockpit they left, leaving him to complete his historic journey alone.[2]

Against all odds, thirty-three and a half hours after his take off, Lindbergh touched down at Paris's Le Bourget airfield. He expected a bit of trouble because he had no visa and but a few cents in his pocket but he did not expect the exuberant welcome that greeted him. Tens of thousands of starstruck French citizens came streaming at him "as if," wrote the poet Harry Crosby "all the hands in the world are . . . trying to touch the new Christ."[3]

The next day the delighted American ambassador to France wrote back to Washington about the young flier's "divine genius." Paris lionized him. In London, just a few days later, the British abandoned all reserve in welcoming Lindbergh. All this was prelude to the unprecedented celebrations waiting for him back home in the United States. One clearly overwrought journalist described the Lindbergh phenomenon as "the greatest event since the Resurrection."[4]

Years ago in a review of *New Yorker* writer Brendan Gill's 1977 biography *Lindbergh Alone*, William F. Buckley, Jr., wrote that despite devoting an entire book to Lindbergh the "sharp-eyed Gill" had somehow failed to "explain why it is probably true . . . that Lindbergh was the most famous man of the 20th century," and why he became "even more famous as the years went by?" And despite hundreds of books that have offered revealing accounts of Lindbergh's life, Buckley's challenge has remained largely unanswered. What was it about this event and this man that so captured the imagination of the world and accounts for his enduring fame?[5]

He cured no deadly diseases. He ended no wars, uncovered no fresh continent; he made no scientific discoveries. He did not invent jazz or write a great novel or stir the American conscience with his eloquence. In fact, Lindbergh's flight across the Atlantic was essentially an endurance stunt, part of a sporting competition that was soon replicated and greatly exceeded.

Nonetheless his daring exploit has achieved a timelessness reserved for those transporting events that capture the spirit of the times. In 1967, forty years after the flight, *Time Magazine*, in a special edition celebrating American heroes, described him as the "first real hero of the machine age and in a sense the last." And today, more than eighty years after his flight, and after a life filled with much controversy, Lindbergh's renown persists. In a time of cyberspace and galactic exploration, this story of a man and his machine challenging and overcoming the elements continues to tug at American memory. Other fliers made records, but he made history.[6]

Each age creates its heroes. In the years after World War I, Americans turned away from grand abstractions and the tainted fields of politics and war, and placed new emphasis on palpable accomplishment. In sport, in art, and in life, bold, riveting action took on great importance. Americans reveled in the pure action of

Babe Ruth sending baseballs screaming out of ball parks, the mighty KOs of a Jack Dempsey, and the iron determination of marathoners sitting alone atop tall flagpoles. But these achievements lacked resonance and Americans quickly wearied of faux transcendence.

In these years as Americans sought surcease in normalcy they tired finally of the narrow mission of prosperity, yearning for a more compelling national signature. "It's as if they'd caught an angel that talks like Coolidge," Ernest Hemingway said of Lindbergh. This son of farm America, who had tinkered in the solitude of the woods and waters, offered a welcome affirmation of pioneer values and grand aspirations. In search of something clean, solid, and upstanding, Americans embraced this young man of singular skill, grace, and courage who after having conquered the sky, refused to be distracted by the pull of easy wealth and purposeless fame, respected Prohibition, had no girl problems, and worked hard for no better reason than to do his chosen task perfectly.[7]

But if his flight captured the world's attention—"Such men," proclaimed the German newspaper *Vossiche Zeitung*, "mark the path of humanity; they are the pacemakers of technical progress; they set the pace for their eras" making it possible for lesser men "to reach the highest mountains without climbing"—it was his transforming influence on American life that accounts for his lasting significance. His flight inaugurated America's Air Age, propelling a nation where trade, travel, and transportation were conveyed by rail and road into the modern aviation era.[8]

In the mid-nineteenth century the United States had committed vast resources to establish the world's most extensive railroad system but years later it refused to do the same for aviation. Despite pouring a huge fortune into building an air force during World War I, the United States allowed its flight industries to wither following the conflict while Europe forged a broad program of subsidized development.

Lindbergh's flight and widely covered air tours made Americans air minded, setting off a vast aviation boom. Air mail surged, new air routes proliferated, aircraft manufacture increased, and passengers flocked to the airports. Overnight college students turned to careers in aeronautics. Investors, ever alert to the fresh new thing, poured millions of dollars into aviation research, development, and production. And in a very brief span of time large new aviation companies formed colossal cartels that catapulted America's air industry to world leadership.

Lindbergh played a critical role in every major step forward, working closely with federal authorities while at the same time directing planning and development for both Pan Am and TAT ("the Lindbergh Line"), the forerunner of TWA. He became not only the voice and face but also the soul of American aviation, insisting on policies that promoted credibility, safety and professional service. His pervasive influence shaped aircraft design, route planning, flight operations, as well as national and international air policy as he helped mold America's air empire.

All his life Lindbergh sought to be in control, to govern his life by his own strict and disciplined plan. The entire flight project was laid out in a series of action lists. His flight plan to Europe was meticulously sketched out. The load he carried was obsessively controlled to the ounce; he even trimmed the margins off of his maps to save weight! Before setting out to find a wife, he prepared a list of traits that he intended to look for. Later he even prepared and orchestrated his own funeral. Touched off by the flight, Lindbergh's renown and influence continued to grow, yet before very long that influence came to be shaped and channeled by others.

Lindbergh foresaw nothing of what occurred after his landing, and for a full year after Paris he laid no more plans as events overtook his every imagined next step. He had hoped that after he won the $25,000 Orteig prize and paid off his debts he would have a little money left over and land a good job; the flight opened a new world for him, one for which he had prepared no guide.

Starting in Paris others' plans took over. The remarkable American ambassador Myron Herrick, took the untutored young flier under his wing, arranging his appearances, helping him with his speeches, and assigning embassy staff to go through the sacks of mail that came pouring in. Herrick's son Parmely arranged an advisory group of responsible men to oversee Lindbergh's financial affairs. In the course of a single hectic week the unsophisticated air mail pilot was transformed into a world-class personality.

Once Lindbergh returned to the States, others took over the task of translating his fame to broader purpose. At first it was the St. Louis coterie that raised the money for his flight. But they were quickly supplanted by an elite high-powered group who were not only committed to advancing American aviation, but also had the wherewithal to make it happen. A J. P. Morgan banker took charge of Lindbergh's finances; a former Assistant War Secretary handled his personal business; and the head of the largest aviation foundation paid him a salary and looked after his welfare. In the countless books about Lindbergh these men—Dwight Morrow, Henry Breckinridge, and Harry Guggenheim, respectively—are mostly portrayed as being motivated by friendship and concern for the young hero.

But there was much more than benevolence and warm regard behind their involvement. Around Lindbergh, these men and their circle constructed their ambitious agenda for aviation. He got to plan his trips and write his own speeches but they orchestrated the larger forces around him to mold Big Aviation.

Lindbergh had insisted that he would not be commodifed, but in this effort he was entirely complicit.

Lindbergh's flight profoundly stirred the imagination of the nation and the world, promoting an era of good feeling and international reconciliation. It raised hopes for an age beyond war even as it recast military strategy and paved the way for America's air dominance, converting, in the words of one scholar, "the disreputable raiment of American aviation . . . into the garment of empire." It launched American commercial aviation and ushered in an era of air monopolies.[9]

"The flight" also distorted his life. It raised him, a poor farm boy from a broken home, to riches and international acclaim. Overnight it brought him into contact with kings, prime ministers, and adoring millions. No one could imagine a more compelling Horatio Alger story as he became the most famous American of his time. As best he could, he tried to ride the tiger of celebrity for the benefit of causes he held dear, aviation at first, and then American isolationism in the run-up to World War II, and later environmentalism. But he was entirely unprepared for the relentless intrusions of the new celebrity age. The media and especially the tabloid press cast him in a spotlight that had never shone with such painful intensity and the attention cost him tragically. Bitter at America's unrestrained press and holding it responsible for his son's kidnapping and death, in the last days of December 1935, eight years after his momentous flight, he secretly packed his family and belongings and fled America for Europe.

The Lindbergh era was over. The man whose flight symbolized the élan of 1920s optimism had little to offer a depressed America in the 1930s. He was no longer innocent, bold, and gallant. He had suffered tragedy but unlike, for example, Franklin Roosevelt (with whom he clashed bitterly), he could take nothing from his own suffering to inspire his countrymen. His boyish charm had curdled into a corrosive disillusion and dogmatic racism. Not long before, he had represented the most appealing qualities of American life and character. Now, as he expressed a cold disdain for Europe's democratic societies while openly admiring its totalitarian regimes, he flirted with Nazism.

With the Depression widespread and the threat of European fascism looming, Americans faced more immediate problems than corralling new horizons. Even before World War II, the mass bombing of Guernica made clear that the hope that aviation would usher in a brighter age was dashed. Nor were Americans now disposed toward unexamined worship of a rags-to-riches millionaire.

He had come from nowhere, a dark-horse flyboy in a competition that had lasted many years, to become the most popular celebrity of his time, perhaps of all time. Hurdling entrenched barriers of time, space, and distance he conquered the most elusive prize of his day. He achieved the American dream, advanced progress, captured the world's attention, and rose to great influence as he directed America's gaze skyward. Following his flight the airplane recast global geography as essential exchanges in money, travel and trade were speeded and diplomacy accelerated. New industries sprouted. Men and women came to know intimately parts of the globe they had thought of as strange and unfriendly. Humankind thought seriously about a new world without walls. He influenced the aspirations of millions and fortified Americans in their sense of world leadership.

He dominated his times but those times changed. Like his own private world, the world at large became deeply clouded. The nation he had projected as a land of endless progress and optimism became mired in a demoralizing depression and as global conflict loomed he turned his back on its destiny. He would go on to one of the most controversial second acts in American history and fame of an entirely different sort, but in the pivotal span of his influence, in the first iteration of his fame, he made a vast difference.

"I was born," he wrote, when "the great forces of science and technology had already been loosed, but horses still dominated the streets and Orville Wright had not yet made the first power-sustained airplane flight." Born in the heart of a traditional rural world he helped transform, he was a man of powerful ambitions that were shaped by the land and by his nurture. The story of the flight begins with his youth at the dawn of the American Century and the age of manned flight.[10]

THE FLIGHT OF THE CENTURY

YOU'RE YOUR OWN BOSS

AS A YOUNG BOY Charles Augustus Lindbergh lived in one of the most impressive houses in the entire Minnesota lumber region, two miles from the town of Little Falls on 120 acres of lush pinelands. Shortly before Charles's birth in 1902, his father hired workers to clear acres of high woods, taking care to spare the most imposing of the great pines and hardwoods, and to carve out an expansive lawn, lay decorative flower beds, and plant a vegetable garden. In the center of the property they erected a splendid three-story house on high ground at the edge of a bluff overlooking the Mississippi River.[1]

Lindholm Manor boasted thirteen rooms, seven of them bedrooms. Each of the receiving rooms was handsomely appointed and finished in a different fine wood. The house's maple floors were varnished to a high shine; there were two indoor bathrooms, a billiard room, a reception hall, and a large furnace that passed heat through hot-water radiators. The furniture, heavy and expensive, came from Grand Rapids, Michigan. Fronting the grounds, which eventually included a caretaker's house, a barn, and other structures, were imposing black iron gates. In the stillness of the evening one could hear the sound of water and birdsong. Charles's mother, Evangeline, described the setting as "wonderfully peaceful and beautiful."[2]

This house befit the prominent Lindbergh family, headed by the respected attorney, bank director, and successful real estate developer Charles August Lindbergh. He had traced a remarkable success story in the course of a single generation. Brought to the United States as an infant shortly before the Civil War, he grew up not far from Little Falls. His own father, Ola Månsson, had been a small farmer in Sweden who dabbled in politics and won election to the Swedish Parliament in 1847 as a supporter of progressive change. Ola also directed the

Bank of Sweden's loan office and in 1858, after some of the loans he had guaranteed were not repaid, he was charged with embezzlement.[3]

After all his appeals failed and with jail looming, the fifty-year-old Månsson prepared to flee the country. When his wife of twenty-four years, the mother of his eight children, learned that Ola had fathered a child with a restaurant waitress the year before, she refused to join him. Undeterred, Månsson swept up his twenty-one-year-old mistress and infant son, Karl August, and slipped away to Liverpool. From there they shipped to Quebec and crossed the border into the United States. Settling on a patch of virgin territory edging the frontier in the new state of Minnesota, Ola took a new name, August Lindbergh, and on August 4, 1859, weeks after arriving in Minnesota, he declared before the district court his intention to become a U.S. citizen.[4]

Although Ola had not worked with his hands for a long time, he cleared the land before the cold set in, put up a twelve-by-sixteen-foot log cabin, and prepared the soil for crop farming. With only two other settler families as neighbors amid thousands of Indians in the surrounding territory, he hacked out a new American life. Less than two years after he made his new start, a sawmill blade slashed his arm. A surgeon arrived days later, too late to do anything but amputate. Like many of his compatriots Karl was learning that America's promise would not be claimed without hardship, but also like many he rose to the challenge. He made do with one arm, supporting his growing family and building a solid future.[5]

Karl (now Charles) August, the only one of the seven Lindbergh children born in the Old Country, grew into a strikingly handsome lad, an inch short of six feet, with jet black hair, arresting blue eyes, and a cleft in his chin. His deadly accurate marksmanship brought the family many a supper. As a youth he was a dreamer, often skipping class to wander the woods. At age twenty, faced with the prospect of unrelieved farm work for the rest of his life, he enrolled in a demanding two-year course of preparatory study at the Grove Lake Academy. From there he went on to complete a law program at the University of Michigan at Ann Arbor, financing his studies by hunting and selling small game fowl. The Minnesota bar admitted him in 1883, the year he graduated.[6]

Charles August settled in Little Falls, fifty miles from where he grew up, a compact village community of fewer than five hundred souls, situated near a slight rapid along the Mississippi River. Farming, furs, and pine formed the principal underpinnings of the local economy, with the giant Weyerhaeuser Lumber Company employing many of the Scandinavian and Polish immigrants who pioneered in the area. In 1887 C. A. ("I do not remember my father's friends calling him by any other name than C. A.," Lindbergh later recalled) married Mary LaFond, the daughter of one of Little Falls's original settlers, and went on to build a thriving law practice, specializing in real estate and land sales. The largest companies in the region became his clients, and C. A., privy to information about the best deals, bought local property, turning a nice fortune on his investments. He also bought mortgages and helped found a bank.[7]

By the 1890s Little Falls was bustling with five thousand inhabitants and C. A. Lindbergh was its leading lawyer. But he retained the heart of a yeoman, lecturing his bank colleagues more than once, "To make money, in my opinion, is not the sole purpose of a bank."[8]

C. A. and Mary raised their two young daughters, Lillian and Eva (a third daughter died in infancy), surrounded by the comforts of a prosperous life. In 1898 this life was shattered when doctors found that Mary, not yet thirty-one, had an abdominal tumor. She died of complications following surgery. Inconsolable, C. A. sent his two young daughters to a boarding school, moved out of his large home, and for a long time sought relief in solitude.[9]

In time he met twenty-four-year-old Evangeline Land. University educated, beautiful, and vivacious, she came from the big city of Detroit and a family of doctors. Her father, Dr. Charles H. Land, ran an innovative dental laboratory; her grandfather, Edwin Albert Lodge, was a highly regarded doctor, specializing in homeopathic cures; and three of her uncles were also doctors. When economic reversals forced her father into bankruptcy, Evangeline's mother suggested that she might put her University of Michigan degree in chemistry to practical use. With few opportunities for women scientists, Evangeline inquired at a placement service about teaching jobs and learned of an opening in Little Falls. Evangeline was intrigued by the prospect of teaching miners' children chemistry on the frontier and perhaps even having "a great St. Bernard dog following her back and forth to school." She arrived in Little Falls early in September 1900 but encountered no miners' children and, alas, no St. Bernard, but she did land a job teaching chemistry, physics, and three other science courses.[10]

From the beginning it was clear that she was misplaced in the small town, but she did find one thing to write home about: "the best looking man in Little Falls," C. A. Lindbergh, a man of sterling reputation who did not "drink, chew or smoke." C. A. was equally captivated by this urbane young woman. Her flair and education stood out in the dour frontier community; her charm and spontaneity lifted his spirits, restoring the joy that had gone from his life.[11]

She could ignore the eighteen-year difference in their ages, could promise to make the best of raising two rambunctious girls, but Little Falls she found suffocatingly narrow, with "two saloons for every church and a church for every creed," none of which much interested her. Four months after she began teaching, her job at the high school ended following a confrontation with the school principal. Disappointed with everything in Little Falls but the "brightest lawyer in Minnesota," she wrote her mother, "Surely no matter what becomes of me & my friend the lawyer, Little Falls, Minnesota shall not see so very much more of this chicken." In January they became engaged. Evangeline knew all would be well after they married, moved to Detroit, and lived happily ever after.[12]

They were married on March 27, 1901, at her parents' home in Detroit and then honeymooned for ten weeks, touring Pike's Peak in Colorado, San Francisco, Sacramento, and a good part of the rest of California. They hiked, rafted, and camped out along Oregon's Columbia River and then boarded the Northern Pacific Railroad for Minnesota. Several years before, C. A. had bought a large property where he had gone for walks to ease his sorrow after his wife died. It was a stunning sylvan expanse near the Mississippi's waters, and he commissioned a house for his new bride on this property, hoping that it would convince her of Little Falls's charms.[13]

The elegant couple easily climbed to the top of local society. They entertained the leading families in the county—the Weyerhaeusers, the Williamses, the Tanners, and the Mussers—with games of pinochle and with music and singing. With her "rippling sense of Irish humor," Evangeline put on plays for her guests. One of Lindbergh's early recollections is of his mother nervously pacing in powder and wig preparing one of her skits. He remembered his parents as the "most handsome pair in the city of Little Falls."[14]

Nevertheless, there were few bright lights in Little Falls, and the most popular local male pastime, drinking in bars, did not impress Evangeline. She longed for her family and for Detroit's more vibrant social life. But soon she set these thoughts aside and turned to planning for a new arrival; within two months of her marriage she learned that she was pregnant.

At the end of January, C. A. brought Evangeline to Detroit as they had planned so that her uncle, Dr. Edwin Lodge, could deliver the baby. On February 4, 1902, Evangeline gave birth to a nine-and-a-half-pound boy. C. A. arrived in Detroit two days later to join his wife, proudly announcing that his son's name would be Charles Augustus Lindbergh. He was not a true junior because his father's middle name, August, was one syllable shorter, but he was still often referred to as Charles Jr.[15]

Evangeline hoped to raise young Charles in Detroit, where he could learn much from her father and uncles. There, with a good education and the family's example, he might carry forward the family tradition in medicine. But six weeks after she gave birth, she trekked back to Minnesota. C. A. wanted a different environment for his son: a life shaped by the land and framed by its rough-hewn beauty. He himself felt a strong attachment to nature's prairie rhythms and aggressively defended the virtues of the rustic life. He hoped that the new home he was building for Evangeline would soften her attitude about life on the agrarian frontier.[16]

Little Charles was pampered by servants and housekeepers. Surrounded by a beautiful landscape—he recalled later that as a toddler he could see the Mississippi from his room—his parents kept him outdoors for much of the day, and he played with assorted animals on the farm: goats, horses, cattle, and especially a succession of dogs, who became his closest friends.[17]

His most dramatic recollection was of August 6, 1905, a Sunday: "A huge column of smoke is rising from our house, spreading out and blackening the sky." Amid shouts and panic a nurse called out to the three-year-old child to avert his eyes from the razing of his home. "Charles, you *mustn't* watch," the agitated nurse insisted, inadvertently searing the image in his mind forever. "Our entire house . . . sunk into the stone walls of its basement," he wrote many years later. "Father will build us a new house," his mother said consolingly, though even she did not believe it.[18]

Much more than the house went up in smoke. Soon after the blaze C. A.'s investments suffered reversals. He and a partner had developed properties, anticipating Little Falls's expansion, but they speculated on the wrong side of town and the family fortunes plummeted. It did not take long for expenses and taxes to burn through their savings. Less than six months after the fire he informed Evangeline that they were strapped for cash. "They both, our little daughters, have got to work and it will be better for them," C. A. wrote. He did not have to add that she would have to curtail her own extravagant spending.[19]

For all her gifts and her husband's fine local reputation, Evangeline never felt comfortable in Little Falls. C. A. had not denied her much, but even her frequent shopping binges could not still her growing unhappiness. Small-town life depressed her. She resented the chattering wives and old ladies who criticized her spending sprees, gossiped about her difficulty controlling two resentful stepdaughters (now hardheaded fifteen- and eleven-year-olds), and regaled one another with tales of her temper tantrums. Nor did she appreciate living in the shadow of memories of C. A.'s sweet and unassuming first wife, whom everybody had loved.[20]

Even as a small child Charles realized that his mother felt out of place. He later explained that her "experience and aptitude" had not equipped her for life in Little Falls. She felt roughly handled in the coarse social environment: "My mother's protected family life in Detroit, and her education in an elite girl's school did not form a good background for Minnesota, one-generation-beyond-the frontier life." She quickly lost patience with her husband's unexpressive manner and his crude, at times mean-spirited practical jokes, often at her expense. She resented what had become of her young life, increasingly secluded from the stimulation and excitement of the urbane world that she had left behind.[21]

They were spectacularly mismatched: he a middle-aged man who cherished the agricultural lifestyle with its fixed horizons and daily routines, and she, much younger, craving the quicker tempo and diverse texture of city life; he a serious, intellectually disposed man of stolid temperament, and she a vibrant young woman whose charms lay in her directness and boisterous sense of fun. Her mercurial moods clashed with her husband, "who," C. A.'s biographer reports, "did not show emotion at all."[22]

The house was not going to be rebuilt, and Evangeline knew that her husband, brought low by his reversals, would be too busy fighting off his own demons to make her or her son happy. By the end of 1905 he had stopped trying. Little remained to hold the marriage together beyond C. A.'s refusal to divorce. "Their relationship," Lindbergh later recounted, "was a tragic situation."[23]

Like his father before him, C. A. turned to electoral politics, running for the seat in Minnesota's Sixth Congressional District in 1906. A friend warned him that elective office would mean spending many weeks away from home, little realizing how satisfactory this might prove to C. A.[24]

C. A. was a striking presence on the campaign trail. He had helped subdue the wilderness as part of the frontier generation and held a genuine regard for the agrarian way of life. He spoke forcefully, bridling with outrage at modern America's dismissive treatment of common farmers and workers and about the need to defend wholesome homespun values against vile urban influences. Around the spirit of populist discontent he molded an articulate program of opposition, exhorting grangers to fight for reforms, including currency inflation and restraints on corporate privilege. "My father loved the farm," Lindbergh would later recollect, "but not to farm." Fixed in Lindbergh's early memory was how different his father was from their neighbors, absorbed by such issues as tariffs, monopolies, and the "Wall Street interests."[25]

C. A. attacked the incumbent congressman, Democrat Clarence B. Buckman, for working private deals with local lumber interests. The erstwhile real estate speculator and banker railed at the "perfidious" eastern banks and dark "money powers" like J. P. Morgan and Kuhn, Loeb. If farmers fail to organize, he warned, "big business will take everything they've got. This country belongs to the people, but they haven't learned how to run it yet." He won the election and went on to serve for five succeeding terms until 1917.[26]

With C. A. immersed in electoral politics and the girls off at school or working and later married, the family of three spent summers in Little Falls and much of the rest of the year in Washington. In Little Falls there was at least the pretense that they were a family but in Washington there was no denying the estrangement. Evangeline and her son lived in a rented apartment or a series of boarding-houses, while C. A. roomed in a hotel or slept in his office. In the summer of 1909, long after the marriage had expired in fact, Evangeline again asked C. A. for a divorce. Fearing the political fallout, he implored her to "let things slide," promising to treat her fairly. Evangeline resigned herself to a sham marriage.[27]

Periodically they would reconcile, only to dissolve into bitter bickering, or worse. C. A. would call Evangeline a "bloodsucker" and on at least one occasion struck her. There were rumors that he had become involved with his stenographer, leading an infuriated Evangeline to hold a gun to his head. (Lindbergh told C. A.'s biographer that his mother never fell in love with another; he could not be as certain about his father.) It was a time when divorce and being raised by a single parent were uncommon, and the situation left deep scars on Lindbergh. "I am awfully sorry for the boy," his father wrote. "He feels so hurt."[28]

Lindbergh lived mostly with his mother, who encouraged him to spend time with his father, but C. A. was consumed by his work. Up at four in the morning, he exercised and breakfasted on an apple or an orange before setting off for his office, often by five. Lindbergh remembered his father as always so preoccupied—composing a speech, meeting with colleagues, or working with constituents—that even when they were in Washington he did not get to see much of him.[29]

Lindbergh also remembered seeing the great men of the nation, catching a glimpse of the portly president William H. Taft taking his morning exercise; meeting Theodore Roosevelt, whom his father supported in his 1912 bid for the presidency; and witnessing Woodrow Wilson sign a bill at the White House that his father had sponsored. He would wander the halls of Congress, causing mischief, gliding through the corridors of the Capitol on skates or locking toilet doors from the inside. Once he dropped lightbulbs one by one from atop the House Office Building to the street below.[30]

Neither parent did much disciplining, and he took full advantage of all the immunities granted to the cute son of a sitting congressman. Congress never impressed him. It was too somber a place and too much like church, another place to which he was dragged once his father became elected. Both places were full of talk: "Sometimes you got a headache as you listened." And both were "too hot, [and] rather stuffy," when the really interesting things were outside.[31]

His mother understood his urge for the outdoors and for freedom from structure. She would pull him out of class every once in a while to take him for hikes in the woods or through the Rock Creek Park Zoo; other trips included visits to national shrines and museums, which he enjoyed, especially the Smithsonian, which filled him with a sense of wonder. Mostly, though, he liked to play alone in Washington's vacant lots, spending hours daydreaming and digging for rocks and artifacts that he imagined were fossils millions of years old. He would gaze in fascination as the wind caught a sheet of paper and sent it soaring through the air. Why, he wondered, was it more complicated getting rocks and scraps of wood airborne, while a shingle, despite its weight, would float up in a draft?[32]

In the end nothing in Washington could really take the place of his home in Little Falls. Charles disliked the capital's crowded rows of unappealing redbrick houses, the snarl of traffic that filled the streets with an unnatural cacophony, the rushed hullabaloo, the tall structures that blocked the sunsets, the artificiality of the man-made environment. City life was a prison. He missed Little Falls's uncluttered rusticity, the "feel of branch to muscle," the solitude and open woodlands. He yearned for late spring and his annual return to the high blue skies of the Minnesota farm.[33]

Years later, in a book devoted to his flight to Paris, Lindbergh vividly reconstructed virtually every step of his return to his "extraordinarily beautiful" home in Minnesota. He described walking two miles from the railroad station, past local shops and saloons, stopping in at the grocer's, and then, after passing the last of the towering telephone poles, arriving at "real country," where he made his way down a woodland path, past a white cedar fence, a gray horse barn, and thick honeysuckle bushes before catching a reassuring glimpse of the modest dwelling that had replaced the razed mansion. He would rush to his room, remove his city duds, don overalls, grab his dog Dingo, and take off to run barefoot in the woods.[34]

Charles loved to hunt, fish, swim, and skip over logjams created by the drifting Norway pine sent downstream by the large timber companies up north. He would lie naked in the sun, stretched out on one of the stalled logs, and even in the late fall he would dip into the icy waters, relishing the afterglow: "You can walk along the beach afterward, in well below freezing air, and still feel warm, completely naked. It is a wonderful experience." In his memories the country formed an idyllic past.[35]

He and his mother would plant a vegetable garden, raising sweet corn, potatoes, peas, beans, tomatoes, and other vegetables. C. A. would visit for a few days and while there do his best to detach the boy from his mother's apron strings. In the little time that he shared with Charles he strove to make him manly and resilient, rushing the hardening process, sometimes to the point of tears. Boys, he would say, "must get knocked and knock back in order to stand the world's knocking later."[36]

C. A. presented his son with a .22 caliber Savage hunting rifle when he was seven. When he was "almost old enough to hold it to [his] shoulder," about a year later, Charles graduated to a Winchester twelve-gauge automatic. Father and son would go off to shoot wild fowl and deer near the Mississippi. For all his mixed emotions, Lindbergh reveled in his father's trust, recalling, "[C. A.] let me walk behind him with a loaded shotgun at seven, use an axe as soon as I had strength enough to swing it, drive his Ford car anywhere at twelve. . . . My freedom was complete."[37]

C. A. also taught the boy to swim: "Father didn't have much use for water wings." When Lindbergh was around eight his father took him to the river bank; there Charles dropped his clothes and waded "neck-deep in the slimy, smooth-stone bottom, and slipped into a hole that was over [his] head." Suddenly he was tumbling, splashing, and swallowing water while struggling to surface. Finally he came up, coughing and quite shaken. He expected to see his father running toward him, but instead C. A. stood at the shore laughing. Decades later, the sting of his father's unconcern remained fresh, but he had passed a test and he was proud of winning his father's regard: "I realized that I was swimming by myself. . . . Now that I could both shoot and swim, I became his partner." When Charles was older C. A. would take him rafting through rapids on the headwaters of the Mississippi and camping with a band of Chippewa.[38]

Each excursion had a subtext: to stiffen the boy so that he would be able to care for himself when his father was not there to protect him. "YOU and I," C. A. told his son, "are able to take hard knocks. . . . We'll get along no matter what happens." There were times when they roughhoused when the boy could hardly catch his breath, but he kept quiet: "I was proud of not needing much help." Some criticized C. A. as too demanding, even austere, but Lindbergh internalized his father's outlook and remembered him as an intellectual, a warm, even witty man in whom he felt "the deepest kind of love."[39]

The strained family situation and his father's frequent absences contributed to a painful shyness in the youngster. Evangeline, concerned that Charles made few friends, even paid some local boys to come over and play with him. But he pursued his solitary diversions, hammering together a flat-bottomed boat for excursions along the river, reading, collecting stamps, rocks, and coins, and wandering through the woods and along the water, filling his days making friends with nature. He could seclude himself in a small tree house for hours: "I loved to stand up on the high branches in a wind, while the tree swayed and the leaves fluttered." It was not that he had a "'zone of gloom' around [him]," Lindbergh later explained, but that he genuinely preferred solitude, spending hours on his back in the tall bushes, "hidden from passersby, watching white cumulus clouds drift overhead, staring into the sky." "How wonderful it would be," he dreamed, "if I had an airplane. . . . I could fly up to the clouds and explore their caves and canyons."[40]

Though he spent only a few months a year on the farm, Lindbergh would always remember himself as a farm boy, dwelling among "secret, violet guarded dells," where he learned to respect the "the value of water, trees and sky—and solitude." Anyone who did not delight in these elements, he thought, "had not really lived."[41]

One day a pilot flew into town in a biplane, offering air rides for a dollar a minute, but Evangeline was too scared to allow Charles to go up. He too had fears and uncertainties. They came out in the dark in nightmares filled with drowning bodies along the river, thieves and violent men hidden in the woods, and dangerous animals and deadly snakes.[42]

Twice a year, on the way to Washington and back, mother and son would stop off to visit her family in Detroit for about two weeks. Charles would be excited to see his beloved grandpa Charles H. Land, the inventive, unorthodox dentist who met them at the train station, "face beaming, [with his] familiar white mustache and gold-rimmed spectacles," and took them to the aging gray frame house at 64 West Elizabeth Street.[43]

Grandfather Land's house was like a quaint museum filled with artifacts collected by an eccentric curator. Natural curiosities shared space with the mounted head of a Rocky Mountain sheep. One box held a human skull, another a preserved tarantula and a horned toad; piles of old *National Geographic* magazines lined the walls, offering transporting profiles of faraway places. In a corner a curio cabinet exhibited polished stones, mounted butterflies, fossils, and even part of a mammoth's tooth. Off in another corner stood toy soldiers, fire engines, and an entire arsenal for Charles's war games. There was also the Stevens single-shot .22 caliber rifle that the boy fired at a range that Grandpa Land set up for him in the basement.[44]

Charles was equally fascinated by the fully equipped laboratory where Dr. Land crafted his dental inventions. He remembered the absorption with which he watched his formidable grandfather, whose hands seemed capable of making and fixing anything. From this lab emerged new techniques in restorative dentistry, anesthesia, and silver amalgam technology. Strewn with dental refuse, porcelain pieces, and old teeth, the lab struck the boy as a wizard's workshop. Dr. Land gave his grandson the run of the place, withholding only the most delicate instruments and dangerous chemicals. He indulged the endlessly curious child, answering his questions, teaching him how to cast metal and work with electricity, and instructing him in the biology of various birds, plants, and flowers.[45]

Talk at the Land dinner table engaged the boy in discussions about science and theories that could be put to real tests in the downstairs laboratory. Nature's mysteries seemed so much more meaningful than politics or sermons (another of his least favorite things). Science was firm, factual, and empirical. "Your experiment either works or it doesn't," regardless of whether you are a true believer or not, a Republican or a Democrat. Recalling the conversations at the Land home, Lindbergh would later write, "Science is the key to all mystery. With this key man can become a god himself. Science is truth; science is knowledge; science is power."[46]

Land helped him understand the layered complexity of progress. Yes, moving pictures were a great innovation, but they also exposed youngsters to temptations that were unwise and even dangerous. Technical advances in automobile technology were breathtaking, but at the same time they raised immeasurably the destructive potential of a common accident, and Land predicted they would multiply greatly the loss of human life. Charles decided that he wanted to study biology and perhaps become a doctor.[47]

His schooling, however, could best be described as episodic. At first he was home-schooled. Then in 1909 Evangeline enrolled Charles in the second grade. His single strongest memory of that year was "waiting, waiting, waiting for the school to close." His subsequent education was a peripatetic affair, stitched together from irregular attendance at no fewer than twelve different schools. Not until college did he spend a full academic year in one school.[48]

Usually Evangeline would bring him to Washington after classes had already begun and take him off to Detroit before finals were completed in the spring. She did not hesitate to remove him from class for mother-son trips, sometimes for as long as ten days at a time. Two and three times a year Charles would change schools, requiring round after uncomfortable round of painful adjustments to new teachers and classmates.[49]

He made few friends among his classmates and usually avoided school games and activities, dismissing it all as boring. He preferred excavating empty lots and staring up at the sky or tinkering in his grandfather's laboratory. A teacher recalled that "while not eccentric, he was what you might call 'individual' in the extreme." Once, when the teacher called on the class to form a circle for a demonstration, Charles refused to hold anyone's hand. He did not seem much concerned with the impression this left, and his classmates responded in kind, calling him "Limburger" or just "cheese." Little wonder that he "thoroughly disliked school . . . [and] had little interest in [his] teachers." He applied himself to his studies rather sparingly, consistently finishing the school year at or close to the bottom of the class. In his early autobiography, *We*, Lindbergh devoted fewer than two hundred words to the first eighteen years of his life.[50]

The truth, as he himself admitted later, was that, like his father, he was a loner who "didn't feel dependent on friends at all." Isolation may also have been his way to protect the secret of his broken home, or maybe an even more sensitive matter. Evangeline suffered from a family strain of mental instability. Describing her stepmother's behavior, one of C. A.'s daughters insisted, "Only insanity explains it."[51]

If Charles's formal schooling was weak, Evangeline nonetheless did her best to expose him to more of the world than was common for the average schoolboy. In addition to their regular Minneapolis-Washington-Detroit loop, she took him to Philadelphia, New York, Atlantic City, and, for an entire semester, to California. In January 1913, when he was not yet eleven, she took Charles for a three-week junket to Panama, traveling through forests and jungles, observing the wildlife firsthand, visiting old castles and dungeons, and watching as powerful mechanical shovels reduced imposing mountains to rubble to gouge out the Panama Canal. Charles remembered, "We walked over the concrete bottom of the still-empty Miraflores locks, stared at the rusting hulks of machines the French engineers had abandoned to the jungle . . . and hired a horse and buggy to take us to Pirate Morgan's Castle." The year before, he attended the Aeronautical Trials at Fort Myer, Virginia, where he saw an airplane race an automobile around an oval track.[52]

Education-poor but experience-rich, he learned to drive C. A.'s Ford Tourabout (they named her "Maria"), which remained on the farm for much of the year. Evangeline would have eleven-year-old Charles drive her around town, and soon enough he did the same for C. A. during the campaign season.[53]

In the fall of 1915 C. A., aiming for higher office, ran in the Senate primary. Now fourteen, Charles was pulled from his classes in Washington to drive his father around Minnesota. At these campaign stops he was exposed to his father's political views, which C. A. also spelled out in several books. In *The Economic Pinch* he wrote, "We must unshackle ourselves from the arbitrary domination of property privilege over human right." Firmly in the western progressive tradition, he lashed out at the "rigged" economic system and called for urgent reform. His son found driving along the rude paths and unfinished roadways by far the most interesting part of the campaign.[54]

Though progressive in so many respects, C. A held a number of regressive views as well. He believed that America's black population, albeit the "happiest of all races," was hopelessly inferior and destined to a subordinate role in social and political life. He thought that African Americans came from a climate that disposed them toward sluggishness and did not deserve the vote. As for Catholics, he worried that they might be conspiring to bring the United States under papal domination, and in a House speech demanded a "true and impartial investigation" of these claims. C. A.'s notions about race left a deep imprint on Charles's thinking.[55]

Yet it was not race but war that dominated the 1915 campaign, with C. A. taking an impassioned stand against American involvement in World War I. As national policy tilted from strict neutrality toward preparedness and support for the Allies, he joined the isolationist bloc in Congress, accusing "Wall Street's profiteers" of fanning war hysteria to make profit from the conflict. "At no time in the world's history," he thundered, "has deceit been so bold and aggressive as now in attempting to engulf all humanity in the maelstrom of hell."[56]

The speeches had little effect on Charles. "I was not old enough to understand the war's basic issues," he later wrote, "yet I felt a pride in the realization that my country was now powerful and influential enough to take a major part in world crises. We would fight for good and right, and for freedom of the seas." His father's indignant criticisms he later dismissed as courageous but ill-informed. Most voters agreed. In the four-way primary race early in 1916 Representative Lindbergh garnered the fewest votes of any candidate. The seat went to the well-known trust buster, preparedness advocate, and future secretary of state Frank B. Kellogg.[57]

Few were surprised by C. A.'s defeat. He had by this time become an annoying scourge, out of step with his times. Even admirers conceded his irrelevance. On March 3, 1917, two days after joining a tiny minority to vote against arming U.S. merchant ships (the bill passed 403–14), he closed his congressional office and returned to Minnesota, to author another attack on the money trust and the war, *Banking and Currency and Why Is Your Country at War?* The tract proved so offensive to the U.S. Justice Department that, according to some accounts, federal agents had the publisher destroy every copy.[58]

That year Evangeline and Charles did not return to Washington. Almost as soon as he registered for his junior year at Little Falls High School his mother decided that they should drive out to Redondo Beach, California. Charles did all the driving for the forty-day journey and did not begin class there until late October. Despite all the days he had already missed, Evangeline withdrew him from class for a tour of the West Coast stretching from San Diego to San Francisco.[59]

Charles did not know that Evangeline made the trip to Redondo Beach to visit C. A.'s ailing twenty-nine-year-old daughter, Lillian. She had contracted tuberculosis and gone to the West Coast with her husband, Dr. Loren Roberts, in search of a cure. There was no cure, and Evangeline hoped to see her one last time. However, younger sister Eva, still bitter toward her stepmother, barred Evangeline from seeing the dying Lillian. C. A. wrote Eva that he would not interfere with her decision. He took the occasion to tell her how badly he felt about having left Charles, but he "would rather be dead one hundred times" than live with Evangeline, who "was a slave to her moods and her demons." He closed the letter by imploring his daughter to yield a little for Charles's sake, telling her how sorry he felt for the boy. But the bitterness ran too deep and she would not relent. Years later Eva admitted, "Charles was hurt terribly."[60]

Once more mother and son picked up and left in the middle of the school year, returning to Little Falls to care for Evangeline's mother on the farm during the last months of her life. Isolated with her son and dying mother on a lonely farm, Evangeline became more and more fearful. She slept with a loaded Smith & Wesson revolver under her pillow and came to depend more than ever on Charles to protect her emotionally and physically. He helped her with the housework, drove her where she needed to go, and learned to deal with her moods. Lightning terrified her; at the sound of thunder he would scramble to her side to hold her hand. When on several occasions local hooligans sent bullets whizzing across the river for amusement, Charles drove them off with a combination of rifle shots and a round from a ten-gauge saluting canon. But for all of his devoted care the relationship never broke through its fixed boundaries of reserve. The closest thing to emotion between them was when Evangeline shook her only son's hand good night.[61]

C. A.'s political career was over, but he had no intention of going back to the farm. He tried to return to practicing law but spent more time writing cantankerous books about the money trust, publishing a progressive magazine, and fashioning quixotic plans for his political comeback. None of these efforts brought much success, and he no longer provided Evangeline and Charles with regular support. He did stock the farm with some heifers and sheep while he kept deeding small slices of the property to Charles, pushing the teenager to assume responsibility for providing for his mother and himself.[62]

Charles did his best to make a go of the farm, adding some milk cows and purebred rams, tending the livestock, working the land, and maintaining the property. Martin Engstrom, who ran the town's hardware store taught young Lindbergh how to carry out many of the countless tasks that fall to a small farmer. Charles would steal away from the farm to spend hours at Engstrom's workshop, absorbed in learning about farm technology. Lindbergh ordered all the latest mechanical equipment, including a tractor, a gangplow, and the first milking machine in Morrison County. Engstrom remembered being impressed with the teenager's aptitude for machine mechanics.[63]

Meanwhile Charles still had a year of school to complete, and the responsibilities kept piling up. As he began the fall semester of his senior year he had to prepare the farm for the winter, bring in the crops, fill the lofts with hay, and thicken the walls to insulate against the coming cold, all while he trekked two miles to and from classes each day. To pull in some extra cash he took on work as the local agent for the Empire Milking Machine Company.[64]

With so many fathers off at war this problem of overburdened students was not lost on the school administration. Little Falls High School adopted a Food for Victory Program, promising each member of the senior class graduation credit for all their courses if they spent the year farming the land. Charles took up the offer, later recounting, "I was among the first to leave school." He did not return until he came to claim his diploma in June. Later, when journalists sought to fill in his background by interviewing his schoolmates, they were surprised to find that few actually knew him because he spent so little time in class. Even when he did attend he usually ran home right after the bell to work on the farm. He did not date or participate in the social scene. The son of a man who had become more notorious than famous, he was not interested in discussing his father. "I guess I knew him as well as anyone," Roy Larson of the class of 1918 told an interviewer, "but I didn't know him well. He always kept to himself." C. A. wrote Charles that he admired his ability "to buck the world alone": "I love that quality in you as a person."[65]

Charles was working so hard that he did not even have time to help C. A. with another campaign. This one, for governor in 1918, turned ugly.[66]

C. A. tended to get carried away on the stump, and failure and frustration loosened his tongue even more as he accused the president, leading citizens, and supporters of the war effort of various dark conspiracies. In return he was denounced as a traitor and pro-German. In the fevered war atmosphere this led to some nasty confrontations. Mobs broke up his speeches, pelting him with eggs. He was dragged from platforms, run out of several towns, and hanged in effigy.[67]

Not entirely sympathetic, Charles wondered if his father didn't "spend too much time thinking about problems he [didn't] have to solve." What was the point of being so different, so at odds with the rest of the community? Later in life Lindbergh tried to capture his father's essence for a biographer, beginning with perfunctory praise, "He himself was, I think, a great man," and concluding that in certain ways C. A. reminded him of Henry Ford, the automobile mastermind whose "erraticism," Lindbergh wrote, "was, I think, fully as great as his genius."[68]

Little about his father's career appealed to him. C. A.'s conspiratorial view of American society he found too sour and unpersuasive. He also dismissed his notions about the government's ability to achieve large goals and improve lives on a vast scale. He granted that his father "felt closely allied to the 'common man'—to the farmer, the wage-earner, the small businessman, and he was constantly endeavoring to advance their welfare," but he was hard-pressed to explain how C. A. actually made a practical difference in their lives.[69]

Exactly how little his father's antiwar politics appealed to him became clear in his plan to join the armed forces as soon as he turned eighteen. If the war continued he wanted to be trained as an army pilot. His father and mother both disapproved, but the signing of an armistice in November 1918 wrecked his plans and, his parents hoped, put an end to his notions of flying in dangerous airships.[70]

He thought this was silly. If it was physical danger that they feared, the farm was not without its own hazards. A malfunctioning gangplow had come within inches of crushing him once, and on another occasion a collapsed ditch submerged him in sod up to his neck so that he had to claw his way out inch by inch. Then a horse team he was driving was felled right under him by lightning. An eventful life, he liked to think, was full of dangers.[71]

From the annealing experience of his youth Charles Lindbergh emerged with a sense of discipline and fearlessness, a risk-taking loner with a gift for mastering mechanical processes and complex details. From his mother he took a sense of wonder and inquisitiveness, and from his father a strong code of midwestern rectitude and exacting standards. His father had hardened him with a regimen that affirmed the boy's sense of isolation as a manly and soul-satisfying solitude. From his mother's parents he inherited a regard for the age's fresh ways of knowing, for scientific theory, empirical wisdom, and practical technology. He came to respect technological precision; it provided a shape and structure that his home life lacked.

He had put together enough of a high school education to earn a diploma and he had the farm. But the farm was not making money. The world market for produce collapsed with peace, depressing prices. The best a small farmer could do was scratch out a living. But this generation of farm boys was no longer satisfied to be scraping by. "After leaving it, I always missed the farm," he wrote later, but the sentiment sounded almost dutiful. Farm life had drained the joy from Evangeline's years in Little Falls, and the clotted, bucolic environment threatened to severely pinch his own future as well. The day of the small farmer was passing. In the fall of 1920 he leased the farm to tenants who worked the land.[72]

If not farming, and not politics, and no army training, then what? C. A. invited Charles into his law practice, though exactly what there was to share in that dead office was a real question. In any event Charles was not interested. C. A., the erstwhile enemy of speculating wealth, then tried his hand at investing in Florida property, hoping, like William Jennings Bryan, another good populist with a yen for a quick buck in Florida real estate, to hit the jackpot in unearned increments. He invited Charles to join him. They could easily clear $100,000, he promised. But C. A. was living out of his aging Buick, eating from tin cans, and sleeping in a folding tent under the open sky, all of which failed to convince Charles of the great possibilities.[73]

His parents agreed on precious little, but on one thing they saw eye-to-eye: if Charles was not going to make the farm his future he must go to college. It is true that on the evidence of his poor grades and uneven application to formal school-work it would be bold to call him a promising student. Nonetheless he was an excellent "learner," with a methodical, retentive mind; higher education could open a fresh path for him. He agreed. He would pursue a degree in mechanical engineering.[74]

From his days in Grandpa Land's basement of wonders, Charles had been cap-tivated by machines and instruments. Bicycles, cars, boats, motorcycles, and all kinds of mechanical devices, especially those that provided rapid transport, fasci-nated him. He took them apart and put them back together to learn how they worked. Driving the family car in those years meant keeping a complicated machine in good repair by yourself, and he also learned a lot from Mr. Engstrom's workshops. In this heyday of the dabbler savant, of Edison, Ford, and the Wright brothers, Charles was entranced by the promise of machinery.[75]

Technology was transforming the world around him ("You are living in an extraordinary time," he recalled his father telling him), and its significance extended beyond the new inventions and labor-saving appliances. The new spirit of speculative thought and imaginative experimentation made far more of the world accessible, replacing an inscrutable cosmos filled with biblical miracles with one anchored in empirical knowledge.[76]

Science and mathematics he barely understood, but the precision of gears and shafts and pistons working in unison to shape man's new environment captured his imagination. Riding a motorcycle enthralled him, and not just for its speed in getting from here to there. He was beguiled by the "mechanical perfection" of his Excelsior motorcycle: "I liked the feel of its power, and its response to my control. Eventually it seemed like an extension of my own body, muscles and movements." Intuitively he grasped that machines expanded life's reach and the scope of what was possible.[77]

He was particularly interested in aeronautical engineering. The idea of flight touched him in ways that no profession could: "I could work hard to understand magic in the contours of a wing." The best place for such training was at the Mas-sachusetts Institute of Technology, where he had no hope of passing the entrance exams. So late in the summer of 1920, eighteen-year-old Lindbergh motorcycled off to the University of Wisconsin at Madison, where he was accepted into the engineering program.[78]

He had grown into a lanky six-foot-two-and-a-half-inch young man, strikingly handsome, with blond hair, a dimpled chin, clear blue eyes, and a winning smile. He remained withdrawn—others would call him painfully shy—and very attached to his mother. Never a particularly motivated student, he expected that college would be different. However, his reason for choosing the University of Wisconsin did not augur well for his new seriousness: "My primary reason for choosing the University of Wisconsin lay in the fact that it was located on the edge of a lake. I loved water, and didn't like to think of spending four years away from it."[79]

Nor did it did bode well for his independence that Evangeline beat him to Madison, taking a job in a junior high school there and renting an apartment a short distance from the campus for them to share.[80]

Soon college education seemed a poor second choice to his dreams of designing charmed vehicles that carried men through the air. He could not summon the will to crack the books; he bristled at the idea of required courses. He had hoped that college would allow him to fashion his own education, but it was the same story as in high school: uninteresting courses foisted upon him by an unyielding curriculum. Of the eleven schools he had gone to before college he said, "There's not one that I have enjoyed. Their memory chafes like a slipping rope against the flesh of childhood." Now number twelve promised little improvement. Not the idea of college, not the serious level of his classmates, not the renown of the professors who taught him—none of this changed his notion that education must be practical and hold his interest. He wanted to "stop taking English and concentrate on engineering . . . maybe . . . take an aeronautical engineering course." Only there was no such course at UMW.[81]

Classes became a chore, and he often failed to do his assigned work or relied on his mother to write his assigned papers. He was unaccustomed to sustained effort: "The long hours of study at college were very trying for me." A short burst of thought would send his mind wandering, pining for the outdoors. He'd get up from his books and go off to swim or ride his motorcycle on the country roads. Lacking the poise for social intercourse, he kept mostly to himself: "I thoroughly disapproved of many phases of college life, and my motorcycle was a means of getting away from a life I did not like."[82]

His best college work, Lindbergh later recalled, "was on the rifle team." He joined Wisconsin's Reserve Officers Training Corps team in his freshman year and was assigned to field artillery: "[I spent] every minute I could steal from my studies in the shooting gallery and on the range." The student who recoiled at the demands of the classroom took easily to ROTC's disciplined regimentation. College courses that sought to introduce doubt or complexity did not appeal to him. ROTC, on the other hand, offered certainty, rules, and a prescribed regimen with a tested leader barking the orders. Charles thrived during the grueling six weeks of field artillery training at Camp Knox in Kentucky. It offered a break from life with his mother and an opportunity for male bonding and physical challenges.[83]

For the first time someone held him to a schedule with no option to go off dreaming in the woods: "I learned to know the imperative note and thrill of the bugle. We rose early, worked hard, slept soundly. The strictness of discipline amazed me, but I enjoyed it, and realized its value in military life." And there was the fillip of danger when he and his companions took chances shooting twenty-five-cent pieces out of each other's fingers at a range of fifty feet. His rifle team took first place in the national ROTC competition and he took home the prize as the best marksman on the team.[84]

ROTC commendations and the fact that the severely straitlaced Lindbergh avoided cigarettes, booze, and chasing coeds were not enough to warrant continued matriculation, though. After three semesters, two of them on probation, his most noteworthy achievements remained on the rifle range.[85]

To no one's surprise, at the end of the third semester, in February 1922, Evangeline received a letter from the registrar informing her that "the record made by Carl [sic]" was "very discouraging," with failing grades in a number of subjects. "It seems to me," the registrar continued, "that Carl is quite immature, and that a boy of his temperament might do better in some less technical courses than engineering. In my conversation with him during the semester he seemed to agree with me on that point." As a result of this "poor record, the Sophomore Adviser Committee decided . . . that Carl should be dropped from the University."[86]

Charles was less than devastated. His greatest regret was losing ROTC: "Ten years of school were like that—mining for knowledge, burying life—studying in grade school so I could pass examinations so I could get into high school—studying in high school so I could get into college—studying in college so—but there I broke the chain. Why should I continue studying to pass examinations to get into a life I didn't want to lead—a life of factories, and drawing boards, and desks."[87]

All along it was something else he wanted: "to enter aviation and learn to fly. I had become fascinated by airplanes." Later he rhapsodized about this epiphany: "Science, freedom, beauty, adventure: what more could you ask of life. Aviation combined all of the elements I loved."[88]

His father thought the occupation was too dangerous. Even Charles had to admit that the image of pilots was not the best. They were thought of as daredevils with nerves of steel, "wild with drink and women, and who placed no value on their lives." But Charles was determined, and C. A. finally accepted his son's choice, telling him, "You're your own boss."[89]

ACOLYTE OF THE AIR

WHEN IT WAS FIRST wheeled onto the historical stage late in 1903, the awkward contraption hardly seemed like an agent of far-reaching change. Assembled from wood, fabric, wire, and glue (lots of it), this primitive flying machine—a glider with an attached power source—nonetheless augured aviation's future, ushering in an age of air travel whose potential for trade, diplomacy, communication, war, and exploration was as yet unimaginable.[1]

Notions of flight had beguiled human society from ancient times. Apollo's son Phaeton rode a sun chariot through the skies, while Sinbad of Baghdad cut through the air mounted on his great bird Roc, and the flying horse Pegasus carried Perseus through the ether. Daedalus fashioned wings to escape the island of Crete with his son, Icarus, only to have the enterprise turn tragic when the youth passed too close to the sun. Leonardo da Vinci's notebooks show his great mind working out the possibilities of human flight.[2]

By the end of the nineteenth century, advances in engineering, materials science, and aerodynamics removed flight from the realm of mythology. George Cayley, Otto Lilienthal, and Francis Herbert Wenham offered explanations of such concepts as lift, control, structure, and propulsion, and the journal *Aeronautical Annual* made fresh research and new data widely available. Based on his studies of how birds remained aloft Lilienthal created curved wings with which he glided off mountains and hilltops. After about two thousand experiments in this early form of hang gliding the aeronautical pioneer finally crashed in 1896, breaking his back. He died the next day with the words "Sacrifices must be made" on his lips.[3]

Two ambitious bicycle manufacturers with no formal training solved the riddle of sustained powered flight in a heavier-than-air vehicle. Even before the turn of the twentieth century Wilbur and Orville Wright of Dayton, Ohio, had become obsessed with creating an air transport vehicle. The Wright brothers did not graduate high school but followed the latest discoveries in aeronautics through voracious reading in the technical literature, as well as their correspondence with aviation researchers, such as the aeronautical pioneer Octave Chanute, author of the classic text *Progress in Flying Machines*.[4]

In principle flight technology had already solved the question of how to power a plane into the air. The Wrights focused on how to control powered flight once it was airborne. They would steal time away from building bicycles in their shop to perfect a glider, but in time this effort made way for the more ambitious work of creating a flying machine. By 1900 they had hired a mechanic to run their bicycle business so that they could seclude themselves in their flight workshop on the sand dunes in Kitty Hawk, North Carolina, where the climate offered a fine environment for their experiments. Later, in what turned out to be a pivotal development, they erected a wind tunnel of their own design to better control test conditions.[5]

Financed by profits from bicycle sales and from a print shop they owned, the Wrights designed, built, and tested seven successive flying machines, moving from simple kites to gliders and then versions of powered airplanes large enough to carry a passenger into the air. Ultimately they settled on a biplane with two parallel sets of wings on top and bottom that by means of a system of wires that twisted the tips of the wings could be kept straight and level and be made to bank and turn.[6]

On December 14, 1903, at Kitty Hawk twenty-seven-year-old Wilbur Wright was strapped into the third version of the Wright airplane, a 605-pound craft powered by a gasoline engine of the brothers' own manufacture. The plane stalled almost immediately on takeoff, dropping to the ground with a disappointing thud that damaged the rudder. It took three days to complete the repairs and prepare for a second test. This time it was twenty-three-year-old Orville who got into the harness on Thursday, December 17, 1903.[7]

On this cold winter day with fierce 27-mph winds, Orville lay prone on the lower wing of the biplane and started the twelve-horsepower engine. Released from its moorings the plane, with Wilbur running alongside, accelerated along the launching track and then lifted into the sky, moving forward under Orville's control for 120 feet. The flight lasted no more than twelve seconds, but the brothers were elated. Later the same day Wilbur managed to keep the craft aloft over a distance of 852 feet for just under a minute. The question of whether controlled powered flight in a heavier-than-air vehicle was possible had been settled; what remained was to extend the distance and make the machine practical and safe.[8]

Over the next two years the Wright brothers increased time aloft so that it was no longer measured in seconds and feet but in minutes and miles. By 1905 their Flyer III, capable of banking and making a full circle turn, flew for more than half an hour over a space of twenty-five miles. To Charles Edouard Jeanneret-Gris, then a student in Paris and later better known as the famed modernist Le Corbusier, the airplane represented "the vanguard of the conquering armies of the New Age."[9]

The Wrights had notified many newspapers of their impending flight in 1903, but they were ignored, and for the next five years their breakthroughs remained uncelebrated. In 1907 the U.S. Army passed on studying or buying the flying machine. But by late 1908, after the Wrights had tested an improved biplane that stayed aloft for an hour, the world began to take notice. Orville carried out trials for the War Department at Ft. Myer in Virginia while Wilbur demonstrated his Flyer before enthusiastic crowds in Europe that included the kings of Spain and England. By year's end the Flyer had completed a seventy-eight-mile trip in two hours and twenty minutes.[10]

Aeronautics was the new thing, and aviation news was covered on the front page (with pictures!). The *New York World* took on a full-time reporter to cover the air beat and soon other dailies followed suit. Popular magazines published articles about aviation firsts, competitions, and the parade of exciting advances. Millions read about the dramatic new "air ships" that moved in all three dimensions, like a bird. In 1909 an estimated one million New Yorkers witnessed Wilbur Wright fly past the Statue of Liberty, and Orville declared the dawn of a new era, "the Age of Flight."[11]

In July the French airman Louis Blériot flew a monoplane (one set of wings instead of two, cutting down on resistance and facilitating greater speed) of his own design from Calais, France, across the English Channel to Dover, England, a flight of thirty-seven minutes. He claimed a prize of £1,000, a princely sum.[12]

From the beginning it was clear that aviation needed to accomplish two not entirely unrelated aims: advance its technology and convince the public that these flying machines had practical potential. To increase public awareness and showcase progress aviation enthusiasts sponsored contests, offering substantial awards and attracting a coterie of "fancy fliers" and birdmen. Instead of funding research and development, promoters, aiming to improve a particular aspect of aircraft design or operation, would announce a prize, spurring others to invest their own time and money on perfecting improvements and innovative techniques. These contests were actually flight tests in which the pilots sometimes paid with their lives for bad theories or poor design.[13]

The various contests helped Europe take the initiative in flight away from the United States. By 1910 aviation offered more than $1,000,000 in prize money, and much of it was from European promoters. *Scientific American* magazine, an early aviation advocate, attributed the rapid progress in French aviation to "the encouragement received from wealthy men, manufacturers and newspapers, in the shape of large prizes for performing feats in the air."[14]

Newspapers often sponsored these contests. Publishers knew that sensation sold papers and that columns on men racing through the air, defying death in pursuit of large purses, did wonders for circulation. In 1906 the British press baron Lord Northcliffe, Alfred Charles William Harmsworth, owner of both the *London Daily Mail* and the *London Times,* offered £1,000 to the first flier to cross the Channel from Calais to Dover (the prize claimed by Blériot). He offered ten times as much for the first to complete the trip from London to Manchester; in 1910 this honor also went to a Frenchman. Another of his prizes went to the first airman to make a circuit around England. In 1913 Harmsworth announced a prize of £10,000 for crossing the Atlantic from the United States, Canada, or Newfoundland to Great Britain or Ireland within seventy-two hours.[15]

American publishers joined in promoting these air contests. The *New York Times, New York World,* and *New York American* each offered prizes ranging from $1,000 to $50,000 for flight breakthroughs. Even the Automobile Club of America gave a prize for the best-performing aircraft motor. One sponsor offered $15,000 for the "machine equipped with multimotors and multipropellers that makes the best performance in a flight of one hour." In 1910, when Glenn Curtiss, the Wrights' great rival in the early airplane business, flew 150 miles from Albany, New York, to New York City's Governor's Island to claim a $10,000 prize, the *New York Times* devoted six pages to the feat.[16]

Shortly thereafter the *Times* ran a story describing American fliers drawing huge crowds around the country to their races and air acrobatics. Some of these airmen earned from $500 to $2,000 a week—very handsome salaries in 1910—plus bonuses. John Moissant, perhaps the best known of these daredevils, was reputed to have brought in $500,000 in 1910. Like others in the flying brotherhood, he competed not for money alone, but also to demonstrate the power and safety of flight.[17]

Another of these intrepid fliers, the charismatic, six-foot-four-inch cigar-chomping Calbraith P. Rodgers set his sights on the $50,000 that newspaper publisher William Randolph Hearst promised to the first person to fly across the United States in less than thirty days. Taking off from Brooklyn's Sheepshead Bay on September 17, 1911, Rodgers was trailed on the ground by a special railroad train carrying his wife, food supplies, and spare parts as well as his mother-in-law. Ten times along the way his engine failed and he lost twenty-five days to bad weather, repair stops, and mechanical problems. In the end he covered 4,321 miles over a period of 103 hours in the air, surviving a dozen crack-ups, a broken leg and collarbone, and an arm injured by steel splinters from an exploding part. He landed in Pasadena, California, to a tumultuous welcome on November 4, too late to claim the prize. But Rodgers picked up a substantial check from the firms that underwrote his trip. In this emerging age of celebrity, flamboyant failure was almost as fungible—and profitable—as success.[18]

A few months later Rodgers dipped his craft as he flew in an exhibition over Long Beach, California, raising his arms to wave to the crowd. He had performed similar feats many times, righting the craft at the last moment. This time the plane did not adjust in time and took him straight down. The engine landed on top of him, killing him instantly.[19]

Scientific American warned about excessive exuberance regarding this new conveyance. Yes, in a very short time air technology and pilot skills improved greatly so that the flying machines covered a distance of 350 miles before landing. But the "aeroplane" was still a primitive apparatus, a "combination of a Chinese box kite, an automobile motor, a restaurant fan, balloon rudders, junior bicycle wheels and ski runners, the whole strung together with piano wire and safeguarded with adhesive tape, and mammoth rubber bands." Though the plane did remarkable things, not "a single new fundamental idea to supplement or correct its original design" had been added since Kitty Hawk, and "between times it has exacted sacrificial offerings to the demons of the atmosphere."[20]

In 1910 alone there were more than thirty deaths and close to 150 accidents attributed to the "fancy fliers." And fatalities were not limited to the inexperienced. Only a few months before Rodgers's death two other popular aviators perished in competitions. On December 31, 1910, John B. Moissant was thrown from his plane as it fell into a dive, and a few hours later Archie Hoxsey, the world record holder for altitude, plummeted to his death. Not infrequently planes exploded in midair or had their wings collapse under the stress daredevils put them through.[21]

Robert T. Collier, the president of the Aero Club of America (founded in 1905), condemned the "useless and reckless exhibitions"; *Scientific American* described airplanes as "[part] flying machine, part death trap"; and the Wrights, who trained an early generation of aviators to perform at carnivals, circuses, and country fairs, withdrew their stable of fliers from participating in these exhibitions. Drawn into the debate over air safety, H. G. Wells observed that the time would come when flying would become routine, but for the moment it remained "a means of display."[22]

In Europe the shadow of war hastened progress. The leading countries took aviation much more seriously, moving the industry beyond its "rambunctious adolescence." Governments subsidized air manufacturers and poured funds into development and production. When war broke out in August 1914 Britain had 110 planes on hand and France 130. Germany, described by Modris Eksteins in *The Great War and the Birth of the Modern Age* as "the very embodiment of vitalism and technical brilliance," boasted 230 aircraft.[23]

Warring powers initially employed airplanes defensively, to scout behind enemy lines, but soon they put them to offensive uses, including the famed "dogfights," a term that came into use in 1919 to describe air-to-air combat. Between incinerated fliers and civilians who perished from aerial bombardment the new airplanes brought death in their wake, but aviators somehow escaped responsibility. They were celebrated as gallant warriors, their dogfights as chivalric clashes conducted high above the nasty war of attrition on the ground. Adversaries would drop wreaths over their kills in homage, and the press made heroes of aces such as the French flier René Fonck, the Red Baron, Manfred von Richthofen, and later America's Eddie Rickenbacker, who scored twenty-six air victories. By war's end the British alone had built an air force of 290,000 men and 22,000 aircraft.[24]

Only as the United States moved toward war did Washington finally press the aviation industry to set aside patent battles, close a series of cross-licensing agreements, and transform the manufacture of aircraft from small-scale custom work to a national operation capable of mass-producing airplanes. Convinced that air flight could be a critical factor in warfare, on July 24, 1917, Congress jumpstarted domestic aviation, committing $640 million, the largest single targeted appropriation in American history to that time. Domestic airline production shot up, from 411 ships in 1916 to 2,148 the following year and more than 14,000 in 1918.[25]

The fevered effort was plagued by war-time shortages, unreliable production, and inexperienced personnel. Between April 1917 and November 1918 175,000 workers were rushed into service turning out airplanes. Despite the $1.25 billion ultimately committed to these efforts, the scramble to meet war quotas resulted in massive graft, unseemly profiteering, and shoddy work. Combined with the hurried muster of negligibly trained pilots, this resulted in many fatalities. So unreliable were the American-manufactured planes that a special army commission recommended that only foreign-built aircraft be assigned to the battlefront. Of the 14,000 domestically produced craft delivered, only 196 de Havillands were put to restricted use as observation planes. They became known as "flaming coffins," as their fuel tanks were prone to explode in crash landings.[26]

Nevertheless the press of war forged an industry. In just a few months scores of companies geared up to produce thousands of planes. Ten thousand aviators and another ten thousand aircraft mechanics were trained. And from the bitter experience of a hastily drawn air service came a host of safety improvements and the replacement of flimsy wood, fabric, and wire construction with sturdy metals. Wings were streamlined and engine power steadily enhanced. By the end of the war planes were faster, more durable, and more maneuverable. The U.S.-produced Liberty engine won plaudits for its endurance and power.[27]

Within a year and a half the United States had built a real air service, numbering 195,000 personnel and more than 8,000 airplanes, with an additional 2,000 craft under naval and marine control. By war's end the airplane was no longer an experimental device. The *New York Times* wrote that aviation stood "on the threshold of a new age whose developments the most imaginative [could] hardly imagine."[28]

With one eye peeled on a future war, Europe took up the challenge, making aviation a priority. Despite strapped treasuries, the leading European powers subsidized the construction of elaborate airway systems while combining smaller private fleets into large national airlines, such as Britain's Imperial Airways. Competition among the European nations spurred technological advances, leading to the use of new alloys, more sophisticated instruments, new construction methods, and more powerful motors.[29]

In the United States the aviation age lagged behind, forced to wait upon the profit motive. Dismayed by the unreliability of war-time aircraft and revolted by the industry's profiteering, Washington withdrew its support of aviation. Within days of signing the Armistice, military orders—the American air industry's lifeline—came to an abrupt halt. Before the ink on the document was dry Washington canceled $100 million in aviation contracts, buckling the elaborate aviation infrastructure erected during the war. With military procurement frozen and other government funds unavailable, so long as it was cheaper to run the speedier and more secure railroads few investors ventured capital on the air. Within a year after hostilities ended, the automobile firms that had diverted production lines to build planes or components for the war effort turned back to exclusively producing cars, and most of the twenty-four aircraft manufacturers in existence at the end of the war had closed down; wartime production capacity evaporated to below 10 percent of what it had been at the war's height.[30]

Despite a host of advantages—a strong investment economy, an immense unbroken land mass where airlines did not have to contend with customs and regulation barriers, a national fixation on progress and speed, and a continental railroad system that would be vastly enhanced by integration with an air network—the infant industry made little progress in the immediate postwar period. The Air Service, America's potential air offense in war, was reduced to assigning pilots to patrol for forest fires and border crossings and sending a "flying circus" around the country to publicize loan drives. With its fleet of deteriorating planes rapidly turning obsolete, the Air Service's nine hundred active pilots and observers suffered 330 crashes resulting in serious injury or death (nearly one hundred airmen were killed in one year alone).[31]

Critics of this policy of obsolescence pleaded the urgency of air power. Within a year of the industry's shutdown Brigadier General Billy Mitchell, chief of training and operations for the U.S. Air Service, warned that given its "few paltry squadrons," it would take the army a year and a half to hit its stride in a war. Mitchell's outspoken advocacy of strategic air offense brought him into conflict with the military leadership, who continued to rely primarily on sea power to defend North America. Mitchell argued that advances in aviation rendered battleships vulnerable. In a series of bombing trials involving captured German warships and decommissioned naval vessels his pilots easily sank the heavily armored vessels from the air, proving his point.[32]

Mitchell and others argued for government assistance short of direct subsidies, including assistance with mapping, radio research, weather reporting, airport construction, and, most important, developing an aviation strategy for the military. But conservatives in the military feared that an air program would cost them their battleships. Shortly after General Mitchell shared his thinking with a journalist, the chief of the Air Service had him removed from his post. The top brass further marginalized aviation by dumping large supplies of surplus airplanes on the civilian market.[33]

So while the airplane was revolutionizing European travel, in the United States it was limited to speeding the delivery of mail and barnstorming displays. Once more American aviation became a fancy distraction. A hard core of about six hundred fliers, trained during the war and determined to keep flying, bought discounted surplus war planes, such as the two-seat Curtiss JN-4, to put on flying-circus shows. The unregulated pilots doing tricks in bad planes drove the industry's casualty toll sky high. In 1923 the Aeronautical Chamber of Commerce estimated that barnstormers were involved in 179 crashes, resulting in 85 deaths and 162 injuries.[34]

Anyone who could get his hands on a plane and dared to fly could. The 1920 U.S. Census reported 1,312 "aeronauts," including eight women. The casualty rate remained high. In 1924 reliable estimates attributed two out of every three flying fatalities to these showmen. These "flying gypsies" traveled about the country, diving over open pastures, spiraling into loops and spins, hanging upside down outside cockpits, and offering joyrides at county fairs and open air shows for a few dollars a head. They kept dreaming up fresh stunts—walking out on the wing or climbing out of one plane in midflight and clambering onto another. Spectators competed for the honor of giving the daredevils a meal and putting them up overnight. Reckless and daring, these flyboys were also admired as acolytes of the air. Claude Ryan, one of the early aircraft manufacturers, was certain that he could turn any individual into a supporter of air travel by taking him up for a taste of heaven. These early fliers, wrote one observer, represented "a lively example of a romantic profession unhampered by precedents and unrestricted by man-made law—a direct contradiction to the plea that romance no longer exists in our day."[35]

While the U.S. air industry sputtered along in these years, among a small group of enthusiasts flying took on almost sacred significance. It is not possible to fully appreciate the meaning flight held for the aviation community without taking this romantic idealism into account. Pilots viewed themselves as a select breed, purified by the rituals of danger. Controlling the heavily vibrating craft took power and skill as pilots struggled to steer through turbulent air and strained to keep their machines aloft. In their open cockpits they tasted the spray as they passed over water and endured fierce winds, driving rains, blinding blizzards, and penetrating chill. To escape humdrum normalcy they endured discomforts and dangers, the snares of closed valleys and sudden fogbanks, and most of all the constant imminence of death.[36]

Like the early sea voyagers and wilderness pioneers they were awestruck by the vastness they discovered and by their sense of privileged access. Their narratives are filled with a rhetoric of awe and wonder, straining to transmit the rapture of the fresh sky's ethereal peacefulness and fierce beauty. The early enthusiasts believed in flight's power to transform, to usher in a more peaceful world and shape a more profound intelligence. The women's rights theorist Charlotte Perkins Gilman thought that humans would no longer think from the perspective of a "worm of the dust, but as butterfly psyche, the risen soul," leading to "human intercourse on a new plane." When the crowd caught sight of the first plane to fly over Chicago, "not a man but felt that this was the beginning of such a mighty era that no tongue could tell its import," wrote Mary M. Parker, "and those who gazed were awestruck, as though they had torn aside the veil of the future and looked into the very Holy of Holies . . . and hope sprang eternal for the great new future of the world."[37]

Aviation, writes J. J. Corn in *The Winged Gospel*, was seen as "an instrument of reform, regeneration and salvation, a substitute for politics, revolution or even religion," ushering in an "era not only of untrammeled movement for everyone in three dimensions but also of peace and harmony, of culture and humanity." Flight would resolve the conflicts of industrial capitalism, unclog cities, reconfigure the countryside, and reduce racial inequalities, opening "an air age of dazzling prospects." Even Rockefeller, "with all his power," noted one air ideologue, "has not been able to control the air."[38]

Long before all this, an adolescent Charles Lindbergh had come under the spell of the "heroic brotherhood" and dreamed of becoming a fighter pilot. In the summer of 1912 Evangeline Lindbergh took young Charles to attend an exhibition of air trials at Ft. Myer in Virginia. He remembered the experience later as "so intense and fascinating" that it left him entranced with flight. During the war he followed with great interest the feats of the gallant aces and he thrilled to fictional accounts describing the hot-blooded adventures of "Tam o' the Scouts," a fictional fighter pilot who became a World War I ace. Now, dropped from the University of Wisconsin's engineering program, Charles decided that though he had never been close enough to a plane to touch one, he would "study aeronautics in earnest, and if . . . it appeared to have a good future" would take it up as "a life work."[39]

A career among the "flying gypsies" carried more than a whiff of disreputability and escapism; one writer compared his decision to running off to join the circus. But Charles saw it differently: "The life of the aviator seemed to me ideal. . . . Mechanical engineers were fettered to factories and drafting boards, while pilots had the freedom of wind in the expanse of sky. I could spiral the desolation of a mountain peak, explore the caverns of a cloud, or land on a city flying field." Precious little about his earlier years was special—not the broken home, not his abysmal school career, not his experience on the farm. From the vantage of lofty air he could "look down on earth like a god." For this he was willing to buckle down and study hard.[40]

Charles sought out information on flying schools and learned that the Nebraska Aircraft Corporation offered instruction in building, flying, and maintaining aircraft and boasted that they placed their graduates in good paying jobs, all for a fee of $500; moreover, as he recalled later, "the name 'Nebraska' was full of romance." In March 1922 he rode off on his motorcycle for Lincoln to learn how to fly. This time he left his mother behind. Later she would return to Detroit to teach high school science.[41]

The school's proprietor, Ray Page, welcomed the twenty-year-old Lindbergh early in April, took his check, and sent him off to begin his training on the factory floor. Charles learned a little bit of everything that had to do with building a plane. He found it all absorbing, participating as the delicate wings were attached in pairs by means of slender wires and wooden struts to the fuselages. He helped apply layers of the acetate and nitrate dope material to the wing fabric to stiffen it and assisted with installing the compact engines that powered the planes. He was fascinated by the way simple fabric, steel wire, and wood were metamorphosed into sky chariots. He had come, however, not to build planes but to fly them. Page told him to be patient.[42]

Otto Timm, the plant supervisor, took pity on the eager young observer who so badly wanted to get off the ground and took him up in one of the planes.

Standing just over six feet tall and weighing 150 pounds, Lindbergh, nicknamed "Slim," donned a leather helmet, strapped on his goggles, and secured himself to the seat. A mechanic twisted the propeller, sending a cough through the motor and a surge of excitement through Lindbergh. "How clearly I remember that first flight," he wrote. Mechanics removed the chocks holding the wheels in place, freeing the plane to move along the rough turf and accelerate rapidly toward the field's perimeter. The roar in the cabin turned deafening, the ride smoothed, the horizon tilted forward, and they were "resting on the air." He recalled the sensation vividly: "I lose all conscious connection with the past. I live only in the moment in this strange unmortal space, crowded with beauty, pierced with danger."[43]

In his first weeks Lindbergh witnessed two "washouts." In the first, a wing broke off during a loop and two men perished. In the other the pilot and his passenger barely escaped death. But he was not scared off by the danger. The possibility of death invested every action with greater import; the smallest error could cost a life. His training took on an importance for him that college courses never had: "Behind every movement, word and detail, one felt the strength of life, the presence of death." The stakes demanded a precision and a discipline that he had never given anything in the past. And, as he later wrote, he relished that instant when "immortality is touched through danger, where life meets death on an equal plane; where man is more than man, and existence both supreme and valueless at the same moment."[44]

Slim got only eight of the promised ten hours of air instruction before the school's one dual-control training plane was sold to a local barnstormer named Erold G. Bahl. Bahl agreed to take the eager trainee on a month-long barnstorming junket through southeastern Nebraska so long as Lindbergh paid his own expenses and helped sell tickets by doing some air stunts. He had never been hesitant about showing off with his motorcycle and doing car stunts, and he took easily to air showmanship. Lindbergh built a repertoire of aerial tricks, including stepping out on the wing of a flying aircraft—like "climb[ing] up through the branches of a high tree"—and proved such a crowd pleaser that Bahl picked up all of his expenses.[45]

The tour ended in May and Lindbergh returned to Lincoln, doing odd jobs at the airplane factory and hoping to stir some attention. When the parachute makers Charles and Kathryn Harden came to town in June to promote their handmade $100 parachutes he watched Chuck Harden descend in one of the silk chutes and talked him into letting him try one. Lindbergh pulled off a complicated double jump, with two chutes opening one after the other; decades later he still cherished those first moments of "exhilarated calmness" floating through the air. Curiously, this jump also cured him of his nightmares about drowning bodies and violent men.[46]

His jump caught the attention of seasoned fliers: "I'd stepped suddenly to the highest level of daring—a level above even that which airplane pilots could attain." One of the local fliers, Harold Lynch, signed him on as a parachute jumper for a four-month barnstorming tour out west. By this time he had the out-of-cockpit stunts down pat, and Lynch taught him the rudiments of flying, as well as how to make some money on the thrill tour. First you had to grab people's attention. Lynch once tossed a lifelike dummy out of the plane into the Yellowstone River to attract a crowd. "DAREDEVIL LINDBERGH," as he was billed, would startle locals by parachuting out of the plane as they came to town.[47]

There was some artifice under the bravado. Lindbergh might seem to be suspended over the ground, hanging onto a strap by nothing more than his teeth, but despite the grimacing and jaw clenching his weight was supported by a thin steel cable attached to a harness under his flying suit. When Lynch put the plane through loops and dives with his young partner perched on the top wing, heel cups and cables leading from the wing's hinges held him secure. Lindbergh loved the work. To his mother, who was taking courses at Columbia University in New York that summer, he wrote, "This is sure a great life."[48]

He and Lynch were resting in the plane's shade near the town of Red Lodge, Montana, one scorching afternoon when a brightly painted touring car came up the road. A rancher jumped out and asked, "What'll ya charge to fly me over the town?" For $10 they promised to make him happy. The rancher stepped into the cabin and once they got up into the air began shouting "Take me low down the main street." The plane dropped to barely one hundred feet above the ground, drawing the gaze of earthbound townsfolk, when the man drew two pistols and started firing at the ground, exulting, "I shot this town up a'foot, an' I shot this town up a'hossback, an' now I shot this town up from an airplane." Another man paid to be flown over his hometown so that he could urinate over it from up high.[49]

Lynch's circuit took them through Nebraska, Kansas, Colorado, Wyoming, and Montana before returning to Little Falls for the winter. By spring Lindbergh had abandoned his earlier thoughts about a career in airplane design, telling his parents that he was ready to fly his "own ship." With money borrowed from his father and from his own savings he made his way to Souther Field in Americus, Georgia, where the government sold surplus World War I aircraft. He selected a two-seat Curtiss JN-4D "Jenny" that was capable of reaching up 60 to 70 mph at low altitudes. These planes (originally produced for $10,000) were being cleared out for $1,000. Lindbergh bargained the price down to $500, with a new ninety-horsepower OX-5 engine thrown in. "You know what you want," a resigned

Evangeline wrote from Detroit, but could not resist asking, "[Is] a plane a wise investment & has the occupation of pilot any future?"[50]

He had not been in a plane since October, and he had never taken one up alone. With eight hours of instruction and a lot of experience flying on the outside of a plane but precious little behind the controls, he fired up the engine and succeeded in bringing the underpowered craft up. Landing, it became clear, would be more difficult. He came down hard on one wheel and one wing, bouncing down the field before he could bring the ship to a halt. "Nothing broke," he noted, "[but] what an exhibition I'd made!" Sheepishly he eased his way back to the hangar, hoping that no one had noticed.[51]

Someone had—an old hand who sauntered over to the green pilot and offered him a bit of free instruction. He guided him through several takeoffs and landings. After a week more of practice Charles began making his way back home, hoping to make some barnstorming money along the way. He decided to take a route through Texas, which brought him over "some of the worst flying country in the south," where even practiced pilots would be hard put to bring down a plane in an emergency amid the rough terrain. Why did he choose this hazardous route? Because Texas was "the badge of the profession. . . . Why miss it?"[52]

On the second day of his flight on May 17, Lindbergh lost his bearings in bad weather and wandered 125 miles north instead of west. Unable to make out a clear expanse amid the swamps and trees, he brought the ship down in a small pasture. It rolled for a short stretch before dropping into a marsh and ended up standing almost perpendicular in the air. Lindbergh was only slightly shaken, but the plane suffered damage, including a cracked propeller.[53]

He ordered parts and within three days they were delivered to nearby Maben, Georgia. It took another few days for him to complete the repairs. By then word of the downed Jenny had attracted crowds curious for a firsthand look at the plane and the tall young flier who had survived the crash. Not one to let an opportunity pass, Lindbergh began selling five-minute rides, pulling in enough in one day to pay for the repairs and the hotel bill. He stayed for another two weeks drawing thrill seekers from the entire region. But one elderly woman who came up to him he could not accommodate. She asked how much he would charge to take her up to heaven and leave her there.[54]

Despite several more mishaps along the way Lindbergh made it back to Minnesota, in time to help out with C. A.'s last hurrah, another ill-fated campaign for the U.S. Senate. He flew his father to several campaign stops before suffering yet another crack-up.[55]

After applying for a job with the Tela Railroad, a subsidiary of United Fruit in Honduras, and being turned down because of his inexperience, Lindbergh stopped at the International Air Races at Lambert Field near St. Louis. With more than four hundred flight exhibitions and contests, the races featured the most experienced pilots racing their advanced aircraft. It also allowed him to mingle with the air jockeys, exchanging information about jobs, competitions, and industry gossip.[56]

He had thought to go south for the next few months, but they warned him away. Virtually the entire air-performing community would be there. Instead he sold his Jenny and began offering instruction to wealthy flying buffs through one of the mechanical shops at Lambert Field. His buddies were settling down to build families. Page, Bahl, and Lynch were married or engaged, but the closest he got to a woman was when he took his mother along for ten days of barnstorming. Other friends had retired from air tramping after suffering injuries or having finally moved past the thrill stage into mundane jobs on terra firma. But Lindbergh kept chasing "the shouting wind . . . through footless halls of air"; he still wanted nothing more than to soar in the "untrammeled sky."[57]

However, even the brash Slim knew that if he wanted to make a serious future in aviation he needed more training. He had learned while barnstorming in Minnesota that the army ran a pilot school. It would allow him to "hold four hundred horses on [the] throttle," a marked contrast to the underpowered Jennies. As uncomfortable as he was with formal instruction he knew that a year of rigorous army training would make a credentialed pilot of him. But he needed to take an entrance examination, and he was pretty certain that he could not pass it. Here finally was the answer to the question of what possible benefit he could derive from his coursework at Wisconsin. It exempted him from the test and, with letters of reference arranged through his father, he completed the application, easily passed his physical exam, and was notified to report to Brooks Field in San Antonio, Texas, in March.[58]

In the interim he joined a car dealer named Leon Klink to fly Klink's modified Jenny cross-country. They experienced a number of memorable mishaps, including one when after a forced landing they took off from the middle of a town square with "daredevil Slim" threading the needle between telephone poles forty-six feet apart; the plane's wing span measured forty-four feet. The takeoff was only a few inches off, but as a result Lindbergh crashed down the walls of a local hardware store, shattered his propeller, and sent pots and pans flying down the main street. Miraculously the two men escaped injury. After squaring everything away—the owner, delighted with the notoriety that promised to attract customers from the entire region, refused payment—and patching up the ragged old flier they took off again, this time successfully. On March 15, 1924, Lindbergh reported to Brooks Field with an entering class of 103 other cadets to begin the year-long training curriculum. They practiced aerial acrobatics in the morning, took ground-school courses in the afternoon, and in the evening (unbeknown to his training officers) Lindbergh offered private instruction to make some money on the side.[59]

The contrast between the demanding army environment, "where every button on your uniform was properly inserted in its hole," and the private airfields he was used to could not be plainer. On the private fields flyboys drank, smoked, and dressed sloppily, taking all the risks they dared, flying any craft that could make it past gravity. Nonetheless Lindbergh responded well to the army's discipline and high expectations. Two-thirds of each class typically washed out, and when he got a 72 on an early exam he took it as a warning, studying with a determination that had eluded him before. In school and at college he never saw the connection between studying and practical, real life. Studying for his pilot's wings was different. Here was a clear goal, a "silver passport to the realm of light." Between March and September he completed courses on photography, motors, map-making, field service regulations, radio theory, military law—twenty-five courses in all. He studied through weekends and into the night, at times reading by the faint glow of the field latrine after lights were shut off in his barracks.[60]

In the early weeks of his training his father was hospitalized with an inoperable brain tumor. He was determined to visit, though it was not altogether certain that he would receive permission. "I may be 'washed out,' for leaving," he wrote to a friend, "but that can't be helped." Fortunately he obtained a leave and rushed off late in April for an emotional good-bye to C. A. at the Mayo Clinic in Rochester, Minnesota. The elder Lindbergh was barely able to speak. A month later, on May 24, he died at age sixty-five. Certain that a second absence would drop him from the program Charles did not go to the funeral. C. A. was cremated and Charles was entrusted with his father's ashes and his father's wish to have the remains "spread to the winds." For reasons as complex as their relationship itself, he waited ten years till he got around to it.[61]

Determined to succeed, Lindbergh surprised even himself with his diligence, raising his average first into the 80s and then the 90s. At the end of the semester, of the hand-picked entering class of 104, seventy-one cadets washed out; Lindbergh not only passed his courses, but he compiled the second-highest grade average in the class. In his flight group, where he was one of six, only he made the cut.[62]

Reserved and straitlaced—he did not smoke, drink, or even date, and he suffered taunts for his daily letters from his mother—he nevertheless participated wholeheartedly in barracks high jinks: "I took my full part in it—probably more than most." The boisterous, if sometimes pitiless camaraderie of the barracks offered him welcome release. Those who overslept, snored, or thought too much of themselves were fair game, and every once in a while, "when the powder woofed and the smoke shot upward"—Lindbergh recalled, unapologetically, about a cut shotgun shell he had placed underneath a cadet's chair—"there would be a delightful reaction."[63]

In the second semester the class, now numbering thirty-three, transferred to Kelly Field for six months of advanced training. Flying the difficult de Havilland airplanes, they took classes in gunnery, photography, and bombing and learned the basic elements of navigation. After completing basic training in combat flying the cadets declared specialties. Lindbergh found his métier in what was called "pursuit flying," reveling in the fancy maneuvers, deft evasions, and "strange field approaches," which tested pilots' ability to land unexpectedly in unfamiliar territory. Over the months he developed into a fine airman, with quick instincts, good judgment, and a subtle flying hand. He participated in precision formations where less than ten feet separated his wing tips from other planes as they dived in unison, practicing swooping down on an enemy. [64]

On one occasion, flying solo in low visibility, he reverted to his barnstorming days, putting his plane through an assortment of stunt moves, all of them forbidden. He assumed that no one could see him through the fog, only to discover that an instructor in a nearby plane was observing his "washout offense" rather intently. For an entire week he feared that he would be dropped from the program, but the instructor turned out to be a good sport, never reporting the violation.[65]

His closest brush with death came shortly before graduation. On March 6, 1925, piloting a pursuit plane as part of a nine-plane attack formation at an altitude of about five thousand feet, he nosed his craft down toward the "enemy," cutting swiftly through the air from the left, while Lieutenant Charles D. McAllister piloted another craft attacking from the right. Passing above the target, he "felt a slight jolt followed by a crash." His wing had collided with McAllister's. "My head was thrown forward against the cowling," Lindbergh wrote in his official report. His plane was spun around and the two de Havillands hooked together, seeming to "hang nearly motionless for an instant." His "right wing commenced vibrating . . . striking [his] head at the bottom of each oscillation." Pulling off his safety harness, he climbed out past the edge "of the damaged wing, and with [his] feet on the cowling on the right side of the cockpit, which was then in a nearly vertical position," jumped backward, away from the entwined wreckage. Parachuting down, he saw the crippled craft pass about a hundred yards to his side and burst into flame several seconds later as it hit the ground. McAllister managed to parachute to safety as well.[66]

This was the first class to go through training at Kelly Field with parachutes. A year earlier the fliers would have plunged to almost certain death. The first to survive a midair collision, the two pilots were inducted into the Caterpillar Club, the flying brotherhood whose lives were saved by parachutes. An hour after the near-catastrophe Lindbergh was back in the air. "I accepted danger," he replied to those who thought him reckless, "[but] I had no craving for it." McAllister registered a complaint about the incident; Lindbergh did not.[67]

Eight days later, on March 14, 1925, one of eighteen of the original thirty-three cadets who began advanced flight training, Second Lieutenant Reserve Charles Lindbergh graduated at the head of the class. But his mother's old question, "Has the occupation of pilot any future?" remained apt. With the United States uninterested in building an air defense in peacetime and American commercial aviation dormant, there was not much call for highly trained pilots with a second lieutenant's commission in the U.S. Air Reserve, even those able, in Lindbergh's own words, "to put a plane through any acrobatic maneuver it was capable of." In May he wrote a friend, "There is still money to be made barnstorming," but the paydays were irregular. "Sometimes you clean up several hundred a month and again you may strike poor weather, a bad terratory [sic] or crack up and loose [sic] more than you have made." He dismissed the idea of buying another plane when he learned that bargains were no longer available. There was a cotton-dusting job in Georgia, but it paid only $200 a month. He applied for a commission in the regular Army Air Service, but withdrew the application. He could not overcome his fear of failing a written exam.[68]

Some have argued that at the time Lindbergh was still finding himself, holding on to a kind of suspended youth, pursuing his muse in air. Lindbergh himself dismissed these notions: "I had no sense of in-betweenness." He maintained that he had a definite goal and was "well satisfied" with his progress toward it. Before his death, C.A. had spied a vast potential in his "unassuming and kindly" son. "He does seem like the real stuff," he wrote: "[Charles had the] making of a big man, and these are times we need them. In the line of work he is at I do not suppose there is a chance for a big man, and yet there may be." Lindbergh himself was less uncertain. He believed that aviation would grow into an important industry and provide a large future for him. Anonymity did not interest him.[69]

He needed a breakthrough. He thought he might fly to Alaska. Then he looked into some air competitions. Newspapers were reporting on the adventurous pilots who were extending flight's frontiers. Navy Commander Richard E. Byrd was laying plans to fly to the North Pole in the spring of 1926. With more than 1,100 hours of flight experience in thirty different types of aircraft, Lindbergh applied to join the expedition—too late, as it turned out, as the crew was already set.

In July he joined the 110th Observation Squadron of the 35th Division, Missouri National Guard, teaching veteran pilots maneuvers "too dangerous for our civil aircraft" and lecturing on navigation. Within weeks the commanding officer, Major Charles R. Wassall, recommended him for a first lieutenant's commission, writing, "He will successfully complete everything he undertakes. He is an intelligent, industrious young man and displays an unusual interest in his work." A few months later he was promoted again, to the rank of captain.[70]

Meanwhile, for the first time in years Lindbergh decided to stay in one place. He settled into a boardinghouse near Lambert Field, taking on several flight students and doing some barnstorming. St. Louis was a budding crossroads for aviation where many fliers congregated. The city's Chamber of Commerce, led by its aviation-minded president, Harold Bixby, enthusiastically promoted local ambitions to make St. Louis into a hub for aircraft operations, beginning with bringing an airmail franchise to the city.[71]

The U.S. Postal Service had initially relied on railroads to carry the mail over long distances. As early as 1911 the service carried out some test runs with airplanes and soon after the end of World War I inaugurated airmail on a route connecting New York City, Philadelphia, and Washington. The maiden effort on May 15, 1918, began rather inauspiciously. With President Woodrow Wilson looking on, the JN-4 mail plane could not get off the ground. Once the mechanics remembered to pour gasoline into the tanks and the plane did take off, the pilot wandered off in the wrong direction and less than twenty-five miles later crash landed. Despite difficulties the Postal Service managed to build a mail fleet that it operated with its own pilots, and within two years it boasted a transcontinental air service that delivered millions of letters and packages each year.[72]

As a vice president of the State National Bank of St. Louis, Harold Bixby directly experienced the advantages of the airmail system which by speeding checks and financial documents to their destinations cut a full day or more of interest on bank paper by reducing the "float" period. In 1923 Bixby approved a loan for the local Robertson Aircraft Corporation, founded by Frank and William B. Robertson on a shoestring budget of $15,000 two years earlier. In 1925, when the U.S. Postal Service began turning its airmail system over to the private sector, the Robertsons applied for and eventually won a regional franchise to deliver the mail between St. Louis and Chicago.[73]

Even before the contract's official award, the Robertsons appointed Slim Lindbergh chief pilot for their company. They had first noticed him at the Lambert Field's International Air Races in 1923 and observed his progress "in the air and on the ground" ever since. He "showed so much, both as [a] pilot and as a man," recalled Frank Robertson, that they virtually handed the twenty-three-year-old captain full operational control over their airmail business. Lindbergh would lay out the routes, plan the flight schedules, select the landing fields, and hire his own team of associate pilots.[74]

While waiting for official approval of the franchise he took on other assignments. He joined a flying circus, offered flight instruction, and test-flew new aircraft. Billed as the U.S. Army lieutenant "who saved his life by jumping from an aerial collision," he barnstormed over Missouri, Iowa, and Illinois. In June he survived another midair accident when the plane he was testing failed to respond as he was putting it through a tailspin. He struggled to try to save the plane before finally jumping late in the dive. Fortunately his chute worked perfectly, though he landed hard in a fierce wind that dragged him across a field before he could collapse the billowing chute. Bloodied and left with a painfully dislocated shoulder, he had once again cheated death. "Yours is the first case on record in which a man has been saved more than once from a disabled airplane," the War Department wired. "My gosh man," a friend exclaimed. "Saved . . . twice in the same year . . . incredible."[75]

In August J. Wray Vaughan, president of Mil-Hi Airways and Flying Circus in Denver, sent him a telegram: "COME IMMEDIATELY AT FOUR HUNDRED MONTHLY." His circus wanted a "pilot with plenty of nerve who knows his business" to navigate Colorado's canyons and ridges, where the sudden downdrafts pressed down on a plane "like giant hands." Vaughan needed a master pilot and the Robertsons recommended Lindbergh, who had not yet begun his duties with them. Anticipating a stylish ace in a leather jacket with flowing scarf, Vaughan was surprised to find instead "a tall gangling kid in a misfit blue suit, about three sizes too small," carrying a cardboard suitcase. "If this kid is a pilot," Vaughan thought, "then I'm a horse." Then he watched him in a plane. "I was wrong. There was never another like him."[76]

Lindbergh performed a stunt repertoire for the circus during the day and put on fireworks displays in the evenings, sometimes with no more than the beam of a car's lights or even some flashlights to guide him. In early October he and Vaughan entered the transcontinental "On to New York" National Air Races, but a series of mishaps and mechanical difficulties forced them to give it up. Lindbergh inquired about other contests, anxious to make a reputation and set some flight records; he was also not unaware of the high stakes that competitive fliers were able to claim.[77]

In these months before taking the helm of the airmail operation, Lindbergh learned to maneuver through the turbulent air zones among the western mountains and valleys, came to know intimately the strengths and weakness of half a dozen of the most common airships, and expanded his bag of performing tricks.

One favorite was the breakaway, where he swung off the wingtip and into the air held up only by a set of cables connected to the landing gear. Another thriller was a plane-switch, where he changed planes in midair, usually making sure to fail on his first two tries in order to make it look harder, and then finally pulling himself up a rope ladder to a second plane, before parachuting off to close the show.[78]

The hard flying provided Lindbergh with experience that served him well as he assumed the demanding airmail responsibilities. Flying American airmail was one of the most hazardous jobs in a very hazardous profession. The British aviation editor C. G. Grey explained the difference between American and European companies and their approaches to piloting in a single pithy sentence: "You cannot scare a mailbag." U.S. commercial aviation, for all practical purposes, consisted of making haste over a wide geographic expanse to deliver bags of mail, while European airlines flew paying passengers. As a result U.S. carriers took more risks, flew in turbulent weather, and introduced the most daring innovations.[79]

It was said of Otto Praeger, the hard-driving assistant postmaster general who directed airmail operations, that as long as he could see the Capitol dome out his window in Washington, he allowed no postponements of flights anywhere in the nation. Once, when two successive pilots refused to take off from New York because of terrible weather, Praeger fired off a wire to local officials: "Fly by compass. Visibility not necessary." The pilots, fearing for their safety, refused. The next wire commanded, "Discharge both pilots."[80]

With similar equanimity the Postal Service introduced night flight. Initially mail and parcels sent cross-country were loaded on a plane, then handed off to a rail carrier for night transport and returned to the air during the daylight. This patchwork system brought down the time for transcontinental delivery to under seventy-nine hours, almost an entire day faster than surface delivery. In 1923 the postal system made a critical breakthrough by introducing rotating beacons that offered illumination for a fifty-mile radius, and in the following year, on July, 1, 1924, instituted night flights, which promised to cut the time for cross-country deliveries even more dramatically, to less than thirty-three hours.[81]

With the Robertson operations set to start in the spring of 1926 Lindbergh, who was paid $300 a month plus whatever he earned on the side, turned to preparing the necessary equipment, carefully studying the terrain and laying out the 285-mile route between St. Louis and Chicago. The government's plan to install beacon lighting at regular intervals progressed only fitfully and had not reached their territory yet. Pilots flying at night were reduced to relying on the distant glow of towns and isolated farmhouses, so Lindbergh visited towns along the route, asking officials to paint identifying signs on top of tall rooftops and keep some lights on at night.[82]

Even during the day pilots had little more than eye, ear, and feel to guide them. They were forced to navigate at low altitudes and often followed the "iron compass"—railroad tracks that guided them to their destinations. This had to be done with caution. One pilot flying low in a storm fixed his course on the railroad tracks only to find them coming to an abrupt halt before a mountain tunnel. Only by jerking the plane into a last-minute ascent did he avoid becoming part of the scenery.[83]

Lindbergh studied the air routes along the franchise to eliminate such last-minute surprises. He pieced together his own maps, flight charts, and direction books, taking note of tall steeples and high wires. He recorded the location of open fields and farms that were equipped with telephones for pilots who needed to bring down their ships and make urgent contact in emergencies.[84]

Entirely absorbed in his work—one of the private clients he flew around for many hours remarked that the young man talked to him about nothing but flying—Slim Lindbergh displayed little appetite for the diversions that attracted the others. "As a normal thing," one of the mail jockeys recalled, "we worked two or three days a week, five or six hours a day, plus standing reserve perhaps one day a week. . . . I spent my time as unproductively as possible, learning to play golf, chasing girls; investigating dives and joints in the area." Craig Isbell, a young pilot trainee who watched the young Lindbergh prepare for a flight, still remembered many years later his intense focus and easy confidence.[85]

But when "the [four] DH-4s with which [they] were to fly the mail" were delivered to the Robertsons with shredded wings and damaged fuselages Lindbergh first realized the scale of the problem he faced. The army had rejected these craft as unfit and actually put an axe to critical parts of the ships to make sure that they would not be flown again. For a few hundred dollars the Robertsons, who were forced to pinch every penny, had reclaimed these planes from the slag heap and reconditioned them. Asked to run the route with this "pile of refuse," Lindbergh stipulated that each pilot be equipped with an emergency parachute and not be penalized for using it.[86]

On April 1, 1926, Lindbergh completed a trial run and two weeks later, on April 15, took off at 5:50 a.m. from Chicago's airmail field in Maywood for the inaugural flight. Later that afternoon two planes departed northward from St. Louis for Peoria and Springfield.[87]

Airmail pilots were still considered members of a "suicide club." If you survived the everyday hazards of flying the open-cockpit biplanes, the punishing winter frost left you numb with cold and impaired judgment. One flier recounted that after a winter flight he would just remain seated for minutes, waiting for his senses to recover and his shaking to stop before he could talk sensibly. A large part of preparing for a trip involved honing flight instincts and making decisions without thinking, because as often as not pilots' minds were so fogged by the combination of sleep deprivation, freezing cold, and monotony that clear thought was impossible once they were in the air.[88]

Wing walking and skydiving may have appeared dangerous, but airmail delivery was the real thing. The thrills were not staged and there were no bystanders to shine their headlights if things went bad. "Practically everyone on Lambert Field knew the risks we took in flying the mail," Lindbergh wrote, "averag[ing] an engine failure about every 70 hours." In a day when weather forecasting was a synonym for fancy guesswork and radio guidance did not exist, pilots took off when local conditions permitted and flew as far as they could, bringing the plane down as they hit bad weather or mechanical trouble. "The forced landing was a way of life," wrote Dean Smith, one of the early airmail pilots. It was Smith who won modest fame with this pithy dispatch: "Flying low. Engine quit. Only place to land on cow. Killed cow. Wrecked plane. Scared me. Smith."[89]

The airmail pilots cultivated an élan of bravado, of fatalistic flyboys who scorned death, partied tirelessly, and took off into the sunrise to duel with the forces of nature while dealing with a hangover. Dean Smith again: "I knew that I could fly well and this skill set me apart from the run of the mill. I certainly had no wish to get killed, but I was not afraid of it. I would have been frightened if I thought I would get maimed or crippled for life, but there was little chance of that. A mail pilot was usually killed outright. Then too, sometimes I was called a hero, and I liked that." Lindbergh was told that he "could look forward to some nine hundred hours in the air as the average pilot's lifetime." He wrote his last will and testament.[90]

There was good reason for the fatalism. Lindbergh's letters to his buddies mention crashes and near misses with a chilling casualness: "Gathercoal . . . left Chicago for Detroit with two passengers. . . . As far as I know not one of them has been found altho I believe that part of some wreckage was located." How dangerous was airmail piloting? In 1925, when the U.S. Post Office turned over the air express business to private lines, thirty-one of the original forty-pilot crew hired in 1918 had not survived to witness the transition. Not a month passed, Lindbergh later recounted, without incidents, crash landings, and near misses, when he had to quickly maneuver his plane down to land.[91]

On September 16, less than six months after launching the run, even before the bad weather season set in, Lindbergh left Peoria for Chicago shortly after six in the afternoon with about half an hour of light before him. His DH-4 lacked night-flying equipment, and as darkness began to descend he encountered a fog bank that obscured his vision. Unable to see the ground he continued in the direction of Chicago, hoping to catch sight of its powerful beacon. But the eight-hundred-foot-thick fog covered any ground illumination. He continued circling, seeking a clear patch. Two and a half hours after takeoff, his fuel supply depleted and flying off his reserve gas tank, the engine finally puttered out at five thousand feet. He directed the plane toward open country, stepped out from his cockpit, and bailed into the open sky.[92]

He released a parachute flare to help him see where he was landing, but it was useless in the deep fog. He was falling blind. He had neglected to cut the engine switches before jumping, and as the craft began its own twisting descent for a long moment it seemed he might be struck down by his own abandoned ship, until it passed him by. He instinctively crossed his legs to keep from being caught straddling a branch or wire on his descent. Luckily he landed in a cornfield. Shaken but unhurt he rushed to find the wreck and locate the mail pouches. He made his way to a farmhouse and called for a mail truck to pick up the bags and hurry them to the railroad. Later he learned that the ship's 110-gallon capacity gas tank had been removed for repairs and replaced with an 85-gallon tank. The mechanic had neglected to notify anyone.[93]

Staff Sergeant August Thiemann of the 41st Squadron at Kelly Field wired, "You are the only man in the U.S. who has successfully jumped from a plane [three times] and lived to tell of your experiences." Less than two months later, blinded by snow, Lindbergh came down near Peoria, landing on a barbed wire fence, saved from serious damage by his padded flight suit. The flying fraternity was small enough to keep score, and once again Sergeant Thiemann congratulated him: "It appears to me that you are favored by the angels." Lindbergh went on to make a total of eighteen jumps over the next few years.[94]

In the span of three years Lindbergh had made himself into an excellent pilot. Lieutenant B. H. Littlefield, who knew him from the National Guard, described Slim Lindbergh as "one of the outstanding fliers in the whole Army Air Force." A ground mechanic marveled, "He sets 'em down at night like you would a toy, without any field lights at all." His bosses were equally impressed, observing, "The worse the weather the better he seemed to like it." He seemed inexhaustible to boot, and his discipline made him stand out from the crowd. One pilot recalled that Lindbergh was the only flier he knew who did not drink.[95]

But if he was unusual in his habits he shared with the airborne brotherhood their addiction to flight. Like them he looked upon aviators as prodigals, lustily pursuing their art. Released from narrow concerns and decisions of little consequence fliers occupied "a higher plane than the skeptics on the ground." Adventuring in the uncurbed sky they tasted the "wine of the gods." He had only disdain for the common mass that experienced life in "antlike" portions. Their bland lives lacked the spark of heroism: "If I could fly for ten years before I was killed in a crash, it would be a worthwhile trade for an ordinary life."[96]

Lindbergh wanted above all to avoid an "ordinary life." Many years later, made more contemplative by experience and tragedy, he arrived at a more complex, more textured conclusion about flight, voicing concerns that he had entirely overlooked in his youthful passion: "Is aviation too arrogant? . . . Is man encroaching on a forbidden realm? Is aviation dangerous because the sky was never meant for him? When one obtains too great a vision is there some power that draws one from mortal life forever?" But for now, Lindbergh was charmed by flight's magic promises.[97]

Back on earth the Robertsons were having a hard time with the grim economics of the airmail business. They had begun with four planes; two of them had been wrecked (as it happened, by their chief pilot); one of their other pilots had to take a leave because of disabling pain from an injury suffered in a crash the year before. It was a struggle to make ends meet. Lindbergh wanted more than this for himself, but also for American aviation. In Europe airlines ran regularly scheduled passenger flights, connecting London, Paris, Rome, Berlin, and a host of other cities. In the United States aviation was only now beginning to show some signs of progress.

In the stillness of the high sky on one fall day Lindbergh took to pondering his future, and the most challenging of all aviation prizes.[98]

AVIATION TAKES FLIGHT

"OF ALL THE AGENCIES that influenced men's minds that made the average man in 1925 intellectually different from him of 1900," the journalist Mark Sullivan wrote in his popular 1930s chronicle *Our Times*, "by far the greatest was the sight of a human being in an airplane." The technological wonders for the turn-of-the-century generation were steel, the telephone, moving pictures, and the Ford automobile; flight remained a fantasy. But for those who reached maturity after the Great War, air travel stood at the front of modern achievements. And, as with steel, motion pictures, and automobiles, they naturally expected the United States to take the lead in aviation.[1]

Instead, as we've seen, following World War I the United States fell way behind in aviation technology. The war-time initiative, deeply flawed to begin with, was abandoned altogether soon after the Armistice, and Congress, with little interest in the sloppy business of incubating a new industry, cut off funding, refusing to provide even minimal structural support such as licensing, weather research, or building airports. The government did not even collect data on air crashes. Regarding American air space a former Air Service official wrote early in 1921, "The thing is of a wild nature . . . in the eye of the law." To Representative Randolph Perkins of New Jersey the effect of all this was as plain as it was unfortunate: "We are behind England, France, Italy and Japan in air power." America's air industry was rapidly disappearing.[2]

On June 1, 1922, as President Warren Harding was delivering a speech before the Lincoln Memorial, a pilot circled overhead, drowning him out. The brazen overflight alarmed the audience and embarrassed the president. "Anybody may buy a machine and fly at his own sweet will," the *New York Times* editorialized. "There is no Federal law governing aeronautics." President Harding, though no one's idea of a visionary, agreed that the "whole course of the United States in dealing with aeronautics has been absurd and devoid of credit to the country." It was the Roaring Twenties, and with so much else going on, so many other opportunities to make money on the ground, Americans focused their sights below the horizon.[3]

The story was of course different in Europe, where national rivalries spurred aviation progress. Countries there viewed aviation much the way they had viewed maritime growth centuries before: it was good for trade in peace and essential in war. Despite an oppressive postwar economic squeeze, the French government supported eight separate airlines, providing generous allowances to train pilots and subsidize passenger flights while covering up to 50 percent of construction costs for twin-engine commercial craft. In Le Bourget, near Paris, the French boasted the greatest airport and aviation research center in the world. In 1922 alone the French government committed $12,000,000 to airdromes, labs, meteorological services, and direct airline subsidies.[4]

Convinced that its "future [lay] in the air," Germany dodged treaty limitations to expand its commercial aviation business fourfold from 1921 to 1924, merging fifty separate companies into the powerful Luft Hansa (air guild) combination. With night flights, sleeping accommodations, onboard screenings of motion pictures, and "passengers whirring through the air at 100 miles an hour . . . [as they] listen[ed] in to radio through headphones placed near each seat," the Germans threatened, in the words of one expert, to take "unchallenged control of the air lanes under the very noses of the nations which vanquished them in the World War." France responded by multiplying its air-related spending many times over to rush the production of a new generation of aircraft.[5]

Supported by such subsidies European lines planned to girdle the globe with as many as thirty thousand miles in air routes, while Americans were reduced to flying war disposal aircraft. As European airlines compiled enviable safety records, reducing accidents and fatalities to a level lower than those for railroads, American air travel remained so dangerous that insurers refused to cover flights in their basic policies. "We who gave the airplane to the world," the chief of the Army Air Service lamented, "who lead in nearly all phases of research and development and who hold nearly every important record in the air, trail far behind the commercial application of this new medium of transportation."[6]

Italy was already spending $50,000,000 a year on its infant industry in the early 1920s, when Mussolini came to power and ordered a tripling of the nation's air capacity. To acclimate the Italian public to air travel he sent planes to 127 cities, offering free rides. Meanwhile in the United States fear of flying held stubborn sway, holding back what Mussolini called the "aeronautical conscience." By the middle of the decade Colombia and Japan had surpassed American spending on new aircraft. "It is quite unspeakable," cried the *Washington Post.* Laissez-faire capitalism's foremost champion, the *Wall Street Journal,* even floated the possibility of government subsidies to get some American planes in the air. "This country is the only large nation without a clearly defined aeronautical policy," reproved the *New York Times.* The president of Curtiss Aeroplane, C. M. Keys, testified before Congress that the American air industry was demoralized: "Tell me who in the business would not like to get out?"[7]

The one bright spot was the U.S. postal airmail system, which built a national air network of impressive scope. From the time it was launched in 1918 it continued to expand, knitting together more than 2,600 miles of linked service, the longest continuous air route in the world. The system was far from ideal, plagued as it was by inadequate facilities and obsolete aircraft, but by 1925 it was delivering fourteen million letters and packages a year.[8]

More important, the service saw its mission in broad terms that went well beyond speeding mail across the country. Its aim, in Postmaster General Harry S. New's words, was nothing less than "to encourage and stimulate the creation in this country of an industry capable of engaging successfully in commercial aviation and to build the planes and equipment necessary to that end." In pursuit of these goals the service built an air fleet, pioneered new routes, and nursed America's air system through its difficult infancy until its viability was established. Then, in the 1925 Kelly Air-mail Act, Congress turned over the entire system to private companies, handing over an expensive aviation infrastructure with airfields, established routes, and a half-million dollars in night flying equipment. And to ensure profitability, it paid the private air transporters very generous fees to deliver the mail at a much higher cost than before. Over just four years the base rate per pound paid to the new carriers went from 22.6 cents a mile in 1926 to $1.09 in 1929.[9]

Stimulated in part by these developments, interest in flight spread beyond the small circle of aviation boosters. Here and there airplanes were used to hustle VIPs to meetings, provide bird's-eye perspectives for highway planners, and search for lost vessels at sea. Airplanes entered the popular culture. Thomas Hart Benton featured them in his paintings; popular songs and novels incorporated flight themes. The film *Plane Crazy* featured Mickey Mouse at the controls, and Ormer Locklear thrilled viewers with his wing-walking and dramatic leaps between planes in *The Great Train Robbery* and *The Skyman.* Tom Mix and Hoot Gibson's westerns introduced the public to aerial cowboys.[10]

In 1919, when *Aerial Age* forecast that "the aeroplane air route will bring that commingling of nations" and a "modern Utopia," it represented the isolated voice of a booster periodical. By 1924 the widely admired commentator and journalist Lowell Thomas lauded flight's revolutionary potential, and the popular historian Will Durant wrote, "Long chained, like Prometheus, to the earth, we have freed ourselves at last, and now we can look the skylark in the face." The literary critic Gilbert Seldes declared the airplane a triumph of the human spirit, "something better than machinery and better than man."[11]

Billy Mitchell's dramatic trial stirred more public attention. Over the years he had kept up a relentless attack on the army command, releasing memos, articles, interviews, and books criticizing the War Department's refusals to erect an air defense. Now, early in 1925, in fiery congressional testimony, Mitchell called the Army Air Service incompetent and ranked it a humiliating fifth among the world's air forces. He accused the navy of deliberately subverting efforts to strengthen the air force. When his appointment as assistant chief of Air Service expired the army sent him to serve as a lowly air officer in out-of-the-way San Antonio, Texas. The demotion failed to quiet him, however, and in September, when a navy dirigible went down with many casualties, Mitchell unleashed a scathing indictment of the brass's "incompetency, criminal negligence, and almost treasonable administration of the national defense." In a dramatic seven-week trial he was found guilty of insubordination and court-marshaled, but his impassioned demand for modernizing American aviation caught the public's interest.[12]

Despite the glacial pace of progress, American aviation also attracted some of the world's foremost airplane manufacturers, including the Italian-born expert Giuseppe M. Bellanca; Igor Sikorsky, who fled Russia after the Revolution to make world-class planes in a corner of New York's Roosevelt Field; and the Dutch-born design genius Anthony Fokker, who had directed German aircraft design and production during World War I. Indeed an entire class of German engineers, prohibited by the Versailles Treaty from producing German military aircraft, came to the United States in search of work.[13]

The industry managed to make important advances, developing more efficient craft. Lighter, longer running, air-cooled engines such as the Wright Whirlwind replaced the heavy, water-cooled Hispano-Suiza and the notoriously unreliable Liberty motors of just a few years before. The Wright engines increased power output from 100 to 200 and then 450 horsepower, raising cruising speed to 110 mph.[14]

Similar strides were made in aerodynamics. In 1914 Glenn Curtiss had designed a plane to cross the Atlantic Ocean, but it couldn't actually fly. Its thin flat wings were based on the theory that a plane slid over the air surface like a kite. Subsequent research demonstrated that planes got their lift from the vacuum created on the wing's topside by the curve of the wing as it was drawn through the airstream by the propeller. New plane wings featured delicately cantilevered tapering so that the varying wing thickness and curving surfaces promoted efficient lift.[15]

If slowly, by the mid-1920s aviation was starting to attract money. A business reporter noted that up to that point American business had sat back and "cannily allowed . . . much of the trial work to be done, and . . . many of the risks to be taken, by [the post office]." Now businessmen stood ready to invest. Together with "well known men of New England," William Rockefeller, Henry Davison, and Cornelius Vanderbilt Whitney formed Colonial Air Transport, Inc., to carry mail between Boston, Hartford, and New York. They planned to move into passenger service soon after. Clement M. Keys and William Wrigley founded National Air Transport with $10,000,000 in startup capital to run an overnight express service from New York to Chicago. And in October 1925 Postmaster-General Harry S. New announced the awarding of the Detroit-Chicago-Cleveland airmail route to Henry Ford and his son Edsel. The dour car genius's interest in aviation created a sensation.[16]

Characteristically the Fords were interested in much more than an air transport contract. They had become intrigued by William Stout's work on an all-metal aircraft. Stout had studied Germany's novel Junkers airplanes, which were the first to utilize an all-metal design (first steel and then corrugated duraluminum) to replace the conventional construction of wood frame covered with fabric. The Junkers was one of the most durable and fastest planes of its day. Stout added his own improvements, and the Fords, eager to move into airplane production, bought out Stout's operation and installed him at the head of their own airplane factory, producing Ford aircraft that featured internally braced wings and Wright Whirlwind motors. Soon dubbed the Tin Goose, the plane set a new standard for performance.[17]

Henry Ford's enthusiastic involvement gave a boost to an industry still dominated by small boutique shops and greatly in need of credibility; all the more so when his son Edsel, backed by the vast resources of the Ford Company, set out to do for aircraft what his father had accomplished for cars. He aimed to massproduce a standard flying "machine . . . as comparatively cheap as [Ford] pleasure cars," making aviation a common form of public transportation. With capital finally engaged, Frank L. Lahm, vice president of the Fédération Aéronautique Internationale, exulted that "the U.S. is on the eve of a great awakening as regards aerial transportation."[18]

One very large impediment remained. "Putting flying within reach of every one," Edsel Ford told President Calvin Coolidge, "is primarily a matter of solving the safety equation" and its corollary, public confidence. On his visit to America,

Prince William of Sweden noted in an interview that the United States lagged behind Europe: "We feel as safe climbing into our airplanes as boarding a train." Germany's Luft Hansa boasted of having transported eighty-five thousand passengers with not a single serious air accident. This safety record had consequences. In early 1927 Germany announced plans for regular transatlantic air service to South America, to be followed by a North Atlantic service. "It is predicted," the *Washington Post* reported, "that within two years airplanes will be in regular operation between New York and Germany." The planes, it went without saying, would be German, mocking Commerce Secretary Herbert Hoover's promise to "put [America] far ahead of all other nations in the use of the air for transport of passengers, mail and goods" within three years. Air flight in the United States continued to struggle to get out from under the shadow of accidents and casualties.[19]

Earlier in the century Henry Ford had run "reliability tours" to publicize automobile safety. Starting in 1925 Edsel Ford put together similar tours for airplanes, offering the most reliable performing planes a silver trophy and a $20,000 purse. These competitions stressed passenger safely and craft dependability. Anthony Fokker, for example, added two additional Wright engines to his standard single-engine monoplane to demonstrate how designers could improve safety by increasing power. The combination of the Ford name, prize money, and exciting new machines drew hundreds of thousands from around the country to these contests. Newspapers and magazines devoted feature columns to aviation, further stimulating public interest. "Flying," Henry Ford exclaimed, "is now 90 per cent man and 10 per cent machine," meaning that it took great skill to fly the current breed of low-tech aircraft. He aimed to make it "90 per cent machine and 10 per cent man."[20]

Finally Washington considered taking a larger role in aviation beyond airmail. Anticipating an adverse reaction to the Billy Mitchell trial and interested in shaping aviation policy to his own small-government views, President Calvin Coolidge appointed a Wall Street banker, Dwight Morrow, an old college friend from Amherst, to take a fresh look at aviation with respect to both military and civilian applications. Morrow, who had served during World War I as a member of the Allied Transport Council and chief civilian aide to General John J. Pershing, commander of the American Expeditionary Force, put together a board of military, political, and civilian experts to examine all aspects of American aviation with a view toward creating a comprehensive new framework for nurturing growth.[21]

After completing its study, the Morrow Committee recommended the creation of an air corps within the army and a larger role for aviation in defense planning.

Most important from the point of view of commercial aviation, the report called for the creation of the Bureau of Air Navigation to license pilots, register aircraft, allocate air routes, and regulate air traffic. The British had established a Department of Civil Aviation to do all this and more seven years earlier; France and Italy had followed, giving Europe a well-organized system of airways. Guided by the Morrow Report, Congress finally passed the Air Commerce Act in May 1926, granting to aviation the basic support that had been given to marine navigation long before.[22]

Congress also approved funding for a modern air force and outlined other steps designed to establish a solid long-term basis for development. "You may say," one observer noted, "that what General William Mitchell was unable to accomplish by direct means—too direct means as it turned out—has been accomplished indirectly." Aircraft manufacture doubled from $7,000,000 to $14,000,000 within two years.[23]

Other prominent figures took up the cause of advancing American aviation. One was Harry Guggenheim, a former navy pilot whose father, Daniel, had built a vast mining and smelting empire. In 1923 Daniel Guggenheim sold off the family's extensive Chilean copper holdings for $70,000,000. Now close to seventy and seeking to be remembered for something greater than digging out mineral wealth, Guggenheim established the Daniel and Florence Guggenheim Foundation to advance the "well being of mankind throughout the world." In the air service during World War I, Harry had become beguiled by aviation's humanitarian potential. He convinced his father to endow the Guggenheim School of Aeronautics at New York University with a grant of $500,000. At the groundbreaking in October 1925 Guggenheim Senior announced that he considered aviation the "greatest road to opportunity which lies before the science and commerce of the civilized countries of the earth today."[24]

A man not given to small enthusiasms, Daniel Guggenheim aimed to mobilize America's air industry by awakening "the American public, especially . . . business men, to the advantages and possibility of commercial aircraft." Harry engaged Orville Wright and others prominent in aviation circles to join his board. In December 1925 his friend Dwight Morrow brought Harry to the White House to fill President Coolidge in on the plans. The president was apparently not initially impressed by what he heard. "What," he asked, "was the use of getting there quicker, if you haven't got something better to say when you arrive?" Nonetheless Coolidge was sufficiently impressed to summon Commerce Secretary Hoover to join them for lunch, and after the meeting to give the effort his blessing.[25]

On January 18, 1926, Daniel Guggenheim launched the Fund for the Promotion of Aeronautics, charging Harry with dispensing $2,500,000 in seed money to advance research and inspire public trust. Before setting specific goals for the Fund, Harry made a three-month overseas tour and brought back from Europe an intriguing set of findings. Europe's substantial lead in the numbers of routes, planes, and airports, he was convinced, could be overcome. The United States had the resources and the capital to accomplish this, but only if the American public was put at ease about air travel. They must be persuaded "by actual demonstration that airplanes are inherently no more dangerous than steamships or railroads." Almost at the same moment that Congress passed the Air Commerce Act Guggenheim began selecting projects to promote aviation.[26]

Proposals for staging transatlantic flights he rejected as too risky, but when Commander Richard Byrd returned to a hero's welcome from the North Pole the Fund showcased the event by sending Byrd's Fokker trimotor (the craft was powered by three engines) on a six-week reliability tour of forty-five cities. An estimated half-million Americans, many of whom had never seen an airplane before, flocked to the traveling exhibit. In June the Fund committed a large chunk of its endowment to removing "the single obstacle to the development of aviation": the "age-old fear of the air."[27]

Nonetheless almost from the moment that planes could stay aloft and move forward at the same time, crossing the big ocean was seen as the ultimate fulfillment of air travel's promise. The trip still typically took from eight to twelve days on the water (though speedy steamships could do it in less time). The journey remained uncomfortable and far from routine, even for seasoned travelers. Critical for trade, intellectual exchange, business, banking, science, and diplomacy— for so much of what defined life in the twentieth century—the Atlantic crossing remained at the mercy of weather and the capriciousness of the seas. Air travel could fix that.[28]

As early as 1910 the aeronaut Walter Wellman sought first honors by attempting to glide his twelve-and-a-half-ton dirigible across the ocean, only to be dumped unceremoniously into the sea. By 1912 *Scientific American* magazine was predicting, "The next great conquest of . . . aeroplanes will be the transit of the turbulent Atlantic." The magazine revealed that plans to encourage construction of planes capable of doing that were now "far advanced."[29]

R. W. Wilson, a Harvard professor and a noted expert in nautical astronomy and aerial navigation, outlined the major considerations for such a flight. To reach Europe by air one had two routes to choose from. The safest path was over the Atlantic ship aisles, avoiding the arctic regions. Planes taking this route had available to them the latest weather reports from the ships at sea and could navigate by observing ship direction. In the event of an emergency rescue was more likely. The other route, the "great circle path" from Newfoundland to the continent, was shorter and quicker. It required less fuel, which brought down the carrying weight and made fewer demands on the engine, particularly during the crucial takeoff. Both routes required extensive travel over water without landmarks or other visual cues. Pilots needed to rely on instruments, astronomical observation, and navigational calculations. The trip itself posed three challenges: atmospheric resistance and the wear and tear of long-distance flying on the plane; an extraordinary fuel load; and the sluggishness and reduced maneuverability that resulted from the weight of the fuel. The solution proposed in 1912: build a sturdier plane and outfit the craft with multiple engines to give it more power.[30]

Calling it the "supreme test of aviation," the department store heir Rodman Wanamaker in 1914 financed efforts to launch a 1,600-mile trip of continuous flying from Newfoundland to the Irish coast. He engaged Glenn Curtiss to design and manufacture an "aeroboat," capable of acting as a "small non sinkable boat" on the high seas and maintaining wireless contact with ships. Scheduled for completion in the summer of 1914, the *America* would establish U.S. leadership in transatlantic aviation, claim the $50,000 prize from London's *Daily Mail*, and advance world peace through trade and communication. But all this was pushed aside by the outbreak of World War I.[31]

The drive to fly across the Atlantic resumed after the war, urged on by the *Daily Mail*'s standing prize for crossing the Atlantic between North America and Great Britain or Ireland in seventy-two "continuous hours" or fewer. The U.S. Navy was of course not eligible for the prize, but with few means of keeping its fliers sharp, the navy put them to work competing for air records.[32]

On May 8, 1919, the NC-1 and two newly built sister seaplanes, NC-3 and NC-4 (huge Curtiss ships with wing spans of 126 feet), each outfitted with four Liberty motors and a crew of six, took off from Rockaway, New York. Two of the ships lost their way in the fog and bad weather and were forced down at sea, but Lieutenant Commander Albert C. Read took his NC-4 from Long Island to Nova Scotia and Newfoundland, then in an unbroken journey of 1,200 miles across the Atlantic to the Azores, and finally reached Lisbon on the European mainland on May 27.[33]

This trip cost millions of dollars and required the participation of thousands. The U.S. Navy had strung across the Atlantic as many as sixty destroyers at intervals to provide assistance in navigation and to be on hand for emergencies, leading an English pilot to dismiss the effort as a "Cook's tour across the ocean." In fact Read's had been far from a seamless journey. It took him nineteen days to complete the forty-one hours and fifty-eight minutes of flying. Early into the flight his seaplane dropped into the ocean and relied on its water wings to limp to the safety of the naval air station on Cape Cod. The hydroplane suffered failures to the engine; propellers and other essential components had to be replaced, and it was forced down repeatedly, once for a period of five days, for repairs and replacements. At another point the NC-4 was so engulfed in fog as it crossed the Atlantic that the crew could not see from one end of the ship to the other. The plane went into a terrifying spin until a faint radio message from destroyers below helped the disoriented crew restore their bearings. Only by a very generous stretch of the imagination could this series of air hops be viewed as a single flight.[34]

Two Englishmen, John Alcock and Arthur Whitten Brown, took the Atlantic contest to the next level. Both men had spent time as prisoners of war during the war dreaming about a flight across the Atlantic. On June 14, 1919, they took off from St. Johns, Newfoundland, in a converted World War I Vickers-Vimy bomber powered by two Rolls Royce 350 hp engines and equipped with wireless. After the first hour the radio's generator fell into the water, and three hundred miles out from Newfoundland flames began to shoot from the exhaust until it too finally broke off and fell into the sea. Later, disoriented by a soupy fog and pinned against their seats in the cockpit, the two fliers suddenly realized that they were descending at an alarming rate. They got to about one hundred feet from the water—close enough to hear the roar of the ocean's waves—before jerking the craft back to ascent and safety. Snow, sleet, and hail covered the wings and iced some of the external instruments, forcing Brown to climb onto the decking half a dozen times to chip off the ice. Finally they came crashing down near Clifden on the Irish coast into a peat bog.[35]

Brown and Alcock had flown 1,980 miles nonstop across the ocean in sixteen hours and twelve minutes, the first such transatlantic flight ever. They claimed the *Daily Mail* prize and a knighthood for the "Great British Air Triumph." Tragically Alcock was killed shortly thereafter when a plane he was flying at the Paris air show crashed in fog. Brown never flew again after his partner's death.[36]

That same year, on May 22, 1919, a wealthy French-born New York hotel owner, hoping to turn attention away from England and Ireland to his beloved France, announced his own offer of $25,000 to the first aviator "of any Allied country" who completed a nonstop flight between Paris and New York in a heavier-than-air craft.[37]

Raymond Orteig had been distressed by the horrendous human toll of the Great War, but also by the way war itself had been drained of glory and heroism. It had turned into a brutal contest of mechanized destruction over meaningless inches in forsaken forests. Where was the valor in this mass slaughter? Only in the air did Orteig find transporting acts of personal honor. The duels between the flying aces recalled for him chivalric contests of courage and daring. He was especially moved by the gallant young men of the Lafayette Escadrille, Americans who had volunteered to fly in the French Air Force.[38]

After the war Orteig joined the Aero Club of America and became an early devotee of the winged gospel that anticipated a world knit closer together by air travel. He believed that nothing would advance the process more effectively than a nonstop flight between Paris and New York, bathing both nations in goodwill.[39]

For the first five years there were no takers. Little wonder. After Alcock and Brown had traveled 1,960 miles Alcock had remarked that he was surprised to emerge alive from his "terrible journey." Often they had lost the horizon, and when they put their heads out the cockpit window to get some sense of direction "the sleet chewed bits out of [their] faces." And the Orteig challenge called for almost twice as long a trip. No engine then available could power such a flight. In 1924, when the offer expired, Orteig renewed it in the hope that the advent of lighter, more powerful engines, sturdier construction, and advanced instrumentation would make longer flights feasible. The world's best-known pilots set their sights on Orteig's prize. Several teams began to prepare for the challenge. Newspapers caught the fever, reporting on rumors and leaks about the latest contestants lining up for the New York–Paris flight, especially after Commander Byrd's successful run to the North Pole sent a charge through the aviation world. The Byrd expedition demonstrated the effective use of a flight compass for navigation and the wisdom of equipping long-distance flights with multiple engines. (One of his engines had failed and the other fortunately kicked in.) Moved by Byrd's success, the French pilot René Fonck declared that the new technology made a transatlantic flight practically accident-proof. "Having devoted [himself] to the art of flying for 13–14 years," he announced that he was now ready for the Orteig challenge.[40]

Fonck joined an air company called the Argonauts, who assembled a team for the competition. Heralded for his bravery in World War I, he claimed more than 125 kills without suffering so much as a scratch. Described in the *New York Times* as "unsurpassed . . . as an aviator . . . [with] great knowledge of aeronautics," he was paid $250 a week to oversee planning. The contest, Fonck insisted, was about more than mere prize money; it constituted a gesture that would reunite two grand allies and advance the cause of commercial aviation.[41]

Despite pressure to keep the crew small, Fonck insisted on the right to determine how large a crew he would take with him. More men onboard meant more strain on the engine, a more difficult takeoff, a larger fuel load, and diminished maneuverability but he argued that at minimum he needed a second pilot to relieve him, a radio operator to handle communications with ships and land centers, and a navigator.[42]

If there was much agonizing over the crew, there was none over the lavish trimotor S-35 aircraft designed for the flight by Igor Sikorsky. No expense was spared to create the most luxurious airplane ever built, for an unprecedented sum of $105,000. It included a sofa, chairs, and storage spaces for the many presents and valuables the crew would carry with them. The cabin was lined with panels of Spanish leather and rich mahogany, while the three 160 hp engines promised power, redundancy, and a cruising speed of 110 mph. Sikorsky planned a battery of weight-bearing tests before sending the air behemoth (fourteen tons when fully loaded with fifteen thousand pounds of gasoline) off to Paris. On one of the last tests the plane took a load of twenty thousand pounds to Washington, D.C., and back without incident. A delighted Sikorsky pronounced the craft to be "everything that [he] wanted it to be." The massive trimotor was groomed like "a racehorse before a race, as workers went over the wing surface . . . wiping off dust and polishing the smooth surface." Reports of swift progress by other contenders accelerated their pace.[43]

Colonel H. E. Hartney, vice president and general manager of the Argonauts, protested the rush. He also opposed the choice of the chief pilot. Hartney objected that Fonck had won renown for his dexterity in piloting small craft and for his nimbleness in evasion and attack in battle, but that nothing in his record indicated that he could pilot a colossal Sikorsky across the ocean. Moreover he objected that Fonck was too headstrong and reckless. When his protests fell on deaf ears, Hartney resigned from the organization.[44]

At 2 a.m. on September 15, 1926, the giant Sikorsky, laden with coffee, tea, sandwiches, chocolates, and every possible amenity, was rolled out for its flight from Roosevelt Field on Long Island. President Coolidge sent his best wishes for the "courageous adventure" that would "bind closer together the countries of the world." Despite a load heavier by eight tons than anything the ship had ever carried before, Fonck believed he could compensate for the extra drag by doubling the takeoff distance. On the flight the radio operator Charles Clavier would be gathering weather information from as many as forty ships providing early intelligence on weather problems. With "every possible device known to aviators" at his disposal, Lawrence Curtin, the navigator, would have the benefit of this real-time information to guide the craft over the great circle course to Ireland, England, and then Cherbourg and Paris. A last-minute leak in the fuel tank forced a postponement.[45]

A week later, on September 21 early in the morning, Fonck stepped jauntily from a car in his crisp blue army uniform with the Croix de Guerre pinned to his chest. He removed the uniform coat, had it hung onboard, and donned his flight outfit. Charles Clavier called out, "Dinner in Paris Wednesday night!" A man handed Fonck a box of fresh croissants, a gift from Raymond Orteig for the trip, and the engines were started.[46]

They never got to taste the pastries.

Straining to reach the 80 mph takeoff speed, the Sikorsky lumbered along the runway. After a few moments the ship began trembling ominously. The horrified crowd watched as the tail dragged, tearing a wheel loose. The tire bounced wildly into the air, sending the craft lurching left. A veteran pilot screamed, "Lift the tail, lift her!" as if his words might levitate the plane. Instead the right auxiliary gear tore off and the other wheels went flying. One struck the left rudder, shearing it clear off. Fonck could not lift the ship off the ground, and as onlookers watched in horrified fascination the craft went hurtling down a twenty-foot embankment, crashing into a gully. In the instant the seven tons of highly flammable gasoline ignited, forming a blazing fireball, incinerating Charles Clavier and the Russian-born mechanic Jacob Islamoff. In less than three minutes the most expensive aircraft ever built was transformed into a crumpled, smoldering wreck, sending plumes of billowing black smoke fifty feet into the air.[47]

Then a dazed, blackened, and bleeding Fonck, all trace of swagger gone, staggered bewildered and uncomprehending from the pyre toward the crowd that only moments before had lionized him. Out of the smoke Curtin also emerged. When they were finally able to speak they could explain only what it was no longer necessary to explain. Once the plane started falling apart, Fonck struggled to keep it straight. He hoped to hop over the bluff, but by then the plane had been sent into a cartwheel. He and Curtin were lucky to squeeze out.[48]

Sikorsky was stunned. When he recovered his composure he announced, "We will go ahead. . . . Aviation must be prepared to meet these things. . . . No one who flies ever becomes disappointed by death and discouragement." Fonck agreed, calling the calamity "the fortune of the air. It could not be helped." He would try again, "absolutely." The *New York Times* remarked that catastrophe must not stay the course of progress.[49]

In a postmortem deposition the copilot Curtin swore that Fonck had done his best and that the craft had been properly tested, though it had never taken off with such a load. In his own testimony Fonck blamed the dead mechanic: "Probably Islamoff let go the auxiliary landing gear on the left side." But detached observers laid the responsibility with Fonck and his lack of experience with large aircraft. He had heedlessly overloaded the plane and a quicker thinking pilot might have wrestled the crippled plane to a stop or manipulated its dragging tail to avoid an explosion, or at least turned off the ignition. Hartney swore that Fonck's failure to bring up the plane's tail caused the crash.[50]

Since the summer of 1926 Charles Lindbergh had been following the dramatic efforts to fly across the ocean. He paid them little mind at first, but the numbing routine of his mail route kept returning his thoughts to adventure and break-through. To make matters worse, the Robertsons were struggling to make ends meet. At times the mail sacks weighed more than the letters they carried. Only the fact that they counted as carrying weight, and therefore the Post Office could be charged for them, kept the company in the black. (Lindbergh recalled that the brass padlock on the mail sacks was especially welcome: "The weight of that lock is worth nearly two dollars to us.")[51]

Meanwhile Lindbergh completed five round trips a week, carrying the St. Louis mail to Chicago. He was proud of the company's 99 percent completion record, but the statistic meant taking risks and often disregarding forecasts of bad weather. A certain desperation had crept into his thoughts. He was young, aggressive, experienced, and respected as an expert pilot. But there was no certain career path before him. The Robertsons were far from financially stable, and in any event flying airmail was an invitation to minor-league status and a minor-league life among boozers, womanizers, and no-account air jockeys. He wanted more of a future than doing five rounds of St. Louis to Chicago each week.[52]

"I am working on a new proposition in St. Louis," Lindbergh wrote to his mother in October, "and have been very busy lately." He had read about the Orteig prize in aviation magazines, paying little attention at first, ceding first shots to the older war aces, but the Fonck disaster suggested that this project required not Old World panache but fresh thinking. Little in their dogfighting experience with the primitive fighter planes had prepared the World War I aces for an endurance run of nearly four thousand miles. Fonck's crash also convinced Lindbergh that the conventional approach—essentially compensating for weight by strapping on extra engines—was flawed.[53]

Proving that he could pilot such a flight became a consuming passion. He reconstructed his thoughts in his 1953 memoir: "Why shouldn't I fly from New York to Paris? I'm almost twenty-five. I have more than four years of aviation behind me, and close to two thousand hours in the air. I've barnstormed over half of the forty-eight states. I've flown my mail through the worst of nights. . . . I'm a Captain in the 110th Observation Squadron of Missouri's National Guard. Why am I not qualified for such a flight?"[54]

He had more than aerial challenges to overcome. Some thought that focusing on impossible challenges was his way of avoiding getting on with his own career. Others gossiped that his newfound interest in transatlantic contests was prompted by his declining status at Lambert Field. After all, his parachute bailouts had lost two of Robertson's four planes, sorry examples of the state of the art though they might have been. Years later these charges still drew a bristling retort: "No pilot at Lambert Field had a higher standing than I did." He was "well satisfied" with where he stood and what he had achieved. He had grown more mature. And the parachute jumps only "added considerably to [his] standing as a pilot."[55]

In fact Lindbergh believed that his interest in the Orteig challenge was eminently practical. A successful flight would demonstrate what modern planes were capable of. It would advance commercial aviation and earn him a reputation, and he would still have a plane at the end of it. *And* the prize would pay for the plane and expenses, leaving enough over to put him on his feet: "I concluded that a nonstop flight between New York and Paris would be less hazardous than flying mail for a single winter with our Liberty- powered D-Hs."[56]

But before he did anything he had to analyze why the Sikorsky had crashed and burned. He concluded that an overconfident Fonck had not prepared for handling an emergency, and when it occurred had not responded quickly enough to avoid disaster. There had been other mistakes: Sikorsky had overloaded the plane with luxurious amenities—upholstery, furniture, beds, and even a kitchen—and Fonck had allowed the disputes over crew size and who was to select the team to become a dangerous distraction. Then, as competition loomed, the Argonauts had hurried their tests and cut corners.

Gradually Lindbergh's strategy took shape. He would keep the plane light, simple, and inexpensive. "A plane that got to break the world's record for nonstop flying should be stripped of every excess ounce of weight." If he found upholstery in the cabin, he would "tear it out for the flight" to cut down on weight, and devote every extra pound of capacity to gasoline. More radical was his idea that "it certainly doesn't take four men to fly a plane across the ocean."[57]

He began to consider flying alone. His father had warned him about "depending too heavily on others." The old Minnesota settlers had a saying: "One boy's a boy. Two boys are half a boy. Three boys are no boy at all." Flying alone meant less weight and less fuel, and it would give him full control. But could he carry out the tasks of pilot, navigator, and mechanic, keeping awake and sharp for close to forty hours straight? That was the question.[58]

4

INTRICATE PERFECTION

LINDBERGH WAS CONFIDENT THAT he could fly the ocean. But he would have to move swiftly; several teams were already well advanced in their preparations. For starters he needed a special plane and could not hope to buy one for the couple of thousand dollars that he had scraped together by living frugally. He needed a sponsor, but pilots looking to fly on other people's money were a dime a dozen. He needed a plan for funding, and quickly.[1]

There were some positive signs. The national mood seemed upbeat yet hungry for grandeur. The media were promoting a number of short-term, small-bore celebrities and their accomplishments—the flagpole sitters, marathon dancers, home-run hitters, screen stars, and pugilists—leaving unsatisfied a real thirst for feats of a more heroic scale. And aviation was finally rising to the first level of attention. Newspapers ran stories almost daily about new flight records. In this prosperous era, investors such as Henry Ford were finally paying attention, plunging unprecedented fortunes into dream projects. Lindbergh needed to link his private dream to those projects. Fortunately for him, he could start in his own backyard.

For much of the nineteenth century, writes the historian William Cronon, St. Louis was primed to become the gateway to western trade. Located at the confluence of the Missouri and Mississippi Rivers, it carried on a high-volume exchange of finished products for produce with New Orleans, supplied the frontier hinterlands in Missouri, southern Illinois, and eastern Iowa, and brought handsome incomes to its leading families from a highly profitable fur trade that reached deep into the developing West. The city's natural advantages at the head of a well-developed system of waterways seemed to assure its continued dominance over regional trade and to ensure that it would remain the chief metropolis of the midcontinent.[2]

The railroads upended such assurances, diverting trade to the shorter, cheaper, and less treacherous land routes centered around Chicago. Offering the advantages of faster, year-round service unimpeded by ice or floods, along with a system of innovative grain elevators and commodities markets, Chicago captured the agricultural and livestock markets. Long grown complacent by the river's bounty, St. Louisans took a long time to realize how completely Chicago's modern transportation system would displace their water-based advantage.[3]

St. Louis's leading businessmen were eager to avoid past mistakes once a new system of transportation appeared on the horizon. They aimed to establish St. Louis as a hub for national aviation, and its leading men took a special interest in flight. Harry H. Knight, a brokerage executive, presided over the St. Louis Flying Club. Banker Harold Bixby, commonly described as one of the "men who [ran] the great city of St. Louis," was part owner of Travel Air, a small passenger line operating out of Lambert Field, and later became president of the St. Louis Aviation Corporation. Bixby was one of the first to keep a plane for business use. Earl Thompson, a local insurance executive with his own "golden-winged Laird," was another.[4]

The St. Louis Chamber of Commerce produced a promotional motion picture, undertook an expensive public-relations campaign, and put on international air races at Lambert Field, all to boast St. Louis's prowess as a modern, thriving urban center. This was the moment Lindbergh began looking for support in St. Louis.[5]

There was more than serendipity at work here. Slim Lindbergh had matured. He gave the impression of being a reserved young flier preoccupied with engines and air-inductor compasses, but he had experienced life in the army and thrived among the hard-living barnstorming community. Lindbergh still didn't carouse, smoke, or drink, but he was nonetheless no innocent. The flyboy environment taught him about taking care of himself. In his own words, "Little sense of shyness remained." Place him in a meeting or before a piece of complex equipment and he quickly understood what worked and why. His retentive mind took in everything at the service of a nimble, tactical intelligence.[6]

Lindbergh outlined his strategy for the undertaking. An eight-point "action" list included planning the flight, securing potential backers, and arranging publicity (which he frankly labeled "propaganda"). He understood that newspapers helped stir interest, investment, and confidence; Commander Richard E. Byrd, already famous for his polar flight and well advanced in his own plans for crossing the Atlantic, called newspapers "the biggest thing today in aviation progress." Another list, labeled "Advantages," summarized Lindbergh's pitch to potential backers. A transatlantic flight would demonstrate aviation's reliability and "aid in making America first in the air," as well as "promote nationwide interest in aeronautics." It would also make St. Louis known across the country, boost local interest in aviation, and spur regional business. With one of America's finest commercial airports, St. Louis was already an "aviation city," and it had every reason to aspire to becoming "a hub of the national airways of the future."[7]

The last list was headed "Results." It contained only two possibilities: completing the trip and winning the $25,000 Orteig prize or "complete failure."[8]

Lindbergh called the insurance executive Earl Thompson, to whom he had given flying lessons. Thompson offered to see him in his office right away, but Lindbergh did not want to present his plans to a harried executive over a busy desk. "Besides," he later wrote in his memoirs, "time builds dignity and thought." He made an appointment for a week later at Thompson's home. There he laid out his project and its significance for St. Louis. Thompson had many questions: Wouldn't a seaplane offer added security if the plane was forced down over the water? Lindbergh replied that heavy seaplanes required too much fuel to make it across the ocean nonstop. Thompson questioned Lindbergh's plan to make the flight alone in a single-engine plane, but Lindbergh insisted that he had thought this through. A single pilot cut down on weight; a lighter craft was easier to handle, required less fuel, and dramatically reduced costs; if you add more engines you increase the likelihood of mechanical trouble. More important, if one engine in a trimotor failed over the ocean the remaining engines likely would not be sufficient to power the craft to land. He closed with what he called his "trump card." Multi-engine planes were heavy: "You know Fonck had three engines."[9]

Lindbergh then took his project to Major Albert Bond Lambert, the director of the St. Louis airport. Lambert too had a number of important questions, and he was impressed by Lindbergh's answers. He promised that if Lindbergh pulled "the right fellows together" he would be interested. He pledged $1,000 and would ask his brother for another $1,000.[10]

Shortly thereafter Lindbergh, who was considering using a Fokker airplane for the flight, buttonholed a Fokker Company representative, who came by the Robertsons' office. The representative quoted a price of more than $100,000 for a custom trimotor. Lindbergh explained that what he wanted was a quote on a small, single-engine plane with the capability of crossing the Atlantic. The man looked at him, then stated, "Mr. Fokker wouldn't consider selling a single-engine plane for a flight over the Atlantic Ocean."[11]

The designer Giuseppe Bellanca had produced an aircraft that boasted exceptional short field takeoff, solid endurance, excellent range, and a large fuel capacity. The Wright Company had paired this prototype with its own nine-cylinder Whirlwind engine. Made of cast aluminum alloy and chrome and tungsten steel the motor was the best air-cooled engine available, providing nearly 1 hp of power for every two pounds of its weight. The Wright-Bellanca ship fit Lindbergh's needs perfectly. He resolved to travel to New York to meet with Wright officials.[12]

Aircraft companies with reputations to protect were skittish about who piloted their planes. Lindbergh needed to make a good impression, to come across as mature and serious. He ordered a suit with a matching vest, an overcoat ("just to wear it through the front door"), a gray felt hat, gloves, a silk scarf, and a new suitcase. He probably would never wear any of it again, but he needed that plane. His natty outfit on order, Lindbergh called and secured an appointment.[13]

He arrived in New York by train on November 28, a Sunday. The next day, decked out in custom attire, he went to the Wright Company offices in Paterson, New Jersey. But the company was not interested in selling planes. The one Wright-Bellanca in existence had already been committed to someone else. Even more distressing, the Wright people, who should have been pleased by Lindbergh's confidence in their motor, were not at all keen on his idea of crossing the ocean with a single engine, even if it were their Whirlwind. They did, however, promise to introduce him to Giuseppe Bellanca.[14]

Lindbergh met the slender, dark-haired designer the next day at New York's Waldorf-Astoria Hotel. He liked the man's frank and friendly manner and trusted him instantly. Bellanca seemed to understand his plan and informed Lindbergh that he could produce a single-engine plane with an extra-large gas tank, enabling it to stay aloft for more than fifty hours. As for landing gear—a sheared landing gear had contributed to the Fonck disaster—he informed the young pilot that his planes were quite up to carrying the extraordinary fuel load and then coming safely back to earth. Lindbergh was delighted. He boarded the train that night confident that he had made an important friend and that they would come to an agreement. When he reached St. Louis he wired Bellanca and asked for definite assurances.[15]

Bellanca's response arrived several days later. He encouraged Lindbergh to try again with the Wright company and promised to help. If that failed he could build Lindbergh a three-engine plane, "exceptionally adapted for the Paris flight," for $29,000. In mid-December, Lindbergh received a telegram from Wright officials rejecting his offer. They wanted nothing to do with a potential calamity. Instead they sold the plane to another Orteig hopeful, the Columbia Aircraft Corporation, headed by Charles Levine. Lindbergh informed Bellanca and asked him for a single-engine craft, not the triple-engine behemoth Bellanca had suggested.[16]

Weeks passed and Lindbergh had neither a plane nor more than a single pledge of $1,000. To come up with funding he considered selling shares in his venture to St. Louisans for $10 a piece, but he quickly dismissed the idea of taking on a thousand partners. He went to the Robertsons with a new plan to attract sponsors.

Although they were just scraping by and he could not expect money, they could help in other ways; he needed to take a leave from his airmail duties. The Robertsons agreed to help. Bill Robertson brought him to the *St. Louis Post Dispatch* offices hoping to garner some press support for the undertaking, but they were met by deep skepticism. "We couldn't possibly be associated with such a venture," the *Dispatch* editors told him.[17]

By the New Year newspapers were reporting on a handful of Orteig contenders who were making progress while Lindbergh was still looking for backers. And he still had no plane. On January 9 Robertson brought him to Harry H. Knight, the brokerage executive and Flying Club president. Knight liked the idea right away and told Lindbergh to turn all his attention to the flight and let him and others "worry . . . about raising money." Knight called the Commerce Chamber president Harold Bixby and had Lindbergh run through his spiel. "Lindbergh was a pretty good talker," Bixby later recalled, but the thing that won him over was that "all of [Lindbergh's] preparations were predicated on success, rather than any thought of failure." He was young, confident, and extraordinarily gifted, and "even then you could see he was a master at that game."[18]

Bixby joined the team and promised to develop funding for the project. Within a week he had assembled a consortium of St. Louis boosters and air enthusiasts. He suggested that the plane—when there was one—be named *Spirit of St. Louis* to convey the metropolis's "urge to create, progress and conquer" and sent a note to his bank's directors: "Charles A. Lindbergh, Air Mail Pilot on the St. Louis–Chicago Route, wants to make the first aeroplane flight from New York to Paris. . . . Will the State National Bank lend Harry Knight and me $15,000, we to endorse the note personally?" The answer was yes.[19]

Lindbergh had not heard from Bellanca in weeks. Bixby later remembered, "Other fellows, Coli, Fonck, Byrd, Davis and so on, were getting hot and bothered about this flight to Paris." With lavish funding, top-of-the-line airplanes, and large crews chances were very good that one of them would reach Paris first. But the St. Louis group was "prepared to go ahead anyway." Lindbergh inquired about ordering a plane from the Travel Air company in Wichita. They turned him down flat.[20]

He had read about Ryan Aeronautical, a small company in San Diego whose high-wing planes were used along the West Coast to deliver the mail. Ryan was not as well known as the other manufacturers he had looked into, but Lindbergh himself noted, "I'm no longer in a position to ask for perfection." Desperate, he dashed off a telegram on February 3 and received back a telegram the very next day, his twenty-fifth birthday. Ryan could produce a single-engine monoplane for him with the necessary adjustments for $6,000 plus the cost of a motor and instruments, for delivery in "about three months." He wired back, "CAN YOU CONSTRUCT PLANE IN LESS THAN THREE MONTHS STOP." The reply came the same day: "CAN COMPLETE IN TWO MONTHS FROM DATE OF ORDER."[21]

On February 13 Lindbergh completed his last mail flight from St. Louis to Chicago for the Robertsons and prepared to fly to San Diego to discuss arrangements when he finally received a response from Bellanca: "WILLING TO MAKE ATTRACTIVE PROPOSITION. . . . SUGGEST YOU COME TO NEW YORK SOON POSSIBLE SO WE CAN GET TOGETHER IN QUICKEST MANNER." He consulted his backers and, rather than heading to California, hastened to New York.[22]

Bellanca met Lindbergh at the Woolworth Building in Manhattan and introduced him to Charles Levine, chairman of the board of Columbia Aircraft Corporation. Turning to another man, Levine said, "This is Mr. Chamberlin, our pilot." Lindbergh didn't quite understand what Levine meant, but said nothing. Levine told Lindbergh that his company had purchased rights to the design and now owned the Wright-Bellanca prototype. He was open to discussing its sale. He was asking for $25,000 but would accept an offer of $15,000 from the St. Louis consortium. It was a bit more than Lindbergh had anticipated, but he felt confident that his backers would agree to the price. Aboard the train back to St. Louis he wrote his mother of his plans to announce a late fall date for the flight, while actually hoping to take off much earlier. Arriving in St. Louis he reported to his patrons, who agreed to raise the extra money. They cut him a check and sent him back to New York to buy the Bellanca.[23]

On February 19 Lindbergh met again with Levine in his office. Anxious to complete the deal, he laid the check on Levine's desk. Before picking it up Levine said, "We will sell our plane, but of course we reserve the right to select the crew that flies it." Only then did Lindbergh understand what Bellanca had meant by introducing Clarence Chamberlin as "our pilot." Lindbergh was simultaneously dumbstruck and incensed. Fifteen thousand dollars for the privilege of painting Spirit of St. Louis on the fuselage? He told Levine that unless the right to pick the crew came with the sale there would be no deal. Levine tried to persuade him to think about it and finally asked Lindbergh to call him the next morning at eleven.[24]

When Lindbergh called Levine asked him whether he had changed his mind. Harold Bixby recalled that Lindbergh was "mad as hell" so mad that he did not trust himself to say anything. He hung up the phone. An entire week had been wasted and he was no closer to a plane than he had been on February 6. He tried another manufacturer, Beech, but they proved as reluctant as the others to take a chance on an unknown flier with a shoestring budget. Lindbergh turned back to Ryan.[25]

Even if Ryan managed to complete the plane in two months, Lindbergh's chances of getting to Paris first were decidedly slim. Chamberlin was already running tests on the Bellanca. Lieutenant Commander Noel Davis's *American Legion* team was close to ready with its own trimotor, and Richard E. Byrd's spanking new $100,000 Fokker was to come out of assembly any day. Meanwhile Igor Sikorsky was building René Fonck a new luxury ship. France itself had five expeditions under way. "American Airmen Will Race French across the Ocean," announced headlines. The Orteig prize, designed to nurture comity and good feelings between the two nations, had turned into a competition over national honor.[26]

For a brief moment a despairing Lindbergh turned to thoughts of an alternative flight over the Pacific via Honolulu to Australia, until Knight got him to focus again on the Paris flight. No other course compared to the New York–Paris route, not for excitement, publicity, or honor. The Orteig had become the most coveted of all prizes. The potential benefits of a successful flight were incalculable: economic dividends from enhanced trade; a huge boost to aviation and St. Louis; and for those firms lucky enough to have their engine, motor oil, or directional instruments used on the charmed plane, there could be no more valuable endorsement. As for the pilot who landed at Le Bourget, success in this emerging age of celebrity would bring fame, fortune, and enormous satisfaction.[27]

The early favorite to take the prize was, of course, Commander Richard E. Byrd. Scion of a Virginia first family, Byrd had earned his wings during World War I and participated in the NC-4's transatlantic crossing in 1919. His flight in 1926 to the North Pole electrified the country and brought him the Congressional Medal of Honor. Porter Adams, president of the National Aeronautic Association, called Byrd "one of the finest if not the finest navigator in the world today." His pilot was the highly regarded Floyd Bennett, and the deep-pocketed department store heir Rodman Wanamaker was underwriting the project. Byrd's plane, a modified version of his North Pole Fokker, had a majestic seventy-three-foot wingspan and was powered by three 225-hp Wright motors. Like Wanamaker's prewar seaplane, which never made it across the ocean, it carried the name *America*. Insisting that he was solely interested in scientific investigation and promoting the cause of aviation, Byrd did not deign to file officially for the Orteig.[28]

Fresh out of the factory, on April 16 the *America* came to startling grief. The plane actually flew well on its maiden turn, but as Tony Fokker, who was piloting the ship, brought it down for landing the craft tipped forward into a somersault. Crushed by the engine, Floyd Bennett was sidelined for months with serious injuries. Byrd fractured his wrist. Another crew member, radio man Lieutenant

George Noville, suffered internal injuries. Only Fokker escaped without a scratch. The flinty designer announced that he would have the plane repaired and ready in days, but Byrd knew it would be weeks.[29]

Press attention now turned to Lieutenant Commander Noel Davis, who like Byrd was an expert navigator. Davis planned to take his Keystone Pathfinder, the *American Legion*, by way of the great circle route to Paris in about forty-two hours. Chastened by the Fonck disaster, Davis limited the load on his triple engine plane to fourteen pounds per square foot (Fonck's Sikorsky held twenty-seven). Davis planned to collect real-time weather information by wireless radio and to climb out of his biplane cabin once every hour and crawl along the exterior lower wing to a navigator's hatch. There he would make fresh navigational observations and adjustments to guide his pilot, Lieutenant Stanton Hall Wooster.[30]

The most frankly outspoken of the competitors, Davis called his the true "all-American" effort that would prove that American manufacturers and engine makers were top tier. He did not like the idea of "a French pilot and French motors making the first crossing." The most promising of the French teams, led by Charles Nungesser, the great World War I ace, was equally nationalistic. With copilot François Coli, Nungesser planned to take the more challenging route, from Paris to New York. With "a French plane, French motors, and all materials French," he insisted, it was only right to take off from France.[31]

On April 24 Clarence Chamberlin, piloting Charles Levine's Bellanca, newly christened *Columbia,* took up two young girls age nine and fifteen in the plane for a demonstration before five thousand spectators in Mineola, New York. As the plane rose during takeoff a bolt was sheared off the landing gear. Several planes quickly scrambled and rose alongside the Columbia, one holding a sign out the side to alert Chamberlin. The pilot sent a mechanic out to repair the strut in midair, but to no avail. Chamberlin brought the stricken craft down on one wheel. Fortunately no one was hurt but the ship careened and smashed its left wing upon landing.[32]

Two days later the *American Legion* team, led by Davis and Wooster, carried out a heavy-load test over Messick, Virginia. Declaring that he was restless to go, Davis assured all that the flight to Paris was "perfectly safe." But his plane was much heavier than he had hoped. For this load test it weighed seventeen thousand pounds and had trouble rising. The pilot kicked the rudder bar to avert treetops, causing the air speed to drop and freezing the engine. The stalled plane plummeted into a marsh. Carried forward for more than a hundred feet by its momentum the wounded craft dug its propeller into the ground, upending the plane, crumpling its wings, and smashing the cockpit. Davis and Wooster were killed.[33]

Accident and tragedy continued to stalk the large trimotors. The multi-engine paradigm had been favored for its redundancy, which gave it greater power, but the extra weight came at a great price. The deadly crashes recalled the words of the *Scientific American* writer more than a decade before, who lamented "this machine which does so much and falls so treacherously. . . . Hundreds who trusted . . . its designers and their own skill have fallen back to earth . . . to lie on a couch of pain for months. . . . Monuments have been erected over the graves of . . . young men who have thought the air was conquered."[34]

Another grim statistic underscored the perils of flight. Sixteen deaths were attributed to naval aviation alone for the month of April. "Seems to me," Evangeline Lindbergh wrote to her son, "some of the N.Y.-Paris people have already been in too much of a hurry."[35]

Charles Nungesser did not need to be reminded about the capriciousness of the air. He had suffered seventeen wounds in battle and had been reassembled by surgeons, who replaced shattered bone in his skull, elbows, thigh, knees, and foot with platinum. He was a testament to the power that flight held over these flyboys. After participating in forty-five combat duels he "often [had to be] carried to his machine," but he refused to retire from the sky. Reduced for a while after the war to putting on exhibitions in the United States as "an acrobat of the air," he returned to France in search of a grand project and joined with Coli, a much decorated navigator, to compete for the Orteig.[36]

At forty-six François Coli was the oldest of the Orteig contenders. During the war he had resigned his navy commission in search of more action and enlisted as an infantryman, ultimately reaching the rank of captain. Wounded twice, he was declared unfit for duty, only to transfer to the Aviation Corps, where, despite five more wounds and the loss of an eye, he made a notable flying career. He too had caught the Atlantic Fever.[37]

Both men were cut from the same cloth, given to a studied nonchalance about danger. Comrades had little doubt that Nungesser was "willing to lose his life in an attempt to reach New York." On the fuselage of their white, single-engine Levasseur plane, *l'Oiseau Blanc* (the *White Bird*), they emblazoned a grisly insignia from old dogfighting days: a black ace of spades with a coffin, skull, and crossbones framed by two lit candles. Experts estimated that the trip from Paris to New York was "20 per cent" more difficult than its reverse because the plane flew against the prevailing winds and had to carry more gasoline. The Frenchmen were unfazed. They eliminated the radio and much of the emergency survival equipment to cut down their carrying weight. Flying from Le Bourget they also enjoyed the advantage of the world's best takeoff field, with its two-mile-long runway.[38]

Meanwhile the repaired *Columbia*'s tests were going well and the Brooklyn Chamber of Commerce promised an extra $15,000 if the Bellanca made it first to Paris. Ready to go, the crew waited only upon good weather. The press reported,

"Every American in Paris is planning to be at Le Bourget [to greet the *Columbia*]."[39]

In France the press ballyhooed *le match Franco-Americain,* while the communist organ *l'Humanité* denounced as "chauvinist hysteria" the frenzy that pushed men to risk their lives to advance the modern technology of capitalism. Learning of *Columbia's* readiness, Nungesser cut some corners to hasten his departure by the end of the first week in May. He and Coli stopped weight testing at seven thousand pounds, though the *White Bird* planned to carry a dead-weight load well in excess of five tons.[40]

May 8 was a holiday Sunday in Paris, honoring Joan of Arc. The night before, celebrants filled the streets, carrying colorful banners; others prepared for the festive reopening of the Cathedral of Rheims. After eight years of painstaking repairs the thirteenth-century structure, left in ruins after the war, was going to hold services. And all France waited for the *White Bird.*[41]

Starting at three in the morning Le Bourget stirred with activity as Coli busily gathered weather information from the French Navy and other sources. "Never has the weather been such a subject of discussion," began a *New York Times* dispatch, describing the tense wait on both sides of the Atlantic as the rivals readied for takeoff, waiting only for a clear day. Sifting the latest data Coli learned of clearing weather on the European side but unfavorable conditions over the mid-Atlantic and closer to Newfoundland; he decided they would go.[42]

The *White Bird* was wheeled out and filled with 880 gallons of fuel. The engine tested perfectly, easily reaching 10,000 rpm. The crowd, which eventually grew to about five thousand and included such celebrities as Maurice Chevalier and the world- class boxer Georges Carpentier, waited anxiously for the fliers, who finally emerged dressed in full regalia around 5 a.m. Slated to pilot the entire flight, Nungesser had taken an injection of caffeine to stay awake. They packed some bananas, caviar, cola, and coffee but refused the emergency food rations, also leaving behind their safety jackets and a rubber dinghy. "A strong heart doesn't fear death," Nungesser announced.[43]

At 5:18 a.m. they took off to cross the Atlantic. For a moment the ship evoked some gasps as it strained to lift off. "The most pathetic figure on the whole field," wrote one observer, "was the chief engineer." Standing so close to the plane as it took off that he was nearly thrown to the ground by the backwash, he kept running behind the taxiing craft, "shouting hysterically." When the first attempt to lift the plane failed, "his anguish was terrible." After it finally rose into the sky, "he broke down completely." Four planes escorted the *White Bird* to the coast and then peeled off, leaving the fliers to their appointed goal: Long Island's Mitchell Field by noon on Monday. The leading French daily, *Le Matin,* wrote that Nungesser and Coli bore with them "the total admiration of France" as they pursued "the triumph of French aviation and energy."[44]

Five hours later word came that the plane had passed the coast of Ireland. Traveling by way of the great circle course meant that once over the ocean they were out of sight of the shipping lanes, and as they had no radio there would be no word about their progress for a number of anxious hours. American aviators wished them well; some expressed surprise that they had taken off despite reports of bad weather.[45]

Hours later came reports of sightings off Newfoundland, setting off jubilation in France. But the celebration turned out to be premature; the sightings proved false. In fact the *White Bird* had vanished without a trace. More than two days after departure it could not be located. Some speculated that it had encountered a fog bank or a storm, others that ice had formed on the wings, undermining the craft's stability. "Ice formation," warned one expert, "brings down a plane almost quicker than anything else." Fears grew that instead of the "greatest of all glories to French aviation" Nungesser and Coli had become two more victims of the ruthless Atlantic course and that the "secret of their failure may always lie beneath the gray, grim waters of the North Atlantic."[46]

Anguish and disappointment engulfed France. No event since the war had so shaken emotions. The aviation expert General Duval questioned whether it had been worth it. Such a feat promised no benefits. Aviation had simply not advanced far enough to support such travel on a regular basis. For men to risk their lives for no scientific gain was unconscionable. Some lashed out at the United States, charging (falsely) that its weather sources had withheld information about potential storms. American papers reported unruly crowds pulling down the U.S. flag outside *Le Matin*'s offices and venting their anger at the newspaper for having originally reported that Nungesser and Coli had completed the flight safely. The U.S. State Department released a cable from Ambassador Myron T. Herrick suggesting that American efforts to cross the ocean at this sensitive moment might be "misunderstood and misinterpreted" and that discretion dictated that such attempts should be suspended for the time being.[47]

But nothing could dampen the Atlantic Fever. Side by side with reports of "grave anxiety . . . for Nungesser and Coli" ran headlines announcing "Bellanca's Plane Is Ready to Start." If Paris did not want them, the contenders were said to be ready to fly over France and land in England. "They hoped to get the jump on us," the *Columbia*'s copilot Lloyd Bertraud declared rather unsentimentally about the missing fliers. "Now it is our turn. Let's go."[48]

Only sporadically did coverage of the "New York to Paris Air Derby" take notice of a young pilot from the St. Louis–Chicago airmail route who had also filed the

$250 entry fee. He lacked the distinction of the others, all of whom had served in the Great War. Indeed his greatest claim to fame was that he had cheated death by opening his parachute. His unorthodox plan to pilot a small, single-engine craft alone was dismissed at first as misguided, if not worse; his name (often misspelled) appeared in articles about the Orteig contestants as an afterthought, if at all.[49]

But the great men had failed tragically, and in retrospect it seems shocking how many of them had been so reckless in their preparations. None of them had questioned the conventional approach to long-distance flight: clap on another engine and pour in more fuel. Veterans of a process in which toughing it out had won them medals, they were blind to new strategies. Even after six deaths and losses that approached half a million dollars, they refused to rethink the process.

Lindbergh, by contrast, was not invested in memories. He continued to pursue a different strategy: loading a stripped-down ship with enough fuel to fly across the ocean; ignoring comfort, sleep, food, emergency equipment, and communication devices; skipping the navigator, cutting down on the motors, and doing everything to save on weight, including tearing the margins off the maps. It was a strategy built around endurance and efficiency.

Four manufacturers had turned him down. The Ryan Company was his last hope. In the last week of February he traveled out to San Diego, and what he saw at first inspired little confidence. The ramshackle plant stood on a bleak waterfront amid warehouses, factories, and food-processing plants. Over everything hung the odor of dead fish from a nearby cannery. The large dilapidated work shed had no flying field near it, no hangar, nothing to impress an aviator. But the people seemed knowledgeable, and Lindbergh liked their "character." Within an hour he had met the entire management of the company, from its chief engineer and sales manager to its president, Benjamin F. Mahoney, who was not much older than he. The production team appeared to be prepared for his visit, having studied issues involving design and durability before answering his telegram. They told him that they could produce a plane with large fuel capacity, one rugged enough to withstand the stresses of a transatlantic flight and yet light enough to rely on a single engine.[50]

Lindbergh felt an immediate connection with Mahoney and with Donald Hall, the chief designer responsible for all the calculations. Like him, the twenty-eight-year-old engineer had trained at Brooks Field in Austin, and Lindbergh admired his no-nonsense attitude and obvious enthusiasm for the project. Mahoney told Lindbergh that the company was too small to offer guarantees, especially on such a high-risk venture. They would do the best they could. However, Mahoney did assure Lindbergh that his plane would be ready in two months.[51]

"I believe in Hall's ability; I like Mahoney's enthusiasm," Lindbergh wrote. "They're as anxious to build a plane that will fly to Paris as I am to fly it there." The price, $6,000 for the plane plus the cost of the Wright J-5 engine and instruments, $10,580 total, was a fraction of what his competitors were laying out, but he informed the St. Louis group that he thought the plane would work. Within a day they approved the Ryan deal.[52]

Lindbergh's competitors had been too removed from the production and design of their planes. In Davis's case the plane was delivered at a half ton over the specified weight. Lindbergh resolved to remain in San Diego to oversee the making of his ship, writing, "I can inspect each detail before it is covered with fabric and fairings." More than just supervising he intended to mold his own vision into the ship.[53]

Hall began by modifying a stock model, making changes in the landing gear and lengthening the wing span by about ten feet to provide greater lift for the extraordinarily large takeoff load. He added auxiliary gas tanks and, to cut down wind resistance, designed a trimmer fuselage of tubular steel with an enclosed cockpit streamlined into the line of the airplane's body. Lindbergh calculated that this step alone would increase cruising speed, saving about fifty gallons of fuel.[54]

For part of his time in San Diego Lindbergh roomed at the YMCA with Hall. They discussed plans and adjustments late into the night. One of the adjustments dealt with the placement of the main gas tank. In most machines it was set behind the cockpit. However, a number of the fuel-heavy planes headed for Paris had suffered front-end crashes. Lindbergh wanted the main gas tank set directly behind the engine in front of the cockpit. In the event of a minor crash it would lessen the chances of his getting crushed between the engine and the huge fuel tank. Placing the tank in the front, however, would also block direct forward vision, but he could lean out the side windows for a view. In any case he expected to be guided by his instruments. And, of course, he did not have to be concerned about running into another plane over the Atlantic. He would have the air to himself.[55]

Hall suggested a wider tail to provide more cruising stability. Lindbergh objected that it would increase resistance and use more fuel: "Let's put everything into range. I don't need a very stable plane." In fact, he argued, a plane that lurched at the smallest easing up on the controls would keep him awake and alert. Regarding the propeller, a low blade angle enhanced horsepower, providing greater thrust on takeoff, but once the plane was cruising such a setting used more fuel. Confident that the takeoff would not be more difficult than the ones he managed in the low-power planes he had wrestled while barnstorming, Lindbergh again chose fuel efficiency, setting the propeller at a higher angle.[56]

Hall asked where to place the seat for the navigator and was taken aback by Lindbergh's reply: "I'd rather have extra gasoline than an extra man." Hall questioned the decision, given that Lindbergh had "practically no technical knowledge of navigation." Lindbergh told him that he was going to learn. Finally the radical simplicity of Lindbergh's plan became clear to Hall. Lindbergh basically wanted a covered plank with fuel tanks. By the time the *Spirit of St. Louis* was done, Lindbergh recalled, "every part of it . . . [was] designed for a single purpose, every line fashioned to the Paris flight."[57]

Given variable weather and flight conditions it was not possible to calculate precisely how much fuel would be needed. What Lindbergh did know was that he needed to eliminate every unnecessary ounce so that he would not have to carry as much fuel as the other competitors. Radio equipment weighed forty pounds or more; he decided to do without it. He also nixed night-flying lights, a parachute, and even fuel gauges; none was worth its weight. Based on Hall's analysis of fuel-to-distance ratios they agreed that 425 gallons of gasoline should support a range of 4,100 miles—enough to get to Paris plus a 500-mile reserve.[58]

There were improvisations along the way. To give Lindbergh at least some forward vision, A. C. Randolph, a veteran of the submarine service, crafted a periscope that slid back and forth from the side window. The press later reported that the device helped with takeoff and landing, which was not really accurate, but it did allow the pilot to see rooftops and hills when he flew low.[59]

When the Wright Company received the Ryan order for a "super inspected" Whirlwind engine, Manager J. T. Hartson hesitated. This was for the same Lindbergh whom they had turned down for the Wright-Bellanca, and they were no more confident in his prospects now. "We might not want to in any way encourage a Trans-Atlantic-Flight with a single motor airplane," Hartson wrote in a memo dated March 1. "This has been our policy in the past." But company officials realized that they could not prevent Ryan from purchasing a conventional J-5 engine, and they had supplied Byrd, Davis, and Chamberlin with premium motors. They set aside their qualms about Lindbergh's "many opportunities for failure" and filled the order.[60]

The precision-tuned motor arrived on April 8 with instructions to not "fuss with it," just install and test. They all gathered around as it was unpacked from the crate, marveling, as though witnessing an art unveiling, which in a way it was. "Here," Lindbergh remembered thinking, "is the ultimate lightness of weight and power—two hundred and twenty-three horses compressed into nine delicate fin-covered cylinders of aluminum and steel." This five-hundred-pound contraption of connecting rods, cams, gears, and bearings would have to spin faultlessly many thousand times a minute for close to forty hours to deliver him safely to Paris.[61]

Harm von Linde, Ryan's chief mechanic, was not sure it was worth all the effort, then one day he watched Lindbergh put a standard Ryan through its paces.

"This young boy . . . flew that ship for about an hour, wrung it out like nothing I'd ever seen," he said. Lindbergh won over the Ryan staff with his interest in every detail. He came into the factory every day, often staying till late in the night, making them feel like they were a part of his team. During the first weeks of production, Don Hall recalled, Lindbergh participated in every aspect of the plane's construction, "and he did not leave San Diego until he was absolutely sure that the smallest part, the weakest link in the mechanism of his ship was strong enough to withstand strain before which other planes had succumbed."[62]

One day, as the engine oil lines were being fitted, Lindbergh observed workers installing a single length of pipe. A single line might crack from vibrations during a forced landing; he asked that it be replaced by eighteen-inch lengths of pipe connected at the joints. Later this became standard procedure. Ryan's order for the *Spirit*'s fuel tanks, the vendor recalled, specified that they be delivered *without a scratch* lest "vibrations . . . set in and create a leak." Hall told the shop superintendent to hold fuselage fairings to an accuracy of one thirty-second of an inch. The work crew grumbled that they had never been held to so exacting a standard, but later in the day Lindbergh saw the work being inspected to that standard.[63]

Hall often came in at five in the morning to check the work that had been completed the day before and to adjust his designs for the day ahead before the staff arrived. He put in ninety-hour weeks, working thirty-six hours straight over one stretch, striving to keep Lindbergh in the race. A grateful Lindbergh later calculated that Hall worked an incredible 775 hours over the eight weeks of production. Work on other Ryan orders virtually stopped; every hand was put to this project. The men earned about sixty-five cents an hour; the women received as much as twenty-five cents less. Overtime was out of the question. Nonetheless, inspired by Hall's single-mindedness, they bent to meet the promised delivery date. In all, 850 hours of engineering and another 3,000 shop hours were squeezed into less than eight weeks. On some nights the factory lights did not go out at all.[64]

Lindbergh still worried that the other Orteig contenders were far ahead. "I'm clearly in a race against time," he remembered telling himself, "with odds against me." But three weeks after he had walked into Mahoney's office a steel skeleton of the fuselage and wings took shape. His formal application to the National Aeronautic Association for the Orteig competition was accepted, but he needed to wait sixty days from the date of filing to be eligible at the end of May. He did not think this would make much of a difference. He planned on taking off early in June, when a full moon would provide the most light.[65]

With much of the design work done Lindbergh turned to navigation. For much of April he devoted practically all of his waking hours to gathering maps, studying weather patterns, and familiarizing himself with the landmarks over the dry parts of his route. He had gotten only the most rudimentary grasp of navigation from the army's flight training school, not nearly enough to plot a course across the ocean. Still, afraid to show them that the kid who was challenging world-class navigators like Byrd was *just now* learning the essential skills for his journey, he decided against consulting the naval experts stationed in San Diego. Instead he pored over navigational texts at the local library, talked with sailors and ship chandlers on the waterfront, and taught himself to set a compass course and interpret navigational charts. The college dropout mastered enough spherical mathematics and trigonometry to lay out his great circle route in hundred-mile segments, with compass corrections for the distortion of the earth's curvature introduced by plotting on a flat map.[66]

By April Lindbergh was appearing in news articles, described simply as the "dark horse," so dark that if he were to make it across the water, in the words of one report, his "venture would be perhaps the most spectacular of all." A small stream of the curious began to visit the Ryan works to catch a glimpse of the *Spirit of St. Louis* and to hear him discuss his plans. Meanwhile Clarence Chamberlin and Bert Acosta broke the world endurance record for aircraft, keeping their Bellanca in the air for more than fifty-one hours. Their total mileage during this feat exceeded the distance to Paris. Lindbergh was left to ponder soberly the fact that for him to succeed "almost everyone else would have to fail." For an instant his thoughts turned again to a Pacific flight by way of the Hawaiian Islands, but they quickly turned back to Paris.[67]

On April 28, two days after Davis and Wooster's ill-fated test flight ended in their deaths and exactly sixty days after work began, the *Spirit of St. Louis* was completed. The fuselage was rolled out through the large opening of the workshop's ground floor, but the wing, completed in the loft space above the work floor and measuring forty-six feet across, did not fit through the doors. Before breaking through walls the Ryan team hit upon the idea of removing a pair of double doors and tipping the wing just so to maneuver it out of the second story onto a boxcar that had been moved into place outside the factory, and from there onto the ground. The entire Ryan staff signed their names behind the cone of the propeller and attached a swastika (an ancient symbol of good fortune before it took on its Nazi overtones) "for luck."[68]

At a hangar on San Diego's outskirts workmen attached the wing to the top of the chassis and installed the cockpit instruments. Less than ten feet tall and twenty-seven feet, eight inches long, with a thin skin of silver gray cotton stretched over the wing and fuselage (and lacquered with cellulose acetate dope to waterproof and tauten the fabric), the trim craft of wood, cloth, and metal weighed a mere 2,180 pounds. Its duraluminum propeller consisted of two blades, eight feet, nine inches long, pitched to conserve fuel during the flight. To carry the fuel there were five fuel tanks: a huge 210-gallon main tank at the front of the fuselage and four auxiliary tanks, one in the nose cone and three arrayed along the wing to hold an additional 240 gallons (the total exceeding by twenty-five gallons the initial design for 425). On the rudder was painted "Ryan NYP," representing the New York–Paris course, and on either side of the plane's faceted metal front hood was emblazoned in black *Spirit of St. Louis*. The craft's powerhouse was its prized air-cooled nine-cylinder 223-hp engine. "On this intricate perfection," Lindbergh mused upon first seeing the cosmoline-painted motor, "I'm to trust my life across the Atlantic Ocean."[69]

Lindbergh turned immediately to a program of testing. As he had anticipated, when he settled into the lightweight wicker pilot's seat for the first time his forward vision was entirely obstructed, but he could see out the side windows and found the view "not much worse than" his DH-4 mail plane. Then he signaled the young mechanic, Douglas Corrigan (who would claim his own page in aviation history in 1938 as "Wrong Way Corrigan" when he set off for California from New York City without maps, radio, or much instrumentation, only to land at Baldonell Airport in Dublin), to remove the chocks blocking the wheels. He took off and put the plane through its paces, reaching a top speed of 130 mph. Over the next ten days he carried out close to twenty-eight hours of testing, including a series of load trials (with as much as three hundred gallons of gasoline).[70]

Lindbergh was the only one to fly the plane after it left the factory floor. He completed the final exercises on May 4, never having tested the *Spirit* with a full 425-gallon load because the results of the tests had exceeded expectations. Doing so would have involved landing with more than a ton of gasoline, putting tremendous pressure on the tires and ball bearings, especially on the rough landing field that he was using. In Paris he would be landing with fuel tanks empty. In any event, the cross- country flight to New York would be more than test enough.[71]

For Lindbergh the final stages brought a blissful contentment. "What freedom lies in flying!" he later remembered thinking. "What godlike power it gives to man." Clarence M. Young, Lindbergh's former commanding officer and now head of the Aeronautics Division's air regulation branch, flew out to San Diego to inspect the *Spirit* for registration and assigned an NX prefix, "N" for "U.S. craft" and "X" for "experimental," which permitted modifications without prior approval. While Ryan engineers busily fine-tuned the craft, Lindbergh took up other planes, behaving like a prizefighter fearful of losing his edge. Even on the ground he kept testing himself with different scenarios, responding in his mind to various emergencies: determining where he might detour at different points along the route; calculating how far out on the ocean he could go and still turn back; how to handle being forced down at sea; how to locate Paris in the dark; and every other possibility that his overdriven imagination could project. He planned to hop to St. Louis on Friday, May 6, and then to New York. "My bills are paid, my bank account is closed," he wrote. "Tires are pumped. . . . The . . . tank is full." But a storm over the Rockies kept him on the ground.[72]

On Sunday, May 8, he learned that Nungesser and Coli had left Paris and were expected to arrive in New York the following day. A glum Lindbergh drew out the charts he had prepared for a Pacific flight (if he was beaten to Paris) and devoted the day to studying charts to Honolulu and points farther west.[73]

The next day brought conflicting reports. Some said the French fliers had been sighted, while other reports declared them missing. By late Sunday it appeared certain that they were lost and by now also out of fuel. Lindbergh put away the Pacific charts and decided to proceed to St. Louis, where his patrons planned a gala welcome and plane christening. On May 10, with the weather clearing and no fresh news about Nungesser and Coli (and Levine's Bellanca delayed, while Byrd's Fokker was still undergoing repairs), Lindbergh thanked the Ryan factory team and bade them good-bye. He waited until late in the afternoon to take off so that he would cover the bulk of the 1,550-mile trip to St. Louis at night to sharpen his "blind" flying skills, that is, relying purely on instrument guidance. He also wanted to reassure his backers, who had come under increasing criticism for encouraging so inexperienced a pilot to make a flight that had already cost at least four lives. A successful night flight over the Rocky Mountains would give his supporters a boost. Escorted by two army observation planes and a Ryan monoplane with Hall onboard, he circled North Island, saluted the Ryan works, and, as the accompanying planes dipped their wings and peeled off, made his way across the coastal range past the Colorado River to Arizona.[74]

Three hours into the flight, while over "one of the wildest regions of Arizona" and in the frigid climate above eight thousand feet, he felt the engine jolt and begin to vibrate. The craft lost altitude and shook violently as the motor began sputtering. He circled for a while and considered turning back but decided to keep going; if he had to, he would land in the mountains, hoping to find a canyon clearing by moonlight. The distressing cough persisted, but slowly, as the plane regained altitude, the shaking stopped and he felt more power in the motor. Considering how carefully the engine was checked and the gasoline filtered he concluded that the problem had to be a combination of altitude and cold mountain air. He allowed the engine to work through the problem and made a mental note to install a carburetor heater once he reached New York.[75]

Lindbergh arrived over St. Louis at 8 a.m. Central Standard Time, completing the 1,550-mile solo journey over mountains, desert, and prairie through the dark in fourteen hours and five minutes. No pilot had flown so far alone in so short a time. Keeping a promise to his backers, he circled the business district before touching down twenty minutes later. Bill Robertson handed him a Bureau of Aeronautics envelope with his assigned pilot's license, number 69. "Right side up or upside down—the same," someone remarked. "Just fits you."[76]

He asked about Nungesser and Coli and learned that the American embassy had urged a moratorium on Atlantic flights. He was certain that the *Columbia* would proceed anyway, but put off making his own decision until he was in New York. Anxious to hasten there, he begged off from the St. Louis celebrations. The press was less accommodating. By now they were very interested in the dark horse from the West. "It looks as though I won't have to bother much about adequate publicity from now on," he noted sardonically, as a mob of journalists surrounded him. They wanted to know about his plans if he came down in the ocean. He told them that the plane's wings would keep the craft afloat for a while, allowing him to empty the gas canisters, which he would then use as large buoys to keep the plane afloat. What about emergency equipment? "Could anything I carry save my life?" Every safety measure came with a cost in weight, reducing his margin of safety even *if nothing untoward happened*. He was keeping his emergency supplies to a minimum. Instead of water at eight pounds a gallon he was taking an Armbrust Cup that condensed moisture into water. He would also carry a collapsible rubber raft, some flares, a hunting knife, a hacksaw blade, a fishing line with hooks, a ball of string, matches, and a sewing needle with thread. If he came down into water he would fish for food, and with the needle and thread would sew a kite from the wing canvas and set it aloft to alert searchers.[77]

Organizations and individuals accosted him to carry small parcels, mail and specially marked envelopes, even offering $1,000 for one pound of mail. But he refused, keeping to his plan to "hold down every ounce of excess weight." He did make an exception for letters of introduction to the U.S. ambassador to France, Myron T. Herrick (including one from Colonel Theodore Roosevelt, the former president's son), but otherwise he refused anything extra, even from his St. Louis backers.[78]

After a hearty steak breakfast on the morning of May 12 he took off from Lambert Field at 8:13 a.m., arriving over Manhattan ("I feel cooped up just looking at it") seven hours later and landing at Curtiss Airfield in Mineola, Long Island, at 3:35, Central Standard Time. He had completed the 950-mile trip in seven hours and twenty-two minutes (averaging close to 120 mph), another milestone. His total flying time from coast to coast, twenty-one hours and twenty minutes, shaved five and a half hours off the old record, set in 1923.[79]

"Dramatically," writes the historian J. J. Corn, he "flew into the public's gaze," with his record-breaking race between the coasts. The airfield was a mob scene.

Photographers and the press were milling around. "I've never seen such excitement and disorder around aircraft," Lindbergh later commented. One old-timer was overheard saying as the plane arrived, "Flying all alone, eh? Must have got away from his keeper." But once he swooped down, spectators cheered from all sides. "A window opened and the smiling face of a man who seemed little more than a boy appeared," the next day's *New York Times* reported. The article celebrated the handsome young flier's "sheer audacity and speed," his trim little plane, and his determination to be the last man standing.[80]

The new face captured the front pages. The accompanying articles described "throngs of women and girls" chasing after the "tall, handsome, blond youngster from the Middle West" for a glimpse or, better yet, to touch him. "No one ever more perfectly personified youthful adventure," gushed the smitten *New York Times*, "than the youthful knight of the air." He was "easily the lion of the hour . . . modest . . . handsome and confident." The report concluded, "He is as clean looking a specimen of man as could be found."[81]

And an open contrast with his competitors. No expense had been spared on Byrd's mission. With more than thirty mechanics, telegraph operators, artisans, and staffers, the *America* enterprise resembled nothing so much as a corporate venture, with its own mogul patron (and pestering ninny), Rodman Wanamaker. As befit so well-heeled a venture, the *America* project boasted luxurious executive offices, top-level consulting services, and field operations outfitted with every possible gadget and amenity. Lindbergh also contrasted with the *Columbia* group. They became enmeshed in unseemly quarrels over how to divide the Orteig prize money and over providing insurance for the pilots' families. Things got nastier when Charles Levine put himself on the crew, replacing the experienced navigator. He also dismissed copilot Lloyd Bertraud, who promptly retaliated with a court injunction preventing the *Columbia* from taking off.[82]

Arriving alone and out of nowhere, Lindbergh changed the competition from a tawdry contest over money and personal pride into something nobler. He provided wonderful drama and the example—all the more striking in the midst of the materialistic twenties—of a life fixed upon heroic conquest. When Lindbergh wired Harry Knight that in order to steal a march on the *Columbia* he might have to take off before completing the sixty-day wait required to qualify for the Orteig, Knight responded, "To hell with the money. When you are ready to take off, go ahead." Sleek and focused, Lindbergh's operation better personified the winged ideal than did the old Goliaths, with their bloated support crews and massive ships.[83]

Overnight Lindbergh became the favorite, winning the hearts of the public who cheered him on, hoping he "would get away first." For the press he was a godsend, opening a new dimension to what had become a tiresome loop of stories about weather and delays. They took hold of the fresh material, filling columns with his varied nicknames, tales of his daring mail flights, and descriptions of his "remarkable instinct, like that of a homing pigeon, for direction in his flying." Around him they shaped a narrative of the farm-bred all-American boy, fighting the odds with pluck, strong values, and a confident humility. Good American "boys," even in their mid-twenties, loved Mom. So while he was quite happy to have Evangeline safely tucked away in Detroit ("For the first time in my life," she wrote in one of her letters, "I realize that Columbus also had a mother") so that he could concentrate on the flight, reporters in New York and Detroit stirred into their stories the indomitable widow facing her son's death-defying flight with quiet courage. So persistently did they pester her about the dangers and describe how experienced fliers had died in previous efforts that she finally decided that she needed to come to New York to spend a day with him. "ARRIVE NEW YORK TOMORROW MORNING," she wired on May 13.[84]

The last place he wanted his mother in these tense days was at his side. But the story overtook him. The media framed the visit as the son who would not take off until he got Mom's blessing. (His father did not make it into the stories, though one would think a congressman father, even if deceased, deserved some notice. But mentioning C. A. would complicate the golden boy narrative by invoking the parents' estrangement.) Evangeline arrived on the May 14, providing a spate of front-page inanity. (Q: *"Was your son a good boy?"* A: *"Just look at him."* Q: *"You had no trouble raising him?"*) She returned home the following day. As mother and son parted she patted him on the back and wished him good luck. Photographers begged for an embrace and a kiss. "I wouldn't mind if we were used to that," she replied, "[but] we come from an undemonstrative Nordic race." Some tabloids put together a fake composite to provide the desired kiss.[85]

He had become a valuable piece of copy and the press was playing with different representations. Landing after a test flight he was forced to veer suddenly to avoid hitting a cameraman and cracked his tail skid. Tabloid accounts presented a laid-back if lovable kid, who drove a bit recklessly and almost killed a bystander. "Undismayed by this accident, which he considers trivial," one sheet wrote, he hopped up with a big smile, declaring, "Boys, she's ready and rarin' to go!" He was not pleased. "These fellows must think I'm a cowpuncher, just transferred to aviation . . . calling me a lanky demon of the air from the wide open spaces." Others simply manufactured facts, reporting on a "device" that would allow him to snooze as he flew to Paris.[86]

He could not hide his discomfort with the new creative journalism: "Accuracy means something to me. It's vital to my sense of values. I've learned not to trust people who are inaccurate. . . . In my profession life itself depends on accuracy." But there was no denying that he had originally sought the attention: "I wanted publicity on this flight. That was part of my program. Newspapers are important. I wanted their help. I wanted headlines." However, he was put off by the mindless questions and rude intrusions. He deplored the focus on "silly stories," the fabrications, "the constant photographing": "There's never a free moment except when I'm in my room." And not even then; one pair of photographers burst into his hotel room to steal a shot of Lindy in his pajamas, shaving.[87]

Fortunately he acquired a friend. One of the first people to greet him after he landed in New York was Richard Blythe of Wright Aircraft. The engine manufacturer, no longer hesitant about associating with Lindbergh, had assigned Blythe to "protect him from the exploiters and the mob." Wright also assigned its ace mechanic, Ed Mulligan, to service his engine. (After a few days with Lindbergh, Mulligan remarked to Joe Hartson, the Wright official who had originally questioned the Lindbergh project, "Joe, this boy's going to make it! I tell you he is!") The Mobil, Pioneer, and Curtiss companies also sent their best men to the Orteig competitors to provide service, replacement parts, and repairs—all at no cost. The aviation industry grasped that this highly publicized contest might prove its big break, and these firms wanted a role in it. Blythe, with his partner Harold Bruno, were responsible for handling public relations and to shield Lindbergh from the press.[88]

The first day Lindbergh did not utter a word to Blythe, though they shared a room at the Garden City Hotel. Only on the third morning did Lindbergh offer a welcome of sorts by pulling back Blythe's blanket at five o'clock in the morning and dousing the terrified flack with ice. "I liked him," Lindbergh later wrote, "and he was a tremendous help to me." The proof of that came a few mornings later, when poor Blythe, who had a tendency to sleep past dawn, woke up to find the lanky flier bent over him with shaving cream and a razor, intent on claiming half his mustache. Blythe managed to struggle free, but their friendship was confirmed.[89]

Blythe was a "tremendous help." He helped Lindbergh understand that the story he had become part of had overtaken everything else and could prove extremely valuable to aviation in general. Since he arrived in New York he had "taken the show." So naturally did he draw media interest that the *New York Times* offered him a deal to write a column about his flight once he landed in Paris. A mere flyboy who had failed English, he was overwhelmed that for exclusive rights the respected daily was offering "several thousand dollars! That's a huge amount of money for a little writing."[90]

Everything had changed in seventy-two hours. Just days earlier Lindbergh's anonymity had seemed secure. Now he had a contract to write for the *Times*, the Wright Company was doing everything to help him, and all the aviation stars came by to welcome him and wish him well. Richard Byrd was especially gracious, making his way over to Lindbergh's hangar at Curtiss Field to congratulate him on his record flight from San Diego. He also invited Lindbergh to use his private Roosevelt Field runway for the Paris flight. Byrd had extended and refinished the strip at considerable expense, making it the best takeoff lane in the region. He also made available the weather reports prepared for him by his meteorological expert, James H. "Doc" Kimball. Lindbergh, who found the patrician Byrd "most courteous and considerate," accepted the offer.[91]

Just days earlier Lindbergh had despaired of making it to New York in time to compete, but bad weather and internal dissension had delayed the *Columbia*. Now both Byrd and he were ready, and the press was trumpeting "the most spectacular race ever held," speculating that all three planes might soon be taking off at the same time.[92]

Lindbergh had a question for Bill MacCracken, assistant secretary of commerce for aeronautics, when he dropped by. New federal regulations required navigation lights for night flights. He had eliminated them to save weight. Was that a problem? MacCracken had to smile at the earnest query, especially since it was unlikely that the *Spirit of St. Louis* was going to run into anyone else along the way. Harry Guggenheim also paid a visit. He was struck by the young flier's "great dignity and modesty in an age of showmen." He praised the "calm assurance, controlled enthusiasm, his faith absolute." But as he left a profound sadness overtook Guggenheim. The errand that the daring aviator had assigned himself, "sitting unrelieved, almost motionless, at the controls of an airplane for over thirty hours," was "doomed."[93]

The grounded fliers remained the top story for days. Lindbergh was receiving more than a hundred letters a day. On Sunday, May 15, thirty thousand people traipsed out to Long Island for a glimpse of the planes. While forecasts called for several more days of stormy weather over the Atlantic, with dangerous squalls, Lindbergh took the time to talk with Byrd's meteorologist, Doc Kimball, who tried to persuade him to take the safer ship-lane route; weather forecasts for the great circle route were much more of a guess. But Lindbergh believed it was too late to change his plans. Nonetheless he did take from Kimball fresh data about weather patterns around Newfoundland and the North Atlantic.[94]

While he waited Lindbergh worked off his nervous energy by horsing around with what had become his team, including Blythe, some of the Wright mechanics, and Ryan's president, Ben Mahoney, who had come east to witness the flight. They spent a day at Brooklyn's Coney Island amusement park, enjoying the rides, hot dogs, and carnival atmosphere until he was spotted. As a crowd began to form they scurried off.[95]

Thursday, May 19, was another rainy day. Lindbergh left the *Spirit* under guard and planned to spend the evening watching the play *Rio Rita* from backstage. Around four in the afternoon Blythe checked with Doc Kimball, who surprised him with a new forecast: the weather over the Atlantic was clearing, and the low pressure system over Newfoundland was dissipating. Over the next two days the entire route should clear. Lindbergh decided to forgo the Broadway play and drove out to Curtiss Field. They found no one stirring from the Byrd or Chamberlin camps. Lindbergh ordered the team to begin preparations for a morning departure.[96]

Two men were assigned to go over the engine. Blythe and Mahoney went to settle arrangements for Roosevelt Field and to locate a National Aeronautic Association official to affix the official barograph that would certify that the flight followed the Orteig rules. Wright chief engineer Kenneth Lane began the laborious task of filling the tanks with gasoline filtered through mesh to eliminate particles that might clog the engine. Half the capacity of 450 gallons were to be filled now and the rest once the *Spirit* was taxied over to Roosevelt for takeoff.[97]

Lindbergh was told that French emotions still ran high over the loss of Nungesser and Coli, but he had already decided that he would proceed nonetheless. The remark did remind him that eagerness to get into the air might have pushed Nungesser and Coli to downplay reports of turbulent weather. Still, he needed an edge. If he waited for perfect weather all three planes would be up and ready. He would leave at daybreak.[98]

He wanted to start early in the morning so that once he was in the air he could count on a full day of sunlight and still reach Newfoundland before dusk. If things went as planned he would arrive over Ireland before nightfall, and then finding well-lit Paris should not be much of a challenge, even in the dark. His fuel supply provided him a safe margin of error of about five hundred miles. Even if he was driven off course over the ocean as far as northern Scandinavia or southern Spain he would still have sufficient gasoline to make his way to Paris.[99]

With everything in motion Lindbergh headed back to the Garden City Hotel for a few hours of sleep. Reporters had already learned that something was brewing, and a number of them were milling in the lobby despite the late hour. There were also men proffering deals, one for a motion picture contract on the spot, for $250,000; another offered $50,000 for a series of stage appearances. It was close to midnight, and all he wanted to do now was get an hour or two of sleep. He asked his old friend George Stumpf to stay outside his door to make sure that he was not disturbed until about two o'clock.[100]

Sleep did not come immediately. His mind raced though contingencies. He also thought about the fact that he was starting out before the sixty-day qualification period for the Orteig. Jumping the gun meant that he might be disqualified from the prize, but if he did not steal a step on his competitors he was certain to lose even the opportunity to be first. Without the Orteig money, how would he pay off the $15,000 to his St. Louis backers? Just as he finally began to doze, he heard a rap on the door. It was George Stumpf. His friend sat down at the edge of the bed. By now all drowsiness was gone. "Slim," he asked haltingly, "what am I going to do when you are gone?" Lindbergh could not believe the "fool question." He calmed poor Stumpf and got him out the door, but he was already "twenty-three hours without sleep," and sleep was now impossible. He would have to rely on adrenaline to keep awake. Shortly before 3 in the morning he was driven by the editor and publisher of *Aero Digest* out to Long Island.[101]

He had successfully completed 7,190 flights by his own count. Perhaps as many as fifty people might have actually cared about those flights. This one would be different.[102]

FLIGHT OF THE CENTURY

FRIDAY, MAY 20, 1927, dawned misty and drizzling. Heavy showers through the night had turned the ground muddy and soft. Nonetheless weather stations from New York to Newfoundland predicted improvement and lifting fog. *New York Times* reports being phoned in regularly were encouraging. Lindbergh told Kenneth Lane that if the clouds left room "to slip beneath" he would start at daybreak.[1]

Lane had arranged to truck the *Spirit* from Curtiss to the five-thousand-foot-long Byrd airstrip at Roosevelt Field. Attached to a tow the covered plane appeared slight and vulnerable, not at all a machine that would be asked to defy gravity and fight the elements for 3,600 miles. In the near distance, barely visible in the pre-dawn darkness, was a blackened remnant from the Fonck crash. Usually exuberant around planes and airfields, Lindbergh was uncharacteristically subdued as he watched the procession escorting the shrouded craft. As it passed, one man remarked that what they were watching had "all the dreams of a boy," but a pensive Lindbergh noted that it was all "more like a funeral procession than the beginning of a flight to Paris." Lloyd's of London, insurers of every conceivable risk, refused to quote a price on Lindbergh's chances.[2]

Wright engineers who had warmed up the engine through the night reported that it was running at about thirty revolutions slower than usual, likely due to the cool, moist weather. They went over every inch of the engine and pronounced it perfect. After a final check of the plane's instruments and moving parts, the last steps involved oiling the wheel bearings and smearing the tires with grease to prevent the tarmac mud from sticking. Byrd came by. "Good luck to you, old man," he said to Lindbergh. Clutching his canteens and a bag of sandwiches, the Lone Eagle told reporters, "If I get to Paris I won't need any more and if I don't get to Paris I won't need any more either."[3]

A few minutes before eight, sheathed in a brown cotton twill coverall flying suit with fur collar, Lindbergh eased his six-foot-two-and-a-half-inch frame into the single-engine Ryan monoplane's cabin. He scanned the instruments set into a plywood dash: an earth inductor compass; aneroid barometer to indicate altitude; Pitot tube air speed indicator; tachometer showing engine revolutions per minute; inclinometer, measuring ascent, descent, and direction; and the bank and turn indicator. He buckled the safety belt, stuffed cotton in his ears, adjusted his goggles, and pulled on his leather helmet. If in the first few seconds anything did not feel right he planned to abandon the flight.[4]

His wheels sank deeply into the soft clay of the wet runway and for the first time he wondered if the plane had enough power. He reviewed the elements that he must keep in balance throughout the flight: wind, weather, power, and load. The *Spirit's* wings were going to have to lift more than they ever had before (empty, the plane weighed barely a ton; with gasoline poured to the brim it bulked up to 5,250 pounds). Don Hall had assured him that the weight would present no problem. Lindbergh trusted Hall, but wondered what effect the mist, soft runway, and slowed engine movement were going to have. The horizon remained hidden.[5]

The *Spirit of St. Louis* was a flying fuel tank; downfield men stood prepared with fire extinguishers, just in case. Finally, with nothing left to check, Lindbergh steeled himself—"What do you say—let's try it"—signaled for the chocks to be removed, and pushed the throttle wide open, rushing a mixture of air and fuel to the engine. The ground crew ran alongside, pushing on the wing struts to help the plane gain momentum. Lindbergh thought the plane felt sluggish, "more like an overloaded truck than an airplane." The tires did not so much wheel across the runway as rut through it, and for a split second takeoff seemed hopeless. He could tell that the engine was working hard, but there was no surge of power. "Nothing about my plane has the magic quality of flight," he recalled thinking. But then he had never piloted a plane with more than a ton of fuel in its tanks.[6]

"Men watched it with anguish in their gaze," the *New York Times* reported a little breathlessly in the next edition, as "death lay but a few seconds ahead of him. . . . He gambled for his life against a hazard which had already killed four men." Kenneth Lane was running behind the plane, chasing after it for a reason that he could not explain. He later recounted that he had "died three times" in those seconds before the plane rose into the air. The tail skid was still dragging through the mud after several hundred feet. Lindbergh had to lift his plane or he would crash like the others.[7]

Here, as in the rest of this account, the narrative relies on Lindbergh's own reconstruction of these events, published years later and based on his own records and meticulous research into a story that never lost its fascination for him.

The turf became a blur, stilling apprehensions about the engine's power, but Lindbergh continued to worry. Could the landing gear take the combined weight and speed; could the wheels absorb the friction? The plane had to be kept perfectly straight. If one wheel tilted ever so slightly the *Spirit* could splinter in the mud. As he passed the one-thousand-foot mark he began to sense resistance in the stick, the controls coming alive in his hands. With the load shifting from the wheels to the wings the skid supporting the plane's tail and acting as a brake rose off the ground. As the engine turned faster and the propeller kicked in he concentrated on holding the plane straight on the narrow runway. He pulled back the stick lifting the wheels off the ground, only to come bumping back down. With nearly two thousand feet of runway ahead he brought the wings up and took another hop, this one longer, only to come down once more.[8]

After a "last bow to the earth," as Lindbergh later described it, touching the ground lightly in a parting "gesture of humility," the plane, "5000 pounds balanced on a blast of air," vaulted gracefully over the telephone wires and into the heavens. "The spirit of unconquerable youth had won," the *Times* recounted the next day, "and 'Slim' Lindbergh" was launched on a historic marathon of endurance, conquest, and skill.[9]

Clarence Chamberlin remembered that his heart was in his throat as he watched the takeoff. "It seemed impossible for it to get off and get into the air," he said, calling it "one of the most courageous efforts ever made at long distance flight."[10]

With the *Spirit of St. Louis* in the air, reporters polled the experts on Lindbergh's chances. Commander Byrd cautiously allowed that he thought he would "probably get there." Tony Fokker remarked that the chances were good for him to make it to Europe, but he doubted that he would actually reach Paris. Bert Acosta, who had joined the Byrd crew, called it a "long chance": "You must remember he is alone and has only one motor."[11]

It is 7:54 a.m., two minutes after takeoff, and the plane is performing optimally as Lindbergh commences the first of the thirty-six hundred-mile segments he has laid out for the great circle route. He glides over the great estates of Long Island and then the farms and woodlands of the undeveloped east, barely skimming the treetops. At fifteen minutes he makes the first of his planned fuel tank changes, from the center wing tank to the nose tank. (With five tanks he needs to rotate their use to keep the craft balanced.) In the first minutes he feels nothing and thinks of nothing but his next step. Gradually the anxiety dissipates, the pinpoint focus eases. The flying instinct takes over and the plane becomes an extension of his body.[12]

Only now, as he began to relax, did Lindbergh notice that news photographers followed him into the air in order to capture him at the controls. The press was intruding into a sky that he had thought was his alone this day. But soon the last of the planes dipped off and he settled into the snug environment of the fabric-lined cockpit. It had been designed with great economy so that there was not an extra inch. He could touch both sides of the fuselage with his extended elbows, and the roof was hollowed a bit to leave room for his helmeted head. Creature comforts were minimal, but it felt right, fitting him like "a suit of clothes."[13]

The steady whir of the engine and the stable control readings reassured him in his solitude. He exulted in the lightness of being alone and independent, of making a decision at midnight to fly and taking off at dawn. One hundred miles out he had passed over the states of New York and Connecticut and by 9:05 was over East Greenwich in Rhode Island. Accustomed to the generous spaces of the West and the Mississippi Valley's vast farms, he wondered at the density of life he saw below: small fields with cattle, boulders, and crops pushed close together; highways and villages with people everywhere. In the time it takes to walk a single mile he had flown over Rhode Island. A half hour later the sun broke through the clouds as he passed over Halifax, Massachusetts. In another half hour he reached the Atlantic coast headed for Nova Scotia. He faced his first real challenge: two hours of flying over water.[14]

In Detroit, Evangeline Lindbergh received steady updates from the *Detroit Free Press*. She had wanted to avoid the spotlight but reluctantly released a statement: "Tomorrow, Saturday, a holiday for me, will be either the happiest day of my whole life, or the saddest. . . . But I know I shall receive word that my boy has successfully covered the long journey."[15]

Over water, with no landmarks to guide him, he navigates by his instruments, confident that "a swinging compass needle will lead [him] to land and safety." When he reaches Nova Scotia he will be able to check how accurately he has held direction. He drops the plane down to almost twenty feet above the watery surface, allowing it to skim the air cushion over the ocean. Only once in his life has he been this far from land, when he was eleven and Evangeline took him on a boat to the Panama Canal. Even the lifeboats were larger than his plane.[16]

He continued to do the mental exercise of going through possible emergencies. In his prize-winning account of the flight, *The Spirit of St. Louis*, he revealed that his plans "included the probability of having to turn back en route and mak[ing] more than one start from New York before [he] got through to Paris." But though he had given thought to many possible hazards, he had not considered sheer exhaustion. By eleven o'clock he felt the effects of his lack of sleep and the exertions of the morning. His cramping body had been stuck in a single position for three hours with the control stick between his legs. And the ache, he knew, would get worse before his body made peace with its mortification.[17]

He sipped some water but refrained from biting into his sandwich, concerned that eating would only make him more tired. With at least thirty-three more hours to Paris he needed to stay alert. As he took in some air from the window he noticed a clod of mud stuck to the bottom of one wing, too far out for him to reach it. This meant carrying extra weight all the way to Paris, and it irritated him no end. He had torn leaves from a notebook to keep the weight down, even made his own flying boots from a light material and cut the margins off his charts to save fractions of ounces, and now he was carrying this useless clump over the ocean![18]

With so much to worry about, why was Lindbergh so concerned about something so trivial? His answer was this: "There's an intangible value in striving for perfection—a value that can't be measured on such material standards as pounds of weight or resistance." His entire preparation had been an exercise in obsession, setting goals and refusing to compromise on any of them, and he refused to distinguish between demanding perfection from an airplane engine and obsessing about an extra ounce of unplanned cargo weight.[19]

Nova Scotia came into view, its expanse of spruce and pine stretching as far as he could see. He had set the province as his test: if he made it over the waters to Nova Scotia reasonably on course by relying on his instruments it would confirm his calculations and reassure him about flying blind across the Atlantic. Even if he were forced to make the rest of his way in fog he could continue. But if he found himself far off course he would have to turn back. From one thousand feet above he matched the terrain with his map. Four hundred forty miles into his trip he was, remarkably, within two degrees of his course! There was no need to turn back.[20]

At one o'clock he set his chart down on his knee to take a swig of water. A puff of wind almost blew the paper away, reminding him how tenuous his adventure was. If he lost the chart, with no radio and no directions he would have to turn back. He started to snap plastic windows in place to keep out the gusts, but then he changed his mind. He needed the connection with the elements; he did not want to be sealed off from the heavens, insulated "from the crystal clarity of communion with water, land and sky," a connection, he felt certain, he would need to rely upon before his flight was over.[21]

It is almost three o'clock, the beginning of the eighth hour. His legs no longer feel pain. Piloting through a storm with gales of 50 mph winds whipping his plane releases a fresh surge of adrenalin, relieving his drowsiness. Clear of the storm, he passes through a gauzy "sheet of blinding white" near the Nova Scotia coast, only to emerge from the thick haze into a clear azure sky. He thinks, "I don't believe in taking foolish chances; but nothing can be accomplished without taking any chances at all." He cannot imagine a healthy civilization that takes no chances: "What justifies the risk of life? Some answer . . . knowledge. Some say wealth or power. . . . I believe the risks I take are justified by the sheer love of the life I lead." He lowers the plane above the water, watching the rushing whitecaps, reveling in the solitude of this detached space, hidden in the wide open.[22]

His rigidity about staying on course made every small deviation a major decision. His charted course over the last sections of North America had him flying over unpopulated areas. A slight detour could bring him over St. Johns, Newfoundland, where the *Spirit* would be seen and duly reported, reassuring those back on Long Island who had labored so faithfully at his side as well as his partners in St. Louis, the Ryan staff, his mother, and everyone who had become transfixed by the race. But he initially refused to budge from his plan: "Misdirected sentiment could result in death. . . . The principles I laid down for this flight involve no waste, no luxuries, no following of shore lines." Only after further agonizing did he decide that smoother weather along the detour route made this a safety issue, shifting the priorities and permitting the overflight. News of his progress was quickly passed back to the States.[23]

Assessing the first eleven hours, aerologists pronounced his flight amazingly accurate, tracking precisely the route that he had laid out. In France Air Minister Laurent Eynac, anticipating the flight's success, quoted Goethe: "From this day at this place will date a new era in world history." In Britain the flight overshadowed everything, including an even longer course by British fliers from England to India; nothing compared with crossing the Atlantic. Aviators interviewed in Paris still believed the effort "foolish." They predicted Lindbergh's greatest challenge would be staying awake.[24]

That night forty thousand fans gathered in New York's Yankee Stadium to watch a heavyweight championship match between Jack Sharkey and Tom Maloney. The announcer, Joe Humphrey, delivered a message to the crowd: "I want you to rise to your feet and think about a boy up there tonight who is carrying the hopes of all true-blooded Americans. Say a little prayer for Charles Lindbergh." The stadium erupted in applause. The humorist Will Rogers began his piece for the next day's *Los Angeles Times,* "No jokes today. An odd, tall, slim, smiling, bashful boy is somewhere out there over the middle of the ocean, where no lone human being has ever been before. . . . If he is lost it will be the most universally regretted single loss we ever had. But this kid ain't going to fail." The *New York Times* received ten thousand calls inquiring about his progress.[25]

Around 7:15 p.m. Lindbergh threaded through the last mountain pass in Newfoundland and on to the Atlantic Ocean. Once he passed St. John's Lloyd's of London, which had refused to offer odds before, changed its position now, quoting

10–3 odds against a successful flight. On the New York Stock Exchange Wright Aeronautical Corporation, normally a slow-moving stock, trading no more than seven hundred shares a day, shot up from 29¾ to 34⅜ in the abbreviated two-hour Saturday morning session, as thirteen thousand shares changed hands.[26]

The Atlantic's limitless "expanse, its depth, its power, its wild and open water" are with him now for the next two thousand miles. There are no landmarks, only the navigation charts he prepared in San Diego. The sinking sun ushers in the darkness and a heavy weariness washes over him once again. His eyes "feel dry and hard as stones. The lids pull down with pounds of weight against their muscles." He has been crunched in one position for more than nine hours. He tries shaking himself, raising and flexing his arms and legs to regain some feeling; even a surge of pain would be welcome. "The very exertion of staying awake" exhausts him. Nothing is more desirable now than sleep, not even life itself. The craft jerks momentarily, sensitive to his slightest slack in piloting.[27]

Suddenly there appeared before him a series of awesome bleached forms. Between Nova Scotia and Newfoundland he had encountered ice fields, but for the first time he now beheld enormous icebergs. These luminous "sentries of the Arctic" were first dispersed in pools of water, but soon the sea itself became an immense block of shimmering white, striking his eyes with a painful brightness. No ships passed these "forbidden latitudes." Trespassing into a place where "no man has ever been before," he was roused to hyperawareness and his mind began racing through a series of what-if exercises: What would he do if the engine failed now? How would he handle a forced landing amid the ice floes? What steps would he take to keep afloat in the frigid environment? The combination of dazzling light, the wild, eerie beauty of the untrafficked heavens, and the biting cold along with the alertness brought on by thinking about emergencies once again cleared away his drowsiness.[28]

About a third of the way through the flight Lindbergh was content with his progress, even a bit disappointed that the flight had turned into a test of endurance. He had hoped it would be more of a challenge, telling himself, "If I make the whole flight without meeting anything worse than those scattered squalls in Nova Scotia, I'll feel as though I'd been cheating, as though I hadn't earned success, as though the evil spirits of the sky had disdained to sally forth in battle." He wanted no easy ribbons.[29]

A soupy fog put an end to his reveries about insufficient challenge. He tried to fly above it, but even at fifteen thousand feet he could not escape the persistently obscuring haze that blotted out the sea below and the guiding stars above. He was truly flying blind, dependent entirely on his instruments. In this type of flying the pilot has to disregard his senses. No matter how much he might feel that his craft is turning or a wing dipping he has to ignore his sensations and be guided only by the black dials before him.[30]

Now, at more than thirteen hours he encountered a storm that surrounded him with "great shadowy forms . . . dwarfing earthly mountains with their magnitude, awesome in their weird, fantastic shapes." Confronted by these vast thunderheads rising thousands of feet he decided that rather than try to fly around them he would fly directly into them. On land a pilot knows to avoid the ridges and mountains, but these summits, "alluring in their softness," drew him into their vaporous forms only to make him captive to their turmoil. Many years later he recollected the terror of being caught in storming ice clouds thousands of feet above ground: "They enmesh intruders. They are barbaric in their methods. They toss you in their inner turbulence . . . poison you with freezing mist." Try as he might to escape, he could not.[31]

Caged in by ice-filled clouds and pelted by hailstones the plane is freezing cold in the pitch dark. His compasses behave erratically. Then, shining his flashlight on a strut outside the cockpit, he finds there what every pilot dreads: ice. Soon the ice will freeze his guidance systems. If the turn indicator freezes he will lose control over direction, making it impossible to fly blind. He thinks of turning back, but he is too far along for that to be an easy option. His decides to keep to his course, struggling to escape the turbulence and descend to the warmer latitudes to melt the ice. But urgent as it is for him to drop down he must avoid too steep a descent; that could send the plane spinning out of control.[32]

He managed to ease the plane to the warmer temperatures, and as he passed from the frigid Labrador Current to the more temperate Gulf Stream the ice melted and he was able to stabilize his craft. His earth inductor and conventional compasses returned to normal. Chastened, Lindbergh resolved not to battle nature so offhandedly, even if it meant deviating from his charted path. His fears about failing "to sally forth" were put to rest. By 11 p.m. he had completed 1,500 miles, not quite half the journey.[33]

Awake for thirty-nine hours straight, calmed by the steady drone of the engine and the monotony of the unchanging ocean, he feels fatigue again clamp down on him. Only the conviction that sleep is death staves off the menacing somnolence, but only barely. Reaching out the cockpit window he directs the current from the slipstream toward his face, gulping huge drafts of cool air to break the trance. But sleep's sheer physical force is overpowering. Desperately he pries his eyes open with his fingers. He had chosen solitude; he is paying the price. "I've lost control of my eyelids. . . . Every cell in my body is on strike . . . in protest, claiming that nothing, nothing in the world, could be worth such effort."[34]

In more than 760 hours of flying Lindbergh had honed an instinct for survival, and he called upon that experience to get him though. He forced himself to do some tasks, checking the gauges and the wing struts. The ice was all gone. He bounced up and down in his seat and dropped one and then the other wing to bring fresh air into the cabin and change the pressure on his body. Finally he brokered a kind of compromise between his body and his mind. His intellect would not demand full awareness, in return for which his body would not insist on sleep. He piloted the *Spirit* in a twilight consciousness. When he closed his eyes for a few seconds the plane's sudden dive or veer called him back: "I'm asleep and awake at the same time." He had not eaten, but his body did not crave food, not even drink. He knew that once the sun rose he would be able to shake the stupor, but he needed to hold on to alertness until then. He thought of only two things: failure was death, and he had to keep traveling eastward.[35]

At three in the morning he caught a glimpse of the sun's rays and brought the *Spirit* down in a controlled descent through the clouds at a cruising speed of 140 mph over the rippled waters. The water current indicated that there was a strong tailwind behind him, that for all the drama he had been given a friendly push forward through the night.[36]

Nosing down to within fifty feet over the huge breakers he is forced back up to above a thousand feet by the fog. Only now he has company. "I feel no surprise at their coming": "ghostly presences" crowd the cabin behind him. He sees them clearly without turning around. They speak to him in human voices, vanishing and reappearing at will, passing through the walls of the fuselage. They comment on the flight and his navigation, "giving [him] messages of importance unattainable in ordinary life." He feels as if he is one with them, weightless, shape-shifting, losing his sense of physical presence. The phantoms, he knows, are "emanations from the experience of ages, inhabitants of a universe closed to mortal men." He himself feels he inhabits the liminal: "I'm on the border line of life and a greater realm beyond." He feels weightless: "The feeling of flesh is gone. . . . I'm almost one with the vaporlike forms behind me." He wonders if he has discovered some new dimension of existence, or perhaps this is death. The phantoms are familiar, channeled from some "past incarnation," and he wonders if they hopped on board when he passed through the thunderheads. Or maybe they are emissaries of the night who hitched onto his chariot to escape the dark realm. He senses a connection with these spirits, with the past, the present, and the future. Has the extreme sleep deprivation taken over his mind, or has he pierced the deep mystery of higher air? Then at some point they disappear from his cockpit. Twenty-six years after the flight he still speaks of these fellow travelers with vivid conviction.[37]

Twenty-four hours into the flight he was no longer conserving water but he still had not taken a bite of his sandwich. He stopped keeping his detailed log of readings and fuel tank changes on the back of his flying charts. Flying on instinct he closed his eyes for seconds at a time. He tried slapping himself hard, but even that failed to get rid of the numbness. Only after bringing the craft low and sticking his head out the window into the spray of the waves did he finally shake off the sleepiness.[38]

At the flight's twenty-seventh hour he caught sight of a porpoise leaping out of the water and slipping back in one unbroken motion. The sight refreshed him. He was back in the temporal world he feared he might have left behind. He was again part of a familiar universe of life and grace and beauty. He broke an ammonia capsule and brought it to his nose, but he sensed nothing, his eyes experienced no sting, there were no tears. He inhaled again—nothing. Noticing a speck on the water he brought the plane down and recognized a boat. Swooping down closer he saw more boats, an entire fleet of what appeared to be fishing boats. He realized that he was close to land![39]

He brought the *Spirit* close enough to call down "Which way is Ireland?" There was no response. He flew to the next boat and shouted his query again. Once more there was no reply. No one came out on deck. Either they did not hear him or they were spooked by the flying machine. But it vexed him; he needed to reconnect. "I want an earthly greeting. I deserve a welcome back to the fellowship of men."[40]

At about 11 a.m., after sixteen hours over the ocean, he saw a cloud or a low fog bank in the northeast distance. He realized that it was likely more substantial than that, but after the phantoms and mirages he was no longer confident in his vision. His plans had allowed for eighteen and a half hours from Newfoundland to Ireland. But the coast line with its irregular shore, lush rolling fields, and tall mountains was unmistakably Ireland. More than two hours early!

He takes the Spirit up to two thousand feet for a wide view and checks his map. There is no mistake: the tapering bay leading to an island of small farms and large boulders is Dingle Bay, located on Ireland's southwestern coast. Despite his detours, the thunderheads, the winds, the visions, and his dazed piloting he has kept to the precise course he had outlined in San Diego, well ahead of schedule. This time the people on the ground wave up to him and he drinks in the sight of earth and men. Everything is sharper than normal; the green turf is vividly verdant, greener than anything he has ever seen. He can see sheep grazing, even the small cottages and trim gardens of the local farmers. He exults, "I've never seen such beauty before— fields so green, people so human, a village so attractive." He had been "to eternity and back": "I know how the dead would feel to live again."[41]

After Ireland Lindbergh had another six hundred miles to cover to reach Paris. For a moment, for the only time during the flight, he lost his bearings and banked away from the mainland, but he quickly corrected himself and flew over the reassuring hilltop communities, sloping pastures, green glens, and scenic dales with their rock fences and low stone houses. Not only were the phantoms gone, but he could not recall a single word from their conversation. Also gone was the overpowering fatigue. From this point forward he took in every wrinkle of the unfolding scene.[42]

At about 5:30 p.m. local time he came to the English coast over Cornwall, then Plymouth, from whence the Pilgrims had set out at the dawn of American history. It took them two months; he did it in less than thirty hours.[43]

The English farms appeared to him as miniatures. "A hundred of these fields would fit into a single Kansas wheat ranch," he thought. The men and women he saw below represented Old World traditions, tilling the same fields, preparing the same foods as their ancestors; he felt a sharp sense of difference as "a child of those who left" to make a new world. It was not just the style of life that was different; it was also the scale. Europe was so much smaller: "All England is no larger than one of our Midwestern states."[44]

In New York thousands followed the latest bulletins outside the newspaper offices near Times Square, while Paris on this balmy Saturday was preoccupied with a tennis match pitting the American Bill Tilden and his partner against the world champion French doubles team. Informed that the American aviator had been sighted over Ireland the crowd broke into cheers. The American ambassador Myron T. Herrick, who was attending the match, acknowledged the *beau geste* and slipped out to make plans for receiving the American flier, who should be landing around 10 p.m.[45]

Darkness descends as he crosses the English Channel. At thirty-two hours he is two thousand feet over Cherbourg. Crossing the Seine at about 9:20 he sees people looking up and waving. Only now does he reach for one of the sandwiches, taking his first bite since New York, but he tastes nothing. He may as well be eating a piece of his cabin. Just thirteen days before, Nungesser and Coli passed here on their ill-fated pursuit of the same goal. They too boarded "a magic carpet," only theirs lost its enchantment. He turns to thoughts about his plane, not the people who designed or built it but the plane itself: "It's like a living creature . . . as though a successful flight means as much to it as to me, as though we shared our experiences together, each feeling beauty, life and death as keenly, each dependent on the other's loyalty. We have made this flight across the ocean, not I or it."[46]

These words of tribute to the *Spirit of St. Louis* were not the words of an exhausted Lindbergh, half crazed by lack of sleep. They were written in the 1950s, after enough time had passed to consider that the *Spirit of St. Louis* was the product of individuals like Don Hall, Ben Mahoney, and the Ryan and Wright teams, and to consider the role his St. Louis backers had played in the project. After having thought about all aspects of the flight for more than twenty-six years Lindbergh reserved his deepest gratitude for his machine.

More than thirty-three hours after he left New York he leveled out at four thousand feet, searching for Paris: "I struck France at the Cap de la Hague, with the sun about to set. The Seine wound in from the north, before nightfall, to guide me." He glimpsed the broad boulevards, brightly lit streets, historic buildings and monuments of Paris, circled over the Eiffel Tower, and turned northeast toward Le Bourget.[47]

There is no longer any ache or stiffness, nothing except anticipation. On this cool night, poised on the threshold of history, he is serene. Lack of sleep no longer intimidates him and he is in no hurry to land. He lets the facts of his accomplishment wash over him. Ignoring conventional aviation thinking, he has taken a small, single-engine monoplane alone across the ocean. He has fought off fog, storms, ice, phantoms, and sleep to accomplish alone what crews of two, three, and four had died trying to achieve. He has woven through black night and thunderclouds, through storm and turbulence, past the chilled Labrador Current and monumental icebergs. His little sprite of a plane has carried him where no other craft, no matter how expensive, how big, and how well powered, has gone. He has put himself through as demanding a test of skill, concentration, planning, and sheer endurance as any man of his time. And now he wants to revel in his achievement: "I almost wish Paris were a few more hours away. It's a shame to land with the night so clear and so much fuel in my tanks."[48]

Over Paris Lindbergh began looking for Le Bourget. He thought it should not be difficult to locate the world's largest airport, but the place where the airfield should have been was speckled with pinpoints of light, which took him by surprise. Le Bourget was not in the middle of the city. He circled once more back over Paris, to make sure of his bearings. Ten minutes later he returned, this time certain that it was Le Bourget. He spiraled down and caught sight of the large hangars and saw the source of all those beams of light.[49]

He begins to think of the next steps. After landing he will need to find a place to sleep—that is, if they allow him to stay in the country. He is afraid that he may have a problem because he carries no visa and has made no arrangements. He needs food, clothing, a toothbrush, some cash.[50]

At the official time (recorded by the Fédération Aéronautique Internationale) of 33 hours, 30 minutes, 29.8 seconds Lindbergh landed the *Spirit of St. Louis*. His tanks had a reserve of eighty-five gallons of gasoline, enough for another 1,040 miles. His senses were frozen. He moved mechanically: "[I was as] uncoordinated as though I were coming down at the end of my first solo."[51] Nothing in his past prepared him for the full force of global celebrity that was about to descend on him.

France had been following his flight since he was spotted over Ireland. Those pinpoints of light were the headlights of thousands of automobiles, part of an enormous line backed up for miles. Thousands had driven as far as they could and then, hopelessly bottled up in traffic, simply abandoned their cars, traipsing to the field on foot. Authorities had intended to provide an orderly reception and assigned extra guards to the airfield; they planned to have a committee offer greetings and have Lindbergh meet the press for pictures and some words. Upon learning that thousands of French citizens were driving to Le Bourget to see the American, the government sent two companies of troops to reinforce the police.[52]

Even before Lindbergh stopped the plane the field was swarming with people. When his tires hit the ground a wave of pandemonium washed over the airfield. Tens of thousands smashed through the fences, toppling the restraining barriers and running over the pitifully outnumbered guards. Lindbergh's first concern was to avoid "mowing a swath through his well wishers," who charged the plane.[53]

He had been warned that French feelings had been rubbed raw, not only by the events of the previous ten days but also by the history of bruised feelings since the war. But this was all swept aside. The French had so wanted Nungesser and Coli to achieve this breakthrough, but they had also invested great emotion in the achievement itself. All the agony over their lost fliers made the crossing and what it had come to stand for even more important. Any hard feelings were supplanted by respect for Lindbergh's valor and accomplishment.

Seconds after he cut the motor the surging crowd rushed toward the plane shouting his name, anxious for a glimpse. Afraid "of killing people with [the] propeller," he quickly brought the *Spirit* to a stop. As he got out of the plane the crowd descended upon him, "as if," wrote the poet Harry Crosby "all the hands in the world [were] . . . trying to touch the new Christ." His log of the trip was snatched away and the frenzied crowd tore at his flight uniform. They snapped off scraps of wood from the propellers, ripped fabric from the fuselage, broke slivers from the fittings. The plane reeled from the press of the crowd and Lindbergh could hear wood cracking behind him. He asked for mechanics to protect the plane, hoping to save it from more rough handling. Only swift action by the French police prevented the entire *Spirit of St. Louis* from being reduced to splintered souvenirs.[54]

"The reception was the most dangerous part of the trip. Never in my life have I seen anything like that human sea," he later wrote. The crowd was shouting and bouncing him up and down, lifting him above their heads so that he lay prone as he was carried forward by hundreds of hands reaching to touch him. Try as he might to sit up he was too stiff from the flight. It was futile; he was in their hands. Then someone jerked his helmet off and suddenly he was standing on the ground, being pulled along by two French airmen. A well-meaning man intending to clear a path for him started swinging a club and caught the flier on the back of his head.[55]

His helmet ended up on the head of an American reporter, who became the crowd's new hero, while Lindbergh's escorts, who seemed familiar with Le Bourget, assured him that the *Spirit* would be safer with him out of the picture as they hustled him to a darkened hangar. After inquiring thoughtfully whether there was any new word about Nungesser and Coli, he appeared most concerned about details like customs, his lack of a visa, and a place to stay for the night. So began *la Folle Nuit*, the Crazy Night.[56]

VIVE LINDBERGH! VIVE L'AMÉRICAIN!

LINDBERGH DID NOT EXPECT what greeted him upon his arrival, let alone what his flight would come to represent to Europeans—or anyone else. Only the day before, the *Chicago Tribune*'s chief Paris correspondent was still asking, "Who the devil was Charles Lindbergh?"[1]

Many of the professionals had dismissed Lindbergh. In fact most were certain that a lone pilot in a one-engine plane was on a suicide mission. At best, he might land in Spain, Portugal, North Africa, perhaps even Norway if he were really lucky. If anyone succeeded it would be the well-funded Byrd. But the French, still in shock over the tragedy of Nungesser and Coli, became caught up in Lindbergh, the dark horse who had nerved his little machine across the ocean and, without sophisticated navigating instruments or radio guidance, arrived precisely on target. Despite themselves, and by all evidence entirely spontaneously, they were drawn by the drama of the underdog and, confounding all expectations, embraced his success as if somehow it ennobled the failed effort of their own aviators.[2]

Only Paris could have reacted this way. The Wrights made the first successful flights in the United States, but it was the French who gave their heart and soul to aviation, priding themselves on being the "winged nation, par excellence." France staged the first flight exhibitions. Its Aero Club funded the early aviation competitions, and the Frenchman Louis Blériot was the first to fly across the Channel. France opened the first flight training schools. Even before the war it led the world in the manufacture of airplanes. Years before, the Russian poet-aviator Vasily Kamensky had written that Paris was the "capital of Europe, the capital of art, the capital of aviation." Flying a plane "required imagination, valor, daring, elegance, subtlety, élan and a sense of adventure: were these not," Robert Wohl asks, in his study of aviation and the Western imagination, "quintessentially French qualities?" Who but the French, asked the novelist André Lichtenberger, should take up the challenge of avenging the fall of Icarus?[3]

When news began filtering through that the *Spirit of St. Louis* had been seen over Ireland, thirty thousand people crowded the Place de l'Opera and Square du Havre to follow the latest bulletins. Not since the Armistice had Paris buzzed with such joy and excitement. *Le Matin*'s posting of a sighting over Cherbourg set off choruses of "Vive Lindbergh! Vive l'Américain!" on the streets. "Every one in Paris who had a car, or could get one," commented Edwin James, the *New York Times* Paris bureau chief, "conceived the bright idea of going out to Le Bourget . . . [to] shake hands" with Lindbergh. Raymond Orteig too rushed to Paris, from the south of France, only to miss the landing by about fifteen minutes because of the traffic. His words of praise for "the modesty of this hero, who in silence prepared for his magnificent effort," were delivered hours after the landing, later that night.[4]

Lindbergh's landing awakened sympathies submerged by years of bickering. Even the most nationalist of the French papers, *Liberté,* was caught up in the fever of excitement: "Paris, always impassioned by courage; Paris, which has not forgotten its emotion of joy, when in 1917, it saw the first American regiments in the streets, will unite this evening in one fervent thought, the names of Lindbergh, Nungesser and Coli." Minister of War Paul Painleve, calling Lindbergh "this daring human bird," celebrated the flight as a "magnificent human triumph . . . a stimulant for invention." News of his landing touched off the "mightiest pro-American demonstration seen in France since the days of the war."[5]

Beyond trying to delay it, the American Embassy had given little thought to the flight. On the chance that Lindbergh might be successful the staff had prepared a small reception, inviting a few French officials and prominent figures from the American colony in Paris. Ambassador Myron T. Herrick, however, was worried that a severely overtired Lindbergh might say something that could exacerbate the already tense relationship between the two countries. Prudent diplomats do not leave such possibilities to chance. Elegant, discreet, and above all extremely careful, Herrick was a fine example of old school diplomacy. In his autobiography he wrote that he did not go to Le Bourget with any notion of taking Lindbergh under his wing: "But . . . when I looked at this boy and realized all at once what he had done and what he had been through, it naturally came into my head to take him home with me." It was a stroke of diplomatic genius. And it was not as unplanned as Herrick let on.[6]

Most accounts of Lindbergh's landing at Le Bourget draw on his own spare description, summarized in the previous pages. He told most of the story in news accounts and in a series of articles published under his byline. Some twenty-six years later, at the urging of his publisher, he pulled the story together in a coda to his *Spirit of St. Louis* memoirs. Standard accounts speak of his extraordinary week in Paris, depicting Ambassador Herrick as but a minor player in the story. The ambassador himself did nothing to challenge this. However, nothing in Lindbergh's past pointed to the subtle and sophisticated way in which he would carry himself for the week, much less explain how he would conquer France so completely. For four years he had focused almost exclusively on flying planes and associated with barnstormers and flyboys. His humor was coarse, his manner reticent and awkward, his learning sketchy; his poise and confidence were limited to the cockpit. Yet suddenly he had mastered a complex diplomatic environment where every word he said was parsed, every action was described in a display of press coverage unparalleled in history. Clearly Myron Herrick had a lot to do with this.[7]

When Herrick first met Lindbergh at Le Bourget the flier struck him as a genuine innocent. Lindbergh had left New York with modest hopes to make it across the ocean, collect the Orteig prize, win attention in aeronautical circles, and advance the cause of American aviation. He did not expect the rest of the world to take much notice. The scene at the airfield overwhelmed him. It also surprised Herrick, but he was quick to grasp its import. He understood how touched the French were by the flight and realized that the reticent midwesterner could help counter the unappealing image of Americans as blustering, willful, and crude. Moreover Herrick knew that Lindbergh's striking good looks, instinctive gallantry, and self-effacing personality would go over well in France.[8]

The ambassador himself was a much admired figure, somewhat exceptional for an American in 1920s Paris. Still imposing and vigorous at more than seventy years of age, Herrick had the weathered good looks and graceful mien of a New World patrician. In 1914, during the early months of the Great War, when it appeared as if the Germans might march into Paris, Herrick had refused to leave, even as many French officials as well as much of the foreign diplomatic corps evacuated their offices and transferred to Bordeaux. His act of courage and defiance earned him a permanent place in the hearts of the French.[9]

Herrick returned for a second tour of duty from 1921 to 1929. *Le Matin* described his welcome as a celebration "such . . . as ha[d] never yet been accorded to any ambassador," adding warmly, "A friend, and a very dear friend, has come back to us." Presenting his credentials to the president of France, Herrick declared that he was honored to be greeted by "the orphans of men who gave their lives that their children might live in peace." It did not diminish his popularity when he declared, "Germany's decision to take forcibly what did not belong to her, her ruthlessness . . . outraged me as a man and a diplomat." "I did not wait till 1917," he continued, in pointed reference to the reviled (in France, at any rate) neutrality policies of Woodrow Wilson, "to decide that we ought to oppose . . . [Germany] with something more than words."[10]

The history of French-American relations in the years following the Great War were marred by bad feeling about America's aloofness from the peace treaty, the League of Nations debate, and acrimonious squabbles over the debts accrued by the war. The very same year of Lindbergh's flight, Transportation Minister and future prime minister André Tardieu published a study of French-American relations in which he detailed the layered sources of French anger: the Americans had failed to recognize France's sacrifices, made a unilateral peace with Germany, crafted postwar peace plans with severe consequences for the French navy and her colonies, and most disturbing of all had refused to grant the French the same benefits guaranteed to German debtors. The fact that the postwar world had been rearranged in America's favor only added to the resentment. "Of one fact we are certain," André Siegfried wrote in his study *America*, "in 1914 the Americans were in debt to Europe and now Europe is in debt to them." "Everything that Europe has lost," Tardieu complained in a biting conclusion, "America has gained." Uncle Sam had morphed into Uncle Shylock.[11]

Herrick consistently and openly rejected this image, advocating generosity toward the French. At a speech commemorating the dead of both countries at the Battle of Champagne, he asked, "Why [are] young Americans buried here on the Champagne battlefields if we have no part in the rehabilitation of this broken world?" His words warmed the French and provoked consternation in the U.S. State Department.[12]

Despite Herrick's efforts, relations continued to worsen. France was in the thick of the worldwide protest against America's decision to execute Niccola Sacco and Bartolomeo Vanzetti, two Italian immigrant radicals who had been found guilty of murder in a tainted trial. A package addressed to Herrick exploded at the embassy, causing serious injury to the valet who opened it; this was followed by death threats directed at the ambassador. The disappearance of Nungesser and Coli only exacerbated tensions, especially after the false claims regarding America's withholding of weather information. Reports of angry crowds jostling American tourists along the Champs Elysées and tearing down an American flag led Herrick to plead for a delay of any attempts to cross the Atlantic.[13] The French appeared in no mood to have their noses rubbed in the tragic failure by Americans rushing across the ocean in unseemly pursuit of the Orteig.[14]

Indeed for weeks Rodman Wanamaker had been peppering the embassy with telegrams announcing Commander Byrd's imminent departure, and it was Byrd whom Herrick was thinking of when he sent his message asking for a hold on flights. He had paid little mind to "the youngster" who had set himself up in

California, far from the main action, to build and test his single-engine plane. When he learned that *le fou Volant* ("the flying fool") had ignored his advisory about "lamentable effects" and taken off for Paris just thirteen days after the ill-fated *White Bird* disappeared, he felt little excitement. After he was informed that the *Spirit of St. Louis* had passed over Ireland, Herrick took his time getting out to the airport. He was as surprised as anyone to find the airfield teeming with excited throngs.[15]

Weeks before, Wanamaker had sent over a representative to orchestrate a welcome for Commander Byrd; Herrick now drew on those plans to arrange the Lindbergh reception. But Byrd had been tested by the ordeals of celebrity and survived them. He was a veteran of the prying questions of the international press corps. Moreover as an officer in active service he could be counted on to speak with discretion and tact. About Lindbergh Herrick knew very little, and he feared that the young man might face "a situation here where one remark could . . . [lead to] international complications." So the plan was to keep Lindbergh sequestered until he could be briefed and prepared for the delicate diplomatic environment. The plan was simple enough: he would be met at the airport and cordoned off by rows of police, escorted to a brief welcoming ceremony away from the crowds and the reporters and, after he had slept, given some cautionary pointers about what to say.[16]

Meanwhile the *New York Times*, which had secured rights to the Lindbergh story, busily laid the logistics for exploiting their exclusive. Paris bureau chief Edwin James was instructed from New York to "isolate" Lindbergh as soon as he landed. "Oh, it was a wonderful plan," James later recalled ruefully. A team of reporters drove out to the field at six in the evening. They prepared complicated telephone hookups and extensive relay plans to rush the first part of the story from Le Bourget to Paris. They also arranged for an automobile to whisk the flier away. After Lindbergh had completed a few obligatory words to a small welcoming crowd, the *Times* men would debrief him during the drive to central Paris. And once Lindbergh arrived there a battery of stenographers would take down his story in his own words while the reporters prepared copy and photographers snapped pictures.[17]

Alerted to the *Times*'s plan to spirit Lindbergh away, the *Chicago Tribune*'s hard- boiled Paris chief Henry Wales had no intention of allowing Jimmy James and his staff to kidnap Lindbergh and hide him in some hotel, then "milk his story to the last detail." Wales had written some speeches for Herrick in the past and played on the ambassador's fear of a serious faux pas during an unsupervised session with the *Times*, encouraging Herrick to frustrate the paper's hopes for a long private interview.[18]

For all of its advantages over the other airports, Le Bourget was still a fairly simple airfield. Military planes and hangars stood on one side of the field, and the facilities for civilian planes, mostly mail planes, were at the other. Around this latter area, near the administration building, the receiving committee had arranged chairs and a backdrop of flags, in front of which was set up a bank of press and motion picture cameras. Major Pierre Weiss, commander of a French bomber unit based at the airfield, had coordinated the logistics with the local police and the American Embassy. As soon as Lindbergh landed his men would detach the flier from the crowd and bring him to Herrick. Weiss had arranged for about seven hundred gendarmes supplemented by a regiment of soldiers, but by nightfall, as we've seen, it was all too plain that the officers were overmatched by the torrent of humanity descending on Le Bourget. They would have to be quick and resourceful to make the plan work.[19]

Herrick arrived at the airport and stationed himself at his appointed spot in the administration building. For a while the crowd actually turned gloomy, fearful that the silence meant that Lindbergh had run into difficulty. Then, around 10 o'clock, the sounds of a motor above electrified the crowd, but it faded. Only later did they learn that Lindbergh had made a first pass and, uncertain because of all the lights as to whether he was actually over Le Bourget, decided to circle once more. Then the silvery craft returned and landed. Wrote Herrick, "Pandemonium broke loose," not the manufactured frenzy one sees "at political conventions, but the real thing," sweeping away the soldiers and police and even a "stout fence" that was supposed to hold back the crowd.[20]

Lindbergh's first words upon landing were to inquire whether any mechanics were on hand to take responsibility for his plane's safety. (Lindbergh himself remembered his first words as "Are there any mechanics here?" Wales, who claimed to have witnessed the landing, remembered the first words as "Careful there; don't break it.") As it happened, one of the first to reach the plane was the chief of aircraft maintenance for one of the airlines based at Le Bourget, and he remained with the plane.[21]

Meanwhile the *Times* team, led by James, was expecting Lindbergh at another part of the field. They began sprinting toward his landing spot, but as James wrote shortly thereafter, "the men from the military side of the field" —Weiss's men— reached him first, "pulling him from the plane." By then the crowd had leveled "the very strongest fences, some seven feet high with spikes on their top," surging toward the new hero. Lindbergh recounted the terrifying crush of the crowd and how fortuitously "two French aviators—the military pilot Detroyat and the civil pilot Delage—" came up and whisked him away from the crowd. Actually, this was no random happenstance. Major Weiss was there, directing his men to snatch the besieged flier away from the excited throng.[22]

Once Lindbergh was safely in hand, his leather helmet was ripped off and, in his words "had somehow gotten onto the head of an American reporter," to whom someone pointed, perhaps not entirely by mistake, and began shouting "There is Lindbergh! There is Lindbergh!" James and his associates got there in time to see a helmeted figure being carried on the shoulders of a mob of men with thousands bearing down on them. The hero and the exclusive had slipped through the *Times* reporters' fingers. All they could produce was an account of his arrival, which got tied up in a traffic jam of monumental proportions on its way to Paris. It was, recalled James, "the tortures of the damned."[23]

Meanwhile Delage threw a uniform jacket over Lindbergh and, with Detroyat, in James's words, "wormed him" out of the crowd's path to a waiting Renault car and spirited their guest to a nearby hangar. There they turned out the lights to avoid drawing attention. From there they led him to Weiss's office. *Times* reporter Russell Owen later wrote of Lindbergh being "hidden" for two hours before being "smuggled into Paris."[24]

Herrick was stationed at the reception area when a man (a reporter), "half torn to pieces," managed to bring him the aviator's headgear. It had been given to him by Major Weiss with orders to get it to the ambassador. "This," Herrick later explained, referring to the idea of placing the helmet on another man's head, "was done to deceive the crowd and get them clear of Lindbergh and his ship." For the two hours that it took to locate the ambassador and bring him to Lindbergh, the man of the hour was protected by a guard of recruits that Weiss had put together in advance for just this purpose. The Belgian air attaché, who somehow got into Weiss's office, found the flier in the borrowed jacket, unhappy about having lost his helmet and concerned about where he would be sleeping that night. To Lindbergh all of this—his rescue by two Frenchmen, his helmet landing on some-one else's head and diverting the crowd, his being hidden in a hangar—appeared unplanned. In Lindbergh's account one of his rescuers went out to find a high-ranking officer, and "in the midst of the crowd he came upon Major Weiss of the Bombardment Group of the 34th A.F. Regiment," who could not believe that Lindbergh "was sitting in a hangar's darkened room" and had them take the flier to his own office about a mile away.[25]

Finally, at close to one in the morning, Ambassador Herrick was brought to Weiss's office along with his son Parmely and some others. By this time Lindbergh had not slept for sixty hours. One of the Frenchmen offered Lindbergh a chair. "Thank you," he said dryly, "I have been sitting." Perfectly calm, he refused to be seen by a doctor and seemed not at all fatigued or drawn. He also had no idea what a celebrity he had become. The first thing he did, to Herrick's amusement, was hand the diplomat several letters of introduction. Herrick was impressed by the young man's modesty, all the more reason to prepare him for what, it was now clear, would be the most intense burst of attention anybody had ever experienced.

He took Lindbergh by the hand, telling him, "My boy, come with me, I am going to take you home and look after you."[26]

Lindbergh was touched. Still anxious about being in a foreign country without a visa and with no idea of where he might sleep that night, he welcomed the invitation. Staying at the embassy would solve his concerns about visas, hotels, and meals (he had no more than a few coins with him). From this point forward no matter how much Secretary of State Frank B. Kellogg (who had defeated Lindbergh's father in the race for senator from Minnesota in 1916) would insist that Lindbergh was Herrick's "personal guest" and that the government had nothing to do with him, the pilot became, perforce, an extension of American diplomacy.[27]

Lindbergh wanted to see his plane before leaving Le Bourget. The French hesitated. They knew that the plane had been damaged by the crowd and did not want to upset him. But he insisted, later writing, "The sides of the fuselage were full of gaping holes." Also some fittings had been pulled off, but he was relieved to find no serious damage, and the French promised to make the repairs.[28]

He was led back to the small Renault by Weiss, Detroyat, and Delage. Taking rough side roads to avoid the traffic, they made good time back to the city. When they reached central Paris Weiss stopped at the Claridge Hotel and commanded the doorman there to round up some flowers from the dining room. Back in the car they passed the Place de l'Opera, where tens of thousands had gathered during the day to cheer the Lone Eagle's progress. They drove down the long avenue and stopped the car. Weiss handed the flowers to Lindbergh as they all got out and walked to the Arc de Triomphe. There Lindbergh stood in silence for some moments before the Tomb of the Unknown Soldier.[29]

After his grueling trip, three nights without sleep, and with a sketchy sense of history, it is not likely that Lindbergh was thinking about a tribute to the French war dead. He himself would explain simply why he was driven to the Arc: "*They wanted my first stop in Paris to be at the Arc de Triomphe.*" But Major Weiss, describing the event a year later, stuck to the script, insisting that the American had asked them to stop, "walked to the tomb and bowed in silence . . . shedding a laurel leaf from the crown still fresh on his brow. No spectacle of such solemn grandeur has been witnessed in this generation." Weiss continued in this vein, glorifying the moment: "That night we understood of what stuff a nation's glory is made of. The America pictured by novelists with its factories, monster cities, [and] banks . . . was all fiction. The reality was the man who discovered within himself the strength, courage and skill to mock earthly slavishness and conquer the immensities of time and space."[30]

The Renault arrived at the embassy well ahead of Herrick, who, tied up in the congested traffic out of Le Bourget, did not return until around 3 a.m. By then

Lindbergh had supped on bouillon and eggs, bathed, and stuffed his tall frame into a pair of ill-fitting pajamas and a robe provided to him by the staff. A small crowd of reporters were gathered outside the embassy hoping to hear from the new hero, and Herrick invited them in for a few supervised words with Lindbergh, who hesitated at first; he still owed the *Times* an exclusive. Parmely Herrick called over the *Times* correspondent Carlisle MacDonald and ever so diplomatically pressed him into waiving his rights and sharing the man of the hour with his colleagues for a few minutes of questioning. Once satisfied that he was not breaking any agreements, Lindbergh began by expressing "great sorrow" over the "noble failure" of the two Frenchmen Nungesser and Coli and then took a few questions. Waverly Root, reporting for the *Chicago Tribune*, recalled that the young flier appeared a bit tongue-tied and allowed Herrick to answer most of the questions for him.[31]

After bidding the gentlemen of the press a good night, Herrick handed Lindbergh a congratulatory note from President Calvin Coolidge, who was sailing on the Potomac when he received the news of the landing at Le Bourget. The president's message, no doubt shaped by the ambassador's own advice and the recognition that it would be reprinted in all the newspapers, artfully combined praise for "the brilliant termination of [the] heroic flight" with an "assurance of [America's] admiration for those intrepid Frenchmen, Nungesser and Coli, whose bold spirits first ventured on [Lindbergh's] exploit." The president expressed continued anxiety about the fate of the missing French fliers.[32]

Sixty-three hours after his last sleep in New York the exhausted flier went to bed in Paris at the American Embassy.

That night a much relieved Herrick sent Secretary of State Kellogg a cable for the president's attention. After thanking Coolidge for his "worthy tribute" he told the president that Lindbergh was admirably suited to the task set for him: "[Had the United States] deliberately sought a type to represent the youth, the intrepid adventure of America and the immortal bravery of Nungesser and Coli, we could not have fared as well as in this boy of divine genius and simple courage."[33] Then, before retiring, he sent off a cable to Evangeline Lindbergh in Detroit: "YOUR INCOMPARABLE SON HAS HONORED ME BY BECOMING MY GUEST. HE IS IN FINE CONDITION AND SLEEPING SWEETLY UNDER UNCLE SAM'S ROOF. MYRON HERRICK."[34]

While Lindbergh slept the first reports began to appear in the French press. "The man, almost a boy," marveled *Le Matin*, "has done the one thing which the most experienced experts could not have done." There was no one to relieve him; he had no companion but his courage, "and it conquered . . . passing through death which he defeated by daring." The French papers devoted their front pages to the extraordinary scene at the airfield and his midnight visit to the Tomb of the Unknown Soldier, featuring the exhausted flier's homage in headlines. Clearly, the papers suggested, despite recent trying moments, America had not forgotten the sacrifices of their French allies.[35]

When Lindbergh arose next afternoon the embassy staff arranged for an international phone call to Evangeline Lindbergh. Later Lindbergh would admit, "I knew there would be a lot of silly publicity about it." He would rather not have made the call but felt constrained to do so, given that all the arrangements were made. In a few words he assured his mother of his health and that the trip had been wonderful.[36]

From the moment Lindbergh completed that phone call until he left Paris, Myron Herrick did not leave his side, accompanying him to all his visits, standing alongside him during press conferences, and calling them to an end when he decided enough had been said. L'Humanité took to calling Lindbergh Herrick's "cher enfant" (beloved child). Neither man has left a record of what Herrick told Lindbergh or how he prepared him, but the result captivated Paris. When thousands gathered before the American Embassy that afternoon for a glimpse of the man who had done the impossible, Herrick took Lindbergh by the arm and led him to the portico. Responding to the cheers Lindy called out "Vive la France" and unfurled a French tricoleur. The crowd went wild. Over the next few days news reporters noticed the effect Herrick had on his young charge. Lindbergh assumed a gravity he did not have when he first landed. His smile was no longer so spontaneous, his jaw was more firmly set, and his answers to press questions took longer in coming as he thought a bit before he replied. The press too reflected the new seriousness, no longer referring to him as Slim, Lindy, or Charlie but more formally as "Mr. Lindbergh" and "Captain Lindbergh."[37]

Paris took on a holiday mood and invitations began pouring in. Government officials, American groups, aeronautical organizations, and heads of state all sought to honor him. French Minister Aristide Briand ordered the Foreign Office to fly the American flag, an honor heretofore reserved only for visiting heads of state. Word arrived that the French president would award him the French Cross of the Legion of Honor. A blind war veteran came to greet Lindbergh, clasped his hands, and told him his greatest sorrow: "I cannot see you for you are the bravest man in the world."[38]

The press was anxious to see him too, but this time Lindbergh insisted on meeting with the New York Times first. In a suit borrowed from Parmely Herrick, Lindbergh sat for an interview with the Times's Edwin James. The paper also ran a story under Lindbergh's byline. These articles, Lindbergh later explained to a biographer, were ghost-written: "The phraseology is usually considerably, or vastly different than mine." He would talk to a reporter, who then churned out the copy. It is here that he mentions for the first time that during the sleet storm he thought for a moment of turning back because of the weather. But he assured his readers that there was nothing foolhardy about his flight.[39]

At the press conference, as he recounted stories about his experiences over the ocean, he repeatedly used the term "we" in referring to his flight. Herrick interrupted to explain that he meant the plane and himself. One of the men posed a question about flying by dead reckoning (that is, flying by instruments alone), explaining, "I am a flier myself; my name is Cobham, and I flew over here from London a few minutes ago to see you and to tell you, you have done the greatest thing I have ever heard of." The remarks caused a sensation: this was Sir Alan Cobham, known as "the greatest of British long-distance aviators," who had pioneered routes to far-flung regions of the British Empire.[40]

That afternoon Lindbergh called on Captain Nungesser's elderly mother. News of the "private visit" leaked out, bringing thousands to the surrounding streets. Several girls tried to kiss the bashful hero, whom Herrick described as "scared to death." With the elderly ambassador in tow, Lindbergh climbed six flights of rickety stairs to the small apartment, where Madame Nungesser embraced Lindbergh, calling him a "brave young man," and through tears begged him to find her son. The daily *Le Temps* wrote that everyone was touched by the visit, and the *Times* reported that the courtesy to the grieving mother won the "undying affection of the whole French nation."[41]

The enchantment was well under way. The Communist paper *L'Humanité* (which had earlier denounced the Atlantic competition as a capitalist scheme) joined the homage, exclaiming, "In Lindbergh we greet A MAN of the very best stamp." The *Christian Science Monitor* reported with pride that Lindbergh's appeal extended beyond the common people of France: "The intellectuals are paying him tribute as well."[42]

The ambassador and the flier next stopped at the Chamber of Deputies, filled to overflowing in honor of the "most audacious feat of the century." The president of the Chamber's Army Commission celebrated Lindbergh's youth, innocence, and daring while raising the hallowed memories of the Great War, emphasizing the spilled blood that linked the two nations. Herrick motioned for Lindbergh to respond, but the aviator deferred to the diplomat. Rising to the occasion, Herrick told the deputies that he had long wanted to show France the heart and spirit of the real America that had been hidden for too long from Europeans. With the extraordinary young man at his side that was now possible. "Gentlemen," the ambassador closed with a twinkle, "I present to you this new Ambassador of the United States, whom France has so warmly taken to its heart."[43]

Lindbergh stepped forward. He waited for the applause to die down, and then waited some more—so long that Herrick feared he had become tongue-tied, this being the first public speech of his life. Finally he began: "Gentlemen, one hundred and thirty-two years ago Benjamin Franklin was asked: 'But what good is your balloon? What will it accomplish?' And he replied: 'What good is your newborn baby?'" It was a story that Herrick had told him, and he used it to perfect effect. He went on to predict, "[This flight is] the forerunner of a great air service from America to France, from America to Europe, which will bring our peoples together." And then he sat down.[44]

His third day in France began with a predawn visit to Le Bourget to check on the repairs to his plane. Then President Gaston Doumergue received the American party in full formal dress at the Elysée Palace. Lindbergh was still in borrowed clothes (the next day he would receive a delivery of suits and formal wear made to his measurements), and an embassy aide apologized. "Oh that's nothing," replied Doumergue, "it is this remarkable *boy* here I am interested in." Kissing him on both cheeks, the president pinned the Cross of the Legion of Honor on Lindbergh's lapel. When they returned to the embassy Herrick helped Lindbergh read through the more important cables and draft responses.[45]

In the afternoon Herrick took him to the historic Aero Club, where the leading figures in French aviation welcomed him enthusiastically. When the officers offered a champagne toast to his mother the teetotaling son of Prohibition America stood uncertainly holding his glass until Herrick signaled him to drink and he gingerly touched the fluid to his lips. "The other day, I flew over to Paris from New York," he began. Then he spoke of Nungesser and Coli, who by attempting to fly from Paris to New York had attempted a "greater thing." Herrick followed, calling him "this Lochinvar from out of the west," and explained why Lindbergh's trip was so important: "It was needed at this moment that the love of these two great peoples should manifest itself and it is this young boy who has brought that about."[46]

Madame Rana Deutsch de la Meurthe, widow of a former president of the Aero Club, gave the Club two gifts, one of 150,000 francs (roughly $6,000) and another of 200,000, directing that the first be given to Lindbergh and the second to be divided between the families of Nungesser and Coli. Declaring, "I could not take these francs to America, because I understand the sorrow of the French for their intrepid airmen and because I share their grief," Lindbergh used the gift to start a fund for the widows of French aviators who had died in the air: "[I do so] as an indication of my affection for France and my appreciation for her generous welcome."[47]

He visited the war heroes Marshall Foch and Marshall Joffre, who received him with great warmth. Standing next to Lindbergh for a picture, Foch admonished the American to stretch to his full height: "[That way] the world can see you are bigger than I am." Lindy chatted for more than an hour with the assembled French aces, sketching on the tablecloth to illustrate some of his thoughts to the rapt airmen surrounding him. He told an admiring Louis Blériot, "I shall always regard you as my master." The "father of Old World aviation" interrupted, "Ah, but you are my son, you are the prophet of a new era when flying will be as common as motor steamship traffic is today." They next stopped—a Herrick grace note, no doubt—at Les Invalides, where war veterans, many badly disfigured, had gathered for a visit.[48]

On Friday, May 27, Lindbergh rose early in the morning to sneak out to Le Bourget. Escorted by the airport commander he boarded a French fighting plane, impatiently replying "Oui oui" to all the instructions, and took the controls. He executed a perfect takeoff, made some fancy curves, and headed for Paris's Trocadero neighborhood, where he swept down to salute Ambassador Herrick, then circled the Eiffel Tower and soared over the Arc de Triomphe. He and an accompanying plane then turned back to Le Bourget, where he made as if to land, only to ascend for some stunts, looping the loop, doing side drifts, headspins, and assorted fancy turns. After twenty minutes the commander signaled for the planes to descend. The companion plane came down, but Lindbergh, happy as a puppy with a bone, remained airborne for another half hour, delighting the crowd by skimming the earth and then closing the performance with an air dance. As he looked over the side of the open cockpit during one of the stunts the wind blew off the leather helmet that had been retrieved for him after the tumultuous night at Le Bourget.[49]

"The days that followed were carbon copies of the first," Waverly Root reported, with two press conferences a day to feed the "mercilessly hungry" media. No detail of Lindbergh's reception, his clothing, his admirers, or even his breakfast was too trivial. Root complained that the press followed like sheep wherever Herrick led them, from award ceremonies to receptions, banquets, and speeches, all unfailingly banal. "Lindbergh was moved through this labyrinth of ceremony like a puppet wearing a perpetual expression of bewilderment," the newsman recalled, "like a wide eyed adolescent." That the succession of events struck a jaded "seen it all" correspondent as trite is not surprising; Herrick was not aiming for subtlety. He wanted to recapture the French heart and to repair relations between the allies, and Lindbergh provided him with the means.[50]

Banal it might have been, but the performance won over the French. Given Lindbergh's slim experience and education and the magnitude of the challenge, "banal" was an impressive achievement, in fact quite extraordinary. Lindbergh's performance was a tour de force of intelligent restraint. He used every opportunity to turn honors directed at him into tributes to French aviators and war heroes. He repeatedly referred to Nungesser and Coli's venture as "the greatest attempt of all." Asked to explain the choice of name for his plane, which in Paris conjured notions of the medieval French monarch, he intimated that it was meant as a sign of regard for "the people of France." "Royalty itself could not have been given a more ceremonious or more popular greeting," the *Times* of London wrote. The strain between the two nations vanished in the glow of the "greatest unofficial diplomat America ha[d] ever sent abroad," added the *New York Times,* concluding: "What he has done for Franco-American relations cannot be reckoned."[51]

Lindbergh delivered the message of America's ascent in a modest wrapper, offsetting his powerful achievement with a personal modesty that the French found irresistible. He mourned with them over their losses and helped them dress the lingering wounds of war by sharing his achievement with France's past masters. In acknowledging their pioneering contributions to aviation he encouraged the French to view the flight as a shared triumph. No one needed to be reminded that the moment belonged to America, but Lindbergh laid out an inclusive, palatable basis for a dignified transition to American leadership, in grace and not in anger.[52]

Coached by Herrick he navigated a delicate path between two distinct but not unrelated imperatives. He needed to recognize and respect the overweening shadow of the war, with its stories of courage and loss. He took great pains to honor France's leadership in World War I, recalling its valor and gallantry. At the same time, too young to have been in the war and therefore free of its taint, he represented a future beyond war. Those qualities that make heroes in war— courage, purity of purpose, bold disregard for personal safety, coming to the end of one's endurance and pushing beyond it, fighting forces stronger than oneself— he harnessed to the peaceful conquest of a new dimension. "It means so much . . . [that] it has been done by just such a hero as this *tired world* has been looking for," declared one of the elderly members of the Chamber of Deputies. "There seems a new inspiration to live and to see other marvels since this has been accomplished."[53]

"He brought you the spirit of America," Herrick told Parisians, and it is striking how many of the stories about Lindbergh emphasized that this spirit had to do with youth, innocence, and guilelessness. The letter of introduction that he handed Herrick from Theodore Roosevelt Jr. read in part, "Rupert of the Rhine said that for a desperate venture give him an army of boys; and Charles Lindbergh personifies the daring of youth." What made the story "immortal," explained the *New York Times,* was the spirit of "fearless youth . . . post-war youth, giving humanity a new hope in the person of this clear-headed, clean-lived, modest but daring son of America, who *even in peace* contemned death and drew the peoples of many nations together in their concentration of their common and supreme admiration."[54]

Hailed as a Roland, an Icarus, an eagle of peace, *le conquérant Américain*, Lindbergh made Paris "his personal possession." Day after day the French papers delivered their front pages to him. "Everyone has talked Lindbergh, thought Lindbergh, cheered Lindbergh and even dreamed Lindbergh," the *New York Times* reported."[55]

Herrick might deny his own role, but those paid to analyze the news knew that he deserved much credit for the achievement. With tongue in cheek, editorial writers cheered at solving the puzzle of what ambassadors were good for: they made heroes. "It is safe to say," the *New York Times* editorialized, that without Herrick's firm guidance "Captain Lindbergh could not have displayed such exquisite tact and sense of propriety in the things which he did and said. The promptings of his fine, ingenuous nature needed such skilled direction as was given to him and as he was sensible enough to accept." In one of his dispatches from Paris Lindbergh wrote, "I would have been lost without him."[56]

Invitations arrived from all over Europe; Lindbergh agreed to visit Belgium and England. Before leaving for Brussels on May 28 he took off in the refurbished *Spirit of St. Louis* and performed an air show for Paris, capped by a message on embassy stationery dropped from the air: "Good-bye, dear Paris. Ten thousand thanks for your kindness to me. Charles A. Lindbergh." A battery of French airplanes escorted him to the Belgian border, where he was greeted by two squadrons of Belgian army planes.[57]

Thousands, led by Belgium's King Albert and Queen Elizabeth, welcomed him to Brussels. Herrick's absence was evident immediately in Lindbergh's lightheaded comments: "I have met my first King and if they are all like him, believe me, I am for Kings." After taking the warm and animated Albert of the Belgians and his queen on a private tour of the *Spirit* early next morning Lindbergh reported, "[I have] changed all the ideas I ever had about Kings. . . . [They are much] more democratic than a lot of other people I know who aren't Kings."[58]

With all the pomp of a visiting head of state, Lindbergh visited the Belgian Tomb of the Unknown Solider and the monument to airmen lost in battle, placing tributary wreaths at both. He told the Belgians that he would never forget them. Elderly Brussels Burgomaster Adolphe Max, cherished for his valor in the war, greeted Lindbergh in the ornate Guild Hall before the city fathers, emotionally thanking him for his triumph on behalf of humanity. In halting English he closed, "I salute you, dear Captain Lindbergh, a noble son of your great nation, which at an hour when civilization was in danger, came to its help and with us, conquered."

Again Lindbergh managed to symbolize at once both the vaunted future and the hallowed past.[59]

Henry Wales imagined that after the American ambassador to England, Alanson Houghton, grasped the transforming power of Lindbergh's celebrity he rang up Herrick, insisting, "We must have this chap come over to see London, you know." Lindbergh at first considered staying at the home of an English aviator, but Herrick strongly advised Houghton to host him at the embassy. Doing so would make it easier for the embassy to control his schedule and shape his message.[60]

Lindbergh arrived on Sunday, May 29, to a rather un-British welcome. More than a hundred thousand had gathered to wait for him at Croydon Airport, and as his silver craft slipped slowly from the sky they began to stampede, crashing through barriers, knocking down women, spilling toddlers from carriages, and swatting aside the police cordons. To avoid decapitating his frenzied fans Lindbergh ascended and circled until the ground could be cleared. "Every shed, roof and watertower held persons on precarious footholds," reported the London *Times*. The police made a path for him to touch down, but as his wheels hit the ground the crowd broke through again, engulfing the plane, the official party, and everything in their path. Only with the greatest of difficulty did the bobbies manage to get Lindbergh safely into a car and deliver him to the administration building; Ambassador Houghton and British officials were all swept aside by the crowds moving Lindbergh to declare, that Croydon was "worse, or should I say better" than his frenzied night at Le Bourget. British reserve, he assured his readers, was vastly overstated.[61]

While a later generation would become familiar with chaotic scenes of this sort, this was the largest, wildest, most disorderly, and most enthusiastic gathering ever to welcome anyone on British soil. The first such welcome for a modern world celebrity led some to deplore the excitement as a "semi-hysterical . . . symptom of modern popular tendencies." In England, Lindbergh wrote, "[I felt] a sensation which had missed me during the entire Atlantic flight—I was downright afraid for the first time since leaving New York."[62]

King George V he found no less a capital fellow than his new buddy King Albert. "Interestingly," he mused, "I was able to observe that what interested the King about flying over the Atlantic was just about what interested everyone else." He wanted to know "How do you pee?" He was introduced to the royal family, including the king's baby granddaughter, Princess Elizabeth. Winston Churchill, chancellor of the Exchequer, who said of Lindbergh "He represents all a man should say, all that a man should do and all that a man should be," arrived smoking a big cigar and took him aside for a lengthy conversation about aeronautics. Later that night at a dinner several young women asked him to dance. He surprised them by refusing outright: "Absolutely nothing doing. I am here as an onlooker." His speeches lauded Alcock and Brown as "the first men to fly the Atlantic," and he went on to make the obligatory round of tributary visits to the Tomb of the Unknown and the graves of those who died in the war.[63]

Despite disappointing his hosts with his open disinterest in the Epsom Derby, his reception in England was no less enthusiastic than in France. During his five days in London Lindbergh was cheered, celebrated, and awarded every conceivable honor, but there was a difference. There was no overlay of rapprochement and rekindled comity between allies that gave his welcome in Paris a deeper resonance. British perceptions of the United States, wrote the *New York Times* London correspondent Ernest Marshall, "remain[ed] exactly where they stood."[64]

At dawn on June 3 he left Croydon for Paris, making good on his promise to return to France before leaving Europe for home. The next day, as Lindbergh boarded the USS *Memphis* in Cherbourg, Clarence Chamberlin took off in the *Columbia* from Roosevelt Field, landing a day later in Germany. The flight exceeded Lindbergh's record-setting distance by five hundred miles. In the same month Commander Richard E. Byrd made his long-awaited trip as well, taking off on June 29. Both aviators were celebrated for their brilliant crossings, and yet their triumphs, coming so soon after Lindbergh's, did nothing to diminish the afterglow of his flight. Why? First, neither of the others flew alone. Byrd took along two pilots and a navigator and served more as flight coordinator than pilot. With Wanamaker's backing he had endless resources at his disposal, and the entire enterprise appeared more bloodless corporate effort than intrepid pioneering. Moreover the Byrd team insistently downplayed the aviation challenges, emphasizing instead the scientific potential of the venture: studying air currents, weather changes, and engine performance. As for Chamberlin's *Columbia* flight, the court cases and ugly personal recriminations dimmed its luster. Both Chamberlin and Byrd were experienced airmen with established reputations, men of the war generation, solid professionals whose ships were equipped to the nines with every conceivable gadget and instrument. Lindbergh shone with the freshness of youth, his love of flying, his understated craft, his sheer gutsiness in taking a minimally equipped ship that permitted little margin for error on a precise path across the seas.[65]

In the end, despite all their preparation, their huge advantage in time and resources, their crews of experts, and their massive state-of-the-art ships, neither Byrd nor Chamberlin proved as adept at hitting their target. At first Chamberlin did not specify what his destination would be; he would determine that in the air, though he had spoken initially of aiming for Rome. In midflight he switched to Berlin, and then, forced down by empty fuel tanks after forty-six hours and more than four thousand miles in the air, he landed on June 6 in Eisleben, Germany, 110 miles short of his objective. The crew barely avoided serious injury when the plane was brought to a skidding halt in a marsh before tipping over.[66]

Byrd's team struggled with terrible weather. For more than nineteen hours the *America* flew blind through fog, mist, and violent storms with a malfunctioning earth inductor compass. The plane itself became unmanageable over the North Sea, "like riding a bucking bronco." Their flight plan called for landing at Le Bourget, but the *America* failed to reach the French mainland after being "hopelessly lost" (Byrd's words) for hours. The pilot had to bring the three-ton craft down in the sea, near the tiny village of Ver-sur-Mer, hitting the water with such force that the wheels were torn off. It was a struggle to keep the badly damaged plane from capsizing. The entire crew came very close to perishing, and Byrd himself was hurled through a window clear of the plane.[67]

Of neither venture could it be said, as the French minister of war remarked regarding Lindbergh's flight, that it was "an aesthetic triumph, a thing so beautiful that it has gone to the heart of the world as only beauty, and beauty alone, can." That it was Lindbergh instead of Byrd or Chamberlin gave the story its special appeal. "If there had been two aviators," the *Times*'s astute analyst Edwin James explained, "it would have been different. Had there been two engines it might have been different. Had he blustered before starting or boasted after succeeding it might have been different. Had he been ten years older, or had lots of other things been as they were not, Lindbergh might have had another sort of greeting."[68]

There was yet another difference: Lindbergh represented purity of purpose and values. This was a young man raised in 1920s America, when all restraints were supposed to have snapped before Holy Mammon. He arrived in Paris with twenty-seven cents in his pocket, concerned about where he would spend the night. He might have been forgiven for accepting a few movie deals, involving nothing more morally dubious than appearing on celluloid or in vaudeville.[69]

At the end of his very first day in Paris the endorsement deals and entertainment offers added up to over $200,000. By the following day the proposals were stacked high: the First National Film Corporation offered him $500,000; Ellis A. Gimbel offered any air company that employed Lindbergh a subsidy of $100,000; a French tailor wanted the honor of dressing him for free for the rest of his life, and two Parisian restaurants offered him free meals forever. By day three Hollywood came beckoning: Adolph Zukor called with an offer of $300,000, and other movie moguls followed with offers equally enticing. It all added up to more than a million dollars; then came another offer of $400,000 for a vaudeville run. Others dangled money for work in radio, a book contract, magazine and newspaper pieces, product endorsements, lectures and appearances. Even Evangeline was offered a silver screen contract of over $100,000 "to depict the American mother." (She turned it down "decisively," declaring that she had no intention of "commercializing" her son's fame.) One "London theatrical man" promised $2.5 million for Lindbergh to do a promotional tour of the world by air.[70]

All the while letters, telegrams, and gifts rained in on him, including several cars and "a little age-worn box from some unknown French woman containing the Cross of the Legion of Honor won under Napoleon by a member of her family." (Of the cars he accepted one, "a Franklin . . . as a token of their appreciation.") By the time he reached London a group of wealthy Americans had persuaded Secretary of War Dwight F. Davis to form a committee to raise subscriptions for a trust worth $2,000,000 (more than $20,000,000 in twenty-first-century dollars) for the Lone Eagle and his mother.[71]

Will Rogers called for protecting Lindbergh's innocence as a national resource: "This boy is not our usual type hero. He is all the others rolled into one. The government should reward him handsomely with a pension for life. And a high position in our aviation program [instead of having him appear on stage or screen]. We don't ask our retiring presidents to go into vaudeville. England don't allow their prince of Wales to go on paid exhibitions. Well this lad is our biggest asset. He is our president and our prince combined." Rogers offered to play benefits for the rest of his life to save Lindbergh from "having to make exhibitions of himself."[72]

Rogers needn't have worried. In an age when money talked and easy money was reputed to shout, Lindbergh declined the offers. "What sort of figure would I cut," he asked, "in a moving picture love story? I have had suggestions to be a cowboy, sheik, robber and lots of others things—but I am an aviator. . . . Flying is my job, not acting." Just a year before, he was still traveling the barnstorming circuit, but his achievement had given him a new dignity. He turned down the movie moguls and vaudeville men, nor would he continue doing air stunts. The other offers he simply set aside for the moment. The blandishments of cheap fame did not entice him. "I made this flight for the primary purpose of advancing the cause of aviation," he declared, "and not to make money." He had wanted a career in aviation and now that he had flown the Atlantic there was no reason to change that plan. "There has never entered my head any idea of doing anything but being a flying man. That's my job and it's a good enough job for me."[73]

Here too the wise Ambassador Herrick helped steer Lindbergh clear of hazards. He assigned the embassy staff to help Lindbergh with his mail, cables, and personal calls so they could sift the offers and set aside those that were questionable. Parmely Herrick helped Lindbergh begin to think about his future and sought out "a big businessman, a prominent lawyer and a diplomat," to guide Lindbergh in "reap[ing] such financial benefits as he legitimately can," while keeping away the charlatans: "His feat has been such a fine, clean, courageous thing, [and his supporters want] him to remain what he has become—an inspiration to the other young men of the country." Parmely selected Banker's Trust Company to handle Lindbergh's correspondence and personal affairs.[74]

During the long hours of his flight Lindbergh had thought about making a leisurely tour of Europe. Why hurry back home when open air in unfamiliar places beckoned? He was especially interested in studying the leading aviation centers and their airlines so that he could bring back to America ideas about improving pilot training, more effective testing of planes, and tougher standards for aviation manufacturers. And after Europe? "I can . . . fly on around the world through Egypt and India and China. . . . There's no place on earth I can't go."[75]

The extraordinary reaction to the flight had initially caught the White House by surprise. Washington had paid little mind to the unfolding Atlantic competition, until Ambassador Herrick suggested a halt to flights after the disappearance of the French fliers. Only after the passionate reception at Le Bourget, followed by that extraordinary week in Paris, did Washington take serious notice of the young hero. Will Rogers put it well: "I see where Mr. Coolidge says Lindbergh's feat grows on him." But it was the French who "appreciated the feat and honored him . . . waking [America] up to its real importance"[76]

Now the United States wanted him back home soon, his own plans notwithstanding. Deluged by requests from nations around the world, the State Department recognized that the situation was fraught with diplomatic implications. Germany and Russia, for example, wanted the aviator to visit, but such a move would certainly ruffle feathers, especially if he were to go before making the rounds of America's World War I allies. Moreover Americans were impatient to shine their own spotlight on him. President Coolidge, scheduled to soon leave Washington for summer vacation in South Dakota's Black Hills, now wanted to put on a splashy celebration immediately. This irked New York Mayor Jimmy Walker, who "deplored" the nervy intrusion; the flight took off from New York "unsung and unheralded by the Government," and, Walker insisted, it was to New York that Lindbergh should return.[77]

Torn between his desire to "see many countries" and his desire to "do the right thing," Lindbergh met the *Times*'s Edwin James one morning in Brussels and confided that he was going to insist on flying round the world "across Europe, across Siberia, across Behring Straits, over Alaska and back to New York." He did not want to come home yet, and he certainly did not want to return by boat. He thought it was undignified for the *Spirit of St. Louis* to be carted up and shipped home. *They* had flown the Atlantic together to prove that it was practical. Why dilute the message by returning by water?[78]

In London Ambassador Houghton invited Lindbergh to his study on the evening of May 29 and helped him change his mind. The instructions from the State Department, he advised Lindbergh, were unambiguous: he was to come home on the next ship. Celebrations were being planned. Lindbergh stood his ground. He wanted to fly home at a leisurely pace and not have his plane boxed up as ship's baggage. Houghton kept reminding the willful hero that he was wanted in Washington. Lindbergh stubbornly asked if this was an order. It was "the wish of Washington," the diplomat replied; a battleship was on its way.[79]

In the end Lindbergh relented. The destroyer was replaced by an admiral's flagship, the *Memphis*, one of the speediest cruisers in the navy. This did nothing to soften his grumbling about the indignities to his partner. It pained him that the *Spirit of St. Louis* was traveling as freight: "[She] lies tonight in a box like a coffin." It was a rather outsized coffin; the wing alone required a box close to fifty feet long. About his own accommodations—he was given the chief of staff's quarters—there was little to complain.[80]

Lindbergh's flight achieved the unthinkable, toppling barriers of impossibility. He had proved that it could be done, delivering the message that the future of international flight was at hand. The flight showcased modern technology, but it also offered comforting reassurance that even in modern times the miracles of technology waited upon human qualities, such as endurance, persistence, and courage. That was the message in Mussolini's encomium celebrating Lindbergh's "superhuman will." Without the air-cooled motor it could not be done, but it needed a Lindbergh to take the *Spirit of St. Louis* where no plane had ever gone before.[81]

Aside from all else, making it across the ocean alone required mastering a medley of aeronautical skills. For five years Lindbergh had trained with nothing else in mind but flying. He had become entirely self-reliant in the air. He could fix his own plane and plan his own route and possessed remarkable hand-eye coordination. Gregory Brandewiede, federal superintendent of the St. Louis–Chicago route in 1926, explained why he considered Lindbergh an extraordinarily gifted pilot: "He had the terrific engineering knowledge of aircraft: he knows an airplane, he knows just what the limitations are, he's very quick to sense anything that might be wrong in either the aircraft or the engine." His comprehensive knowledge of aircraft prevented him from asking a plane to do more than it could, a caution the other competitors would have done well to heed.[82]

He took off as a daredevil sportsman fired by personal ambition, but from the beginning he also betrayed a larger sense of purpose than just acing the contest or claiming the prize money. Aviation had come to be both life and sport for him. He aspired to transform flight from a thrilling diversion into a conventional mode of transportation and to propel the United States to the forefront of this new field. The fortnightly field letter prepared by the foreign branches of the U.S. Commerce Bureau noted that the flight had stirred "instant interest" in American aviation equipment. Leading aviation manufacturers and engineers from Europe's industrial nations flocked to inspect the *Spirit of St. Louis,* and the bureau predicted rising overseas orders "as a result of these record-breaking exploits."[83]

The *Spirit of St Louis* represented no extraordinary technical breakthroughs. The Wright engine performed as flawlessly as expected, and the Ryan craft held its own against the pressures of takeoff, flew through challenging weather, and then landed cleanly. What Lindbergh did was match the simplicity of the design with faultless execution and singular purpose.

More than a decade of air contests had primed the environment for air drama and the race between nations. The rival crews featured no shortage of operatic personalities fighting over glory, money, and fame. Pompous men were brought down, golden boy heroes and tough air aces died; outrageously expensive machines blew up in spectacular explosions. As the contest pressed forward a succession of failures pushed the stakes higher, making the elusive goal all the more extraordinary. After the disappearance of the French fliers the contest changed from a competition among teams to something greater. Even the French, who no longer had a plane in the race, very much wanted this victory, for human achievement, for aviation, for honor. The frenzied reception at Le Bourget and the remarkable celebrations that followed demonstrated how profoundly this particular course had captured the European imagination. "Lindbergh," wrote one Paris journal, "was sent to us from the sky and nothing shall soil his legend, which will remain for us as noble and pure as a page of Missal."[84]

Like all narratives, history requires transitions. It may be that in the Great War's aftermath the decline of Europe had become obvious. But when President Woodrow Wilson tried to dictate a postwar structure for the globe ("a magnificent Caesar at our expense," the French poet Charles Maurras said of him), one the French thought was cruelly solicitous of the German foe, his plan to assure eternal peace and lay the basis for secure democracy did not fare well. His Olympian pronouncements evinced just the sort of provincial nationalism he sought to avoid. Having failed to craft a mutually acceptable transition to acknowledged American leadership, he learned that there was more to international relations than firm ideals.[85]

One of Lindbergh's essential distinctions was that he was not an American exceptionalist dancing on the graves of old Europe. Nor was he typical of the air heroes familiar to Europeans. The tall flier with the tousled blond hair and chiseled good looks did not strut his medals, boasted no ace's scarf, no monocle, trophy injury, or swagger stick. The aces were wonderful characters, courageous iron men who had endured terrible torment, but they were also killers who had vaporized ten, twenty, even fifty planes in combat. In contrast, Lindbergh was fresh, clean of the war and its wounding memories. After all those celebrations of crippled heroes it was bracing to see a man in full, whole-bodied, smiling, the face of a future where heroes were not forged on battlefields. Under the Lone Eagle's warming glow, resentment faded into rapprochement—even admiration—for an audacious America, vibrant with energy, dash, and enterprise. Not long after the flight, the English writer Mary Borden exclaimed, "The scaffolding of the world of the future is reared against the sky of America."[86]

"I want to do all I can for American aviation," Lindbergh wrote on his way home aboard the *Memphis*. "That is going to be my career." He had of course already done a great deal. Two weeks after the flight Assistant Secretary of War F. Trubee Davison exulted, "American pilots and American planes lead the world." Lindbergh used his new stature as a platform to speak about the future of American aviation, indicating that he had thought about these issues more systematically than the average flyboy. His first and broadest message was simply "Flying is just as safe, if not safer, than motoring on the ground." The Europeans had been serious about air travel for some time now, and the United States had much to learn. He capped his message with a plea to Washington: American aviation would be able to compete with the heavily subsidized foreign airline industry only if the government took a hand in erecting a supportive infrastructure, especially airports.[87]

In these early dispatches Lindbergh laid out a set of ideas about the economics of American aviation that would color his thinking for a long time. He had witnessed the hand-to-mouth struggle of small companies like the Robertsons'; they were not going to carry American aviation to world leadership. The future of free enterprise aviation lay in broad-gauged and well-funded undertakings. Yes, he had made the trip across in a single-engine light aircraft built by a small company, but international travel would require large, expensive, multimotor planes, probably massive hydroplanes that could land on sea-based fueling stations as they made their way across the oceans. The conclusion was plain: only through coordinated, large-scale effort would American aviation rise to prominence. The United States could not hope to supplant the more experienced Europeans through incremental steps fostered in a perfect competitive environment; success would demand big business, big money, big research and development laboratories.[88]

Returning home aboard the *Memphis* Lindbergh faced questions about how to convert his fame into something practical. The Robertsons and his airmail days were history. He had skipped to the highest levels of significance, and investors were discussing substantial backing. Self-effacing in his public speeches, he was anything but modest in his aviation enthusiasms. He was thinking of the next step, "a big, comprehensive commercial . . . air service" that would offer domestic passenger, mail, and parcel services and ultimately extend overseas.[89]

7

IT TOUCHED OFF AVIATION

LATE IN THE AFTERNOON of June 10, 1927, the USS *Memphis* with Charles Lindbergh and the *Spirit of St. Louis* onboard passed through the Virginia Capes, about a hundred miles off the coast of the Unites States. An honor guard of four destroyers, two army blimps, and forty airplanes escorted her up Chesapeake Bay to Piney Point, where she dropped anchor for the night. Standing on the bridge of the ship, taking in the impressive scene, the Minnesota farm boy remarked to the admiral standing at his side, "I wonder if I really deserve all this."[1]

That day Evangeline Lindbergh arrived in Washington and spent the night as the guest of President and Mrs. Coolidge at 15 Dupont Circle, their temporary headquarters while the White House was undergoing renovation. Only one other guest joined them for dinner that night, Coolidge's old college chum Dwight Morrow, the investment banker who had chaired the committee on modernizing American airline policy. News reports noted the irony that Evangeline's late husband probably had not been in agreement about a single policy with the Republican president who hosted her, much less with the Morgan partner who joined them for dinner. (The additional irony, left unsaid of course, was that she and her late husband did not share many ideas either.) Morrow reported to his wife that he was charmed by Evangeline's dignity and simplicity.[2]

Since she last saw him her son had been transformed from an unknown mail pilot into a global hero. He had conquered the sky, and Europe as well, single-handedly recasting what the *Los Angeles Times* called "the accepted 'American type' abroad": "the arrogant, ignorant, purse proud moron." Never had an American achieved such widespread veneration.[3]

Americans, of course, cheered as well. The story about the headstrong loner whose mite of an aircraft ferried him across a quarter of the globe, 6,200 miles from San Diego to Paris in three hops, to win one of the most spectacular races ever held had broad appeal. At first Americans cheered for what Richard Byrd called "one of the greatest individual feats in all history," an extraordinary accomplishment for three men, almost impossible for one. But then Walter Hinton, famous for having piloted the Curtiss NC-4 across the Atlantic back in 1919, observed that Paris taught Americans to view the flight more broadly as a "turn of the road for aviation . . . bring[ing] all people to the realization of the possibilities of human flight." Paris demonstrated aviation's protean power to vault barriers of nationalism, provincialism, even economic competition. Lindbergh was no mere champion, trumpeted the *Baltimore Sun*; he was "the spearhead of the race."[4]

The day after Lindbergh's arrival in Paris the *New York Times* devoted its first five pages to the flight. On the following day stories about him filled every column on the first four pages. The public appetite continued to grow. The *Times* printed thirty thousand extra newspapers for the May 23 edition that featured his first-person account—which began, "Well here I am"—only to have eager readers snap up the entire run of some 420,000 papers. Those who could not get a copy bid up to fifty times the cover price for a coveted paper, and those who could not buy a copy paid to borrow one.[5]

Within two days, a clipping bureau reported, the Lindbergh saga had become the biggest news story in U.S. history. The public clamored for more, exhorting editors to run more Lindbergh stories and fewer about those who filled the jails, the courts, and the morgues. Will Rogers cracked that Lindy's greatest accomplishment "was to show that a person could get the entire front page without murdering someone."[6]

Cynics might dismiss Lindbergh's feat as an ephemeral triumph, akin to a victory in a sporting contest, wrote the *New York Herald Tribune,* but it was in fact "a work of art." This sort of deed, the paper continued, "casts a beam back into the centuries and massive figures standing there take fire and glow again." Even the flinty social critic Heywood Broun took heart from the flight: "Nature can't bully us indefinitely with wind and wave and peril of great oceans. One of our boys has put the angry sea in its place." Wellwood Beal heard about the flight at his fraternity house at the University of Colorado, and it inspired him to make aviation his life's work. "It touched off aviation. It touched me off . . . to be an aeronautical engineer."[7]

"For years," Frederick Lewis Allen wrote in *Only Yesterday,* his retrospective of the 1920s, "the American people had been spiritually starved." Their confidence and ideals had been eroded by the "disappointing aftermath of the war . . . by scientific doctrines, and psychological theories which undermined their religion and ridiculed their sentimental notions," as well as by sordid politics, cheap heroics, scandal, and gangsterism. For a people fearful of being overtaken by impersonal technology and mass society Lindbergh offered an inspiring example of individual courage and skill. Amid their manufactured heroes and cardboard idols they yearned for someone with discipline, and convictions that went deeper than celluloid, whose achievements were real, substantial, and solid, "a Galahad for a generation which had foresworn Galahads."[8]

On June 11, a torrid Saturday, the USS *Memphis* steamed up the Potomac past Alexandria. Among the dignitaries lining the Navy Yard pier to greet the returning hero were the former secretary of state and future chief justice of the Supreme Court Charles Evans Hughes, the secretaries of the navy and of war, the postmaster general, Commander Richard Byrd, and scores of others. Overhead roared a squadron of close to one hundred army and navy planes of every type. Piloted by elite fliers from across the nation, they provided an honor escort as the *Memphis* answered the booms set off by the long guns on the presidential yacht. Church bells pealed, sirens blasted, car horns blared, and whistles pierced the air with joyous welcome.[9]

Evangeline Lindbergh came up the gangplank first to welcome her son for a few minutes alone, followed by a procession of officials. Armed service representatives brought Lindbergh a Missouri National Guard Reserves uniform, hoping that he would appear in khaki for the day's honors. But he decided against it. He had flown as a civilian and insisted that that was how he would accept his honors.[10]

Then the presidential limousine drove Lindbergh and his mother through the streets lined with cheering crowds. A guard of cavalry and detachments from the army and navy followed, while three mail trucks bearing half a million letters addressed to the flier while he was overseas trailed them as the parade made its way to the Washington Monument.[11]

More than five hundred photographers snapped away as Lindbergh arrived at the crest of Potomac Park. Standing by were special trains, trucks, and planes prepared to rush the captured moments for distribution worldwide. On the grounds where, as a boy, Lindbergh had frolicked and rolled on the grass, the president, cabinet, ambassadors, and justices assembled to greet him. Three hundred thousand spectators, stretching out into the far distance, shattered all previous records for such tribute. Men in frock coats and high hats and women in stylish outfits joined office workers, factory hands, and dignitaries from foreign lands in the sweltering heat of the Washington day to honor him.[12]

Lindbergh mounted the grandstand overlooking the monument. President Coolidge took him by the hand to his seat. Then in a lavish encomium uncharacteristic of the tight-lipped president, Coolidge celebrated this "wholesome, earnest, fearless, courageous product of America . . . [who] driven by an unconquerable will and inspired by the . . . spirit of his Viking ancestors . . . set across the dangerous stretches of the North Atlantic." With little fanfare and much courage, "this genial, modest American youth, with the naturalness . . . and the poise of true greatness," accomplished what no man had and "He was alone." He landed in Paris with a message of "peace and good will" and despite offers of riches refused to "become commercialized." He returned to bring his "unsullied fame home." Coolidge presented Lindbergh with the Distinguished Flying Cross and commissioned him a colonel in the Officers' Reserve Corps. Casting aside all protocol, the secretary of the navy whooped, waving his arms over his head while the crowd responded with deafening cheers.[13]

Lindbergh stepped to the podium, at first uncertain. A long minute passed before he leaned into the microphones that carried his words to those assembled and thirty million more radio listeners. He offered not a word about himself, his flight, or the extraordinary reception he had received in Europe. He spoke for less than a minute, delivering a message that he said had been entrusted to him in the European lands that he had visited: tell your countrymen of our affection for the people of America. Then he thanked the crowd and sat down. Unaccustomed to short speeches, the throng waited for a moment before breaking out with peals of sustained applause. "It's as if they caught an angel that talks like Coolidge," wrote Ernest Hemingway.[14]

Lindbergh and his mother joined President and Mrs. Coolidge and Dwight Morrow for lunch. That night at a National Press Club reception the *New York Times* chief Washington correspondent Richard V. Oulahan spoke: "We of the press rub shoulders with all manner of mankind. We see much of good, but we see much of self seeking, sordid motive, as we sit in the wings watching the world's procession pass across the stage." But all cynicism faded before Lindbergh, who proved that "clean living, clean thinking . . . fair play and sportsmanship, modesty of speech and manner, [and] faith in a mother's prayers have a front page value." Postmaster General Harry S. New announced that for the first time in its history the Post Office was issuing a stamp in honor of someone still alive. The ten-cent airmail stamp with the image of the *Spirit of St. Louis* featured his name. It was a distinction, General New told Lindbergh, "worthily won." Closing the evening Secretary of State Frank B. Kellogg declared, "No act of a single individual in our day has ever aroused such universal enthusiasm and admiration."[15]

The next day, Sunday, Lindbergh paid tribute to America's Unknown Soldier, placing a wreath before the monument. Then he toured Walter Reed Army Hospital, visiting wounded veterans. In America as in Europe the war remained the reference point for heroes. During the next two days, filled with official visits and triumphal parades, he took pains to share credit for his flight with those who had nurtured aviation technology in its early years and made his success possible.[16]

On June 13, a Monday, he set off for New York from Washington's Bolling Field in the reassembled *Spirit of St. Louis*. Gotham officials had sought to convince him to come by amphibian craft and land in the water, away from crowds that would surely mob any airfield. He would not hear of it. It was enough that he had been separated from his partner for the return trip across the ocean; he would not add to the indignity by having the *Spirit* brought to New York by rail. Nor would he permit the plane to be brought up by someone else. Leaving it to the committee to work out the details, he added, "My heart is set on it."[17]

Around 10 a.m. Lindbergh settled into his wicker seat and prepared to take off, but the freshly tuned engine did not sound right and the *Spirit of St. Louis* stayed behind in Washington after all. He borrowed a Curtiss P-1 army pursuit biplane and, in the words of one correspondent, proceeded to "make it talk," putting on a stunt show, "play[ing] like an aerial porpoise," before heading off for New York.[18]

Twenty-four Curtiss hawk pursuit airplanes accompanied him to Mitchell Field; he was whisked to an amphibian craft and delivered to Staten Island, where New York's official yacht, the *Macom*, was waiting. Accompanied by four hundred boats and twenty-two planes in battle formation overhead, the *Macom* made its way into the harbor to the Battery. As Lindbergh stepped onto the pier a Frenchman broke through the crowd, ran over, and announced that he was president of the French War Veterans in the United States. He removed the Legion of Honor medal fixed to his lapel and pinned it onto Lindbergh's jacket, declaring, "What is mine is yours."[19]

Escorted by a marching guard of fifteen thousand uniformed servicemen, the hero's limousine moved past skyscrapers and historic buildings decked with bunting and photographs of him. City schools and businesses had closed for the celebration. The Stock Exchange shut down trading and courts were shuttered. From the Battery to City Hall Park a crowd of 300,000 filled the historic canyons with cheers as confetti rained down from the tall buildings, forming a canopy so dense that it completely blocked the summer sun.[20]

At City Hall three white-robed women trumpeted the hero's arrival. New York's "good time mayor" James J. (Jimmy) Walker welcomed the honored guest and thanked him for adding a new "flying pronoun . . . the aeronautical 'we,'" to the lexicon. At this historic gateway to America, the portal to liberty and opportunity, Walker declared, he, the son of one immigrant, was proud to hail the world's greatest hero, the son of another. Pinning the medal of the city on Lindbergh's chest, the urbane mayor told Lindbergh that New York City was his: "I do not give it to you. You have won it."[21]

After Lindbergh declared the New York celebration bigger and more impressive than all the others combined, he and other luminaries motored up to Madison Square, stopping for a tribute at the Eternal Light, commemorating the city's war dead. Then they continued up the six-mile route along Fifth Avenue to Central Park. Four million New Yorkers, some of whom had waited all night for a prime location, packed the streets. Hotels along the parade route rented rooms to those eager to witness this historic day from their windows. Others squatted in building cornices or perched on parapets, in trees, and on statues.[22]

Ten thousand children trilled a welcome as the procession passed the New York Public Library on Forty-second Street. Stopping before St. Patrick's Cathedral Lindbergh climbed up the steps to greet the elderly Patrick Joseph Cardinal Hayes, who rose from a throne placed outside the church to meet him: "I greet you as the first and finest American boy of the day." Then the caravan continued up to Central Park, where Governor Al Smith presented Lindbergh with New York State's Medal of Valor, hailing him as "an example for the youth of America."[23]

That evening the city hosted the largest official banquet ever given in honor of an individual in New York City. Dignitaries from church and state joined leaders of business, culture, and society, "all of masculine New York that counted" (about 3,700 men), to crowd into the Commodore Hotel Ballroom. White-haired justices jostled with members of the clergy and social Brahmins—some standing on chairs—to catch a glimpse of the hero and hear City College of New York President John H. Finley address him as "a composite youth of the best that is and a promise of the best that is to be."[24]

Former secretary of state Charles Evans Hughes spoke:

We measure heroes as we do ships, by their displacement. Colonel Lindbergh has displaced everything. . . . He fills all our thought. He has displaced politics. . . . He has lifted us into the upper air that is his home. He has displaced everything that is petty; that is sordid; that is vulgar. What is money in the presence of Charles A. Lindbergh? . . . He has driven the sensation mongers out of the temple of our thoughts. . . . Where are the stories of crime, of divorce, of the triangles that are never equilateral? For the moment we have forgotten. This is the happiest day. . . . We are all better men and women because of this exhibition in this flight of our young friend. Our boys and girls have before them a stirring, inspiring vision of real manhood. What a wonderful thing it is to live in a time when science and character join hands to lift up humanity with a vision of its own dignity.[25]

It was too much to expect Lindbergh to respond in kind. He was a flier, a man of action, who remained focused on practical matters. Moreover he did not have

Myron Herrick at his side. It would take time for him to assimilate the significance that came to be attached to him. For now he focused on aviation, responding to the praise by telling the august audience, "There is great room for improvement in the United States in aeronautics," especially airports. He urged New York's leading men to invest in the new air industry.[26]

At a dinner celebration put on by the Aeronautical Chamber of Commerce all three government secretaries charged with overseeing air policy spoke of the stimulus the flight gave to aviation. Charles Schwab, the sixty-five-year-old steel czar, journeyed five hundred miles from his home. He would not have made the trip for anyone else, he told the assembled aviation establishment, but "I love this young man."[27]

The next day's *New York Times* filled every inch of the first *sixteen pages* (except for ads) with stories about Lindbergh's triumphal celebration. The *Los Angeles Times* described Gotham as "Joy Mad." Eight miles of city streets were covered to a half inch in ticker tape, 1,800 tons of celebratory detritus left over after the greatest demonstration ever in New York's history. The euphoria continued for the entire four days Lindbergh spent in the city.[28]

On Thursday, June 16, Lindbergh received a check for $25,000 from Raymond Orteig at a formal affair in the Hotel Brevoort. Orteig explained that he had hoped to achieve two goals with his prize: to stimulate aviation and to strengthen U.S.-French relations. He told Lindbergh, "Through you, Colonel Lindbergh, my aspirations have materialized beyond words." Lindbergh, acknowledging that the prize had turned his attention to Paris, observed that such challenges remained critical: "I do not believe any such challenge, within reason, will ever go unanswered."[29]

The Orteig presentation ran late, causing Lindbergh to miss another hero in action. Lindbergh had been scheduled to throw out the first ball at Yankee Stadium. For twenty-five minutes the umpires held up the game, but finally they started without him. The New York Yankees' Babe Ruth was on his way to hitting a record sixty home runs in this year and in the first inning told a teammate that his left ear was itching. "I feel a homer coming on. . . . That's a sure sign." He kept looking to the stands for Lindbergh, but when he got to the batter's box he could delay destiny no longer, and with a count of two strikes he unloaded homer number twenty-two. The "Sultan of Swat" was disappointed, however. "I had been saving that home run for Lindbergh and then he doesn't show up. . . . I held back as long as I could," the Babe told reporters after the game. Lou Gehrig also hit one out of the park before Lindbergh arrived.[30]

Lindbergh did not long agonize over the missed home runs, but something else did put him out of sorts. Unsure about how to report this, the press simply described him as "lonesome for his partner." In the midst of the acclaim of millions he missed his plane. So forlorn did he become that he decided to fly down to Washington to retrieve the *Spirit*. Twice in a pouring rain he went out to Long Island to borrow an army pursuit plane, but army brass nixed a flight in the summer downpours. When he finally did take off, bad weather forced him back down in twenty minutes. Downcast, he returned to the empty hangar at Roosevelt Field.[31]

On Thursday night the weather cleared and he rushed out after an evening benefit in Manhattan, slipped his flying togs over his dinner suit, and at 2:59 a.m. took an army plane to Anacostia Field in Washington. Within half an hour he was blissfully aboard the *Spirit of St. Louis,* returning to Mitchell Field. Arriving at 7:40, he sped back to the Park Avenue apartment where he and his mother were staying, showered, changed, and completed the round of activities set for his last day in New York City, tired but finally happy. He stopped at police headquarters to thank the cops for their work, dropped by the *New York Sun* to acknowledge what had already become one of the most popular newspaper pieces of the era, the editorial "Lindbergh Rides Alone." The rest of the day he spent in Brooklyn being praised as a model for America's youth.[32]

He next flew nine hours to St. Louis, arriving on a drizzling night to find five thousand excited fans waiting to for him at Lambert Field. In the morning he was driven through seven miles of St. Louis streets packed with half a million people. Praised as the pathfinder who had stripped the unknown of "its mystery and peril," he heard the secretary of war call him a "new Columbus."[33]

On June 22, with his triumphal tour finally completed, Lindbergh ducked into Dayton, Ohio, to spend a private evening with Orville Wright at his home. But word of the meeting leaked out, bringing a huge crowd clamoring for the Lone Eagle. They trampled everything under foot, and finally Wright had to ask his visitor to acknowledge the crowd from the balcony to save his property from further damage.[34]

What had begun as spontaneous celebration had given way to frenzied celebrity. Everything Lindbergh did made the front pages: the endless round of receptions, his job offers, his mother, his comings and goings. Suddenly his face was everywhere, on ads for watches, pens, motor oil. The public could not get enough of him. Countless babies were named Charles, or Lindy, or even Lindbergh. Papers reported that one child born in Chicago's Chinatown was given the moniker One Long Hop. Celebratory flags, buttons, miniature *Spirits*, and other trinkets flooded the market. Sandwiches were named after him; so was Chicago's airplane beacon and scores of parks, schools, streets, and even a mountain peak in Colorado. Businesses incorporated under variations of his name, the name of his plane, "Lone Eagle" and "Slim."[35]

The camera loved him from any angle, filling papers, popular magazines, and movie screens with his visage. On his first day in New York film crews devoted more than 7.4 million feet of newsreel film to his activities, more footage than of anyone else in the world. A Hollywood producer told the *Washington Post,* "Women saw in him the perfection of man, what they conceived their husbands to be and what still constitutes their dream. . . . The men in turn experienced quick pulses of the heart and thought wistfully of things they might have done, things they would like to do, things they wished they had the nerve to do."[36]

The *New York Times* received more than five hundred Lindbergh-related letters to the editor (three were negative). Some demanded that a fund be set up for the flier and his mother; others thought that President Coolidge had been ungenerous in making him a mere colonel, that a generalship was in order. One flat out demanded that the president resign in favor of the twenty-five-year-old hero. So many schemes were started to raise money for his benefit that he had to announce publicly that he did not want and would not accept public subscriptions. Later, when William Randolph Hearst nevertheless launched a campaign in the *New York Evening Journal* to collect nickels and dimes from the children of New York as a tribute, Lindbergh asked that the money be returned or given to a hospital.[37]

By this point he had received 3.5 million letters and 100,000 telegrams—with urgent proposals of marriage, business, or breathtaking solutions to the world's problems through flight. Three missives invited him to help reach the moon by "a rocket shot from earth." He received literally tons of presents, including jewelry, antique manuscripts, and lifetime passes to baseball games and Broadway plays. Gifts waiting for him in St. Louis filled twelve crates, creating a dilemma over what to do with it all. He carried medals from France, England, Belgium, the United States, and every city he visited. Merchants refused to cash the checks he signed, and often his laundry had a way of getting lost once it left his quarters. One woman implored the manager at a hotel where he was stay ing (on a later tour) to rent her the room that Lindbergh had used "so she could take a bath in same tub."[38]

In July President Coolidge, having made Lindbergh's notion of ocean-based airports, or seadromes, an important part of his newly ambitious program for international aviation, took pains to inform the public that his program had been cleared by Colonel Lindbergh, who would be given whatever assistance he required "to induce foreign countries to cooperate in the development of landing places and aerial oceanic routes." Indeed the White House announced that the president was prepared to make aviation progress "the great outstanding accomplishment of his administration."[39]

The *Times*'s Russell Owen marveled, "There is something superhuman in Lindbergh's acceptance of honors such as have been paid to few men in the history of the world." Owen's colleague Edwin James, who got to know Lindbergh well in Europe, remarked to him one morning that he was impressed with how his encounters with kings and dignitaries had not swelled his head. "Well, what if I did get a swelled head?" Lindbergh replied. "I might fool somebody else but I couldn't fool myself and so there wouldn't be any real fun in it."[40]

The fun was bound to stop at some point. After making an appearance in Detroit he dashed off to Ottawa, Canada to join the sixtieth-anniversary Dominion Confederation Jubilee. Canadian Prime Minister Mackenzie King was a distant relative and had invited his famous kin to Ottawa. He was trailed by an escort of twelve planes. The air honor guard had become a regular part of his entourage, and as he landed they circled overhead in battle formation, followed by a series of coordinated dives and fancy maneuvers. Suddenly the propeller of one of the planes caught the tail of another, sending it plummeting. The plane was shredded and the pilot died instantly. It was a sobering conclusion to the chapter of celebration as Lindbergh turned to shaping his new future on the ground.[41]

While in Paris he had received timely assistance from Ambassador Herrick and his son Parmely, who had helped him deal with the offers that came rushing in. The offers still kept coming, only there were even more of them with even larger payoffs: deals for films, personal appearances, lectures, endorsements of every type. One benefactor, fearful that sooner or later the odds would catch up with him, offered Lindbergh a million dollars to stop flying. He turned it down, unwilling, he said, to become a living statue. Maurice Howland, director of the Division of Engineering and Industrial Research of the National Research Council, suggested that Lindbergh be appointed America's aviation czar (the "Will Hays of Aviation") to "crystallize the popular enthusiasm and public sentiment of the moment into action" and sell an as yet unconvinced public on aviation.[42]

Only a few months before he had been piloting rickety craft, delivering the mail for the Robertsons. His world had changed not only because he had talked to kings and been cheered by millions. He had become not merely a hero but a symbol. The flight had incalculably expanded his horizon, but now it was up to him to shape it, and to do that he needed knowledgeable guidance.

The St. Louis team that backed his flight, especially Harry Knight, Harold Bixby, Bill Robertson, and Earl Thompson, remained close. Joined by Ryan Air's president Ben Mahoney, they had greeted him in Washington and accompanied him on the other stops as he made his way back to St. Louis. They had tried to protect him from bad deals and helped him respond to some of the invitations and offers. Once things calmed down, they expected him to settle in St. Louis, where entrepreneurs were putting together a number of aviation possibilities for him to choose from.[43]

He also had a public relations team. When Lindbergh was in New York readying for the flight to Paris, as we saw, the Wright Corporation had assigned Richard Blythe and Harold Bruno to help with his mail, the press, and general PR. Before he took off Lindbergh had agreed to a series of penny ante deals for commercials. As the *Spirit of St. Louis* was still winging its way to Paris large newspaper ads informed Americans that the plane featured Goodrich Silvertown tires and AC sparkplugs, that its tanks were filled with Socony-Vacuum's gasoline and lubricated by Gargoyle Mobil oil B. He also backed Waterman fountain pens (the pen used to mark "the route on [his] maps") and Bulova watches (for a fee of $500). These were testimonials to products he actually used and trusted, but he did not want to do more endorsements. Nor was he interested in putting his name to marquee use.[44]

While he was in Paris, Bruno and Blythe continued to handle some of his work and now that he had returned they were looking to build their PR business around him. Wading through stacks of proposals, separating the legitimate from the far-fetched and dubious, they spent "twenty hours a day saying no"—apparently, not often enough. When they brought him a prominent businessman's offer of a life-time endowment, Lindbergh turned indignant: "What do they think I am, philanthropy?" Lindbergh himself wavered between moments when he felt secure about his financial situation and moments when he feared that his bubble might soon burst, sending him back to drawing $300 a month. "With a lot of public appearances coming up," he later wrote, "I foresaw that I must find some way of meeting expenses."[45]

With the blizzard of unsolicited offers also came advice. World heavyweight boxing champion Gene Tunney, no stranger to transient fame, urged the young flier to "commercialize his stunt for every cent that's in it, for in a year from now he will be forgotten." Gertrude Ederle, the first woman to swim across the English Channel and in record-breaking time, agreed: Lindbergh "had better get the money now; later on it may be too late." She had been feted and celebrated immediately after her accomplishment, her name in headlines from coast to coast. Now, barely ten months later, she was making two appearances a day on the small-time vaudeville circuit. Exploit the moment, she urged Lindbergh, for "a great deal of life is the business of making money."[46]

Harold Bixby, the St. Louis banker who had helped Lindbergh finance the flight, feared that Bruno and Blythe were not right for Lindbergh. Dick Blythe might have been helpful, but he was liable to "to take him over, exploit him." Lindbergh did not need publicity; what he needed was sure-footed guidance to chart a rewarding future. Lindbergh himself felt uncomfortable with the promoters, especially after the pair's ham-handed effort to set up a rendezvous for him with a "buxom, heavily powdered and painted blonde" who he concluded was a prostitute.[47]

Lindbergh had much higher regard for the St. Louis coterie. In interviews and discussions he spoke of St. Louis as the home to which he was eager to return and organize his future. Only a virtual government command, he told reporters, could tear him loose. Anticipating his return, his St. Louis backers formed the Spirit of St. Louis Corporation "to promote aviation in St. Louis and vicinity; to promote interest in national and international flights and to foster interest in aviation generally." Earl Thompson took the initiative to develop plans for an airplane manufacturing plant and offered him the presidency. Lindbergh's participation, he was confident, would make St. Louis an aviation center. Others raised $1,000,000 in seed money to establish a passenger airline around the magical Lindbergh name. For his part Lindbergh said that St. Louis belonged "at the top of the aeronautical world." Enrollment in flight classes at Lambert Field rose by 500 percent.[48]

In his recollections, deposited with Columbia University's Oral History Collection, Bixby recounted that Dwight Morrow, whom he knew from Amherst College, contacted him soon after Lindbergh's return from Paris. Morrow wanted to meet him in Washington. On his way to the meeting Bixby ran into another Amherst graduate, President Coolidge, who appeared to know that he was to meet Morrow. "You do whatever he asks you to do, will you?" Coolidge advised him. Highly regarded in establishment circles, Morrow had molded Coolidge's aviation policy and favored a muscular American aeronautical industry. He had met Lindbergh and been impressed, but he was also concerned that the young man was not equipped to deal with the responsibilities and choices that were descending upon him so furiously. This is what he discussed with Bixby, who was no less afraid that Lindbergh might be exploited. Bixby himself was unsure about what to do. Here was a kid who just days before "didn't have a damn thing but an extra pair of socks; all of his savings had gone into the flight." Were they supposed to simply wave away offers of a million dollars? "Who were we to turn it down?"[49]

Morrow had a firmer sense of how to proceed. He told Bixby, "[Lindbergh is going to be] the biggest thing that has ever happened to help aviation, which you're interested in and I'm interested in." He aimed to protect this asset and Bixby, agreeing that Morrow knew much more about "that sort of thing," deferred to him. Morrow promised $10,000 from his Morgan partners to retire what was left of the original bank debt for the purchase of the *Spirit of St. Louis*. He saw to it that Lindbergh's initial investment of $2,000 was returned to him and received Bixby's assurance that the St. Louis group would forgo their shares in the Orteig prize, allowing Lindbergh to keep the entire $25,000. He and Bixby also agreed "to write . . . [Bruno and Blythe] out of the play" and to arrange for all future business offers to be handled through the Guggenheim Fund for Aviation.[50]

Harry Guggenheim was no less taken with Lindbergh than was Morrow. In a book he published in 1930, *The Seven Skies,* Guggenheim attributed the public's rapid embrace of aviation to Lindbergh's "almost superhuman effort." Despite the fact that little new technology resulted from the flight, Guggenheim thought its consequence was of the first order because it broke down the barriers to imagining transatlantic flight: "The world needed a Lindbergh to impress it." Morrow turned to the philanthropist to find something for Lindbergh "to save him from the wolves . . . before he commits himself to some proposition that he might regret."[51]

About a week after Lindbergh touched down in St. Louis, on June 27 he returned to New York and visited the House of Morgan at 23 Wall Street. He lunched with J. P. Morgan Jr. and Dwight Morrow, then spent close to three hours closeted with Morrow, Knight, Bixby, and Bill Robertson in the Morgan offices. They agreed that Lindbergh would let Bruno and Blythe go. He did not need PR; he needed sober advice from refined and deeply informed men of broad vision, men with financial power who could frame a future worthy of him and his goals of advancing aviation. They assured him that he did not need to be concerned about money or feel pressed into unseemly endorsements or projects that could compromise his achievement. The St. Louis debt had been forgiven, the Orteig money was all his, and he was getting back his $2,000. Morrow offered to oversee Lindbergh's investments himself and assured him of a well-paying project with the Guggenheim Fund.[52]

The next day Lindbergh announced that he had accepted the Guggenheim Fund's offer, in cooperation with the Department of Commerce, to make an air tour of the nation to spread word about airplane reliability. He would fly the *Spirit of St. Louis* to every state in the country to stimulate interest in aviation and to encourage support for the development of safe and reliable commercial air flight. The tour would begin in late July, after he had fulfilled his prior commitments, principally finishing a book about his flight to Paris. He intended to work on the book at Falaise, the Guggenheim manorial estate on Sands Point, Long Island.[53]

Instead of hawking Waterman pens and Mobil oil for hundreds of dollars Lindbergh would be representing aviation itself for tens of thousands. How much exactly? Guggenheim asked Morrow (who was a board member of the Guggenheim Fund) to be "good enough to set the fee." Morrow suggested that demand alone made Lindbergh a valuable commodity, far more valuable than the "normal flyer." He pointed out, "Colonel Lindbergh's position has been perfect in not wanting to capitalize his advertising value," and it was important to keep him happy within the aviation family. He suggested the sum of $50,000 for the aviation tour (about $500,000 in 2005 dollars). Guggenheim agreed.[54]

Morrow and Guggenheim also recommended that Lindbergh take on Henry Breckinridge, a friend of the Morrow family and Guggenheim's personal lawyer, to handle his day-to-day affairs. An impeccably credentialed establishment attorney, Breckinridge grew up in Tennessee and went on to a Princeton education and Harvard law degree. He had served as assistant secretary of war during the Wilson administration, resigning his post once war broke out to serve in France, where he befriended Myron Herrick. He returned to service with the War Department after the Armistice and, like Morrow and Guggenheim, sought a large future for American aviation. As Lindbergh's personal attorney and adviser he became the gatekeeper to the franchise.[55]

Meanwhile Lindbergh had a book contract to fulfill. Only now did it occur to him—and no doubt his high-powered aviation circle—that writing a book that regaled readers with tales about the uproarious and dangerous early days of flight might not be the best way to promote the industry.

Lindbergh's book dilemma illustrates how dramatically his situation had changed. In the tumultuous days following his landing in Paris he had still seen himself as the poor flyboy. Despite the nonstop celebrations and loose talk about big money, he carried with him the nagging feeling of insecurity that a salary of $300 a month imparts. Of the many offers brought to him, writing a book struck him as an upstanding and not very taxing exercise. The articles under his byline for the *Times* had been effortless enough, especially as he did not actually have to write them: he spoke his thoughts to a correspondent, who turned his loosely connected ideas into flowing sentences with correct spelling. Reassured that writing a book did not require much more, he had signed with G. P. Putnam's Sons for a volume detailing "his life, his flight to Paris, the reception there, in England and in Belgium, and his views on the future of aviation."[56]

New York Times correspondent Carlisle MacDonald, who had covered Lindbergh in Paris and written many of the pieces that carried Lindbergh's byline, signed on as his amanuensis. MacDonald accompanied Lindbergh across the ocean aboard the *Memphis* and for much of that week they worked on the book. Under great pressure to pull the story together rapidly, MacDonald drew on these talks, available news reports, and Lindbergh's own articles to weave the narrative together. By June 9 Lindbergh reported from sea in his column that he was making good progress on the manuscript, "a true and accurate account of my flight from its inception to the day we get back to the United States."[57]

Then he threw himself into a series of whirlwind celebrations that drove pre-publication interest in the book sky-high. MacDonald holed up in his publisher's home in Rye, New York, with a bevy of secretaries and worked furiously on the text. From there, "hot from MacDonald's typewriter," the pages were rushed into type and, within ten days a life of Lindbergh, titled *We,* was efficiently redacted. George Putnam judged the manuscript "a good job, complete, dignified, well-written." The galleys were rushed to Lindbergh. All that was needed before setting the pages for print and rushing tens of thousands of copies to eager booksellers around the nation was his approval.[58]

Harry H. Knight had negotiated the original contract with the publisher, but now the more discerning Breckinridge was representing Lindbergh and the press began reporting rumors of some difficulty. Lindbergh did not like the draft. Unwilling to dispel the illusion that the famous scribbled their own books, the *Times* obliquely reported that Lindbergh had found much to correct in the manuscript: "The unexpected extent of his fame has made him more critical than ever of his own work." He was double-checking everything for accuracy and making corrections "word by word in his own handwriting," despite the pressures of business deals and a clamoring public. "[His] associates are astonished to find that he writes as well as he does."[59]

In fact Putnam's, extremely skittish about the short shelf life of celebrities and their books, was badly rattled. Lindbergh had shocked the publisher by rejecting the manuscript outright. He offered no more explanation than that he had changed his mind and wanted to do it himself. Actually he did not like the tone of the account, all the first-person pronouns struck him as pompous, and he later described the manuscript as "a poor job of writing." The draft was also flecked with minor inaccuracies, and to Lindbergh there was no such thing as a "minor inaccuracy." More important, he did not want his book filled with sensational yarns about the early flyboys. Of course there were great stories about fliers doing crazy things in the sky with their machines and of barnstormers involved in dramatic crack-ups. Even the buildup to his own Orteig competition was accompanied by tragedy, heartrending disappearances, and spectacular crashes. He himself had survived several near misses, and the airmail system was notorious for its casualty rate, its high-risk élan, and its ragged equipment. But with the help of Messrs. Guggenheim and Breckinridge he now understood the folly in writing a warts-and-all picture of early flying at this particular moment.[60]

He wanted to present a sanitized narrative, one that reassured the public about air safety. If this drained the story of his flight of punch and color, he could live with that. (He seemed unconcerned with what Putnam and MacDonald could live with.) He had projected an image of the pilot as a sober professional, and he wanted that emphasized in the book. He wanted the public to read about solid preparation, careful planning, and the remarkable technology of the new flying machines. Under intense pressure to get the book out the publisher had no choice but accede to Lindbergh's demands.

Lindbergh returned on July 4 from Canada's Dominion Jubilee and on July 20 he was scheduled to launch the Guggenheim Fund tour. He had less than three weeks to rewrite *We*. It was a bold undertaking. He had almost no writing experience, after all. Years later, describing his own father, who seemed to write speeches, articles, and books effortlessly, Lindbergh admitted, "I spend many hours over weeks, sometimes months, writing the text for an address." But he did not lack for determination, and no one doubted that he had the discipline to churn out the words.[61]

Secluded in the calm of the Guggenheims' Norman-style mansion on Long Island, he found surcease from the crowds that followed him everywhere. He set himself a goal of 10,000 words a week, writing in longhand on yellow legal paper. At the top of each sheet he recorded the number of words he had written on the page, as if each page were another hurdle cleared on an onerous obstacle course. Putnam assigned Fitzhugh Green, a retired navy commander and experienced writer with a background in aviation, to edit the volume. Eager to get something that could be slapped between covers, Green praised Lindbergh's submissions, calling the writing "clear, precise and well balanced," when serviceable, unadorned, and superficial would have been more truthful. But even Green asked for some more color with a "personal touch now and then." Meanwhile Harry Guggenheim, apparently much happier with the new version, informed Morrow that Lindbergh was "quietly [re]writing his book," adding, "I think he will do it very well."[62]

Rushing to turn out the manuscript, Lindbergh asked his editor to get someone else to write the section assessing the flight's impact and describing its aftermath. With mere days left to deadline, Green, who had himself ghosted several biographies, reluctantly took on the task of preparing the ten thousand words covering the days after Le Bourget. Uncomfortable about negotiating a fee (which would come out of the author's royalties) Green obliquely mentioned that even for a short article authors took $2,000.[63]

Lindbergh, for his part, focused on his biography. With no time even to reread most of his sentences, he completed a terse sketch of his young life that went directly from first draft to the printer. The self-portrait was one-dimensional; it betrayed no doubts, raised no ambiguities to ponder, offered no complexities to iron out. The publisher slapped on a glowing foreword by Myron Herrick and the polished, if effusive, afterword prepared by Green, and sent it off to the printers.[64]

A quarter-century later Lindbergh admitted that *We* was freighted with ulterior intentions. "Being young and easily embarrassed," he had written a bowdlerized account of his life, censoring his own "errors and sensations" and skipping over "existing weaknesses" in aviation that might hinder its progress. The whole point of the book was to present aviation in the best possible light in order to advance both his own prospects and those of American aeronautics.[65]

He had already done some of this gilding. In an article prepared soon after his flight, Lindbergh praised the earth inductor compass: "This compass behaved so admirably that . . . I knew at every moment where I was going." Later, and more truthfully, he dismissed the contraption as worse than useless, calling it "unreliable and often inaccurate." In *We* he edited out the disquieting moments from his flight to Paris, when terrifying storms forced him to consider turning back, and left out descriptions of the alarming effects of sleep deprivation and of the phantoms that joined him in his cabin. Despite the offensive use of aircraft in the recent war—a foreshadowing of vastly more destructive possibilities that he himself would later come to rue—he refused to consider aviation as anything but an unqualified blessing.[66]

Reviewers were mostly respectful, impressed with the tales of barnstorming, air cadet training, and his months spent transporting the mail for the Robertsons. They praised the author's modesty and lack of pretension. But even supporters compared the tepid narrative to the "bald directness of a report to a superior officer." One reviewer wisecracked, "As an author Lindbergh is the world's foremost aviator."[67]

There remained the question of paying his collaborators. Green arranged for Lindbergh to pay MacDonald $10,000 for his discarded efforts. For his own share in the book Green suggested 10 percent of the royalties. He had contributed one-fourth of the final manuscript but recognized that it was Lindbergh's name that drove sales. The publisher agreed that 10 percent was a fair figure. (Based on ultimate sales this would have yielded $20,000.) Lindbergh, however, stuck to $2,000, the amount Green had offhandedly mentioned as an example of what writers were paid for an article. Exasperated, Green wrote Henry Breckinridge,"[I am offended by] Colonel Lindbergh's curt dismissal of me by an offer so small that it affronts my standing as an editor and a writer."[68]

The exchange continued a bit longer, with Green being forced into undignified appeals for payment and Lindbergh demanding, in lawyerly fashion through Breckinridge, that Green present his case for compensation. Hurt and surprised, Green wrote that he had a great regard for Lindbergh and that he took on the work only to save the book from a delayed delivery that would have damaged sales; he had not thought that a formal contract was necessary. If nothing else, his eighty-five pages raised the book's cover price, increasing Lindbergh's royalties. He was not asking anything close to a proportional share of royalties, only for payment at the going rate for such writing. Nine months later Lindbergh finally forwarded him a check for $4,000.[69]

Charles at age six with his mother, Evangeline Lodge Land Lindbergh, in 1908. After the estrangement between his parents, Charles spent most of his time with his mother, who suffered bouts of depression. *Courtesy Lindbergh Picture Collection, Manuscripts and Archives, Yale University Library. Except where otherwise noted, all images in the book are courtesy the Yale University Library.*

Charles at age nine (circa 1911) with his father, Charles August Lindbergh, who served as an insurgent Republican from Minnesota in the U.S. House of Representatives between 1906 and 1917.

Charles enjoyed his rural upbringing in the solitude of the woods and waters of the nearby Mississippi. Here at about age ten he is playing on a raft.

After completing training with the Army Air Corps, Lindbergh took on assorted flying jobs. Here on June 2, 1925, he prepares for a test flight in St. Louis.

Dark horse Lindbergh takes off for his historic flight on May 20, 1927, in his single-wing *Spirit of St. Louis* from Roosevelt Field, New York.

The Spirit of St. Louis during the first hour of the transatlantic flight that would end thirty-three-and-one-half hours later outside Paris.

Saturday night, May 21, at Le Bourget airport where one hundred thousand came to greet the unsuspecting new hero as he landed.

The day following his landing, Lindbergh, in a borrowed suit, greets the crowds next to Ambassador Herrick at the French Aero Club.

Greeting the crowd before the City Hall in Brussels on May 29.

President Calvin Coolidge welcomes Lindbergh back from Europe on Washington Monument Grounds on June 11. *Courtesy Library of Congress*

Mayor James Walker and Grover Whalen, New York's official greeter, with Lindbergh at the city's ticker-tape parade, June 13, 1927.

Lindbergh, Mexican president Plutarco Calles, and his future father-in-law, Ambassador Dwight Morrow, in the winter of 1927.

With the philanthropist Harry Guggenheim, who underwrote critical aviation research and became a close adviser.

Charles with Anne Morrow Lindbergh prior to their 1931 Pacific survey flight.

Charles and Anne Lindbergh with Hermann Göring, the Commander of the German Air Force. On October 18, 1938, Göring presented Lindbergh with the Cross of the German Eagle. *Courtesy Library of Congress*

Lindbergh, by this time an advocate of environmentalism and a more simple, natural lifestyle, in a reed hut in the Philippines, circa 1970.

Lifting the hero's hem a bit, George Putnam observed that in Lindbergh's "direct metallic mind . . . things are either black or white, right or wrong, with no middle grounds or place for argument or logic or the guidance of experience." Or graciousness.[70]

Putnam later received an offer of $30,000 from a collector for Lindbergh's handwritten manuscript. The publisher wrote to Lindbergh through Breckinridge that it was not clear who had rights to the actual manuscript, so it might be fair to split the money. Lindbergh curtly refused the deal. If in fact the pages belonged to the publisher Putnam could do what he wanted with it; if it was his he was not prepared to sell it. Putnam, perhaps tired of dealing with him by now, simply gave Lindbergh the manuscript. (Lindbergh later turned it over to the Missouri Historical Society Museum.) Putnam concluded that the same "mechanical mind" that had brought Lindbergh great fame also made it difficult for him to be flexible. He had no sense of how to deal with situations outside his own area of experience. His mind occupied a single track, and his "utter absence of imagination" prevented him from interacting normally with the broader world.[71]

We became a huge best-seller, going through six printings in the first month and selling an impresssive 635,000 copies, occupying the best-seller charts for two years. Sales earned the first-time author more than $200,000 in royalties. For all of Putnam's caviling, the extraordinary interest only confirmed the aviation coterie's investment in the young hero.[72]

Lindbergh now turned his full attention to his aviation "reliability tour" under the Guggenheim Fund's auspices. Flying remained not only his first love but his consuming passion and he wanted to return to it. All the celebration had placed a strain on him. He did not enjoy small talk or glad-handing crowds or the constraints placed on him by the endless round of social occasions and tributes. And writing a book turned out to be more of a chore than he had anticipated.[73]

Now as he prepared to return to the air for the Guggenheim tour his future looked very fine. Just a few weeks after the *Spirit of St. Louis* had landed in Paris a Morgan banker was investing Lindbergh's funds, a former assistant secretary of war was handling his personal business, and the head of the largest private aviation foundation was planning his future. They sought to guide him, assure his financial security, and keep his reputation out of harm's reach. This circle of powerful and well-connected men with easy entree to the highest authorities in the nation were committed to advancing American aviation to international leadership, and Lindbergh's popularity made him a perfect vehicle for achieving these goals. They understood that for his value to endure, Lindbergh's mind-boggling popularity needed to be grounded in a cause that would also endure. The tour would do that by linking him with the long-term goal of building American aviation.[74]

Guggenheim was an extraordinarily gracious patron, but in portraying Guggenheim and Morrow as sentimental visionaries selflessly interested in helping America's shining new hero, earlier biographers miss a point: these very shrewd men were not starstruck hero worshippers. They did indeed respect Lindbergh, but they also had larger goals in mind than a single flier's career. These very practical capitalists were less interested in celebrating his past achievement than in cultivating him for the future. Guggenheim, who ran his philanthropic organization with the same single-minded intensity earlier industrial barons like his father had devoted to mining, steel, and oil, did not begrudge Lindbergh's celebrity and he remunerated him generously for his work. But uppermost in his mind, at the very highest level of priority, he aimed to advance American aviation to world leadership. Lindbergh had won the public's heart, no doubt about that. Now Guggenheim and his clique proposed to maneuver a tricky turn: to use Lindbergh's personal popularity to focus attention on the larger implications of his achievement.[75]

The year before, Guggenheim had sponsored a very popular airplane tour featuring Commander Richard Byrd's plane and crew to familiarize Americans with airplanes. Then the flight to Paris magnified public awareness. But even after all the hullabaloo a survey of businessmen, in New York no less, found that many did not even know about airmail. Now the hero himself would bring his *Spirit of St. Louis* to every state in the union to inform a wide public about aviation and its possibilities while dispelling some of the lingering mystery and trepidation surrounding flight. Millions would get to see him fly and witness firsthand the plane that took him across the ocean. They would see close up that the craft was no magical contraption but a well-engineered machine. And the pilot was solid stuff too, a testament to all-American values and clean living.[76]

Meanwhile a growing chorus of admirers, concerned about exposing aviation's talisman to any more danger, wanted Lindbergh grounded. To these faint of heart Lindbergh answered that there was too much still to be done in the air for him to come back down, adding rather off-handedly that if he should die in the course of such work he was "willing to make this sacrifice."[77]

On July 19, four days after turning in his manuscript to Putnam's, Lindbergh hopped off from Mitchell Field to Hartford, Connecticut, on the first leg of his tour. Over the next three months he appeared before huge, enthusiastic crowds in each of the forty-eight states. He spent 260 hours in the air, flew 22,350 miles, and visited eighty-two cities. He also dropped an additional 192 messages from the air over cities that he did not have time to visit on the ground. He paraded over 1,285 miles of procession routes, survived sixty-nine dinners and countless speeches from governors, mayors, and masters of ceremony straining to offer fresh praise.[78]

The point was to emphasize trustworthiness, to prove that planes were not simply playthings for wealthy sportsmen but could get businessmen to urgent meetings quickly and on time. Planned with a formidable exactitude, the tour showed just how dependable flight could be. An earlier transportation pioneer, the manager of New York's Black Ball Line, had revolutionized shipping in the 1810s by keeping departures to a schedule, thus allowing shippers to count on arrival by a certain day. Lindbergh showed that air travel too was predictable. Of his eighty-two stops, every one, except a single stop in Portland, Maine, where the fog forced him to make a detour, was on time. In fair weather and foul he rivaled the record of the best railroad trains. Often he circled over the airfield a minute or two before the scheduled arrival time, invariably landing at exactly two o'clock. Where he arrived early he would put on an aerial show, delighting the crowd, before landing.[79]

Of the eighty-two stops, sixty-nine involved overnight stays and thirteen were "touch stops," with a short talk at the airport and a quick exit. The longer visits opened with a welcome and then a short speech by Lindbergh at an open-air rally, followed by a parade through town. Children let out of school for "Charles Lindbergh Day" would line the streets. Even in inclement weather he rode with the top of the car down so as not to disappoint those who waited for hours to see him. Around five o'clock Lindbergh would break for rest before a two-hour banquet from seven to nine that featured a second brief address. His speeches emphasized the dependability of air flight and urged citizens to use the airmail and to support the construction of airports. Promptly at nine the festivities ended and Lindbergh retired to plan for the next day's flight.[80]

Cities near his flight route often requested a flyover with some friendly sign of recognition, and Lindbergh would ask in return that local authorities commit to painting large signs identifying their city on building rooftops to aid pilots in their navigation. Over these cities he would drop a canvas bag with a signed certificate of his air visit and a printed message patterned on his speeches.[81]

Except for some crunching when crowds broke through barriers in their enthusiasm to reach him, disorder was kept to a minimum. There was one fatality, in Boston, where a man suffered a heart attack during the pushing. But the most disturbing moment came when a press photographer scurried out onto the field just as Lindbergh prepared to take off. In the *Spirit*'s cockpit, with his forward vision blocked, Lindbergh could not see in front of him. As he advanced the throttle, bringing the engine to a roar, and the propeller sliced through the air the eager cameraman stood in harm's way. Only a mechanic's desperate shouting and motioning to Lindbergh prevented a disaster. A fuming Lindbergh jumped out screaming, "Do you know you just missed being killed." Following this incident,

Lindbergh ordered his advance man, Milburn Kusterer, to tighten security and to make sure that his takeoffs were more carefully policed.[82]

Proceeding from city to city with machine-like precision, Lindbergh inspected sites for airports, talked to engineers and politicians, and tried to convince everyone who would listen that aviation had a brilliant future, in which America should lead. While in Michigan he coaxed Henry Ford into making his first airplane trip. The *Spirit* did not have a passenger seat, so the Sage of Dearborn sat "happy and scrunched-up, on the arm rest of [the] pilot's seat." Afterward Ford, pledged to expand his $4,000,000 investment in the air industry and to accelerate production of the all-metal flivvers to the rate of one a day. Ford also laid plans for a one-hundred-seat passenger plane, while joining Lindbergh in calling for a second generation of spacious airports, where passengers would drive up to the field, park their cars, and board waiting planes in comfortable covered areas.[83]

In Los Angeles he exhorted city fathers to build a modern new airfield and inaugurated California's first intercity air service, carrying Will Rogers and other dignitaries between Los Angeles and San Diego. "That kid. . . . eats, sleeps and drinks aviation. He is not particularly interested in anything else," Rogers remarked. In his honor the Los Angeles Chamber of Commerce voted to install a giant beacon on top of the City Hall tower to guide air traffic.[84]

Lindbergh was accompanied on the trip by a couple of buddies, Donald E. Keyhoe, who served as his assistant, and Philip Love, his colleague from Robertson's and with whom he had trained in flight school. Reporters noted that Lindbergh seldom smiled during the parades and that all the earnest homage made him deeply uncomfortable, but when he hit the air with these men he dropped his stiff public persona and enjoyed himself. He would cut up with them, play pranks, and gambol in the air, speeding the *Spirit* through the sky, exuberantly rehearsing the stunts he had learned as a barnstormer.[85]

Thursdays and Saturdays were the tour's off-days and they would make side trips, taking in America's breathtaking natural scenes. Many years later Lindbergh still recalled with delight seeing the country "as no man had ever known it before," flying over "white villages . . . , great lakes . . . , pastel deserts and . . . , deep forests," witnessing awesome mountain ranges, beautiful beaches, and endless prairies. He dove down over Death Valley, "its hot sands ten feet below [his] wheels," spying a village of Indian tents, where one "squaw struggl[ed] to take cover from [the plane's] wings." One of his detours took him over the summer White House in the Black Hills of South Dakota, where he dropped a message for the president.[86]

The press lavished attention on his appearances, tirelessly repeating the pat references to his youth, courage, and humility, his smashing old barriers and prying open new horizons, and his regard for his mother. The one thing they refused to do was lose interest. Did readers tire of the endless descriptions of cheering airport crowds and earnest speeches? Here is one letter to the editor of the *New York Times*: "We only admire him and know him through your paper and we are not prepared to forget him and his wonderful deed for many a day. . . . We want to hear everything we can that concerns him."[87]

The tour attracted so much attention that Harry Guggenheim implored mayors and governors on the itinerary not to weary Lindbergh with private invitations and other demands on his energies: "I am sure you understand there is no commercial aspect connected with this tour and that Colonel Lindbergh is not attending any meetings where admission is charged, nor is he . . . accepting personal invitations." In mid-August, to dispel rumors that he was exhausted and losing weight, Lindbergh had himself examined by two doctors, who pronounced him the picture of health. Evangeline Lindbergh added her own assurances that Charles was holding up very well.[88]

Near the end of his itinerary, in Abilene, he was accorded a Texas-style welcome, including a throne-like seat in the front of the limousine. Lindbergh took one horrified look at the massive chair mounted on the front of the open car and dove into the back. But aside from this and his irritation at the press for the endless questions about his personal life he had reason to be pleased. The *New York World* recalled the early doubts about the tour: "Would he 'blow up'? Would he do or say something foolish that would take his godlike popularity from him? Would his head be turned and his career ruined?" But the tour had gone very well indeed. The turnouts broke all records. His open-air stops drew on average twenty thousand, and by the time he closed the tour in Philadelphia on October 23, after more than three months, he had been seen or heard by thirty million people. Others put the figure closer to fifty million, an amazing 40 percent of the total U.S. population. Countless dubious taxpayers who knew little about aviation and harbored doubts about its value had their minds changed by Lindbergh, about whom it seemed very few had any doubts. More than a third of the country heard him deliver his message about using the airmail, building airports and "spreading the gospel of flight."[89]

Cities around the country took up his call. "There is hardly a good-sized city in the West," the papers reported, "which is not building a flying field." Men and women considered flying for the first time. Joyriders waited in long lines to go up in planes. "Col. Charles Lindbergh is directly responsible for this awakening to the possibilities of aeronautics," declared the *Los Angeles Times*. The use of airmail spiked, the sales of private airplanes increased, and investors underwrote new airline ventures. Towns across the land offered prizes for long-distance flights and air derby competitions. Flying became so popular on the Pacific Coast that flights had to be booked days in advance, and for the first time businessmen found themselves bumped from their regular departures. Demand for aircraft quickly outpaced supply, delaying delivery on new orders for ninety days.[90]

Newspapers added columns on aeronautics and flying. The *New York Times* ran Russell Owen's column "Aviation" and later added "Lindbergh on Flying" as a regular feature. The *Washington Post* titled its aviation column "Flying and Fliers"; in the *Los Angeles Times* it was "Aviation News." In a little more than a year one sample study discovered a sixfold increase in aviation news coverage, and that did not take into consideration the slew of new aviation magazines.[91]

Harry Guggenheim was delighted. The tour had helped transform the frenzy over one flight into something practical "in the form of new airports, improved facilities on the fields, and in the material encouragement given to air mail and other forms of air transportation."[92]

As for Lindbergh, he emerged from the tour as the face of commercial aviation, not simply a heroic and expert flier but a flight expert. Officials from many branches of government, including the State, War, Navy, and Commerce Departments, conferred with him. Congressmen called for a new Department of Aviation to be created and for Lindbergh to be its first secretary. The doors of the White House parted at his very approach, even for "unannounced visits." The rich and powerful in industry and government asked his counsel and compensated him generously.[93]

So what was next? "I have no plans," he maintained, beyond resting and ultimately returning to St. Louis, his "present headquarters."[94]

AIRSHIP DIPLOMACY

OFFERS CONTINUED TO POUR in to New York, where Henry Breckinridge reviewed them and passed on those that seemed to be of interest. Most, like one promising $50,000 for a cigarette endorsement, he rejected out of hand. One they did consider came from the publisher William Randolph Hearst on behalf of MGM Studios, offering Lindbergh $250,000, plus 10 percent of gross receipts (with a guarantee of at least $500,000) to play the lead opposite Hearst's mistress, Marion Davies, in an "aeronautical picture" that Hearst promised would promote aviation and be "filmed with dignity and taste." Breckinridge suggested that this might be a deal worth considering, if Lindbergh could be assured that he would "neither break [his] neck nor hurt [his] reputation." While Breckinridge sent out discreet feelers to a number of experts asking how the public might react to Lindbergh's appearing in a Hearst film, Lindbergh agreed to meet with Hearst.[1]

The publisher greeted him warmly at his elegant Riverside Drive residence in upper Manhattan and after some small talk handed him a contract to sign. Lindbergh wasn't sure what to do. He did not want to do "pictures." Likely he had hoped that he would find a reason to turn down the deal. But Hearst was charmingly persuasive and assured Lindbergh that the film would be "an inspiration" for the new generation. Lindbergh fumbled for a while. He tried to hand the contract back to Hearst, who told him to tear it up if he was uncomfortable signing it, which Lindbergh later remembered doing, to Hearst's "amused astonishment." They talked a bit more, and as Lindbergh was leaving he complimented Hearst on a pair of exquisite silver globes adorning a side table. The next day a messenger arrived with the two rare antiques sculpted by eighteenth-century craftsmen for which Hearst had paid $50,000.[2]

It was not that Lindbergh was indifferent to money or unaware that fame had granted him a ticket to a better life. "Where I had an opportunity to make money in ways acceptable to me, I tried to make it. I saw no reason not to," he later explained. He had collected $65,000 from the *Times* for exclusive reports from Paris and elsewhere. *We* brought him another $200,000 in royalties. The Guggenheim Fund for the Promotion of Aeronautics paid him $50,000 for the national tour. And there was much more. In early 1928 the press speculated that the flight had made him a millionaire. Russell Owen, as close to Lindbergh as anyone in the press, denied this "on the highest possible authority." By his own calculation Owen reckoned that Lindbergh's assets, which stood at around $2,000 in May, had grown to "something over $400,000." These assets were handled by "one of the largest banks in the country . . . and it is entirely possible," Owen allowed, that they would become a million soon enough. "Clearly," as Kenneth S. Davis wrote in his 1959 biography of Lindbergh, "the tangible rewards of virtue had been astonishingly large and swift."[3]

Not only his modest circumstances had changed. His St. Louis sponsors, who had invested in his flight hoping to project St. Louis as a center for the emerging aviation industry, continued to nourish this hope, planning to erect a modern airport and establish several new air industries to make their metropolis into an air hub. But these ventures were vaguely formed and had only limited and uncertain backing while the New York aviation coterie, Guggenheim, Morrow, and Breckinridge and others, promised a much more ambitious agenda and the resources to make it happen. Their plan for galvanizing American aviation, consisted of three parts: shaping a modern aviation policy, forging public air-mindedness, and hastening industrial progress. They had already achieved much through the Morrow board's National Aviation Program and Guggenheim's extensive efforts to foster popular support for aviation. Now as they turned to promoting a vigorous commercial airline industry they wanted Lindbergh onboard.[4]

Moving aviation to the next level involved generating the kind of focused capitalist energy that had built the railroad industry. The St. Louis group could offer little more than dim hopes, whereas the New Yorkers could mobilize behind their efforts the most powerful political and economic figures in the nation, including the president and his much admired commerce secretary, Herbert Hoover, and, increasingly, many from the Wall Street investment community.

Lindbergh put off going back to St. Louis or accepting any other offers that came in from startup aviation companies, waiting for the industry picture to crystallize. Following the advice of his New York backers, he accepted a temporary post with the Guggenheim Fund at 598 Madison Avenue, close by the nerve center of American capitalism. Here he could work his wonders with investors. "His popularity is of such a nature," read an appreciative article in the *New York Times*, "that he will always get a hearing from business men."[5]

Those accustomed to the transient nature of celebrity expressed surprise at Lindbergh's continued popularity. The honors kept coming. On November 14 he flew to the White House to accept the coveted Hubbard Gold Medal from the National Geographic Society. In presenting the medal President Coolidge took note of Lindbergh's new role, calling him an "apostle of aeronautics" who had capitalized on his own fame to promote aeronautical "activity far beyond any dreams of six months ago." On December 8 Lindbergh received the Langley Medal from the Smithsonian Institution.[6]

A couple of days later, when Speaker of the House of Representatives Nicholas Longworth learned that Lindbergh was in Washington testifying before the House Appropriations Committee, he recessed Congress and sent the majority and minority floor leaders over to the committee hearing to invite the flier to the House. As Lindbergh entered the chamber to a storm of applause, Speaker Longworth announced, "I have the honor to present to the House of Representatives America's most attractive citizen." When the applause died down Lindbergh stood alone on the dais and each member filed past to congratulate him. After he left, members passed a bill by acclamation conferring upon him the Congressional Medal of Honor "for displaying heroic courage and skill . . . by which he not only achieved the greatest individual triumph of any American citizen, but demonstrated that travel across the ocean by aircraft was possible." The bill was rushed to the Senate and passed unanimously—and signed by the president two days later.[7]

In September Dwight Morrow accepted an ambassadorship to Mexico. Breckinridge, who tracked Lindbergh's finances, assured Lindbergh that the Morgan firm would continue to look after his investments with "absolute security," adding rather cryptically, "I believe for sentimental reasons they will make money for you." One wonders what sentiment had to do with making successful investments. Only much later did it come out that the Morgan Bank kept a list of favored clients who were singled out for preferential opportunities. Lindbergh was placed on that list.[8]

In mid-November Morrow, already installed in his new post in Mexico City, wrote Harry Guggenheim that he was very pleased with Lindbergh's forty-eight-state tour, adding that "it would be an excellent thing . . . for aviation and for the Foundation and for him" to come to Mexico. But first there were "some complexities" that he needed to work out. One was that the State Department did not approve the flight. Another was the contentiousness of U.S.-Mexican relations.[9]

Dwight Whitney Morrow was a compact, bespectacled man with deep blue eyes, whose ill-fitting suits and unkempt hair might have been described as sloppy in a man of lower standing. It was widely agreed, however, that his unprepossessing appearance and disarming manner "concealed one of the shrewdest political brains in the U.S." Son of an Allegheny, Pennsylvania, schoolteacher, pale and sickly as a child, he proved a whiz in the classroom, graduating high school at age fourteen. During the next four years he took odd jobs to raise the tuition for Amherst College. Once there, he accepted hand-me-down shirts from banker Jacob Schiff's son Mortimer and tutored students to pay his bills. Voted Most Likely to Succeed, he outpolled his classmate Calvin Coolidge, who later described him in his own characteristic syntax as "gifted with an ability that entered the field of genius." Morrow took highest honors at graduation.[10]

After seven years with a Wall Street firm specializing in utility law, the House of Morgan recruited him in 1914, "not merely because of his talent, for talent was plentiful and easy to buy," Coolidge would later recall, "but they wanted him for his character, which was priceless." In less than a year at the largest and most powerful commercial bank in the United States he was promoted to partner. His focus and smarts were legendary, as was his gift for structuring mergers and colossal new corporations. When Morrow finished "Morganizing" the Kennecott Copper conglomerate, mining czar Daniel Guggenheim declared that Morrow had learned more about copper in a few months than he himself had in a lifetime. Through his essays, participation in foreign policy conferences, and service on foundation boards, Morrow was recognized as a formidable legal theorist with a firm grasp of international policy. With his colleague Thomas Lamont he molded Morgan's international banking strategies.[11]

Morrow was by now a very rich man, happily married, the father of three daughters and a son, and widely regarded as "Morgan's philosopher king." He lived with his family on a large estate in Englewood, New Jersey, kept a pied-à-terre in Manhattan, and served as a director on numerous corporate and financial boards that sought the advantage of his good name.[12]

Morrow had been mentioned for top posts when Calvin Coolidge took over the presidency after Warren Harding's death in 1923, but for some reason—some speculated that even in a Republican administration his Morgan affiliation was a liability—Coolidge did not recruit him until late in 1925, when he asked him, "Look into the subject of airplanes for me." Expert in international finance and global business planning, Morrow became the administration's aviation strategist, responsible for crafting a comprehensive aviation policy. When Lindbergh returned from Europe Coolidge invited Morrow to join him in welcoming the hero back home. Also the president had an appointment to discuss with him.[13]

Despite rumors that Morrow was being considered for an ambassadorial post to Russia or England, the president offered him perhaps the most thankless foreign post available: the ambassadorship to Mexico. "The situation [there]," Coolidge later recalled, "was difficult and delicate." The State Department feared that Mexico, which was emerging from a long and bloody revolution, was intent on fostering what it characterized as "a Bolshevik hegemony" on America's front porch. Under Mexico's revolutionary constitution Americans faced the expropri-ation of their extensive mining, railroad, oil, and land holdings, valued at an esti-mated $1.3 billion. (U.S. interests owned more than 130 million acres, about 27 percent of Mexico's land.) These interests demanded Washington's protection. Others denounced the nationalization of church properties, the closing of Catholic schools and the rough treatment of Catholic clerics. Trial balloons floated by President Plutarco Calles about defaulting on foreign debts further roiled rela-tions, leading Secretary of State Kellogg to suggest that the United States might need to intervene to stabilize its unsteady neighbor. This was not just talk, for U.S. Marines had indeed landed in Nicaragua just months before.[14]

Betty Morrow could not hide her disappointment. Her husband was being asked to give up his Morgan partnership for this? Still, Morrow decided to leave the advantages of Wall Street life, folded away his plans for building a dream house in New Jersey, and took on the daunting challenge of representing American interests in Mexico in very difficult times. "I wish I thought it was an adventure," Betty Morrow wrote in her diary. Coolidge's directions were as simple as they were feckless: "My only instructions are to keep us out of war with Mexico." Walter Lippmann, who thought that Morrow was the most gifted public figure of the era, hailed the appointment.[15]

Morrow arrived in Mexico on October 23. President Calles had feared that the appointment of a Morgan banker meant increased pressure on Mexico to pay debts that it was in no position to pay. "After Morrow," declared one paper, "come the Marines." But Morrow took pains to assure Calles that he no longer served a private bank. He cut off all his Morgan involvements and moved to still the bellig-erent talk. "Is there anyone," he asked, "who thinks that if a man owes him money and cannot pay it, there is profit in going out and killing him?" He pushed for pragmatic compromise.[16]

Morrow's diffidence, his lack of airs (early in his tenure he showed up to an official lunch with a mismatched suit, his shoes unlaced and his necktie askew), and his preference for face-to-face discussions over the hectoring official exchanges of the past proved disarming. His respect for local culture made a deep impression, especially as it was so rare among gringo diplomats. Aware that all nations in the hemisphere claimed the title "American," he ordered that hence-forth the embassy be called the *United States* Embassy and he the *United States* ambassador. To the State Department he proposed that it was in the country's interest to have a strong and prosperous neighbor with a stable and orderly government; that a policy asserting U.S. property rights over all others, including Mexican sovereignty, was doomed; and that in the long run U.S. interests in Latin America could best be served through solid bilateral relationships.[17]

When the U.S. Chamber of Commerce protested to him about the potential effects of proposed labor reforms in Mexico, Morrow responded that he was the ambassador of the United States and not the ambassador of its special interests. When his former Morgan colleagues tried to press for the immediate payment of Mexico's debts, heedless of its destabilizing effects, he ignored them, structuring a compromise solution instead. House of Morgan historian Ron Chernow reports that this resulted in "blistering exchanges" between the ambassador and his former colleague Thomas Lamont.[18]

Scholars continue to debate Morrow's impact. Some argue that his pragmatic approach ultimately preempted revolutionary radicalism. But if Morrow aimed to move relations away from the volatile edge toward conversation and compromise, it was a goal shared by the Mexican regime. Eager to demonstrate that he could win peace with the giant northern neighbor on terms that were honorable, Calles too wanted to ease tensions.[19]

And quite unexpectedly there developed between the banker and the revolutionary president a warm personal relationship. Barely a month into Morrow's tenure, Calles, in an unprecedented overture, invited the ambassador to accompany him on a tour of the northern Mexican countryside to explore changes wrought by the revolution. The three-thousand-mile tour began on December 1 and was joined by Will Rogers, whose presence brought wide coverage in the U.S. press. To one Mexican newspaper it seemed that in his first five weeks in office Morrow had done more to bring the two countries together "than all of his predecessors had done in the last one hundred years."[20]

Morrow wanted to cap this progress with a dramatic *geste*. Congratulating Morrow soon after his appointment, Lindbergh had offered his assistance. Now Morrow wrote Lindbergh inviting him to do "a little flying in Latin America." Morrow hoped to use Lindbergh's enormous appeal both to further the thaw in diplomatic relations and to extend profitable prospects for U.S. aviation south of the border. Lindbergh agreed to make the trip.[21]

Several obstacles remained. The United States had an embargo on air flights to Mexico, and, more important, the State Department opposed the trip, fearing that it might set off protests and demonstrations. This was no idle fear. The United States had a huge stake in Latin America—for every four dollars that the United States invested in Europe it had already poured five into its southern backyard, exerting a large, and often resented, influence on banking, extractive industries, agriculture, and railroads—but its relations with these countries were choppy. Earlier in the year, on the pretext of ending a civil war in Nicaragua, the United States had sent gunships and some two thousand marines to press liberal rebels to accept a compromise settlement with the government of President Don Adolfo Diaz. Signed on May 20, just two days before Lindbergh landed at Le Bourget, the Pact of Espino Negro called for marines to train a nonpartisan Nicaraguan national guard and supervise the 1928 elections. Bridling at this intrusion, Augusto César Sandino led a guerrilla campaign against the government and the gringos. The rebels were unable to prevent the occupation, but did succeed in sparking anti-U.S. opposition.[22]

During the previous few years the United States had been sending goodwill flight missions to Latin America, hoping to smooth relations and build air links. "A comprehensive international system of air highways," the *Washington Post* wrote wishfully, could bind "the two Americas inseparably together," opening up isolated regions to U.S. trade while promoting local industrial growth. In this iteration of the "winged gospel" aviation would further unity, economic development, and goodwill. "Just as the transcontinental railroads welded together the United States and made of it a nation," the *Post* continued, "the international air lines will weld together the Americas. . . . May the day be hastened!"[23]

That day was soon coming, but there was no assurance that it would be U.S. airlines doing the welding. With their long domestic experience and ambition to build a worldwide air transport system, Europe's heavily subsidized lines had seized the early initiative. Germany already controlled much of inland South American air transportation, with the German-affiliated, Colombia-based Scadta (Sociedad Colombo Alemana de Transporte Aéreo) the most prominent among these companies, and the French Aéropostale dominated the east coast. The system was still quite rudimentary, but given its foothold it seemed likely that Europe would continue to dominate as it expanded the industry from a local system into a hemispheric network.[24]

In the fall of 1927 Scadta laid plans to launch an airmail line from Colombia to Panama and from there to the rest of Central America. Sensitive about foreign control of the air space over the Canal Zone and spurred by the new attention that the Lindbergh flights had drawn to aviation, the Coolidge administration only now began to formulate a response. A special interdepartmental aviation committee convened in Washington on November 23, 1927, and agreed that for military and strategic reasons, as well as the imperatives of trade and commerce, the United States needed to act decisively to halt European air advances and to develop its own robust air presence in Latin America.[25]

President Coolidge signaled a similar commitment to firming U.S. air salience, telling Lindbergh that he was prepared to provide whatever was needed "to induce foreign countries to cooperate in the development of landing places and aerial oceanic routes." Just a few days before the interdepartmental aviation committee meeting Coolidge referred to aviation as a national priority and on November 29 he approved the interdepartmental committee's recommendations to build air links with Latin America. That same day the State Department removed its opposition to Lindbergh's visit to Mexico, advising Ambassador Morrow that the trip was now advisable.[26]

When Morrow first invited Lindbergh it had seemed simple enough. Morrow wired that he should avoid anything risky, such as trying to do it all in one stop. "You get me invited [and] I will do the flying," Lindbergh had replied. But now the visit took on a much larger importance. Lindbergh was called in to confer with Undersecretary of State Robert E. Olds, and his flight to Mexico was reshaped at the cabinet level to complement the expansive new hemispheric aviation policy. Still fearful of the possibility of a debacle, the State Department, asked Morrow for assurances that the trip would be well received.[27]

Eager for a chance to share the spotlight with the world's new hero and to divert attention from domestic conditions President Calles readily offered these assurances. He sent a long telegram to Lindbergh on December 8 promising the flier a warm reception. Lindbergh responded immediately, pledging to come "on the first clear day."[28]

Two days earlier, in his State of the Union address, President Coolidge announced that private companies were developing aviation services south of the border: "We are particularly solicitous to have the United States take a leading part in this development." Meanwhile the State Department suggested that Lindbergh might consider extending his itinerary with visits to other Latin American countries.[29]

The *New York Times*, an enthusiastic supporter of an aviation agenda, was generally pleased by the contemplated mission. But its publisher, Adolph Ochs, had some concerns that he shared with Morrow. Lindbergh was too valuable a commodity to send him on treacherous journeys in unfriendly places. The idea of a diplomatic tour was fine but it needed to be handled with care. A serious mishap would undermine confidence in aviation so there was good reason to be prudent and conservative. "Everyone on *Times* staff approves this telegram," Ochs added.[30]

Other publications were kept in the dark about Lindbergh's real plans, still thinking that the Lone Eagle was paying a simple courtesy visit to Mexico. Meanwhile, the privileged *Times* dispatched six top reporters with a battery of support services by boat, plane, car, mule, and every other available conveyance to prepare for what had surreptitiously become a Latin-American tour. One of the reporters, Clarence K. Streit, bounced 125 miles by motorcycle at night over roads "as can only be visualized by one who has been in Central America," hastening from Guatemala to El Salvador. As news of the large detail of southern-bound *Times* reporters leaked out some wondered if Ochs had somehow learned of a brewing revolution. In any event, the extensive preparations guaranteed the story wide coverage, especially with the *Times* committed to running a Lindbergh column for the duration of the trip. In the first of his bylined articles Lindbergh aptly captured the dual purposes of diplomacy and business behind the flight: "Aviation Brings People Together . . . Hopes to Demonstrate the Practicability of an Air Route between the Capitals."[31]

In Mexico Will Rogers, just now ending his own visit, described Ambassador Morrow as "the most pleased man in Mexico tonight," as he waited for Lindbergh. The impending visit chased all other news off the front pages as Mexico's newspapers reported that the country had gone "Lindbergh mad."[32]

Arriving at Bolling Field in Washington early on December 13 Lindbergh found the field waterlogged from persistent rains. Flying west in December meant thirteen hours of night flying, and there were reports of storms along the route for the next few days. But he would not hear of delaying the trip. Recalled Bolling's commanding officer Major Burwell, "Lindbergh was in charge of his own arrangements."[33]

He also ignored Morrow's precautions about avoiding risk. No one had ever attempted a nonstop flight from Washington to Mexico City. Convinced that nothing could better demonstrate the benefits of air travel than a quick, clean sprint over 2,100 miles, he rejected a tested course with lighted airways in favor of a direct route that had never been tried before. From crude maps purchased in New York City he pieced together a flight plan and fixed upon taking the *Spirit of St. Louis* once more nonstop and alone, this time for about twenty-three hours, to Mexico City.[34]

Lindbergh tucked away three sandwiches and two canteens of water, walked over every foot of the airfield, marking off soft and soaked areas to avoid during takeoff, clambered aboard, and once again leaped into the front pages. "VIKING OF AIR CONQUERS OBSTACLES" headlined the *Times* in an elegiac column by its chief Washington correspondent Richard Oulahan. In Mexico President Calles declared the morrow a national holiday (the first time such a tribute had been paid a foreigner), closing businesses and many government offices for the visit.[35]

The flight west, uneventful for the first few hours, turned rough over Georgia's hill country. Stormy weather made it difficult for Lindbergh to make out the line between earth and sky. Flying through squalls he reached the Gulf of Mexico in the dark and followed the white surf along the irregular coastline. At fog-blanketed Tampico he climbed above the storm clouds for visibility and set his course for

Mexico City. But his maps lacked ground detail and he found it impossible to fix his location. He kept winding through hills and desert, searching for some landmark to match the crude lines on his map. He could not figure out where to turn. He had enough fuel and the weather had finally calmed, but with nothing more than rudimentary directions he was lost.[36]

In Mexico City the crowd turned apprehensive. Lindbergh was hours late. He carried no radio, and there was no clue about his plane's whereabouts. In New York the two air stocks listed on the New York Stock Exchange, Wright Aeronautical and Curtiss, dropped more than eight points each at the news that there was as yet no trace of the plane. At the airport since eight in the morning, President Calles was chain-smoking and Ambassador Morrow could not stop pacing. The telephone wires between Mexico City and Bolling Field "sizzled," but the only comfort Major Burwell could offer was that Lindy was "too great a pilot to be easily killed in the daytime with a lightly loaded plane."[37]

Lindbergh handled the disorientation with his usual composure. He climbed to fourteen thousand feet for a larger view and finally after another hour of flying glided down over a small town, where he made out a sign reading "Toluca." He was able to find Toluca on his map and set a course east over the foothills. In less than an hour he reached the wide valley where Mexico City was nestled.[38]

Finally Lindbergh arrived, twenty-seven hours after takeoff, more than three hours late. "Something went wrong and I guess it was me," he wrote. The "men in serapes, women in colorful shawls and children kicking in the dust" had waited without food or water for four hours in the broiling sun, setting aside the grim concerns surrounding their hard lives to welcome a flying man. They had feared the worst. Now as they caught sight of the slight silver monoplane slicing through the air 250,000 Mexicans sent up a joyous roar of welcome.[39]

Only now was President Calles able to take something in his mouth. Morrow looked about as "happy as it is given to men to be in this world." On Wall Street airplane stocks shot back up. In Washington where the House of Representatives had been interrupting its business for updates on the lost flier, the chamber filled with jubilation at the news of his arrival. "Wonderful! Good!" exclaimed the secretary of the navy, as he danced around his office.[40]

Amid shouts of "Viva Lindbergh!" Calles threw both arms around the smiling hero in an enthusiastic *embrazo*. The Mexican president called the flight "a priceless Embassy of good-will sent by the people of North America." In Paris they had almost torn his plane apart; in Mexico City hundreds took the *Spirit of St. Louis* on their shoulders and carried it to the hangar like a sacred relic.[41]

For the next six days Lindbergh worked his magic once again. (His mother, flown down on a plane provided by Henry Ford, joined him as a guest of the

Morrows for Christmas.) Squabbles and resentments melted away. The people buried the streets in flowers and the labor unions, not long before denounced by the U.S. State Department as *Bolsheviki*, paraded in his honor. On Sunday afternoon Calles himself escorted Lindbergh to the national stadium, where tens of thousands of schoolchildren put on native dances and Mexico's greatest bull-fighter came out of retirement to perform for him. After making the final kill another matador wrapped the smiling Lindbergh in a crimson and gold *capote*. Back in the United States some questioned his attendance at this bloody sport. "I am a guest of the Mexican Government," he retorted, "and the Mexican people, I think, are perfectly capable of selecting their own national sport."[42]

Lindbergh took up a thrilled President Calles around the capital for his first airplane ride. Twice during this week Calles came personally to visit the U.S. Embassy, a place Mexican presidents had avoided for years. One Mexico City newspaper wrote that this inspired visit had "dispelled mistrust and will . . . conquer for the U.S. glory and love." A delighted Calles telegraphed President Coolidge with "most cordial felicitations." Just several months before Calles had characterized U.S. behavior as "deplorable." Now he agreed to attend the Pan-American Congress in Havana and sit down with the U.S. president. Similarly Secretary of State Kellogg, who had recently denounced Mexico as a communist threat, adopted a mellower tone as the State Department spoke of mutually beneficial relations. News reports predicted that Kellogg would soon lift restrictions on the sale of airplanes and air shipments and, even more significant, on embargoed weapons sales.[43]

Calles was no pushover. He did not shrink from smashing his opposition; Church opponents especially were brutally dispatched. Yet Lindbergh moved him in ways no one ever expected him to be moved. The Morrow initiatives and the Lindbergh visit, Russell Owen reported, "swept [Mexico] with a wave of pro-Americanism." Even such bitter critics of the United States as former president Álvaro Obregon, whom Lindbergh flew over the magnificent Palace of Chapultepec, came away exulting, "There is something which is worth more than money—glory."[44]

Lindbergh spurred progress on his aviation agenda as well. Shortly after he addressed a Mexican Department of Communications luncheon about aviation's possibilities, the agency announced plans to establish airmail routes to important cities and to open a civilian aviation school. Within weeks Calles inaugurated a Department of Civil Aviation. Just days after Lindbergh left Mexico American businessmen, who had earlier been scared off by talk of nationalization and expropriation, arrived to discuss new trade relations. Months later, at the annual May Day parade, for the first time in years observers saw no banners denouncing Yankee imperialism or "dollar diplomacy."[45]

In the United States, Postmaster General New laid plans for opening airmail to Mexico City. Soon he was lobbying Congress to extend airmail to much of Latin America, crediting Lindbergh with having laid the groundwork. And in March 1928 the State Department announced that as a result of President Calles's termination of the "confiscatory oil laws" the ten-year-old oil controversy had reached a satisfactory conclusion. Pledging to "safeguard the interests of foreign capitalists who invest money in Mexico," Calles declared that the United States was "not composed of robbers, but of producers." Secretly, he promised to revisit agrarian reforms that adversely affected U.S. interests and to amicably resolve other disputes.[46]

Pleased with Lindbergh's productive visit to Mexico, President Coolidge signaled his approval for extending the tour to other countries in the region. Going deeper into Latin America involved some risk. Previous U.S. missions had been coolly received, especially in the face of simmering resentment over Nicaragua. With the sixth Pan-American Conference scheduled to take place in Havana in just a few weeks, the administration could ill afford to rouse fresh anger at what radicals would doubtless portray as patronizing gestures of friendship. Moreover professional diplomats understandably hesitated to set international relations on the unstable base of incandescent celebrity.[47]

Nonetheless there was no denying what Lindbergh had accomplished in Paris and Mexico City. His appeal reached down to the grassroots, where much of the anti-U.S. resentment was lodged. Willing to test the waters, the administration advised its Central American legations to solicit invitations; the response exceeded all expectations. Lindbergh had not intended to travel deep into South America, but an invitation from Colombia, where he could review Scadta's operations firsthand and perhaps blunt some of the strongest anti-U.S. sentiment on the continent, proved too attractive to turn down.[48]

There were real hazards in flying over mountainous territory and over forested jungles, often in pitch black night. Lindbergh described some of the perils he himself later encountered: "Tropical storms rushed in from the ocean without warning; rain beat down so heavily a pilot could neither see the ground nor hold his plane in the air." Over the Andes and the endless plains "native huts were often miles apart" providing few landmarks. And if he was forced down in the dense brush, flyboy moxie would not protect him against wild beasts and other dangers. "I was told," he later reported, "it would be inadvisable to get caught by some of the head-hunting tribes in Colombia." He packed a machete and a rifle just in case.[49]

More than once Lindbergh lost his way. Crossing the Honduran mountains he confronted "the roughest [turbulence he had] ever seen," flinging his plane "upward and downward with jerks on its side the whole time." Several times he was thrown against the top of the cabin. Over Belize several cylinders cut out on his motor, forcing him to descend sideways for a hair-raising landing on a narrow polo field. Over Nicaragua he had to scamper up high to dodge bullets from Sandinista guerrillas and again later to avoid ash spewing from active volcanoes. And everywhere on the ground crowds pressed in very close to his landings, creating dangers even greater than the ones in the sky. In Costa Rica police wielding whips and sabers failed to hold back the crowds, and he was forced to drop a note from the air appealing for room to land.[50]

But at each stop in Guatemala, Belize, El Salvador, Costa Rica, Panama, Colombia, Haiti, Cuba, and the Virgin Islands his speeches advocating airmail and the promise of a world made closer, better, and richer through aviation drew enthusiastic cheers from the crowds. He was even celebrated in Nicaragua (Sandinistas or no), and in Santo Domingo he was hailed as the new Columbus, "un muchacho perfecto," a perfect boy. Journalists reported in amazement how much of the Latin American heart he conquered. Puerto Rico's governor Horace M. Towner suggested that Lindbergh appealed to a postwar world because he had made conquest peaceful, applying the devotion, sacrifice, and heroism of war to an achievement that yielded pride without terror and victory without defeat. For this "prophet of a . . . better day" the defining feats of manhood were not won over others but against his own best self.[51]

Lindbergh had become accustomed to being lionized and even adored, but he remained aloof. He lacked the common touch; he did not mingle easily and he spoke with a stern, stiff earnestness, especially in public. He offered no revolutionary new system to eradicate poverty or pestilence, or even inequity. Yet, interestingly, the effect was to make crowds even more effusive and to heighten the impression that he brought them the promise of something greater. "In Mexico," wrote a perceptive observer, "all the unhappiness and uneasiness of a life in which the firing squad was the most common expression of political victory were forgotten for the days that Lindbergh was there."[52]

Throughout Latin America, relations with the United States took on a new luster. Jacobo Varela, the Uruguayan representative, closed the 1928 Pan-American Conference by praising the United States as a "prodigious country which . . . made objects speak through the genius of Edison, and sent with wings, which the Wright brothers created, Lindbergh to conquer the heart of France and Europe." Even those who opposed U.S. policies hesitated to criticize Lindbergh. As a group of Nicaraguans handed him a memorial critical of the United States they took pains to praise him at the same time. Honduras's opposition newspaper, *La Tribuna*, long a critic of Yankee Big Stick diplomacy, hailed the flier and described his reception as "one of the greatest manifestations of sympathy Hondurans have ever bestowed upon a foreigner." In Venezuela President Juan Vicente Gómez called him "a semi-mythical figure, a hero of the age . . . , a new conquistador, a Captain Courageous of the Spanish Main." "Venezuela," he announced, "is his for the asking."[53]

In one of the many guidebooks to Mexico written by American and English travelers, W. E. Carson wrote in 1914 that everywhere one went in Mexico City one encountered Americans "with schemes." The series of articles that carried Lindbergh's byline in the *New York Times* (some ghosted, others written in snatches scribbled on the backs of maps resting on his knee as he flew to his destinations) offered his own guidebook encouraging businessmen and travelers to consider Latin America for trade and tourism. No booster rhetoric sounded sunnier; throughout he reported on "dancing and costumes," jungles and majestic volcanoes, birds of bright plumage, and other exotica. Americans would be comfortable in these surroundings: "an attractive residential section, with golf links, a race course, and avenues lined with trees." In Belize there was basketball and country clubs; in Honduras he found American-style sandwiches and attended a luncheon in the San Jose Rotary Club. In Managua "a large portion of the officials and well-to-do people speak English." The West Indies he advertised as a wonderful opportunity for some flight entrepreneur.[54]

As aggressively as George Babbitt pushed real estate in Zenith, Lindbergh touted south-of-the-border cities, with their well-graded roads and modern office buildings. In his portrayals they consistently measured up to U.S. standards, with a bonus: here one could go hunting for game or even alligators. He stressed the warmth and hospitality of the locals. How much Lindbergh's scheme to stir interest in Latin American trade and aviation led him to suppress his real views became clear years later in his posthumous book, *Autobiography of Values*. There he describes the Latin America he encountered in 1928 as a backward region pocked with poverty and disadvantage. Travel was difficult and primitive and modern means of communication almost nonexistent. The roads were rutted, crude paths, used primarily by donkeys and oxcarts. Children ran around naked, covered with layers of mud and dirt. "I felt the great superiority of our civilization to the north," he wrote. "There seemed to be an unbridgeable chasm between it and Central American culture—in science, in industry, and in political organization. Even the capital cities in Central America were isolated places." Only when he got to the Panama Canal Zone, an area he had visited as a youth, did he find "civilization itself transplanted to the jungle." There he found discipline, cleanliness, fresh paint, and modern equipment. Shops offered the latest fashions and the piers were piled high with imports. "Luxurious hotels and restaurants flourished," and hospitals were staffed with well-trained doctors and nurses: "I sensed the power, the wealth, the accomplishment of my United States of America."[55]

Like his book *We*, the travel reports Lindbergh wrote in 1928 were shaped by an ulterior motive: to promote interchange between nations and dispel fears. A parade of labor unions at the National Palace in Mexico represented "a gratifying expression of friendliness toward the United States" rather than a display of worker solidarity. In Haiti, one of the poorest countries in the world, he focused on the imposing Citadel of la Ferriere, a one-hundred-year-old fortress, and in Port au Prince the Damien Agricultural College and "fields thick with sugar cane." In impoverished Guatemala City he saw a "great number of expensive cars" and new buildings that "give it a modern air." The local populace in the West Indies, he reported, were receptive to trade, cooperative, and English-speaking; the local culture he described as vivid but not discordant; the cities as charming and not without modern conveniences.[56]

Washington had wanted "the sunny eagle of American kindness" to hasten to the Pan-American Conference in Havana, which began on January 16, in order to thwart any movement to declare illegal the sort of intervention that the United States had carried out in Nicaragua, but, aware that his particular type of diplomacy would not work well on a clutch of politicians arguing hard about contending national interests, Lindbergh kept adding tour stops in South America. While Washington fumed a bit and Assistant Commerce Secretary MacCracken complained in a telegram to the Cuban ambassador that Lindbergh was "practically making his own plans" (the word "practically" revealing how much in fact Washington directed his itinerary) Lindbergh explained simply: "[I] wanted to feel my way as I went."[57]

In Colombia, one of the most outspoken opponents of U.S. policy in the region, he was greeted warmly and awarded the nation's highest military award. Even the U.S. State Department had to admit the visit's value. Then, after a tricky flight and being forced to pick his way through clouds and mountain passes during a coastal storm, Lindbergh raced the sun to arrive at the Maracay Airfield in Venezuela before nightfall where strongman Juan Vicente Gómez greeted him as a "cavalier of the skies."[58]

On February 8, three weeks after the conference first convened and bringing it to a close, Lindbergh arrived at the sixth Pan-American Conference to a hero's welcome. An estimated 100,000 turned out to greet the man described in the newspapers as "more universally loved than any other person in the world." The crowds displayed almost equal awe for his fragile partner, vying to touch a plane that for many was a "supernatural machine." The head of the U.S. delegation to the conference, Charles Evans Hughes, underscored the dual nature of Lindbergh's tour, crediting him with "tracing the route that future commerce will follow," while assuring that this course to prosperity would also be "a route of good-will." At the Presidential Palace Lindbergh was met by many of the Pan-American delegates, their conference having adjourned in his honor, and was praised by the Cuban president for advancing "brotherhood among all peoples." After a talk about aviation's power to transform, Lindbergh charmed the delegates with airplane rides. Then he was off, flying home to St. Louis.[59]

Throughout the tour diplomatic spectacle drew much of the press's attention, but those listening to the words and not just the music heard Lindbergh's broader message: that commercial aviation had the power to uplift these nations and the lives of their citizens. "The airplane probably means more to Central and South America than to any other part of the American continents," he insisted. The dense matrix of mountain ranges, jungle terrain, and ramifying waterways had retarded road and railway construction, leaving vast stretches of the region unconnected. The eight hundred miles separating Peru's two largest cities, Iquitos and Lima, might as well be a continent. Trade, conducted on mules or a thirty-day journey by steamer down the Amazon and up the South American coast, was slow, small, and stunted. By air this trip took *nine hours*. In some Central American countries, he noted, mail was transported by runners, horsemen, and oxcarts, taking a day for each hundred miles. Foreign mail was dispatched by steamers that sailed every two or three weeks. In El Salvador, one of the more advanced countries on the itinerary, it took two months for bills, notes, and small parcels to make their way to the United States. Airmail could cut this to forty-eight hours, energizing business and cutting interest costs. Aviation, Lindbergh declared, would "open up" these countries by expanding their economies, raising living standards, and promoting concord. He called it a great "compliment" when he arrived in Panama and learned that they had a built a new airport for his visit. Build the airports and air routes, he declared, and the tourists and business deals will come.[60]

Lindbergh himself actively encouraged U.S. entrepreneurs to invest in Latin America, smoothing access to political leaders and helping with practical advice. While still at the Pan-American Conference he met with a number of Americans interested in taking up his challenge. Of these entrepreneurs the most memorable was Juan Terry Trippe, who sought out Lindbergh to discuss with him his ambitious plans for a hemispheric airline that would compete with the better established European lines. Others, including James H. Rand, president of Remington Rand Typewriter Company, proposed other air ventures but Trippe more than anyone else fully appreciated the scale of what Lindbergh was proposing.[61]

Originally planned as a gesture to assist Morrow's diplomatic initiatives in Mexico, Lindbergh's third historic flight involved 116 hours in the air and covered more than nine thousand miles with stops in sixteen countries. From a simple diplomatic gesture it was transformed into a bold offensive to corner Latin America's aviation business. "[The] motives for my flight," Lindbergh later wrote candidly, "coincided with . . . government policy." Once planes were flying regularly between North and South America, Lindbergh believed, the next step would bring the fulfillment of his Paris flight's promise: "transoceanic communication with Europe."[62]

Over the two months of the tour Lindbergh had been welcomed with almost religious fervor in every country he visited, spreading goodwill and "air mindedness." The routes he developed for this tour would serve as templates for subsequent airline services. Congressman Henry W. Watson of Pennsylvania credited Lindbergh with paving the way for solid commercial relations with "the greatest market in the world for United States products." Following the tour U.S. exports of aeronautical machinery to Latin America rose appreciably and air-related business multiplied more than sixfold. Over the next seven years Latin America accounted for 41 percent of U.S. aviation-related sales. The growth of ancillary markets, such as the Central American cotton trade, was also laid directly to the Lindbergh trip.[63]

There were, of course, scattered complaints. In Haiti, where U.S. gunboat diplomacy remained a matter of controversy and hostility, a local newspaper criticized the United States for commercializing its air hero into "a great traveling salesman of Wall Street." Nonetheless the paper would not criticize the icon himself. Heywood Broun, the social critic, put it all in perspective, writing in *The Nation*, "Even if you say the flight was incorporated into traditional dollar diplomacy I still feel that it was excellent. . . . Big Business, whatever its faults, is preferable to expeditionary forces." Wesley Phillips Newton, the outstanding historian of U.S. aviation diplomacy, credits Lindbergh with helping shift the United States "from hard line gunboat . . . diplomacy to that of the Good Neighbor."[64]

The flight back to the United States on February 13 should have been routine, but it served as a reminder of the dangers that continued to face fliers. Halfway across the Florida straits both of Lindbergh's compasses began spinning erratically, leaving him disoriented in a haze-filled sky. Unable to tell in what direction he was flying, he remained in the air for fifteen and a half hours in "abominable" conditions that took him three hundred miles off course before he found his way back to his destination. Despite the delays and pouring rain, a large crowd was waiting to greet him, and President Coolidge sent greetings.[65]

Lindbergh had grown in stature. No longer the flyboy wonder, he was returning with a portfolio. He had met presidents and a host of leaders in troubled places and calmed tensions by preaching a future made better through aviation. He was no Henry Ford with a quixotic peace ship off on some quirky crusade. His tour on behalf of aviation was buttressed by U.S. policy and large-pocket investors. Assistant Secretary of Commerce for Aeronautics William P. MacCracken called 1927 the year that Lindbergh created an "air psychology."[66]

Lindbergh's forays into diplomacy—first in Paris and the rest of Europe, and then throughout Latin America—signaled a fulfillment of the winged gospel, the notion that the celerity of "higher air" together with easier communication and interaction would dissolve misunderstandings and eliminate jealousies. Aviation "stir[s] a common emotion in all people," he wrote, and it promised a postwar sensibility that could speak with one voice to Paris and Berlin, to Tokyo and Mexico City. The offensive use of planes in World War I was a false start. Flight's true purpose was in the service of world harmony and global prosperity. In a long interview with the *Christian Science Monitor* Lindbergh spoke of the "internationalism of the air" that brought remote regions of the world closer together. Those who fly, he said, fraternize as "citizens of the universe," ignoring the artificial boundaries of nationality while furthering mutual understanding.[67]

Earlier in June, when New York University Chancellor Elmer Ellsworth Brown presented Lindbergh with an honorary degree, he praised the Lone Eagle for giving aviation "a loftier significance" and "making the air above us a highway of good will." Now, following the proven impact of his aviation tours, the distinguished Woodrow Wilson Foundation, with its mission of international peace and understanding, unanimously conferred its prestigious Peace Prize (a medal and $25,000) on Lindbergh. Only twice before had the prize been awarded to an individual: once to Viscount Cecil of Chelwood, an architect of the League of Nations, and the second time to Elihu Root for helping found the World Court. This was no faddish organization taken with transitory celebrity. Recognizing Lindbergh's extraordinary impact for peace, the trustees hailed him "as the greatest ambassador of modern times."[68]

In analyzing the protracted Lindbergh enchantment, scholars have written about the two-sidedness of his appeal: on one side the individualist and on the other the promoter of an industry whose processes and financial structure were large, complex, and corporate. He was a man who tamed nature but did it with a machine. At bottom, however, his appeal rested on something greater than the sum of these ironies. To people in the 1920s Lindbergh's flights represented a fresh, young, and hopeful sensibility, a wisdom of the skies that rejected land-based jealousies and conflicts. The *Denver Rocky Mountain News* wrote that he had "set a love chord moving in the universal ether and changed the spiritual atmosphere of two continents." If this sounds fatuous, then perhaps it offers a sense of the suspension of disbelief that he was able to provoke. His artless innocence, heroic achievement, and promise of new beginnings drew in sophisticates and common folk alike. South American dictators, Mexican radicals, European intellectuals, kings, and workers, all were beguiled by his message of peace and profit through aviation.[69]

Two decades before Lindbergh's transoceanic flight the philosopher William James in an address at Stanford University spoke of the uphill battle of the pacifist, for war exerts a great pull on the human imagination. "The horrors," he said, "make the fascination." He went on to explain: "War is the *strong* life; it is life *in extremis*; war taxes are the only ones men never hesitate to pay, as the budgets of all nations show us." From the cruel history of blood and plunder we take our heroes and our grand narratives of valor and sacrifice. Without primal tests of courage and the bracing tonic of battle, youth would turn soft and dissolute. And so as long as pacifism could offer no "substitute for war's disciplinary function, no *moral equivalent* of war," it failed in its appeal to the human imagination.[70]

In his flights, his diplomacy, and his missions on behalf of aviation Lindbergh projected nothing less than a moral equivalent of war. Through bold conquest that posed no threat to the innocent he carved a dramatic pathway to transcendence, a means to unleash humanity's better future. Linking heroic achievement to the promise of peace and prosperity, he offered the world a challenge worthy of it, without the impetus of fear, empire, or vainglory. Without bullets and bombs, air technology would unleash the promise of a better life.[71]

The papers reported in 1929 on a woman who upon the first pangs of labor rushed to the local airfield and with her husband, her mother, two nurses, and a doctor boarded a plane to give birth in the heavens to Aerogene, a baby daughter. So many couples chose to get married in the air that it stopped being news. For so many, the sky Lindbergh had made unthreatening seemed to promise a special sacral dimension, a different, better future.[72]

THE LINDBERGH ERA

IN TWENTY-FIVE YEARS American aviation passed rapidly through four phases of development: the Wright era, when an unnoticed band of air enthusiasts got off the ground; the era of sustained flight and daring flyboys who tested the planes and taught the industry what worked and tragically what did not; and the Great War, which rushed development and applications and ushered in the airmail system. But the next phase, commercial aviation, remained an idea waiting for its time, especially because the United States (unlike Europe) had a fine railroad system and there seemed no urgency to the project. A common joke went that Americans would go up in the air only so long as they could keep one foot on the ground. As late as 1927 experienced airplane hands thought that it would take years for the public to develop the confidence to fly. Then, the Lindbergh era made flight imaginable; assuring the public that air travel was safe and efficient. As important as the flight were the celebrations and the reliability tour, which broadcast the message to the far reaches of the land.[1]

Because of Lindbergh thousands of college students decided on aeronautical careers. "Every schoolboy is now dreaming of air travel," the magazine *Outlook* reported. In just a few months following the transatlantic flight the number of student pilots in the country multiplied from two thousand to more than fourteen thousand. A month after Paris, Walter Hinton, the pilot for the first transatlantic flight in 1919, wrote, "[The] long and tedious period of waiting . . . is now over." In June Pratt & Whitney, which began manufacturing airplane engines in 1925 in a 2,500-square-foot shed, moved to a quadrangle of modern buildings composed of more than 200,000 square feet of space. In 1927 they produced 267 engines; by the end of 1928 they were turning out a thousand units a year. Their initial roster of twenty-five employees grew to 570 by January 1928 and by

December close to double that. P&W's parent company's stock traded at 29 in January; before the end of the year it reached a high of 93, with a dividend of $24 a share on preferred stock.[2]

Investors poured capital into the industry. "Within three weeks after the Lindbergh flight," Walter Hinton wrote, "[funding] was made available here in the United States to finance almost any kind of aeronautical Project." Bankers who had hesitated to commit funds before opened the gates to every kind of aviation investment. Prominent financiers joined aircraft firm directorates, attracting venture capital to new aviation projects. Aviation consortiums sprang up, leading the *Aircraft Yearbook* to exult, "Money, everywhere, seemed to be available for aviation." Between June 1927 and January 1929 investors committed over a billion dollars to the young industry.[3]

Buoyed by the optimism aviation securities soared to new highs. Individual shares of Curtiss Aeroplane, 19 at the start of 1927, climbed to 46 soon after Lindbergh's flight and hit 69 by mid-December. Weeks before the flight Wright Aeronautical, manufacturer of the *Spirit of St Louis*'s Whirlwind engine, had sold at 25; in December it stood at 94¾ and a year later it reached 245. In October Western Air Express, servicing a regular route between Los Angeles and Salt Lake City, became the first airline company to declare an earned dividend on profits. Early in 1928 the Guggenheim Fund, aviation's Medici, opened a program to assist commercial airlines with start-up capital. Within weeks the fund closed the program, concluding that private "subsidies" were no longer needed. Declaring that interest in aviation "ha[d] been definitely and permanently aroused," Harry Guggenheim reallocated the funds to fundamental research and development in aeronautics.[4]

Manufacturers built more than three thousand planes in 1927, twice the number during the previous year. A few years earlier a road-building craze had gripped the nation once the automobile caught on; now hundreds of cities rushed to construct airfields. In the month following the flight air postage volume jumped 20 percent. By 1929 the post office was delivering 7.7 million pounds of airmail; a little more than a year earlier it had carried about a tenth of that. Attributing the growth to the "Lindbergh effect," Postmaster General Harry S. New added three thousand new route miles to the airmail system, which continued to serve as American commercial aviation's spine. Between mid-1927 and January 1929 the number of air passengers rose from 5,782 to 173,405 (including 13,654 to foreign shores), most of them business travelers. In 1929 aircraft sales receipts climbed from $21,162,000 to $71,153,000. The growth spurt in civil aircraft was particularly striking: 652 units in 1926 multiplied to 5,516 in 1929. By the end of the decade production capacity reached more than fifteen thousand planes a year, and each day American air companies flew more than 120,000 miles.[5]

In 1929 the recently formed United Aircraft and Transport reported a phenomenal return of $10,000,000 on $41,000,000 in assets. The *Wall Street Journal* marveled at how rapidly commercial air services had become essential to many businesses. Only a year after Lindbergh's flight the United States was being held up as the new air standard. When the British complained that their air industry had fallen behind they no longer made comparisons with Germany and France, but with the United States. France sent its largest aviation delegation in history, headed by the famed tire manufacturer Andre Michelin, to study American aviation. Will Rogers joked, "The man that travels on the ground next summer he just don't deserve to get nowhere."[6]

Even amid the Depression, following a shaky period soon after the stock market crash, aircraft assembly lines were kept humming. Revolutions, wars, and threats of war, one insider declared, made aircraft customers. Boeing made an average of 21 percent profit on its navy contracts and 25 percent on its army contracts. Pratt & Whitney did even better, reporting profits of more than 40 percent on its engines. From Lindbergh's flight, T. J. C. Martyn wrote in the *Times* a little more than a year after it had taken place, "dates the growth of a small struggling industry into one now turning over hundreds of millions of dollars."[7]

During that year Lindbergh came to personify aviation, expert in all its branches and at the same time a symbol of its idealistic possibilities. His testimony was sought by legislatures across the country. The president looked to him for counsel in shaping aviation policy, and the most powerful airline companies sought his help. All the while he remained the most popular figure in the land. In March 1928, after his return from Latin America, guards had to be called to clear the crowds and let the senators through when he testified before a congressional committee. He commanded the front pages of the leading newspapers. Articles about him commonly began referring to him as "Colonel Charles Lindbergh, 'Lone Eagle' of the epic, non-stop flight from New York to Paris, which remains," as the *Times* put it, "the most talked-about feat in aeronautics."[8]

Late in March he flew to Washington to receive the Congressional Medal of Honor. The next few days, using two planes—one warming while he took the other up in the air—he devoted to taking lawmakers and their families for jaunts over the Capitol. Congressmen, notorious for their impatience, waited for hours to ride with Lindbergh. The press gleefully reported on the starched VIPs jostling for priority for their ten- to fifteen-minute junkets, while the eighty-seven-year-old chief justice, Oliver Wendell Holmes, watched from a distance and pronounced the scene "simply thrilling." Lindbergh took up a total of 835 officials and relatives, many of them flying for the first time, and put them at ease with aviation. Newspapers around the country printed photographs of local congressmen with the Lone Eagle, broadcasting the message of air reliability far and wide. "Flying is now bound to become the fashion," exclaimed the *Times*. "Who will be afraid? . . . Luring Congress into the air was his master stroke." Before leaving Washington Lindbergh urged his friends in Congress to add even more miles to airmail.[9]

He held more honors than any other living man or woman. A letter to the editor of the *Times* called upon the Nobel Committee to award him the Peace Prize for "having done more for international good will that any other living man." Members of Congress competed with each other to shower him with tributes. They called for medals to be struck in his honor, for converting his childhood home into a national museum, placing his image on U.S. coins, erecting an airport bearing his name, even for publishing his life story and distributing his biography in schools across the country to inspire students to honor and heroism; others wanted to provide him with a subvention. Lindbergh informed the honorable members that the last thing he wanted was to be a state-supported icon.[10]

He seemed ready now for the next stage in his life, but what that would be seemed undecided. He cleared out most of the mementoes that he had received, giving them to two museums. The *Spirit of St. Louis* went to the Smithsonian Institution. (Ryan Aircraft, newly renamed B. F. Mahoney Aircraft Company, replaced his beloved *Spirit* with a four-passenger monoplane that included lighted wings for night landing.) His medals, clippings, and more than $300,000 worth of gifts, including the Hearst silver globes, a thousand-year-old copy of the Koran, a large diamond cut in the form of an airplane, a small casket filled with gold nuggets from Honduras, and assorted swords, relics, objets d'art, and historical artifacts, were placed on permanent display in the Missouri Historical Society Museum in St. Louis.[11]

In the spring of 1928 he accepted the *Times*'s offer to write a weekly column, "Lindbergh on Flying." "It will be worth the attention of all who are interested in the subject—and who today is not?" the *Times* wrote, introducing the new column. "No one knows the parts of a flying machine better than he does, and in its handling and care he is a past master." But this was a sideline, not the large aviation job he had spoken of soon after Paris, when he declared, "I shall keep on working to help make air travel better, safer, and quicker."[12]

He continued to give speeches. Before the Boston school superintendents he proposed adding aviation to the curriculum. This speech was drafted for him by Harry Guggenheim, who remained his closest adviser and continued to shape his career. Businessmen sought his advice and counsel and the pleasure of his company. While he continued flying across the country, testifying before Congress, speeding serum to Ottawa in a vain mission to save the famed pilot Floyd Bennett's life, and "dropping out of the sky, it seemed, as the whim seized him," speculation continued about what he would ultimately choose to make his career. He had flown more than 200,000 miles, made almost eight thousand flights and spent more than 2,500 hours in the air, all in the cause of preparing the public for aviation. Now, remarked an associate, it was his turn to prepare aviation for the country.[13]

Then in May, just a few days short of his flight's first anniversary, the *Washington Post* reported that it had uncovered the logic behind all Lindbergh's apparently aimless flying. It was all part of a vast mapping exercise to develop a system of nationwide airplane routes as Lindbergh prepared to join a "gigantic aeronautical enterprise . . . [that] would startle the world." The ambitious plan brought together the resources of Henry Ford, the Wright Corporation, B. F. Mahoney, the Guggenheim Foundation, and the Curtiss Aeroplane and Motor Company. Lindbergh would not comment beyond saying that he was "not connected with any commercial company." Wall Street, refusing to take him at his word, responded exuberantly to the rumors of a giant air company with Lindbergh at its head. Wright stock shot up "perpendicularly," to 196, and Curtiss, selling under 54 earlier in the year, climbed to over 145.[14]

Actually these discussions had begun only a few days after Lindbergh had returned from Paris, when the attorney for Howard Coffin and Clement M. Keys, directors of the National Air Transport Corporation, contacted him. Coffin, who made his fortune as president of the Hudson Motor Company, had headed the war-time Aircraft Production Board, and Keys, president of Curtiss Aeroplane, was the most dynamic aviation entrepreneur on the scene. They offered him the presidency of a new national airline conglomerate that they intended to launch, hoping to call it "Lindbergh Air Lines." He would receive a one-fifth share in the company plus a handsome salary.[15]

In the course of these deliberations Lindbergh and his St. Louis group flew to Washington to discuss his future with the government's major aviation officials at the home of Commerce Secretary Herbert Hoover. Lindbergh's advisers made clear that he was not interested in a government post. He would, they insisted, be "more useful in private enterprise where he could assist the government by employing his arguments and vivid personality to stimulate commercial and other aviation." They also explained quite candidly that he wanted to make some real money. He was weighing the offer from Coffin and Keys but seemed to prefer a project being put together by Earl Thompson in St. Louis for an airplane-manufacturing firm. Hoover urged Lindbergh to reconsider and to give serious thought to the Keys venture, adding that the administration was prepared to do everything possible to make it a success. The next day papers announced,

"Colonel Charles A. Lindbergh's future has been decided." The twenty-five-year-old flier would soon join a new air conglomerate poised to become the General Motors of the air, making him the "Rockefeller of aviation."[16]

Despite Keys's and Coffin's insistence that the public would take to the air "if they were sure that [Lindbergh] had vouched for the planes and the pilots," and that his name would attract Wall Street financing, Lindbergh remained ambivalent about assuming executive responsibilities for a fledgling airline. Keys and Coffin did what they could to put him at ease, bringing his St. Louis cohorts into the deal and adding a number of highly regarded aviation figures to the staff.[17]

But he kept putting off a decision, appearing preoccupied and unsmiling in public, rebuffing the press, even snapping at a little girl who wanted to shake his hand. To journalists trailing him he seemed distant and unhappy. Finally, telling Breckinridge that National Air Transport had not been "efficient or practical" in the past, he decided to hold off making a decision while he went on the Guggenheim tour and then to Latin America. Meanwhile Breckinridge continued to explore other possibilities, including another motion picture deal (Hollywood did not easily give up on the photogenic hero) that promised to promote aviation—and to bring in a large paycheck.[18]

By the spring of 1928 he had ruled out the movies and politics and had passed on opportunities with some air manufacturing start-ups. Meanwhile the Keys-Coffin venture had evolved into Transcontinental Air Transport Inc. (TAT), a cartel of vertically integrated aviation enterprises, including the Ford, Wright, and Curtiss companies, as well as the Pennsylvania and the Atchison, Topeka & Santa Fe railroad systems. Five banking houses capitalized the new company at $5,000,000.[19]

With rumors of other air conglomerates in the offing, TAT focused on bringing Lindbergh onboard. Bixby and Knight were both made directors of the new corporation, and as a further concession TAT's route to Los Angeles from New York was directed through St. Louis instead of Chicago. To satisfy Lindbergh, his own responsibilities were scaled back, limited to heading TAT's Technical Committee and Keys staffed the committee with experienced airmen of national reputation, keeping business and financial types away. Finally Lindbergh agreed, leading the *Washington Post* to announce a "gigantic aeronautical enterprise."[20]

Years later Lindbergh defended taking inflated corporate pay as honest money, but when he first assumed his post with TAT he wanted to preserve his image as a disinterested spokesman for American aviation. He insisted that he was joining TAT in an advisory capacity on a "part-time basis," not actually assuming administrative or management responsibilities. He refused to acknowledge or discuss questions about his salary and assured reporters that he would pay for any stock that he acquired. In fact he had struck a very attractive deal, collecting an initial retainer of $250,000 in the form of twenty-five thousand shares of TAT at an insider price of $10, with options on twenty-five thousand more shares at the same $10 per share ("[These] warrants," Lindbergh later commented, "became quite valuable as years passed." Keys advised him to hold these securities in others' names so as not to attract attention when he sold them.) This was in addition to an annual salary of $10,000. The agreement specifically allowed him to carry on other activities. The Pennsylvania Railroad, a TAT partner, chipped in another $10,000 retainer for Lindbergh to serve as their consultant as well.[21]

Over the next few years Lindbergh resisted efforts to expand his role at TAT, turning down the position of operations chief and other administrative posts. He underscored his independence by working out of the Guggenheim Fund offices, where he continued as a consultant (for a $5,000 retainer), while also joining other ventures, put together by the large aviation interests. With its gold-plated tag, "The Lindbergh Line," TAT saw its stock, issued at 10, shoot up to 28 within days and then hit 31. The burst of buying sent other air stocks climbing as well. Wright peaked at 245 and Curtiss reached 192.[22]

There was a time when Lindbergh had admired independent entrepreneurs who did whatever it took to build the airplane industry. But his perspective had changed. He now warned repeatedly against the proliferation of small, poorly funded undertakings chasing dreams of overnight fortunes. Aviation needed to avoid the early experience of America's railroads, when a welter of small competing lines engaged in cutthroat competition, finally bringing upon themselves a collapse of spectacular bankruptcies. Exceedingly well treated by wealthy aviation investors and their supporters, he had come to distrust the small men on the make, the wildcatters who cut prices, appropriated industrial innovations, and threatened the giants' profits.[23]

As for those companies that had made the initial investments and built the early firms, companies like Robertson Air that had scrimped and scraped to patch together an airmail run and scramble for a profit, Lindbergh offered them scant sympathy. They may have helped get aviation off the ground, employing young men like him and laying the tracks for later development, but their time was over. "The Robertson brothers," he recalled, "took part in extraordinary opportunities," especially after his flight. Now, however, the industry had passed them by. It was the sleek new corporations that represented the future of aviation. "Personally," he added, "I felt that environment preferable."[24]

His father had wrestled with established politics, taking pride in his career as a midwestern insurgent. But insurgent politics held no appeal for the younger Lindbergh. He warmly endorsed Herbert Hoover and his conservative policies over Al Smith for the presidency in 1928. "YOUR ELECTION IS OF SUPREME

IMPORTANCE TO THE COUNTRY," he wrote in a telegram to the candidate. "WHAT YOU STAND FOR . . . MAKES ME FEEL THAT THE PROBLEMS WHICH WILL COME BEFORE OUR COUNTRY DURING THE NEXT FOUR YEARS WILL BE BEST SOLVED UNDER YOUR LEADERSHIP."[25]

Hoover was a booster of aviation in general. He took pride in the more than twenty-five thousand miles of government-improved airways and hundreds of privately funded airports added by his department while he was commerce secretary. "I felt a personal triumph," he later declared, "with every mile of service we added." As president-elect he retraced some of Lindbergh's own stops on a seven-week goodwill tour of Latin America, meeting with leaders there to project a new mutuality, while encouraging aviation progress. In September 1929 President Hoover appointed the thirty-nine-year-old Harry Guggenheim as ambassador to Cuba, the hub of Latin American aviation.[26]

Hoover was especially friendly toward big aviation. As president he promoted America's air industry through associational networks that brought together government and business in cooperative economic councils. Federal agencies, aviation manufacturers, airline operators, insurance companies, and other involved parties collaborated to mold policies favorable to the large air corporations. He entrusted bureaucrats, who themselves passed through a revolving door from the private to the public sector and back again, with implementing these policies, advancing the interests of the most powerful companies in the industry.[27]

Earlier in the century progressives had agitated against big business monopolies, fearing their impact on society and business. Prosperity Era government took a more benign view of large business consolidations, and in the two years following Lindbergh's flight the aviation industry was monopolized. William Boeing merged a number of transport and aircraft manufacturing companies into Boeing Air and Transport Corporation. United Aircraft and Transport, a new holding company, purchased Pratt & Whitney, then Sikorsky Aircraft in July 1929, and Northrop just a few months later. Through his holding company, North American Aviation, Clement Keys controlled National Air Transport, TAT, and forty-five other aviation properties. A little more than a year later another Keys conglomerate combined the venerable Wright, Curtiss, and Keystone firms with at least nine other companies into the Curtiss-Wright Corporation, the single largest aircraft manufacturing holding company in the United States, capitalized at more than $70,000,000. In March 1929 a collection of Wall Street titans, including the estimable Harriman, Lehman Brothers, and Mellon financial houses, formed the Aviation Corporation (AVCO). By 1930 it controlled about eighty subsidiaries. With remarkable swiftness the train of serial mergers consolidated much of the industry into a very few hands.[28]

Older companies folded before these steamrollers; it was either merge or go down. The pioneering aircraft manufacturer Anthony Fokker, whose Atlantic Aircraft Corporation built some of the best machines in the 1920s, believed that "the Lindbergh boom" had irrevocably changed aviation: "The sudden dumping of $400 millions into the industry, six months after a period in which no aviation company could even get credit, made it imperative that I join forces with a strong financial ally." By 1929 his company merged with General Motors to form General Aviation Manufacturing Corporation, which later merged with North American Aviation. A number of airline moguls entered into secret agreements to avoid competition—"We are desirous of hearty cooperation with . . . other lines," Boeing wrote Keys in June 1928—hoping ultimately for a merger of giants.[29]

In a very short time this young industry, in the words of a later congressional report, "assumed a degree of complexity which would do credit to long-established industries such as the utilities and the railroads." Waves of mergers proceeded with dizzying frequency, resulting in a thick net of cross-invested stockholdings and interlocking holding companies that controlled competition. Control was held in the hands of a few financial interests.[30]

Applying the model developed by J. P. Morgan when he took control of railroads in the 1890s, the consolidated companies sought the benefits of shared planning, coordinated operations, and economies of scale. Leading newspapers, enchanted by the emerging colossus (and its ability to overpower European air companies), focused on the benefits to be derived from linking up the various routes, standardizing equipment, establishing common guidelines, and effectively organizing the system under monopoly control. "Ultimately," the *Washington Post* wrote approvingly, "the Nation's commercial airways will pass into unified control."[31]

Lindbergh agreed. He believed that American aviation needed to be large and unified to compete with Europe. He called upon "capitalists who [were] willing to risk large sums" to build the new aircraft factories, survey new routes, lay airstrips, and develop the new guidance technologies: "Experimentation is our real need and that calls for money, lots of money." Like his coterie of advisers he favored large, secure, lavishly funded air monopolies that could spend millions without cutting corners. Lending his hero's gloss to the effort, he shielded the industry from trustbusters and used his far-reaching celebrity pulpit to give it all a benign inflection.[32]

By mid-1929 United Aircraft and Transport, National Air Transport, and AVCO formed an oligopoly that worked closely with government and readily submitted to federal regulation, which it helped shape. Government contracts for aircraft and federally approved franchises for airline routes remained critical for success in the industry, and these companies won a lion's share of these assignments; the post office granted them practically all its airmail business.[33]

One could imagine Representative C. A. Lindbergh railing at the monopolists and insider profiteers made fat at the expense of the people. Imagine his fury at the Pratt & Whitney treasurer who paid $18 for ninety shares of original stock and then added another 110 shares for $22 in 1926, cashing in his $40 investment in 1929 for $3,367,840; or P&W's president, Fred Rentschler, initially investing $253 for 1,375 P&W shares only to see this original investment multiply into 219,604 shares of United Air and Transport, valued in May 1929 at over $35,000,000. What would he say to the "pyramiding of companies . . . and million per cent profits made by insiders on . . . securities," reported in one careful study of the industry? Congressman Lindbergh had crusaded against Wall Street and big business with a bristling sense of violation, fighting the notions of economic or any other form of royalty. It puzzled former Minnesota governor John Lind that the late congressman's son, the air hero, seemed to get along famously with the monopolists; the "big men" seemed to control him.[34]

In fact Charles had renounced his father's prairie populism. Lindbergh *fils*, who thought that kings were just like you and me, could find little to dislike or distrust in tycoons and the wealthy, whether a Guggenheim, a gaggle of Morgan bankers, or the entire regime of Latin America's despots. And for aviation to succeed, he believed, it needed its millionaires.[35]

By 1929 he himself had become very comfortable, if not a millionaire, then close enough. For one who had so publicly "refused to capitalize his fame for self aggrandizement" he had reaped substantial rewards. He felt no discomfort about that, nor did he apologize for backing the big aviation companies: "I supported the development of aviation as it seemed to me it could best be developed." As for his father's abhorrence of money changers and eastern bankers, Charles told C. A.'s biographer that the country congressman had never really understood big businessmen, had never seen the world from their perspective: "If he had . . . he would have moderated his position in many instances. . . . He saw more devils in the financiers than actually were there." His father's acid diatribes on big business he dismissed as wrongheaded and demagogic. To his father big business was an abstraction "to which he tended to attribute, figuratively speaking, all evil." As for himself, he found the high financiers—Thomas Lamont, Harry Davison, Seward Prosser, and two generations of J. P. Morgans among others—"men of high integrity." Dwight Morrow, for example, was "one of the greatest men I have known, brilliant, perceptive, considerate, honest, a man with the welfare of his country very much at heart."[36]

He had turned down easy money from Hollywood, vaudeville, and the world of endorsements. They were riddled with inauthenticity, with posing, "acting," and if there was anything he despised it was pretending to be what one is not. Businessmen were doers, not posers, men who took chances as much as any farmer. He saw no reason to question the profit motive or the notion that those who succeeded had the right to all the marbles. There was nothing inauthentic about speculation and dealing; it was very much like the chances he took as a flyboy, taking up a plane and doing stunts. If you had the moxie and you were good at it, you had a right to your prize. As for those solid common citizens who avoided risks, the yeomen on whose behalf his father had crusaded, didn't they deserve to be protected from buccaneering monopolists? Frankly he did not give that kind of life much thought. These were the folks who partook of life in "ant-like" miserly portions, preoccupied with protecting rather than experiencing. He had no respect for that kind of life.[37]

Working with powerful men meant that he could move aviation ahead more swiftly than even he had imagined, but he insisted that it be done with care. TAT officials had hoped to inaugurate services in the late fall or early winter of 1928, but Lindbergh, whose committee supervised the preparations, would not be hurried. He took the better part of a year to sign off on the launch. Casey Jones, the famed test pilot, served on Lindbergh's Technical Committee and marveled at the aviator's ability to corral the best men in the field, including Colonel Paul Henderson, "the father of air mail"; Commander Jerome Hunsaker, the pioneering aircraft engineer who designed the NC-4 flying boat and introduced courses in aeronautical engineering at MIT; Major Thomas Lanphier, commander of the U.S. Army Air Corps' crack First Pursuit group; and H. C. Ferguson, an expert in airport design. Barely twenty-six years old, Lindbergh had the confidence to surround himself with the experts who had built American aviation, all of them older and more experienced than he. These experts deferred to him on tough decisions about where to invest, which engines to use, which pilots to hire, how to coordinate the air and rail systems, and dozens of other, equally challenging questions. Jones admired how he took charge, orchestrating their efforts to "put . . . this new transportation system together bit by bit."[38]

In the year leading up to actual passenger service, working from a flying office equipped with a desk, chair, and typewriter outfitted for him by the Ford Company, Lindbergh personally laid out routes, weighing such issues as climate, weather patterns, and access to emergency landing sites. He tested and selected the airplanes, developed guidelines for training and assigning pilots, and arranged for "meteorological stations" (admittedly not much more than a string of railroad agents looking out their windows). His reviews took in the full range of airline activities, extending even to the noise level in cabins, in-flight passenger comforts, and improved navigation instruments.[39]

The old landing fields had been little more than cleared pastures. He laid out new airports to accommodate the large and heavily laden trimotors, added new lighted runways, introduced an array of passenger amenities, and directed the preparation of secondary fields for emergencies along the routes. Aviation's primary attraction for the business traveler was its efficiency, and Lindbergh took pains to protect this premium by carefully synchronizing connections with railroads. With reluctance he also agreed to center TAT's major service facilities in Kansas City instead of St. Louis because this better fit the route grid adopted for TAT's flights.[40]

The decisions he made set precedents well into the future. He was hesitant at first to equip the planes with three hundred pounds of radio equipment, the equivalent of two passengers; ultimately the radios were reduced to sixty pounds and installed. He developed the protocols for shaping a motley crew of flyboys into a disciplined force of sober, conservative passenger pilots. His reports laid the groundwork for night passenger flights, midair refueling, and the preparation of backup systems for emergency power failures. Later he also worked on pressurized cabins for high-altitude flights.[41]

Many of the early advocates of commercial aviation obsessed about the issue of parachutes. They feared that passenger deaths would have a devastating effect on flying and wanted to do whatever was necessary to prevent them. Lindbergh considered what it would take to strap each passenger into a safety device. Aside from making a long trip uncomfortable and adding to the weight load of the craft, being harnessed into a safety chute emphasized to the passenger that he had left his normal environment for a dangerous space with a potential for disaster. This was the wrong message. Moreover parachutes meant that women would have to wear pants to accommodate the leg straps, and the chutes would hamper the elderly and the very young. Nor did he accept as more practical the novel notion of a craft parachute "so large it would let the entire plane down." In the end he nixed this proposal as costly, ineffective, and bad for PR.[42]

He peppered Keys with reports about engine safety and the comparative qualities of different types of passenger planes and various route options. These longhand accounts, scribbled on unlined hotel stationery, the backs of envelopes, and even on the flaps of book jackets, were then typed up by a secretary. He presented his conclusions in an unadorned style, without ambivalence or uncertainty. When he was finally satisfied that the many elements had been pulled together, he carried out a two-week test run in June before signaling Keys that TAT was ready to begin flying operations in July 1929. So impressed was the public with TAT's preparations that more than a thousand applications poured in to the airline for reservations for its maiden flights.[43]

On July 7 Lindbergh, standing at the TAT terminal in Los Angeles, pressed a button at 6:05 p.m. New York time that closed a Western Union circuit and sounded a gong, dispatching the Pennsylvania Railroad's *America* train from Penn Station in New York City with sixteen passengers, launching the Lindbergh Line's operations. The train arrived the next morning seven miles outside of Columbus, Ohio, where passengers transferred to a Ford trimotor and flew to Waynoka, Oklahoma, arriving at 6:30 p.m. There the sixteen passengers deplaned for a Santa Fe Railroad car for a night run across the southwestern desert to Clovis, New Mexico, where they again boarded a TAT aircraft for the last leg of the flight to Los Angeles, arriving at 6:42 p.m., thirty-six hours after leaving New York, all for the price of $350, which included meals, transportation to the airfield, and insurance. (A flier seeking insurance in 1920 paid $90 per $1,000 of insurance, if he could find it; by 1925 the price had fallen to $25; in 1929 the price was between 75 cents and $1.50.)[44]

On July 8 Lindbergh piloted the TAT aircraft *City of Los Angeles*, inaugurating eastbound service on the first leg of its trip to Winslow, Arizona. A few days later he launched the Los Angeles–Oakland route. Opening new routes kept him busy as TAT insisted on his making the opening flights, guaranteeing wide publicity and a "laying on of the hands" credibility.[45]

When disaster struck, which of course it did, it fell to him to reassure the public. Less than two months after the launch, on September 3, the TAT aircraft *City of San Francisco* disappeared over New Mexico. Four days later the badly burned plane was found smashed on the side of Mount Taylor, about twenty minutes from Albuquerque. All eight passengers, seven men and a woman, had perished, their bodies unrecognizable. Initial reports suggested that the pilot had been forced off course by a fierce electrical storm and had crashed into the mountainside. Lindbergh rushed out to investigate. He studied the crash site and the wreckage as well as the reported weather conditions. Then he issued a dispassionate report, concluding that there had been no mechanical malfunction. He praised the pilot's record and TAT's policies, allowing nonetheless that the plane should not have been flying near a mountain during a storm. He theorized that the seasoned pilot was forced to do this in order to avoid the worst of the storm and announced that henceforth pilots would detour around storm areas or, if necessary, turn back to protect the lives of passengers. He closed with assurances that TAT's pilots were the best in the nation.[46]

In January 1929 Lindbergh took on the additional position of technical adviser to Pan Am, another of the giants to come out of this era of airline mergers. Pan Am greatly benefited from the emerging policy that extended the U.S. air defense perimeter over Latin America. Shrewd, tough Juan Trippe, son of a rich New York investment banker, had been bitten by the aviation bug as a teenager. He served as a navy pilot in World War I and after graduating from Yale in 1920 pursued his dream with an unrelenting drive. Underneath his bland mien churned the ruthless creativity of a nineteenth-century robber baron. Ultimately he combined strong financial backing, excellent Washington contacts, and America's new emphasis on blocking foreign carriers like Scadta, into the hemisphere's dominant airline. Six feet tall, weighing almost two hundred pounds, he was once characterized by *Fortune* magazine as a "man with a hell of a lot of energy and an almost psychic grasp of the future." From a single franchise operating trimotor Fokkers between Key West and Havana, Trippe erected an air network covering Central America, the Caribbean, and eventually all of South America.[47]

With his clutch of excellent connections and bruising business style, Trippe coolly dispatched all competitors. Convinced of his ability to get things done, Washington made Pan Am its "chosen instrument" to lock foreign competitors out of Latin America. Early in 1928, for example, the State Department informed Ecuador and Peru that "certain American aeronautical interests, operating with the approval and encouragement of the United States Government," were laying the basis for carrying airmail and passengers along the "West Coast of South America," and asked that exclusive contracts be withheld from others.[48]

After Herbert Hoover took office, his postmaster general, Walter Folger Brown, took this a step further, handing Pan Am the gift of Latin America. When Thomas B. Doe, president of Eastern Air Transport, complained, Brown explained that "it did not seem the part of wisdom to invade each other's territory with competitive service." With Pan Am holding the rights to international service to Mexico, Central and South America, and the West Indies, Brown did not want others to impede its operations. Independents working these routes were frozen out of mail contracts, even when they offered lower bids. And, because the U.S. government was "in partnership" with Pan Am, Brown thought it only natural for the government to advance Pan Am's business interests, larding the company's contracts with a slew of hidden subsidies disguised as high delivery fees. The carrier either crushed or absorbed every one of its competitors.[49]

On February 2, 1928, two days before his twenty-seventh birthday, Lindbergh went fishing on Belle Isle, Florida, and dined with President-elect Hoover, discussing aviation and trade with Latin America. A few weeks later Hoover devoted a section of his first State of the Union Address to the topic. The following year, in August, Lindbergh joined the president and others from the aviation community at Hoover's summer camp in the Blue Ridge Mountains to lay plans for government stimulus to air development. Perched high above reproach, Lindbergh was rarely criticized for conflict of interest, despite the fact that he collected checks from Pan Am, TAT, and the aviation industry while advising the administration on policies that strongly affected his clients.[50]

As he did for TAT, Lindbergh would inaugurate Pan Am's new routes. In July 1929 he piloted a Sikorsky airship from Miami to Cuba, then, hugging the coastline, stopped off in Belize. From there he hopped over jungle woods to Honduras and proceeded for two thousand miles to Nicaragua, Costa Rica, and the Panama Canal Zone, where he launched Pan Am's South America service, setting, in the words of the *Christian Science Monitor,* "fresh pinions to the Monroe Doctrine." Later in the year he opened the 4,500-mile airmail route to Rio de Janeiro and Buenos Aires to enthusiastic welcome.[51]

But Pan Am had greater ambitions than simply monopolizing Latin American skies. It looked to expand into transoceanic service to Europe and Lindbergh made the Caribbean into Pan Am's laboratory for perfecting over-water flights. He surveyed new territories, laid out air routes, and mapped future projects. "We had to decide as we went along," Trippe later recounted, and Lindbergh "encouraged others to look beyond what was possible." Convinced that "flying boats" provided maximum flexibility for expanding in unforeseen directions— amphibious planes allowed the airlines to add new routes "almost overnight, wherever harbors or sheltered water exists"—Lindbergh helped test and perfect America's first four-engine amphibian, the Sikorsky S-40, which became the workhorse of Pan Am's fleet.[52]

In Lindbergh Trippe had found a kindred spirit who shared Pan Am's ambition to carry "the American flag all around the world." Lindbergh met with foreign officials on the company's behalf and boosted the airline on his many trips to the Gulf and Caribbean. At Trippe's behest he also lobbied Congress to support policies critical to the airline's expansion. (Trippe would send drafts of letters for him to send to Congress, cautioning that none must be traced to Pan Am.) Years later when Trippe credited Lindbergh with laying the foundation for international air service over the oceans, he recalled admiringly how Lindbergh brought an intuitive genius to planning a route, factoring in large issues such as foreign trade, diplomacy, and security in addition to strictly aeronautical considerations. Trippe brought Lindbergh into virtually every important decision involving Pan Am's flight operations.[53]

When Pan Am first entered the Latin American air competition, seven different European concerns were running airlines in the region. By 1930 Pan Am dominated its 19,000-mile territory. In September of that year when Pan Am merged with the New York, Rio, and Buenos Aires line to form the largest air transport company in the world Lindbergh cheered the creation of a new air giant.

He continued to draw fawning press attention and huge crowds wherever he went. One New York editor, tired of reporting about perfect landings, on-time arrivals, and wildly enthusiastic crowds—and frustrated by Lindbergh's unwillingness to reveal even a bit of his private life—ordered correspondents to hold off on any more Lindbergh news "unless he crashes."[54]

Then even this editor had to take back his words. On returning from one of his South American jaunts in February 1929, Lindbergh joined a search for two downed fliers. He discussed the mission with reporters, who insisted that they wanted to know about something other than airlines, airmail, and airports. They wanted to hear from him regarding the rumors that he had become engaged to Miss Anne Morrow, the daughter of the U.S. ambassador to Mexico. He brushed aside their questions as irrelevant to aviation. Nonetheless one thing seemed clear: the linear Lindbergh story—of the Lone Eagle, the daring unaccompanied boy, his airplane, and aviation—was turning a corner.[55]

"WE" NOW A TRIO

A METICULOUS AND VERY PRIVATE MAN, Lindbergh approached projects in a manner that bordered on the obsessive. While growing up he would impose discipline and order within a dysfunctional family environment through his taxonomies on rocks, stamps, butterflies, and coins. Shuttled from Minnesota to Washington, Detroit, and California as a child, he formed few close friendships and learned to occupy himself without being dependent on others. His closest relationship was with his dog, and in his twenties with his beloved *Spirit of St Louis*. Lists were his support system. Once he decided on his Paris flight he compiled multiple lists and proceeded methodically to carry out the prescriptions. Once he was in the air he relied on his regimen of recording vital statistics every hour to keep focused.[1]

As we've seen, his life was transformed after Paris—he had in fact become the world's most popular and famous human being—but he remained quite alone. Even with his close associates there remained a reserve, a distant formality. Fame created a real barrier between him and his buddies from the army and barnstorming days. And those who had taken a strong interest in his welfare, such as Harry Guggenheim, Henry Breckinridge, and Dwight Morrow, were respected advisers rather than friends. For a time after Paris his St. Louis backers traveled with him, providing advice and friendly assistance, but once he settled in New York these relationships weakened.

His stressful home life, made more difficult by his mother's suffocating embrace, had also left him emotionally withdrawn and ill at ease with women. Well into his twenties he had never asked a girl out. In college, he said, he had enough trouble with the courses; dealing with women would involve mastering new skills "to learn their language" and to learn to dance, and to take them out to eat and the theater. Riding his bike, he decided, was "a lot cheaper." Despite the best efforts of classmates and later Air Corps cadets and then flyboys on the barnstorming circuit to loosen him up, he refused to join the common prowl for good times, attributing his reticence to Darwin. Loose women and brothels, he was certain, impeded "evolutionary progress." Moreover chastity suited his work ethic, allowing him to save his energies for aviation.[2]

Nonetheless he was enough of a child of his times to think that he might someday marry and have a family of his own. Now at the age of twenty-six, with his other goals well achieved, he turned to what he called his "girl meeting project." Characteristically he employed the dispassionately clinical method that had served him so brilliantly before. Aiming to master matters of the heart by meticulous and systematic analysis, he began searching for someone he "could stay in love with" for a lifetime by "observing young women more carefully."[3]

But this, he soon learned, involved him in silly parlor games and frivolous talk about film actors, tennis, weddings, and fashions. He turned, therefore, to the empirical evidence derived from "breeding animals on [the] farm." Heredity was fundamental. To ignore the influence of family was blind fanaticism. So he compiled a new list, this one with desirable female qualities. He would look for "good health, good form, good sight and hearing." True, some of the girls he encountered were so skillfully painted and styled that it took much effort to penetrate the elaborate covers, but he absorbed a great deal by focusing on a woman's "hip line and the portion of her legs that showed beneath her skirt." What was best was if you could get them to go for a swim. His girl, he was certain, would come from the "Caucasian race," enjoy flying, exhibit "mental attractiveness," and reject dogmatic religion.[4]

Thus equipped, Lindbergh was ready for a mate. Celebrity brought him into contact with business and political leaders interested in aviation, and in their mansions he got to meet well-born daughters from families disposed to technological and economic leadership. Since "like tends to like," he was confident that in one of these families he would find a girl to marry. Several months into his girl-meeting project he met an intelligent, "blue-eyed, dark haired, extremely pretty" young lady from a rich family with an interest in aviation.[5]

During Lindbergh's mission to Mexico in the winter of 1927 Ambassador and Mrs. Dwight Morrow hosted him and his mother for the Christmas holidays. The Morrows' middle daughter, twenty-one-year-old Anne, came south to join her family during holiday break from Smith College, where she was majoring in literature. (There were two more daughters, Elizabeth, the eldest, and the youngest, Constance, as well as an only son, Dwight Jr.) Excited about rejoining her family for the holidays, she was more than a little resentful that the much-ballyhooed guest would be intruding on family time. She held out little hope that he might be interesting. Likely he was one of the modern American heroes, "a baseball player type," all dimwitted bluster and brawn, "not at all an 'intellectual.'" She was surprised when she actually met him; he was more boy than man, "tall, slim . . . very refined . . . very, very young and . . . terribly shy." He spoke nervously, in clipped sentences, and found it hard to carry a conversation, but he was "amazing." He took her breath away with his "personal magnetism." Her father, whom she admired, also "adored" the "beautiful boy."[6]

Anne was a star at Smith, a tart-tongued writer and a published poet able to put into words what others could only conjure in their thoughts. Nonetheless her encounter with Lindbergh left her awestruck and speechless. She so wanted to commit to words some part of the emotion she experienced, but she found herself "too moved—and too ashamed of [her] emotion": "I never felt so *completely* inarticulate." In the presence of this man the usually graceful Anne dropped spoons, bumped into people, and was reduced to stammering. The best she could do when he took the Morrow women for a plane ride over the embassy and across the mountains of Ixtaccihuatl was to pray that she remain conscious so that she would remember the "complete and intense experience" of being his passenger in the air. "I will not be happy," she recorded in her diary, "till it happens again."[7]

Long after he left to complete his tour of Central and South America she could not erase the enchantment. She began reading aviation magazines, pining for "the last of the gods." This "clear straight boy," as she put it, had pushed away all the "pseudo intellectuals, the sophisticates, the posers": "All my life, in fact my world—my little embroidery beribboned world is smashed." Of one thing she remained certain: that her infatuation was entirely unrequited. Still, she was grateful for the experience of learning that "there *is such a person* alive, *that there is such a life*," even if she would never see him again.[8]

Others thought that one of the three Morrow girls might be a good match for the tall aviator, but they had the older sister, Elizabeth, in mind. Elizabeth Morrow was the family beauty. She was outgoing, laughed easily, and had a warm, engaging personality. Brown-haired Anne was plainer looking and somewhat delicate. In an undergraduate poem she portrays a fragile childhood in which she felt small and afraid; grasses seemed to her as forbidding as forests. She had a winning smile but seldom displayed it, counting social intercourse a burden, perpetually afraid of giving affront or taking too much time. Men brought out the best in Elizabeth; they made Anne nervous.[9]

There was about her a certain melancholy as well. "I think one of us will die," she wrote in her diary, about the Morrow siblings. "It won't be me. It ought to be—I am the complete loss in our family. But the useless people never die."

Affronted by her parents' extravagance, she complained about the "waste" and "artificialities" that shaped life behind the "walled garden" created by their wealth and status. And though she referred to herself as "the youngest, shiest, most self conscious adolescent" who had ever lived she exuded an aura of intelligent curiosity and sensitivity that many found attractive.[10]

When she read in the press about a rumored Lindbergh romance with one of the Morrow girls, she was certain it was with her vivacious older sister, Elizabeth. "I don't think I can bear to face it," she wrote in her diary about another Lindbergh visit. "He will come. He will turn quite naturally to E., whom he likes and feels at ease with." She tortured herself with hopes that Lindbergh might like her, only to swat them away: "Fool, fool, fool," she reprimanded herself. Throughout the spring she steeled herself for disappointment, ceding the contest to her sister, describing her own world as "utterly worthless compared to the world of Elizabeth and Colonel Lindbergh—that world I cannot touch, those people I cannot be like."[11]

In fact Lindbergh found Anne's diffidence appealing. "I was deeply impressed with Anne the moment I saw her," he later recalled. After he returned from Latin America he found her occupying more of his thoughts and finally decided to ask her for a date. It took him three months to make the call. Only in October 1928, almost ten months after first meeting the "beautiful boy," did she return late one night to her New Jersey home to a message from her mother's secretary, Jo Graeme, that "Charles Augustus L." had called and was to call again in the morning. The next morning Graeme had to push the phone into Anne's unsteady hands as the caller awkwardly announced in a low voice, "This is . . . Lindbergh himself."[12]

He invited her to go flying with him. She was skeptical, suspecting that he had somehow gotten it in his head that he owed the Morrow girls a sky ride and was dutifully following through. She kept testing to see if he really meant it, giving him ample opportunity to back out before asking him to call back a week later. (Meanwhile she read as much as she could about aviation, certain that the date would be about him and his interests.) When Lindbergh called back she accepted, still certain that it was really Elizabeth he wanted to impress through her. "I'm not used to being treated like a spoonful of medicine that's got to be taken," she wrote to her younger sister, Con, before the date.[13]

By the end of their date her tone had turned softer. "He *really does* like us," she reported. Soon she was gushing about how flight allowed her to see "*beyond*" and about his vision that aviation would vault national barriers to inaugurate an era of peace, prosperity, and brotherhood. While on the subject of peace and brotherhood, he shared with her his technique for dealing with crowds that got too physical: "Just kick their shins—they don't know who's doing it." A couple of days later they went driving through Englewood's back roads, and by the end of the evening he mentioned marriage. Anne protested that he did not know her, and certainly in the sense of his Darwinian mate selection criteria she was right. Anne's immediate family had its share of imperfections, including mental illness, alcoholism, physical frailty, and other serious health issues. But they did have money, status, and power, and Anne's combination of spirit, education, and presence won him over. "Oh, I do know you," he retorted. His confidence reassured her. By the end of the night they shared a secret plan to marry.[14]

They were strikingly different: he an imposing figure of action, she a petite creature given to reflection. He did not read books, had flunked his college courses, and was a stranger to introspection; she wrote poems and probing letters and kept a diary. She liked to fantasize and weave words together for the beauty of their sound; for him words were tools, possessing no more allure than a hammer. He enjoyed coarse practical jokes; she delighted in subtle analysis of emotions and what lay behind them. She was far more able than he to capture the romance and exaltation, the drama and promise of his own celebrity. For him flight was an end in itself; for her it merged with the notion of an escape from the expectations of her station, the pressures of family, and especially her suffocating mother.[15]

Yet, in addition to overweening mothers, they also had much else in common. Both were shy, treasured privacy, and affected an elite scorn for common folk. They both idealized the simple life. And they both adored him. Her concern that he may never have read more than a magazine article melted away before the largeness of his personality and, despite his modest learning, his unshakeable certainties and absorption by aviation, she became helplessly intoxicated, adopting his interests, his views, and ultimately his life. "Colonel L. is the kindest man alive *and* approachable," she raved to Constance.[16]

They told no one of their engagement. Anne was leaving for Mexico and Lindbergh got an invitation to go hunting with an American military attaché in Coahuila, allowing him to follow her south in November. After a few days he made his way to Mexico City to stay with the Morrows at the embassy. They broke the news to her parents together. (He informed his mother, who was out of the country on a visiting teaching appointment in Constantinople, by wire. She wrote back congratulating him and thanking him: "[You are] too fine always in your attitude toward me for me to be even able to write about it.") Betty Morrow was stunned by the news. "I think I can never be surprised again," she scribbled that night, but to her daughter she exclaimed, "Anne, you'll have the sky!—the sky!" The Morrows had their doubts, and Anne was also far from certain about her decision. "He is utterly, utterly different from me," she said to her mother, but she was sure it would be "all right."[17]

They went riding, swimming, and picnicking amid the tropical blooms, and Anne was introduced to the hectoring horde that trailed them everywhere. He tried to lose them in traffic, once even taking a detour through a private lawn. Rumors flashed through the press that he was seeing one of the Morrow girls, often as not identifying her as Elizabeth (who was not even in Mexico). Friends batted down these rumors; one report quoted an aunt saying that "he'd have to give up flying" if he wanted to marry a Morrow. Other reporters questioned whether Lindy had room in his life for a woman besides his mother. As he prepared to leave Mexico he warned Anne never to say or write anything in a letter unless she wanted to see it in the papers. This clamp on her spontaneity she found "smothering": "I, to whom an experience was not finished until it was written or shared in conversation." Before he left he laid down a set of rules for the entire family: they must tell no one, not even their children, of the engagement. It was a foreshadowing of what life would be like with a reluctant global celebrity obsessed with privacy. Betty Morrow remained ambivalent, struggling with the notion that her daughter was not going to live the life they had imagined for her.[18]

Anne could be delightfully free-spirited, but she too wrestled with doubts and hesitation. Over the next few months Lindbergh's long absences, his preoccupations with his flying and aviation work, and her own family's ambivalence raised new qualms. Sensing this, he asked Anne again for her hand, and this time she took a while to think it through. She shared her thinking with a childhood friend and former suitor, Corliss Lamont, confiding in him that "apparently" she was going to marry Charles Lindbergh. This, she allowed, must strike him as "funny" in light of her oft-expressed desire for a "quiet life" and her belief that couples should have much in common. But after setting her mind against all he represented ("There he is—darn it all—the great Western strong-man-open-spaces type and a life of relentless action!") she told Lamont that she would marry Lindbergh. He need not bother to wish her happiness. "I don't expect to be happy," she wrote, "but it's gotten beyond that somehow. Wish me courage and strength and a sense of humor—I will need them all."[19]

In February Dwight Morrow released a message to the press, announcing the engagement from the U.S. Embassy in Mexico. Lindbergh was airborne at the time, and when he landed he refused to answer questions about his private life. Nevertheless the news captured the front pages, creating a sensation. Six Ziegfeld girls excitedly offered to serve as bridesmaids (doing little to still Betty Morrow's anxiety). Journalists trailed the couple through the streets, staked out the Morrow residences, and stalked them with long-range lenses. The more adventurous among the tabloid posse attempted to bribe servants to reveal inside stories and filch photos. Lindbergh simply froze out the more aggressive reporters, but Anne was terrified. With little of substance to report, the tabloids resorted to printing rumors, reporting that Lindbergh planned to settle down, curtail his flying, and take the aviation portfolio in the Hoover cabinet. But Anne knew that was not going to happen. He would not give up the sky for anyone. Directly after the announcement he disappeared to do some flying for TAT and she had to rely on news reports for information about his whereabouts.[20]

But when he returned he brought the excitement she craved. In March he took her on a flying picnic to Mexico City's outskirts. As they were heading back he noticed that the plane had lost a wheel. (A mechanic had neglected to bolt it in place.) Landing would be rough, and the borrowed plane had no safety belts. He circled the air strip for hours to drain the tanks of fuel, minimizing the possibility of explosion upon impact. Then, after padding Anne with seat cushions and instructing her to hold tight to the seat bottom, he brought the crippled craft down slowly on one side, steering the controls with one hand while gripping the cabin with the other. The plane skittered along like a bicycle on two wheels for about thirty yards, and as the axle dug into the ground the plane toppled over. Well cushioned, Anne escaped without harm; Lindbergh was badly banged up and dislocated a shoulder. Mexican patrols, ever solicitous of their visiting celebrity, confiscated press films of the mishap. The next day the couple was back in the air.[21]

Finally, more or less resigned, Betty Morrow ("A beautiful and thrilling life was ahead of them—if only the papers will let them alone," she wrote a friend) began plans for a large church wedding, as befit a socially prominent ambassador's daughter. She would invite the diplomatic corps, Dwight's former colleagues from the Morgan bank, and their many friends and relatives to this first wedding in the family. Charles would have none of it. He insisted that the ceremony must be small and private, with no announcements or formal invitations. Preparations were to proceed with one thought uppermost: to keep it from the press. To guard the secret, Anne's wedding dress was sewn by a local seamstress and her bouquet was picked from the garden. The Morrows were reduced to puzzling over whom to invite to the wedding in their newly constructed mansion, Next Day Hill, in Englewood.[22]

On Monday, May 27, the Morrows invited some friends and relatives over for bridge and lunch in honor of Betty's birthday. Charles flew in with his mother from New York. Late in the afternoon Mrs. Morrow summoned the guests to the living room and Reverend Dr. William Adams Brown strode to the front of the room. Only then did the twenty-two guests realize that Charles and Anne were about to be married. Reverend Brown performed a brief service, and the groom, dressed in a blue business suit, slipped a wedding ring on the bride's finger; the ring was made from gold nuggets that had been presented to him in Honduras. There were no photographs.[23]

Then Charles and Anne hurried upstairs to change and escape on their honeymoon. For weeks the press had laid siege to the Morrow residence, keeping it under round-the-clock surveillance, and Charles had put much thought into avoiding them. To thwart them, the couple hid in Henry Breckinridge's car. Anne later wrote, "I seem to remember lying down in the bottom of a car while passing the crowd of reporters at the gate." Then they switched into Lindbergh's own Franklin and rushed off to board a thirty-eight-foot Elco motor cruiser before the press knew anything. Meanwhile they had left a decoy plane at the airport in Rochester, New York, to further mislead any pursuers.[24]

The papers reported with grudging admiration that secrecy had been so strictly maintained that even the house servants had no clue. The press crew camped outside Next Day Hill first learned of the nuptials two hours after the couple had fled, via a single-sentence press release handed to them. In reviewing Anne's recollections of the day it is hard to escape the sense that the moment was robbed of its joy and grace. The furtiveness of the entire event had stripped it of any pleasure other than putting one over on the press.[25]

After two days on the water they were finally discovered. One persistent newsman pursued them in an airplane and demanded that they come out to pose for him. He had the pilot keep circling around them for seven hours, sending their craft rocking from the turbulence. That night they spent on a fishing bank, where the chopping waves sent the china smashing in the hold.[26]

For a long time Anne blamed the press for preventing them from building their relationship in private. But another of her notes hints at the larger issue. For the entire year after their honeymoon they had no home; they lived in hotels, planes, or other people's houses. Charles resisted domestication. "'We' Now a Trio," announced the press soon after the engagement.[27]

In the months that followed, that was exactly the case; it was Charles, his plane, and Anne. She became his sidekick. They crisscrossed the country regularly, laid out a transcontinental route, launched mail programs to Latin America, and flew over the oceans to test new planes and make new surveys. Wherever they went the great flier and his charming assistant attracted huge crowds and press attention, creating excitement and making high-altitude flight seem routine, helping dispel the lingering "wild birdman" image. Anne aimed to become more independent, but for a while she was willing to lean "on another's strength until [she] discovered [her] own."[28]

Insisting that "women are just as well-fitted to operate a plane as men," Charles molded her into his "devoted page," putting her thorough a rigorous training program. "Charles has been working me very hard this last week," she wrote her mother-in-law in Detroit, "flying every day out at the Aviation Country Club [in Hicksville, Long Island]. . . . Some good days, some bad days, some scoldings etc. You know the way it is." He was relentless and she would not let him down: "I remember going round and round the field alone in that plane, making one hideously bumpy landing after another." She was "infinitely relieved" just to hit the ground safely: "[But Charles] kept insisting that I go around again until I made a decent landing." Then he had one of the outstanding navigators, Harold Gatty, teach Anne aerial navigation. Gatty arrived every morning at ten; they worked until lunch, and then through most of the afternoon. He came back after dinner and they worked until late into the night. In her first year of marriage she learned to pilot and navigate a plane and to operate its communications equipment.[29]

In August Lindbergh joined the Navy High Hat Acrobatic Team at the national air races in Cleveland. There he placed an order with the Lockheed Company for a low-wing Sirius monoplane with tandem cockpit for $18,000. Then he and Anne flew west to survey TAT routes before speeding back to join President Hoover at the Rapidan River presidential retreat on the eastern slope of the Blue Ridge Mountains. In the year and a half following their wedding, Anne joined Charles for eight transcontinental surveys.[30]

On one of his flights between the United States and Central America Lindbergh caught sight of ancient-looking ruins deep in the jungles of Yucatan. After reporting these findings to archaeologists at the Smithsonian in Washington it occurred to him that airplanes provided a unique vantage point for studying archaeological sites and remote ruins. He developed a technique to help researchers locate temple and burial ruins from the air by flying close to the ground over flat terrain, sometimes no more than ten or twenty feet above the jungle canopy, looking for "bumps" that often hid age-old pyramids.[31]

In the summer of 1929, while flying cross-country to the TAT launch, he and Anne observed a complex of constructions in Arizona's Navaho Indian country. They were tucked away so high off the ground that researchers had no record of them. While Anne took the stick, circling around the site, Charles snapped hundreds of photos, capturing a bird's-eye views of these cliff dwellings. The photographs caused a sensation among researchers, pointing to fresh possibilities for mapping ancient sites from the sky.[32]

In the fall of 1929, after completing a seven-thousand-mile Caribbean survey accompanied by Juan and Betty Trippe, Charles and Anne flew the Trippes and a Carnegie Institute archaeology team to explore and photograph the Yucatan jungles. Searching for evidence of Mayan civilizations (described as sites upon which "no white man before had set eyes"), they located an early settlement. There followed front-page reports of their discovering four lost cities around Quintana Roo, deep in the Mexican jungle. Exploration from the air, one delighted expert declared, accomplished more in twenty-five hours than ground researchers could have completed in five years.[33]

Dr. Alfred Kidder, the renowned archaeologist who accompanied them, told reporters that at the Mayan ruin of Tulum they discovered the "only man in the world" who had never heard of Lindbergh. The team had met three chicle gatherers, and Kidder pointed to the tall pilot, saying in Spanish that this was Colonel Lindbergh. Two of the three recognized the name and exclaimed their pleasure, but the third did not. "Fool," one of the others called out, "that is . . . the man who flew around the world in one day." Archaeology experienced a temporary boom because of the attention, but within months came a perverse side effect of fame: the looting of several of the newly discovered ruins.[34]

As an old airmail pilot, Lindbergh was all too familiar with the price of progress. In September he took his young bride with him to search for a downed TAT trimotor that left no survivors. There were two more such tragedies within the next eighteen months, and it fell to Lindbergh as the face of the airline to report on each accident and proceed to reassure the public that aviation was fundamentally safe. On December 5 he joined the search for his old flying buddy Thomas Nelson, who had vanished on an airmail run during a severe storm. He was found dead. The crashes tore at Anne's heart: "Another hideous crash. I can't write any more now." But she was careful to reassure her concerned mother-in-law that "C." had a special knack for avoiding danger: "He is one of those rare people who do their best in an emergency."[35]

In the end her emotions did not matter. If she wanted to be part of Charles's life she needed to join him in the air. In October she claimed her pilot's license. Later that month they learned that she was pregnant. Despite Charles's resolve to cut back on their virtually nonstop travel, they continued to participate in various launches, surveys, and investigations. Homesick for her family, Anne wrote her sister, "When am I going to see you? When I feel better? But Charles has a lot of ideas for 'when I feel better.'"[36]

Early in January they flew to California in an open-cockpit Curtiss Falcon biplane for Charles to oversee the completion of the Sirius monoplane he had ordered. In California Anne took air-gliding lessons and qualified for her glider's license. Because of her condition they cut back on flying but still covered more than thirty thousand miles in less than a year. Flying open cockpits at high altitude and gliding off a mountaintop, she later reflected, were probably not the best activities for a pregnant woman. In fact she wrote that she was "frightened to death" by some of the exploits, but if she did not join Charles in the air she would have been alone most of the time. On the other hand, assuming responsibility for radio communications and navigation strengthened her confidence and sense of self-worth. "All this was liberating," she wrote.[37]

Once in a while she even stood up to her husband. From his days as a boy Lindbergh had delighted in practical jokes and adolescent horseplay that often turned on others' discomfort. He still reveled in the barracks humor from his days at flight school. He thought it was hilarious when he tipped over a canoe that Harry Guggenheim and Henry Breckinridge were paddling and sent both men into the water. On another occasion Anne and a friend of his sat in the back of a car together, reading a copy of the *Paris Herald,* while Charles drove. Turning around, he reached over the car seat and put a match to the paper, enjoying the scene when his wife and his friend began furiously beating the paper to put out the flames.[38]

One evening in California they joined a number of others for dinner at the Hollywood home of Jack Maddux, the chief of Maddux Airlines. Among the guests was Amelia Earhart, the first woman to fly the Atlantic and often referred to as "Lady Lindy." (Anne thought, "She is the most amazing person—just as tremendous as C., I think. It startles me how much alike they are in breadth.") But Earhart had little patience for Lindbergh's pranks and with much pleasure reported an incident to her husband, George Palmer Putnam (who himself had his fill of the hero, having published his book *We*). Charles was standing beside his wife, munching a tomato sandwich, when it struck him that it would be fun to tip his glass so that water dripped slowly onto Anne's blue silk dress. Anne waited a bit, hoping he would stop, but he was having too much fun irritating her. Finally she turned and flung a glass of buttermilk directly at him. Momentarily stunned, he broke out in a big guffaw.[39]

Anne became more comfortable with being in the public eye as well. When a picture of her appeared in the papers with her skirts windblown, she wrote offhandedly, "I suppose that means another thousand letters telling me that I *am* a flapper after all and that the youth of America . . . etc." The next time she wrote of her skirts being caught in the wind she added that it was to "delight from the movie men." Another time she warned her mother not to be shocked but, yes, she had gotten her hair bobbed.[40]

The Lockheed Sirius came out of the factory in April, and on the twentieth of the month they set a new speed record, flying from Glendale, California, to Roosevelt Field in New York in fourteen hours and forty-five minutes. Racing at up to 180 mph they shaved three hours off the previous record. Seven months pregnant, Anne was sickened by the gas exhaust fumes that leaked into the cockpit and was in constant pain for the last four hours of the trip.[41]

On June 22, 1930, Anne gave birth to a baby boy at her parents' home in Engle-wood, where the Morrows had set up a birthing room and nursery. He had the "unmistakable" Lindbergh cleft. Well before his birth Anne had written to Evan-geline Lindbergh to say that if it were a boy there was no question about what he'd be named: "That's been decided from the first: just *exactly* the same [Charles Augustus Lindbergh]."[42]

As headlines announced the "Eaglet's" birth and Charles began planning an overseas survey, Anne in particular became anxious about her baby's security. She wrote her sister that she feared for "emergency situations that arise out of pub-licity": "The house is rather unprotected. The baby sleeps outside. Unless he is watched every second, *anyone could walk in* and photograph him etc." She feared that this sounded silly but she must be careful, so many people behaved strangely. One woman had come to the door and said she had to see the baby—that it was a matter of life or death. And there were always photographers buzzing around, especially after the frequent rumors that the Lindberghs had crashed or disap-peared, anxious to get pictures of the "maybe orphan."[43]

For the first year of marriage they had lived out of suitcases in hotels, planes, and the homes of friends around the country, touching down at the Morrows' Next Day Hill when they came back east. It was comfortable enough at the Morrows' estate, with servants, butlers, and nannies, but the time had come for their own home. Lindbergh's office was in New York, but he hated the city's noise and the hounding of its crowds. They decided to build a home near the Morrows on a secluded 425-acre plot at the foot of the Sourland Mountains, about ten miles north of Princeton, close by the town of Hopewell. The property was accessible only through dense woods by dirt and gravel paths, yet close enough to New York, an hour away by train and two hours by car, and there was room for a generous airstrip. While Anne recuperated, Charles busied himself with plans for the house and chopped down trees as he waited for her to be strong enough to fly.[44]

She would have been happy to settle into a domestic routine and care for her baby. Instead, as she wrote her mother-in-law, "I jumped from bed into a plane, almost. As soon as I was well we started flying." But it was not a choice she made without apprehension: "My how I hate to leave that baby!"[45]

Lindbergh's Paris flight had signaled the promise of regular transatlantic travel, and his work with Pan Am was designed to prepare for that day. To move the process of devising a global aerial network along he planned another great expe-dition deep into Europe and Asia to carry out a comprehensive survey of global aviation. Still very much the pioneer, he also wanted to carve a polar path to the Far East. And he wanted Anne to join him to work the radio and help with the navigation. When he laid out the great circle to Paris he had sought the shortest route; it came at the price of treacherous winds, blinding fog, and frigid storms. He made the same choice again, charting a route by way of the Arctic. This route over unexplored space, was hours shorter than any other across the ocean, but it carried all the dangers of the unknown sky.[46]

He outfitted his Lockheed Sirius with a powerful 575 hp Wright Cyclone engine, large-capacity gas tanks, and pontoons so that they could land on the inland lakes and coastal waters in Alaska, Siberia, and the Japanese islands, where airfields did not exist. This time he had a radio installed, but he remained as obsessive as ever about cargo weight. Anne observed with bemused detachment as he devoted months to packing. He began with nine different lists, among them "Emergency Equipment for Forced Landing on Land," "Forced Landing at Sea," and "Emergency Parachute Jump." He would make separate piles in middle of the room topped with "Do not disturb" signs. Weeks went into arranging and rearranging these piles, pulling out items that did not make the final cut. For the two-month trip he held himself and Anne to sixteen pounds each for personal items not an ounce more. All the while he packed and repacked endlessly, weighing each item and thinking hard about its utility.[47]

"Lindbergh Once More Takes to the Air," the *New York Times* headlined on June 14. Aviation's "Guiding Hand" was again laying routes to the future. Planning for the tour dominated the front pages.[48] Long after his historic flight, in the midst of economic crisis and growing uncertainty on the international scene, the nation could still not get enough of its airborne hero, this time accompanied by his plucky copilot.

They took off at the end of July, touching down in such places as Moose Factory, Ontario; Churchill, Manitoba; and Baker Lake in the Northwest Territories. They camped with natives in Point Barrow, Alaska; secured permission to fly over Soviet Russia; visited Siberia's Karagin Island; and from there made their way to Petropavlovsk, the capital of Kamchatka. Over the fabled Northwest Passage they encountered storms and frost, typhoons and fog worse than anything he had seen on his flight to Paris. Anne later admitted that she dared not write candidly about the hazards and dangerous conditions, for fear of frightening her family and adversely affecting aviation. But she was also overwhelmed by the force and beauty of what she experienced, and she took pride in her work as radio operator and copilot, relieving Charles when he needed to rest.[49]

Despite growing tensions between the United States and Japan, their landing in Tokyo brought one of the greatest demonstrations ever in that city's history. Aviation retained its power to create transcendent heroes. The total air time from Washington was a daunting eighty-four hours and five minutes. Nonetheless Lindbergh promised that before long there would be regular passenger traffic between the two countries, and the newspapers reported this as gospel. The Lindberghs spent more than two weeks in Tokyo touring, celebrating, and taking in the sights. By now, months into the trip, Anne would have been happy to return to her baby and family, but no one was asking her, and Charles still planned to visit China, Africa, and South America.[50]

On September 19 they arrived in Nanking, China, and soon all other thoughts were swept away before the devastating spectacle they witnessed. The Yangtze River had flooded, displacing a vast population. "One dared not think how many lives had been lost," Anne wrote. Millions were left homeless, cut off from food and medicine. So overwhelming was the catastrophe that relief agencies had no idea of its true scope. The only vehicle capable of carrying out an air survey was the Lindbergh Sirius. After meeting with the president, Generalissimo Chiang Kai-shek, they canceled their itinerary and worked with the National Flood Relief Commission to map the flooded areas and provide relief. Anne did much of the piloting while Charles mapped the deluged territories. When they were joined by a Rockefeller Institute relief specialist, Anne gave up her seat and squeezed into the baggage area.[51]

In the walled city of Hinghwa they found flood victims marooned in the center of a large area, twenty-five miles from the nearest dry patch. Leaving Anne behind in Nanking and taking onboard two doctors, Charles loaded the Sirius with urgently needed vaccines, anti-plague serum, and medical supplies. As soon as he set the craft down amid flooded rice fields, famished families in rickety sampans came streaming toward them, hoping for some food. Soon hundreds followed, surrounding the plane, tearing at the parcels of medicine that they were convinced held food. Priceless antitoxins and serums were ripped open as more boats kept pressing in on them, sending the Sirius rocking on its pontoons. Lindbergh kept signaling for the frantic crowd to stand back, to no avail. Only after he drew a .38-caliber revolver and fired a shot into the air and then pointed it directly at the front of the surge did they back off. He pulled the two doctors back into the craft and hastened off, deciding that this was work best left to the military.[52]

The Lindberghs turned to less hazardous labors, sketching the hundreds of small villages that were submerged in the water. On October 2 in Hangkow as their Sirius was being lowered from an airplane carrier into the water it capsized. They struggled out of the damaged plane, and a lifeboat sped over to lift them to safety, but not before Anne, who had been careful to avoid drinking unboiled water throughout the trip, had swallowed a large amount of muddy Yangtze water. Just days later, as their plane was being readied for repair, they received word that Dwight Morrow had died suddenly in his sleep of a cerebral hemorrhage, at age fifty-eight. They decided to return home by ship and have the wounded Sirius sent back to Lockheed for repair.[53]

With Dwight Morrow's death, Lindbergh lost his closest adviser. In ways he only faintly understood, his father-in-law had not merely advised him about diplomacy and finances; he had helped mold his career in aviation. Yet ironically Lindbergh's marriage into the Morrow family led him to a new professional interest entirely apart from aviation and brought him into contact with a man whom Lindbergh later described as "the most stimulating mind I ever came to know well."[54]

Even before Morrow's death Charles had become involved with two visionaries, one in the field of rocket research and the other in the field of biology. Both of the men, Robert H. Goddard and Dr. Alexis Carrel, were unconventional, ridiculed by many of their contemporaries as eccentrics. Goddard's pioneering work on jet propulsion in the 1920s was dismissed as sci-fi fabulism, but Lindbergh took an interest in his experiments and became a strong supporter of his work. He connected Goddard with the Guggenheims, arranging for years of subsidies to support foundational research in rocket-powered flight. His relationship with Carrel was deeper and of a different character. Carrel's influence on Lindbergh came to be pervasive, displacing his ideology of aviation with an outlook that sought the kind of answers others found in religion, in a single integrated vision. Carrel became his mentor and the most important influence on his mature thinking.[55]

Lindbergh liked to maintain that it was a love of science and his curiosity about the universe that prodded him to tour the skies. He would describe his flights as "scientific experiments," tracing his attraction to aviation for its grand possibilities for remaking the world. Yet Lindbergh had also grown somewhat disillusioned by the hype, the air crashes, and the stock bubbles that appeared to be taking aviation in a direction he had never foreseen. Pure as his idea might have been, well intentioned and idealistic as the winged gospel may have seemed, it had become a vehicle for building large businesses, some of which had no interest in uniting the world and advancing goodwill. Some companies had rushed planes into the sky before they were sufficiently tested, endangering lives. So while he continued to fly and make tours, because the open sky continued to enchant him, he was ripe for something new.[56]

Since youth Lindbergh had had a practical interest in biology, though he never pursued a formal program of study. On the farm questions about life and the mechanical aspects of the body had intrigued him. Later, he became especially fascinated by a question that bordered on metaphysics: Did life have to end in death? If aviation had opened the sky, couldn't he do solid work in the lab to open the mysteries of life and death and perhaps immortality? "With science . . . at his disposal," Lindbergh wrote about twentieth-century man, "nothing seemed beyond his grasp."[57]

This was no passing caprice. As early as 1928 this interest led him "to reduce [his] activities in aviation" so that he could study science. Even with his obsession for keeping cabin weight down he took to carrying science texts with him on his flights, poring over them in his extra minutes and hours. He purchased a high-powered microscope and planned a full-scale biology laboratory for the house in Hopewell. In the interim he put together a library of essential texts in physics, chemistry, physiology, cytology, bacteriology, and related subjects that now fascinated him. Henry Breckinridge, a Princeton alumnus, arranged access for him to the university's libraries and science labs. Indeed, one of the reasons he chose to build at the foot of the Sourland Mountains was because of its proximity to Princeton University.[58]

He credited his marriage for transforming this inchoate interest in "life's mysteries" into practical reality, even if inadvertently. Anne's elder sister, Elizabeth, suffered from a heart condition related to childhood rheumatic fever. By now she had grown very weak, and to relieve pressure on her severely damaged heart, doctors prescribed a full year of bed rest. Discussing Elizabeth's condition with Dr. Paluel Flagg, the anesthesiologist who attended Anne during the birth of Charles Jr., Lindbergh inquired whether a deteriorating heart valve could be repaired or even replaced. Dr. Flagg told him that it was not possible to work on the heart without interrupting blood flow. This did not seem to Lindbergh to be an insuperable problem. Why was it not possible to circulate the blood by means of a "mechanical heart" while the heart was being repaired, he wanted to know? Dr. Flagg did not have an answer. He recommended that Lindbergh speak with Dr. Alexis Carrel, an eminent research surgeon and head of Rockefeller University's experimental surgery department. Carrel's specialty was cutting and suturing the tiniest of blood vessels. As a student in France he had once sewn five hundred ultrafine stitches onto a single sheet of cigarette paper. The clearly gifted Carrel had collected a Nobel Prize in 1912 at the age of thirty-nine, the first Nobel Prize awarded to an American scientist, for groundbreaking work in surgery and organ transplantation. Even today, writes David M. Friedman in his monograph, *The Immortalists: Charles Lindbergh, Dr. Alexis Carrel and Their Daring Quest to Live Forever*, his achievement is described as "second only to the discovery of anesthesia" in importance for the field of surgery.[59]

Flagg arranged a visit. Lindbergh came into an immense office where he found a bald, stolid figure, whose unusual look was magnified by a pince-nez. Lindbergh extended his hand. Carrel ignored the outstretched hand and instead rose up on his tiptoes and began closely examining Lindbergh's face, taking in its angles and form. A student of physiognomy, he was scanning the flier to discern his inner qualities from his facial characteristics. If he did not like what he saw on faces, he was known to simply walk away without a word. His examination completed, the doctor announced, "I am Alexis Carrel." He would be happy to be of help with Lindbergh's questions.[60]

Carrel listened to Lindbergh's queries and explained the biological complexities. Even if it were possible to stop the heart long enough to operate on it and to reroute the blood flow the pounding of a pump would damage the delicate red corpuscles that passed through the arterial system; moreover such a pump inevitably raised problems of clotting (brought into contact with foreign substances, the cells rapidly coagulated). And then there was the problem of infection. He himself had been working on these issues for close to two decades, trying to develop a device to keep organs alive with blood while avoiding infection. "Infection," Carrel confided with a sigh to Lindbergh, "always infection."[61]

Carrel was full of original approaches, arcane rituals, and novel experiments, searching for "life's limits and capabilities and to further its meanings." Like Henry Ford's Model T, his operating theater was entirely black. During surgery he wore a black gown and hood; the floor, walls and ceiling, the towels, cabinets, and storage cases, as well as the rubber mats that covered the surgical instruments (boiled for two hours to guarantee asepsis) were all black; so was the operating table. All others in the OR were similarly dressed, in Lindbergh's breathless rendering, "glid[ing] about spectrally" while light streamed in from a large skylight directly above the operating table. Carrel believed that black cut down glare and made it easier to see dust and other particles. Moreover, he thought that "too much light inhibits the brain." This explained much more than his choice of interior design: "Surely you've noticed that the world's great civilizations have formed far above the equator, where there is much less direct sunlight than in tropical regions."[62]

Carrel had not expected to do more than answer a few questions, but he was impressed with the flier's intelligent curiosity (and facial structure). He took Lindbergh around his lab, demonstrating the various experiments his team was carrying out. While Lindbergh was captivated by the work on tissue nutrients and various organ experiments he found the devices being used in the lab crudely engineered. He immediately saw possibilities for improvement. A better-designed pump, for example, might avoid some of the problems with infection. Carrel invited him to create a better one.[63]

Lindbergh was delighted. A hero before the world, he nonetheless wanted to do something more substantial than be a celebrity. He had been looking for an opportunity to "experiment with living material in a laboratory." Now he was invited into the inner sanctum of a world-class research lab, where "more than any other place in the world, perhaps as never before in history, man was achieving an understanding of life in its apparently essential earthly relationships to matter."[64]

The field of bioengineering was still in its infancy. Little systematic thought had gone into designing the flasks, tubes, and various devices used to carry out experiments. Lindbergh would bring his own metal tool box, with hammer, screwdrivers, saws, and assorted screws and nails for his work in the lab. He had always loved to tinker, and he had learned much from visits to his grandfather Land's workshop lab. Now he could devote himself to unraveling the mysteries of life alongside "a man who was a philosopher, a mystic and one of the greatest experimental surgeons in the world." Lindbergh signed on as Carrel's assistant. He replaced his aviation heroes with those of the laboratory, concentrating on biomedical engineering research for which his extraordinary focus, his eye for detail, and his talent for systematic experimentation well suited him.[65]

Carrel's lab had the aura of a scriptorium in a medieval monastery and Lindbergh made the lab at New York City's Rockefeller Institute his home. Contrasted with the frenzy that greeted him upon his flights, he was awestruck by the deliberate and silent way researchers moved about their work. He hated small talk with common people, but he was stimulated by the interchange with the elite Institute team, reveling in the shared experience of experimentation, losing himself in the arcana of lab science. He studied "every detail" of Carrel's experiments and then worked on making them more efficient.[66]

Lindbergh spent weeks sequestered at the lab, devoting much of the two-hour drive each way from New Jersey to thinking about perfecting a pump that would keep tissues alive while organ transplants were being carried out. He would often stare into his microscope well past midnight, watching cells reproduce and live outside their natural environments, to learn about "immortality" at the cellular level, even placing his own semen under the scope. Sometimes, lost in a project, he would not come home for several days. ("I'm sitting here with the dogs," Anne wrote her mother in March 1931, "while waiting for Charles long after supper. I suppose he's at the Rockefeller Institute.") If he could not make it into the city he would drive over to Princeton's labs to continue his work. He had earlier idealized aviation. Now he did the same with science. "In that room mortality was being analyzed in its ultimate physical form. Life sometimes merged with death so closely I could not tell them apart."[67]

Carrel had sought to replace diseased organs with transplanted ones but never solved the problem of rejection. He had turned instead to the notion of removing a diseased organ and repairing it, the key being to keep the organ alive by providing it with its critical nutrients and infusing it with blood. To do this he needed a mechanism what would circulate life-sustaining fluids through the organ's own arterial system. Patiently Lindbergh designed and tested countless versions of a glass pumping apparatus as he tried to solve a series of perplexing issues.[68]

How seriously these men believed they would succeed in these and other experiments to ultimately lengthen and even revive life is revealed in a question Carrel posed to his attorney. "What would be my responsibility if I bring people back to life?" the surgeon queried. The attorney had no idea what he was talking about. What the man in black wanted to know was whether, if he brought someone back to life, he would be responsible for feeding, caring and supporting him. Carrel was confident that once Lindbergh was successful with the perfusion pump he was working on they would be able to move from animal experiments to humans, removing, repairing, and then replacing diseased organs, bringing the day closer when man could achieve immortality.[69]

In 1935 Lindbergh finally perfected his perfusion pump, and in April Carrel used it to cultivate an entire organ in vitro, avoiding the dreaded infection that had doomed other such efforts. The perfusion technique proved valuable for transplantation medicine and other advanced surgical procedures. Carrel told *Time* magazine that the world thought of Lindbergh as a heroic pilot but that he was more than that. "He is a great savant," he declared. "Men who achieve such things are capable of accomplishments in all domains."[70]

It was high praise from a man Lindbergh esteemed above all others. Carrel filled a void left by the loss of Dwight Morrow and by Harry Guggenheim's 1929 departure to serve as U.S. ambassador to Cuba. Carrel formed with him an almost paternal bond. There was no one to whom Lindbergh listened more closely, no one whose thinking he more greatly respected than this surgeon's, whose mind, Lindbergh wrote, "flashed with the speed of light."[71]

Carrel, whom Anne described as a "terrific force, under control," was a member of a dining group that called themselves the Philosophers Club (he soon invited Lindbergh to join him at the sessions). With these colleagues he often shared his less conventional views. He offered theories regarding the dehumanizing effect of factory labor and the frightening implications of a new generation of educated white women choosing careers instead of raising children, thus contributing to the "decline of the white race." He suggested that the source of creativity came from "unassuaged" sexual energy. Democracy, he maintained, was "an error of the brain"; social welfare programs violated the evolutionary imperative by perpetuating the unfit; Americans were endangering their future by allowing the immigration of inferior peoples who threatened to overwhelm the superior Westerners. White nations, he warned, needed to protect their advanced heritage and genetic lineage. In fact his perfusion experiments, designed to ultimately lengthen the lives of people, were actually only for the right sort of people, those who were noble, fit, and white, and thus worthy of perpetuation.[72]

Carrel championed a program of survival of the fittest. He ran a mouse laboratory where he played at breeding a super mouse. The mice were encouraged to
fight among themselves to reveal which was fiercest in combat. Winners were
then used to impregnate females; losers were dissected. If he could do similar
experiments on humans, Carrel was certain, he could produce a man who jumped
twenty feet and lived to be two hundred. He supported eugenics and euthanasia,
declaring that man must rid himself of those sentiments that obstructed progress.
"Philosophical systems and sentimental prejudices" must not be permitted to
stand in the way.[73]

This witch's brew of science and metaphysics appealed to Lindbergh's notions
of order and holistic theory combined with privileged experience. He remembered the moment he entered the black-walled room in his own gown and hood:
"I felt outside the world men ordinarily lived in." The words are reminiscent of his
early delight at flying. With Carrel he felt he had "reached the frontier where the
mystical and the scientific meet, where [he] would see across the indistinct border separating life from death."[74]

As Lindbergh turned thirty his personal life was gradually moving away from
the public stage. He had always thought of courage in physical terms—taking
risks, pushing endurance, challenging the elements—but now he came to look
upon intellectual curiosity as heroic. Carrel had allowed his prodigious mind to
take him where others would not go and he followed its logic, regardless of the
consequences.

Back when he was still a surgical resident in Lyon in 1902 Carrel had accompanied a pilgrimage to the shrine at Lourdes, where a holy spring was said to bring
miraculous cures. He had treated a very sick woman on the train there, adminis-
tering some morphine, but with little hope that she would live more than a few
hours. Upon the return trip he was astounded to see her recovered. She had been
sprinkled with healing waters. He hesitated to call it a miracle, but when he
returned to Lyon he described the case as one that he could not explain medically.
Despite his fine record and the publication of his experimental work, Carrel was
subsequently turned down several times for a staff position at the Lyons medical
college and finally learned that he had been blackballed because of the controversy he had sparked. Catholics were appalled that he did not recognize the miracle, while the scientific community thought he had abandoned good science for
bad mysticism. Controversy followed him the rest of his life, but he shook off the
critics and continued to raise provocative questions.[75]

It was a lesson Lindbergh now took to heart. He himself had always had the gift
of a laser-like focus, albeit a very narrow one. Under Carrel's influence he began to
think more broadly about life and death, man and race. "[Carrel's fascination with]

the overlapping peripheries of mystical and scientific worlds," Lindbergh wrote, "corresponded with and intensified my own." Even more than in his early thinking about aviation, these "peripheries," he believed, contained real possibilities for a radically improved world. He had never lacked for confidence. Now with the ambit of his thinking growing wider and his mind hitched to Carrel's protean imagination, he became more assured about addressing larger issues. This would later emerge with his engagement in world politics and in his own search for "bridges between the physical and mystical." He became interested in telepathy and clairvoyance, even experimenting with suspended animation, never giving up the pursuit of immortality: "After my death, the molecules of my being will return to the earth and the sky. They came from the stars. I am of the stars," he wrote.[76]

When Lindbergh finally designed the pump that managed to fend off infection in a series of experiments, Carrel submitted an article describing this work to the journal *Science*. Lindbergh did not want his name on it, so it was published under the Institute's name. But he signed a subsequent article for the same journal. He was completing the fact-checking for the article when Charles Jr. was kidnapped.[77]

AS ONE GAINS FAME ONE LOSES LIFE

"IN THE SPRING OF '27," wrote F. Scott Fitzgerald describing Lindbergh's flight, "something bright . . . flashed across the sky." The *New York Times*—called the "old grey lady of the press" because of its contempt for fads and short-lived sensations—plastered his story across its entire front page, added a ghostwritten Lindbergh byline, and devoted five pages of its May 22 edition to his flight.[1]

Like the media's embrace, the public's fascination with Lindbergh was unprecedented. He had cured no deadly disease, uncovered no fresh continent or new physical law. He did not write a great novel or stir the American conscience with his eloquence. His flight across the Atlantic was essentially a test of endurance and piloting skill, part of a sporting competition that was very soon outdistanced. Yet it achieved a renown that is reserved for transporting moments of great symbolic power and monumental achievement.

This puzzle was of considerable interest to those engaged in what the historian Frederick Lewis Allen called "this idolization of Lindbergh." What placed Lindbergh so much above saints, presidents, and the greatest intellects of his time? How was it, for example, that in the shadow of Albert Einstein's shattering of Newtonian physics the *New York Evening World* proclaimed Lindbergh's Paris flight to be "the greatest feat of a solitary man in the history of the human race"?[2]

Allen suggested that in a moment when the past was being debunked and the present revealed as sordid, when comforting myths were being stripped away and long-standing idols deemed counterfeit, people were starved for something uplifting, pure, and uncomplicated. To a nation surfeited with faux heroes Lindbergh's simple courage proved riveting, and the massive celebrations to which it gave rise revealed a deep and nearly universal thirst for transcendence.[3]

Allen's reading of Lindbergh's celebrity offers a starting point, but it overlooks the role of the media in this process, and it oversimplifies the complex reaction of the American public. It also says nothing about Lindbergh's own complicity with the star-making mechanics behind his sustained fame, even as he fought to avoid being drawn into a celebrity vortex with ultimately tragic consequences.

In 1839–40 Thomas Carlyle delivered a series of lectures, later published as the book *Heroes, Hero-Worship and the Heroic in History*. He examined such figures as Odin, Mohammed, Shakespeare, Luther, Rousseau, and Napoleon, the hero as divinity, prophet, poet, priest, man of letters, and emperor. But the turn of the twentieth century, the eminent editor William Allen White proclaimed, brought "tremendous change" and recast "the mold in which heroes were made." Twentieth-century America chose different icons—not gods, kings, or poets but grittier heroes responsible for their own success.[4]

The popular press helped advance this conceit by adopting a human interest approach to news reporting. Joseph Pulitzer in particular had his papers communicate complex political, economic, and diplomatic news by means of stories built around individuals, whether elected officials, business moguls, or statesmen. "Please impress upon the men who write our interviews with prominent men," Pulitzer commanded, "the importance of giving a striking, vivid, pen sketch of the subject; also a vivid picture of the domestic environment, his wife, his children, his animal pets, etc. Those are things that will bring him more closely home to the average reader."[5]

The new staple—the "celebrity profile"—favored dramatic portrayals of the personalities behind the headlines, emphasizing personality over character or achievement. When Pulitzer's *New York World* profiled the chief prelate of the Roman Catholic Church in America, it focused on his daily life and peculiar habits. Readers lapped up features about the unknown lives of the famous whose renown, as with the gilded habitués of café society and the new constellation of Hollywood stars, increasingly rested less on outstanding achievement than on heavily promoted "glamour." Not coincidentally, behind the construction of 1920s celebrity often stood a well-financed publicity machine that worked the levers and cued the spotlights.[6]

An individual did not have to make the world better to win press attention. He could also hit mammoth home runs or sit atop a flagpole or dance for twenty-six hours straight. Success came in many guises. Less than enduring significance, the test was whether the story line would intrigue the common reader. The flagpole squatter might not alter the fate of the nation, but Alvin "Shipwreck" Kelly, who skipped from town to town perching atop tall masts to "demonstrate the hardiness of the American posterior," attracted ever larger crowds.[7]

In some ways, therefore, Lindbergh represented a throwback. His sudden fame was spontaneous and unplanned. All his backers hoped to achieve in supporting his flight was to win a place for St. Louis in the unfolding Aviation Age. He himself seemed initially genuinely uninterested in exploiting his fame, holding himself aloof from crowds and intrusions into his private life and turning down astounding sums for assorted endorsement deals. Bruno and Blythe, the public relations team that represented him briefly, was charged with keeping reporters away, not attracting them. His fame was largely sustained by his character.

Many assumed that soon after the celebrations of his flight the euphoria would die down, leaving the young man with fond memories and bitter disappointments. Yet over the succeeding months and years—amid disasters and international tensions, the exploits of Al Capone, and, perhaps most of all, economic crises—Lindbergh remained the lead story. Years after the flight he continued to command the front pages. "In Lindbergh's case, more than in any other," observed the *New York World*, "the full glare of the modern publicity machine with all its blinding light has been suddenly thrown on a single individual. To have attracted and caught this light is another of Lindbergh's records."[8]

It helped that the flight followed a prolonged series of failed attempts and carried all the excitement of an international competition. Moreover the story could be summarized in captivating photographs, beginning with the seemingly tiny *Spirit of St. Louis* taking off from Roosevelt Field in the early morning and landing thirty-three hours later in Paris. The flight and celebration fit the public's attention span, long enough to be record-breaking and yet contained within a two-day news cycle. The fact that at its center was not your average hard-drinking, womanizing, death-defying aeronaut, but an impossibly photogenic man with a doting mother made it irresistible.[9]

Lindbergh's feat refracted the moment. "He has chosen to achieve an aim the whole world can understand and admire," explained one journalist. "Every era has its alleged evangel." In the Middle Ages men built cathedrals. Reformers analyzed the Bible. "Our faith," the writer continued, "is locomotion." Lindbergh was "our Elijah." Not only could he "ascend to heaven in a chariot of fire," but he returned back to earth.[10]

With attention kindled by a series of extraordinary spectacles of welcome, the likes of which had not been seen before, the press flocked to the feel-good story of the decade: the daring small-town boy with the cowlick who beat the well-funded professionals and foreign aces with his small engine that could, all alone. The first broad strokes, presenting Lindbergh as the courageous young hero with perfect manners, modest disposition, and unfailing courtesy, captured a vast audience. His discomfort at the celebrity treatment, his rejection of artifice and seeming eagerness to resume normal life all added to the conviction that he represented the best of yeoman America.

The adulation of Paris introduced a new dimension. The corrosive effect of fame was one of the pervasive themes of celebrity narratives. Would he allow his head to become swelled by the praise, the money, and the women throwing themselves at him? Would he convert his fame into a career on the silver screen or choose to live off endorsing products and speaking for large fees, joining the vast roster of one-week saints? Or would he hold true to his vision for aviation? Would he uphold the great moral investment Americans made in his story?[11]

The story had yet more layers. In an age when America was losing its young farmers to the exciting cities, Lindbergh filled the desire for heroes built from common country stock. To a nation experiencing divisive bouts over monopolies, prohibition, Darwin, and immigration, this modest son of old America, who had tinkered in the solitude of frontier woods, affirmed heartland values of self-reliance and independence. To those who feared that the new urban industrial order was promoting regimentation, threatening to grind down individualism and creativity in favor of bland, corporate orthodoxy, Lindbergh offered eloquent reproach. He reminded the nation, in the historian Leo Braudy's words, that "nineteenth-century America was not dead," that it could thrive even in the new technological age. Standing in America's traditional past he embodied its future.[12]

By the time of the Paris flight the prosperity era was in high gear. The grim atmosphere of war and its after-years in quest of normalcy had made way for the pursuit of wealth, pleasure, pastimes, and intoxicants. "A young Minnesotan who seemed to have nothing to do with his generation did a heroic thing, and for a moment people set down their glasses in country clubs and speakeasies and thought their old best dreams," wrote F. Scott Fitzgerald, himself a Minnesotan. "Above any man of our times," ran an editorial in the *New York Times*, "Colonel Lindbergh has done more to put healthy ambitions, and the traditions of courage and fine development, into the minds of boys."[13]

There was indeed fairly widespread anxiety that the culture of excess was corrupting children. Were they turning soft, abandoning the stiffening discipline of tough tasks accomplished against high odds for the "forced gaiety" of the Jazz Age? The age-old revolt against parental authority proved even more disquieting in this era of automobiles, speakeasies, Freud, flappers, jazz, and religious skepticism.[14]

It was no coincidence that the countless profiles of Lindbergh usually made a point of his never having dated, danced, or been arrested for drunken and disorderly behavior; he did not smoke, he honored his mother, and he poured his healthy energies into work. "No parent can look at him or his picture and not feel a glow of pride and affection," read one letter to the editor of the *New York Times*, "and who doesn't think of his mother, 'blessed art thou amongst women?'" The sentiment was echoed nearly everywhere—by Army Chief of Staff General Charles Summerall before a graduating class of West Point cadets, by Senator William Borah, and by Fifth Avenue Presbyterian's Reverend D. Minot Morgan. This generation needed to aspire to more than a life of empty riches and "necking and drinking parties," the Reverend Dr. Christian Reisner warned. "If the flapper type is to be our model we cannot produce Lindberghs to startle, thrill, awaken, inspire and lead the world on to better things."[15]

"Better things" than (he could easily have meant) Babe Ruth, who matched his astounding feats on the diamond with an awesome passion for food, gambling, and brothel hopping. In the Lindbergh narrative duty trumped pleasure, rural uprightness held fast before urban lassitude, ambitious effort and hard work came before luxuries and leisure. Made cynical by the puffery and inauthenticity of the celebrities they covered, journalists themselves were enchanted by Lindbergh. *Time* magazine, initiating a feature that would become its hallmark, named him Man of the Year for 1927.[16]

The spotlight on Lindbergh was brighter than anyone—celebrity or otherwise—had ever experienced before. He stepped into the glare of world attention with believable humility and grace but entirely unprepared for the loss of independence that came with his new role. Following his landing in Paris, the U.S. Embassy took over his schedule; the president commanded his early return to the States; the press commandeered his story and his byline was slapped over someone else's prose. To the intensely private Lindbergh was cleaved a public figure who right from the beginning was projected as America personified. "[He is] *ours*," declared the *New Republic*, "no longer permitted to be himself. . . . He is the United States."[17]

To be sure, he was far from innocent about publicity. He himself had courted press attention and had always wanted as part of his project to increase his "personal influence and earning capacity." After the flight he found it "exhilarating" to land on the front pages of America's greatest newspapers. And though he was never able to make peace with the notion that those who write the story control it, his career choices openly traded on his fame. If municipal airports were to be built, modern air laws enacted, and postal airmail to continue to serve as the feeding cow for the developing air travel industry, aviation needed public support and he was prepared to use his fame to accomplish this.[18]

Lindbergh's national publicity tour owed much to the structure and intent of a political campaign. Its carefully choreographed spectacles, replete with vast motorcades, huge public assemblies, and processions of notables, stirred national support for aviation. They also carried him to the next level of significance, making him the face of modern aviation. It became difficult even in his own mind to sort out what was mercenary and what was earnest.[19]

Meanwhile, writes the cultural historian Charles L. Ponce De Leon, the local press capitalized on Lindbergh's visits to promote "middle-brow WASP values." Here was a hero for the immigrant and the native, the young and their anxious middle-aged parents. A Cincinnati newspaper, ignoring the crowds of keening teenagers at the Lindbergh reception, focused on a group of solemn matrons in the crowd. Declared one of the gray-haired ladies, "I have experienced most of the thrills of life. I just did not think there was another kick I could get." But the sight of Lindbergh overwhelmed her. Providence had "raised him up at the time when America needs just such a boy to show the world what a boy can be and can do."[20]

Identification is a critical element of hero worship, and in Lindbergh's case this identification was amplified by his apparent lack of affect. There was a kind of endless and fillable void to his personality. Honest, stoical, hard-working, inquisitive, and inventive about some matters, he was utterly accepting and incurious about others. If he did or said nothing surprising he did not disappoint. "He looked like his pictures!" exulted the writer of one article. No one seemed disillusioned that the flesh-and-blood reality seemed scarcely more animated than the Benday image of his face and the Vitaphone recording of his voice. Indeed his very diffidence worked in his favor and helped the press fashion his great popularity.[21]

But within weeks the buoyant joy of his first days in Paris was replaced by an aloof, almost sullen demeanor. At times he appeared more dutiful than happy. The journalist Alva Johnson noticed it quite early: "Once in the air Colonel Lindbergh abandoned the solemn deportment which has marked him on the land. . . . Only in the air did he feel 'at home.'" In Los Angeles more than sixty thousand people turned out in tribute, but an editorial noted that he didn't smile once. So grave was his manner that when he did crack a smile the crowd chorused "Lindy's smiling."[22]

He had grown up in a place where good people avoided the spotlight, and he made a show of ignoring the cheers of the crowd. He could not abide popular ditties like "Lucky Lindy," which bands insisted on playing when he came on stage. He wanted dignity, not cheap lyrics. When a little girl broke through the protective line to shake his hand, he looked at her severely. "No shaking hands," he snapped. He hated the promiscuous use of his identity and the sweaty, adulatory contact of fame. He once told Harold Nicolson that he could not stand the false intimacies of celebrity, the "silly women who bring their kids up to shake hands with me at the railway stations."[23]

Although he needed and wanted the press, he especially resented the intrusive questions that came with its attention. "Is it true, Colonel," one reporter demanded, "that girls don't interest you at all?" Though he insisted on talking about aviation, they refused to be deterred. What color eyes did he like? What were his hobbies? Did he prefer blondes or brunettes, and did he like to dance? It did not help that he had a thin skin and an almost Victorian sense of propriety, taking umbrage at slights both real and imagined. The smallest inaccuracy made him seethe. As for his duty to the inquiring press, he recognized none. Contacts with the press became increasingly distasteful to him. "I felt that interviews and photographs tended to confuse and cheapen life, especially those printed in the 'tabloid' papers," he later wrote. He failed to appreciate the degree to which he had already surrendered custody of his story when he undertook to trade fame for publicity. "I can't stand it," he told one sympathetic reporter. "I am going to quit.[24]

The *Times*'s Russell Owen was one of a small fraternity of newsmen whom Lindbergh actually liked and trusted. In a day with different journalistic boundaries, Owen even accepted a generous check from Lindbergh for helping the aviator write his dispatches from Latin America, while he continued to publish glowing columns about his friend. Owen's *New York Times* colleague Deak Lyman was another good friend. So was the *New York Times* itself, which paid Lindbergh handsomely for his bylined features, provided him with behind-the-scenes advice, and continued to lavish him with flattering front-page exposure for many years after his flight.[25]

The tabloids were another matter, and he made them aware of it. At first the tabloids hesitated from diverging from the hero storyline. Those who did dare to hint at darker shadows received vituperative letters and canceled subscriptions from their readers. Some in the press grumbled that it was not so much his refusal to cooperate that rankled as the fact that he was forcing *them* to cooperate with him, to tell his story on his terms, broadcasting his aviation message while staying away from his personal life, at the same time that he dismissed them as rumormongers.[26]

But the arc of tabloid celebrity caught up with Lindbergh. His fame reached a point where the picture was too good to be true. As John Gregory explained in the journal *Outlook*, "After all there is only so much that can be said for the flawless, while imperfection offers an infinite variety of possibilities." After countless "graceful takeoffs," "perfect landings" "enthusiastic crowds," "modest speeches," and extraordinary welcomes, some papers demanded gamier stuff from their reporters.[27]

Gradually some reporters gingerly began taking potshots, about his having gone "high hat," referring to his standoffishness and arrogance, then about his "violent temper." Initially it was the newsreels that did much of the damage, capturing his glowering looks and evident impatience with the thousands who lined up to see him.[28]

His engagement to Anne Morrow opened a new path for the tabloids. At their first public appearance after the honeymoon Anne and Charles completed a flight demonstration at Mitchell Field on Long Island as part of the Guggenheim project for demonstrating air reliability. As reporters gathered around, one shouted, "Is it true that Mrs. Lindbergh is pregnant?" Lindbergh flushed with anger.[29]

For Anne, whose sheltered existence as the daughter of an international banker and ambassador had been lived behind tall walls, this "blaze of a naked stage" was particularly painful. Five months after the wedding Anne wrote her mother that they were trying to protect themselves from the crowds and press, but their strategy may not work: "At least we will have done our best to live in the United States and will have to try somewhere else." The hounding and relentless scrutiny made Anne intensely unhappy. She could not walk down a street or go to an art gallery without being harassed. Editors offered servants inside the Morrow home thousands to steal photos and snoop into telegrams. One Hearst tabloid tried to bribe a workman to pilfer a collection of Anne's letters. Both Charles and Anne were forced to write in code for fear of having their correspondence leaked. He would don a fake moustache and slick back his hair if they wanted to take in a play. "We never catch people or life unawares," Anne complained. When it came time for her to give birth she refused to go to a hospital, where she would be on display. Charles Jr. was delivered at home.[30]

It became a contest between the Lindberghs and the journalists. He withheld information while they did their best to ferret it out. For their safety and comfort the Lindberghs went out of their way to build a home in a secluded area, hidden from curiosity seekers and cranks. Under the heading "The Lone Eagle Builds a Nest" the *New York Sunday Mirror* published a photograph of the construction site near Hopewell along with detailed floor plans. Other photos showed their temporary residence, guiding the curious and deranged to their door.[31]

So strained did relations become with the press that when their baby was born on June 22, 1930, Lindbergh imposed a blackout on any information. The tabloids, denied access to real news, printed sensational rumors about Anne's mental state and the baby's health, suggesting that he was deformed or deaf from the din caused by airplane engines while Anne was flying. It took all of Dwight Morrow's diplomatic skills to persuade his son-in-law to issue a terse statement about the baby's birth. But Lindbergh allowed no photographs and the news blackout led to even more unfounded horror stories. At last, after first barring five newspapers, including three Hearst publications for their "contemptible" rumormongering, Lindbergh released a single photo that he himself had taken, hoping this would quell the frenzy and keep photographers away from Anne and the baby. A week later he announced that he was finished dealing with the tabloids.[32]

Others suggested to him that instead of trying to outwit the press or duck away he arrive at an agreement about boundaries. He tried, but the deal quickly broke down. Yet, as C. P. Snow observed about Albert Einstein, when the physicist lamented the intrusions on his privacy, it is not impossible to avoid publicity: "If you do not want it you do not get it." Lindbergh did want to stir the American imagination on behalf of aviation and to marry an ambassador's daughter and to enjoy open access to the world's great cities, but he wanted these gifts without the cost. Leo Braudy calls attention to a more serious lacuna: "In nothing that he writes is there the barest indication of any awareness that his fate was other than deserved and that attacks on his later actions and politics were motivated by anything but envy of his natural gifts."[33]

In 1930 the fresh and iconoclastic *New Yorker* magazine ran a piece that asked what all the fuss was about. Lindbergh had been a reckless barnstormer doing stunts for a living just a year before his flight. Yes, he turned down lucrative endorsements and entertainment deals, but through royalties, consulting fees, and stock shares in the new airlines he had become quite comfortable. He had planned shrewdly and capitalized on his fame and become an elitist who was often rude and contemptuous of his adoring fans. For all his youth, he was a humorless, arrogant, and crotchety fellow, "astonishingly uninteresting, grim with a Scandinavian grimness." He was no model for normal boys.[34]

The author of the piece, Morris Markey, a former tabloid writer, reserved the strongest criticism for Lindbergh's program for aviation:

> They say he is responsible for the growth of the aviation industry in America. He is. Yet that growth is about as unhealthy as it could very well be. His Atlantic flight and all his subsequent adventures roused a terrific popular interest in aviation—but practically no interest in airplane riding. The bankers failed to make this distinction and the result is an industry perilously overdeveloped. For all the excitement and the headlines and the haste to invest in aviation stocks, there are less than twelve thousand airplanes in the country—including the hundreds of military and naval planes. A ridiculously small number of people ride the regular transport lines. Only a small fraction of the population has ever been in a flying machine.[35]

The *New Yorker* piece marked a turning point precisely because it reflected the new Depression-era mood. After the bust in aviation equities and the meltdown of the stock market Americans were more skeptical about the agenda that Lindbergh had pushed so relentlessly. What Markey suggested was that stripped of the aura of boom-time America, Lindbergh was a stunt showman sprinkled with fairy dust who complained an awful lot: "He spends his life creating sensations and protests bitterly that the sensations he provokes make life miserable for him."[36]

So here was the irony. Lindbergh had achieved amazing success and wide credibility. Millions followed the unfolding narrative of his life, thrilling at his exploits, taking as gospel his pitch about air travel. They avidly followed his diplomacy, rejoiced in his marriage, and delighted in the birth of his son. An appreciative nation was prepared to offer him any office he wanted, including the highest—even Markey agreed that he could have the presidency for the asking—yet he often complained about the "staggering price of fame."[37]

That price became unbearable when his son was kidnapped. Charles was too cold and austere to be a doting father, but, in the words of one biographer, he "admired the child's good health." Life had rewarded his toughness and discipline and (like his father before him) he was an advocate of rugged nurture, hoping to harden Charles Jr. through exercises of nerve and discipline. To keep the baby from sucking his thumb at night he devised metal thumb guards. Years later the child's nanny would recall that there was a "little bit of sadism" in Lindbergh. When his mother-in-law heard a splash coming from the bathroom followed by the baby's howl she was certain that Lindbergh was "ducking the baby under water to build his courage." Lindbergh once explained to Lady Vita Sackville-West that the world was a brutal place and children had to learn to take care of themselves. One day in the winter he built a large chicken-wire enclosure on his property and ordered the nanny to place young Charles Jr., not yet eighteen months old, into it with a toy and leave him there to "fend for himself." The child was left crying for hours, but when the nanny went to ask Mrs. Lindbergh to rescue the toddler, Anne, close to tears herself, said simply, "There is nothing we can do."[38]

In late February the Lindberghs, who spent much of their time in the Morrow residence now that Anne's sister Elizabeth was gravely ill and her mother widowed, decided to return to their home in Hopewell, where they had not been for weeks. They arrived there late on Saturday afternoon, February 27, 1932. Charles and Anne were dining downstairs on Tuesday night, March 1, when they were summoned by the nurse in a panic. Baby Charles's bed was empty. Lindbergh ran up the stairs, looked into the child's room, and quickly realized that the baby had been taken from his crib. "Anne," he said to his shaken wife, "they have stolen our baby." He later wrote, "I looked at the crib. It was empty. I ran downstairs, grabbed my rifle and ran out into the night."[39]

The case drew unprecedented attention and resources. J. Edgar Hoover had the FBI reach out to underworld sources. President Herbert Hoover committed the resources of the federal government, and the governors of both New Jersey and New York assembled their forces as well. Within twenty-four hours an estimated 100,000 individuals had mobilized to carry out a nationwide dragnet. A bank clerk from Trenton driving home from the west was stopped and pulled over 107 times because his car had New Jersey plates. The Boy Scouts, labor unions, and women's groups all sent their members out to hunt for a child matching the Lindbergh baby's description. World leaders joined tens of thousands of individuals wiring wishes for a safe return. Clergy of all denominations led prayer services.[40]

Two underworld figures combed criminal circles, only to conclude, "This one was pulled by an independent." Al Capone, about to begin a prison term for tax evasion, offered $10,000 for useful information. Others tried to contact the kidnapper, at one point placing an ad in a Bronx newspaper pledging immunity if the child was returned unharmed. In Madison Square Garden they stopped a boxing match and asked everyone to stand for three minutes and pray for the safe return of the baby. Five years before they had done the same thing to pray for a safe landing in Paris. In four weeks the Lindberghs received thirty-eight thousand pieces of mail, five thousand from cranks.[41]

Soon after the child's disappearance Dr. John F. Condon, a seventy-two-year-old former school principal and admirer of the Lindberghs, offered himself as an intermediary and after a flurry of messages delivered through newspaper ads elicited what appeared to be a genuine response; Lindbergh agreed to have him serve as a go-between. Condon was finally instructed, apparently by the kidnapper, to bring the ransom to a cemetery. Accompanied by Lindbergh for part of the way, on April 2 he delivered $50,000 and in exchange was given a note with instructions about where to find the child as the man who collected the money disappeared. There followed a number of efforts to locate a boat on various waters where the note implied they would find the boy. But over the next weeks, while the world followed the developments with rapt attention, the child was not found. Seventy-two days after the abduction, on May 12 a truck driver discovered a tiny body in a shallow grave not far from the Lindbergh home. The denouement was described in stark terms in a letter that Anne sent to her sister: "The baby's body found and identified by skull, hair, teeth, etc., in woods on Hopewell-Mount-Rose road. Killed by a blow on the head."[42]

Lindbergh went alone to identify the partially decomposed body. Parts of the leg and arm were missing, perhaps gnawed away by animals. The child had apparently died the very first night, after he was abducted, likely after having been dropped by the kidnapper as he climbed out onto the ladder he had placed under the second-story bedroom window.[43]

Years later the Lindberghs' daughter, Reeve, thought back on what it meant for her father to make that trip. At first she could not understand: "[How] could you do this at such a time, and then I thought immediately, that's exactly what he would do." Unable to give in to grief or tears or even to discuss the tragedy, he could "examine carefully and clinically." That was, she wrote, how "he got through life."[44]

Throughout the ordeal, straight through to its grisly end, Lindbergh took charge, never allowing his stoic reserve and manly control to crack. "A long sleepless night," Anne recorded in her diary three days after the discovery, "but calm with C. sitting beside me every hour. . . . His terrible patience and sweetness and silence—terrifying." He told her it was "like war"; faith in goodness and security were wiped out. Harold Nicolson, who was staying at the Morrow home working on a biography of Dwight Morrow during these weeks, recalled that Lindbergh handled himself with "real dignity and restraint."[45]

The kidnapping and death threw the Depression-plagued nation into deep anguish. The outpouring of grief and sympathy was unprecedented. "The most famous baby in the world had been brutally killed," remarked Henry Breckinridge, who hardly left Lindbergh's side during the ordeal. Telegrams of condolence flooded into Hopewell from the White House, General and Mrs. Chiang Kai-shek, Benito Mussolini, and 100,000 others expressing the outrage and sorrow of the world. A law was later passed making kidnapping a federal crime punishable by death. In August, taking to the air for the first time since his baby's body was found, Lindbergh quietly flew out over the Atlantic and spread the ashes of his cremated son. They feared a cemetery plot would only lead to macabre incidents and more agony.[46]

On September 19, 1933, while they were in California the Lindberghs were informed by the New Jersey police that more than $13,000 in marked ransom bills had been found in the apartment of a thirty-six-year-old carpenter named Bruno Richard Hauptmann. After nineteen months of the most intense manhunt in history Hauptmann was charged with the kidnapping; the grand jury voted to indict him for murder in the first degree. His trial began on January 2, 1935.

The curious battled for tickets to the "trial of the century" in Flemington, New Jersey. Editors recruited celebrity writers and personalities to cover the proceedings and to profile the participants. More than a hundred photographers and three times that number of print journalists descended on the small town to report on the trial. One enterprising sheriff sold seats, charging $10 for the better spaces on the main floor and half that for those in the balcony. Celebrities from film, radio, and Broadway joined the battalion of onlookers. On Sundays, when the court was not in session, sightseers would cram into buses to visit the courtroom and tour the town.[47]

Despite the show atmosphere, Anne wrote, Lindbergh attended the trial, leaving at nine in the morning and not getting back until seven. He chafed at the media circus. "This morning he opened up his heart to me on the subject of publicity," Harold Nicolson wrote to his wife, Vita Sackville-West. "He absolutely loathes it." Lindbergh told Nicolson that the worst thing about the trial was his becoming front-page news once more. Charles, Nicolson thought, was a very decent man but "absolutely naïve about all this."[48]

In court on January 4, 1935, Lindbergh identified Hauptmann's voice as that of the man he had heard in the cemetery accepting the ransom money from Dr. Condon. The following day, after the prosecutor David T. Wilentz completed his presentation, the crowd was convinced of Hauptmann's guilt. Lindbergh certainly had no doubts. On February 13, after eleven hours and twenty-four minutes of deliberation, the jury unanimously convicted Hauptmann of murder in the first degree and sentenced him to death in the electric chair.[49]

Two days earlier Charles, whom Anne relied upon to be her rock, to fight her depression, lashed out at her for letting her emotions overwhelm her, for allowing the kidnapping to stop her from working on her writing, for failing to bear the pain. Anne turned to her mother. "He loves her," Betty Morrow recorded in her diary. But he wanted her to mold herself to his frame. Betty thought it reflected his narrowness: "What a condemnation of him." She had always feared that they were a mismatch, but never more than now did she understand the terms of their marriage.[50]

Hauptmann's attorneys launched a round of appeals, and New Jersey's governor, Harold G. Hoffman, who held some lingering doubts about the case, secretly visited Hauptmann in prison, bringing more notoriety to the case that seemed unwilling to depart the national stage. On April 3, 1936, after a reprieve granted by the governor and after all his appeals were rejected, Bruno Hauptmann was put to death.[51]

Celebrity had made Lindbergh America's most popular hero, and now it made him its most famous victim. He had conquered the sky but could do nothing to protect his son. It was a bitter lesson. No more practiced at handling tragedy than fame, he responded with quiet dignity. Yet Anne, torn by grief and depression—her letters spoke of little else—and pregnant with a second son, later recalled that she missed something, something she "regretted never witnessing": her husband's tears.[52]

After the trial the Lindberghs could not go back to live in Hopewell. They ultimately gave their home the name High Fields and donated it to the state to serve as a children's home. They settled instead at the Morrow residence in Englewood. Even before the birth of their son Jon in 1932 Anne expressed "an intense yearning for a quiet life, free from publicity—at any price." Yet incredibly with Jon's birth in August 1932, before the trial was even under way, came a new rash of threatening letters; at least a dozen people were arrested for extortion, forcing the Lindberghs to hire a retired detective who carried a sawed-off shotgun to protect the boy. Lindbergh himself took to wearing a Colt .38 under his jacket. Soon after the baby's birth Charles released a plea for privacy to the press, placing the onus of the tragedy on them. He and his wife very much wanted to continue to live in New Jersey: "Obviously however it is impossible for us to subject the life of our second son to the publicity which we feel was in a large measure responsible for the death of our first. . . . I am appealing to the press to permit our children to lead the lives of normal Americans."[53]

In the early years of their marriage Anne had viewed Charles as a larger-than-life hero. His approval and respect was what she craved most. Called to testify in court at the kidnapping trial her foremost concern was to "not disappoint C." But even during the terrible nightmare of the kidnapping they exchanged few words. He would comfort her, reassure her, and then, preoccupied with directing the response, largely ignore her. After the kidnapping their relationship gradually changed. Even "Charles the Invincible" had not been able to prevent the tragedy. Much as she continued to look up to him, she became more independent and over the years turned her attention to her own writing and assumed responsibility for her own fulfillment.[54]

As for Lindbergh, he did not seek emotional support from Anne or his mother. In fact in her regular letters to Mrs. Lindbergh, Anne was in much closer contact with Evangeline than he. His mentor, Alexis Carrel, who had remained in the distance during the kidnapping ordeal, sent a message of condolence expressing his sorrow at the "final blow." But, he wrote his assistant, "life continues": "I wish for you all the future holds in store for all those who possess indomitable courage"[55]

Like Carrel, Lindbergh viewed the kidnapping as a test of his courage and ability to keep focused entirely on the task at hand. What parents and friends were for others—enabling, sustaining, and a means for judging progress through life—rigid, unruffled self-control served for Lindbergh. Converting tragedy into tasks and then handling the tasks professionally was the best he could do.

After the tragedy he returned to his desk at the Rockefeller Institute, designing new flasks for Carrel's tissue experiments. He would devote hours to studying a piece of lab equipment, silently going over its elements and making notes on improving the design. He became absorbed in creating prototypes, running tests of his own devising, and making adjustments, all without the need to talk to a single human being.[56]

This focus on work—not only as work but as solace and fulfillment—to the exclusion of much else was essential for Lindbergh. It also sheathed him in profound solitude. Interestingly, another twentieth-century figure described himself in terms that could easily apply to the Lone Eagle. "I am truly a 'lone traveler,'" Albert Einstein said about himself, "and have never belonged to my country, my home, my friends or even my immediate family, with my whole heart; in the face of all these ties I have never lost a sense of distance and a need for solitude." His heart, a colleague once said about Einstein, though kind, "never bleeds." For both of these men, so different in fundamental ways, immersion in their own work absorbed them. In words that could as easily apply to Lindbergh, the historian Thomas Levenson wrote about Einstein, "He had no gift for empathy, no ability to imagine himself into the emotional life of anyone else."[57]

Lindbergh had always thrived on a regimen of tasks that might drive others to distraction. Anne would marvel at how he prepared for a trip. He would assess each item's utility and possible use in an emergency, weigh it on a baby scale, and deliberate before making a final determination. One rainy day, after spending six hours repairing a piece of machinery on his plane, he came home soaked to the bone, telling her that nothing could make him happier than work like this. It did not occur to him to ask what made her happy. But now he needed more than work, even more than the engineering work he did with Carrel. He needed the sky.[58]

Late in March 1933 Charles and Anne left seven-month-old Jon with her family and an armed guard and flew to California to retrieve the Sirius airplane that had been sent for repairs after the mishap on the Yangtze River. Then in July they appeared on the front pages once more as Charles took off, with Anne serving as navigator and radio operator, on a historic Atlantic survey. Only four planes had ever succeeded in crossing this treacherous northern route. They made their way across unexplored space as he assessed the feasibility of travel to Labrador, Greenland, and Iceland. ("As usual," Lindbergh wrote to Juan Trippe, "in a country where little flying has been done the difficulties have been greatly exaggerated.") He (she helped in the piloting but did none of the consulting) identified bases for refueling and predicted that commercial carriers would be traversing the Atlantic within two years.[59]

Testing new navigational and radio equipment, they twice crossed over the immense Arctic ice cap, with its blinding plates of ice. Then, struggling past snowstorms, hurricanes, and other hazards, they flew to Europe, where they stopped in more than twenty different countries. Everywhere, even in Moscow and Leningrad, the couple were greeted by enthusiastic crowds. The communist press, which had dismissed their earlier flights as "bourgeois stunts and sensationalism," ran front-page stories with large photographs of the flying couple (who were appalled by Russia's poverty and seediness). From there they flew to England, France, and Switzerland to investigate facilities and assess potential demand for air services. Charles met with leading aviation figures laying the groundwork for transatlantic passenger service.[60]

Invigorated by being in his element, Lindbergh gave little thought to returning home, but Anne missed young Jon terribly. More than once during the five-and-a-half-month-long tour she thought of returning home by boat, only to dismiss the idea for fear of upsetting her husband. But she did do something she would never have done before: letting on that she was "terribly anxious to see her baby." It made the newspapers. When the press suggested that it was time Lindbergh took her home he declared, "My time is my own."[61]

He still wanted to survey a southern route over the Atlantic. Setting out from Portugal they dashed to the Azores, and after many difficulties and unscheduled stops completed the sixteen-hundred-mile journey across the ocean, landing in Natal, Brazil, on December 6. Not yet done, he insisted on a detour up the Amazon to Trinidad and Puerto Rico, finally closing the thirty-thousand-mile trip by landing in New York just in time to spend Christmas with Jon.[62]

Even as the Lindberghs were flying the skies to encourage peace and prosperity, it was becoming evident that aviation was not going to bring about the millennium. For all the hope that aviation would serve as the moral equivalence of war, building tracks across cultures and civilizations, Europe was once again building offensive aircraft, and Germany was steadily advancing its air capacity. In the United States where aviation stocks reached historic highs in the flush months before the 1929 stock market crash, aviation-related production stood at 144 on the list of gross industrial output, slightly below the manufacture of corsets, but number 4 in the issue of new securities. The Department of Commerce continued to cradle the new industry with generous mail contracts, and the army and navy awarded the ten leading airline companies close to half a billion dollars in government business. By December 1929 aviation securities had reached a value of a billion dollars on the New York Stock Exchange. And then the Depression hit, all but devastating the nation's aviation industry.[63]

More than the Depression burst aviation's bubble. For all the headlines, the astronomical stock prices, and aviation's escalating glamour quotient, the passenger carriers—as that New Yorker piece by Morris Markey pointed out—never attracted enough passengers. And the issue of safety continued to be a real concern. By hurrying planes into service, companies too often had cut corners. The rapid buildup also quickly outstripped the number of trained pilots and mechanics. Lindbergh may have treated each crash as if it were local and limited, but a rash of accidents revealed that the problem was systemic. While Americans continued to devour articles about Lindbergh and thrilled to each air record being broken, they remained hesitant about actually boarding planes.[64]

But the problem went deeper than that. In the bonanza years the aviation cartels had coasted along paying inflated salaries, issuing generous dividends, and playing fast and loose with the easy money to reward favored officials and friends. The crash, however, forced them to consider the bottom line. TAT reported a net deficit of $986,591 since its beginning. Clement Keys thought the panic would purge the industry of marginal companies, but by December even optimists realized that the entire industry faced a crisis. TAT slashed its ticket prices by 25 percent and dropped them again after the New Year to about the cost of a rail ticket, less than half of what it had been six months earlier. Other companies followed.[65]

Edging toward disaster, airline companies took a cleaver to expenditures. Stock values plummeted. From a peak of just under 20, North American Aviation went to 4; National Air Transport dropped from above 48 to 10; and TAT, "the Lindbergh Line," plunged from above 33 to 6 and verged on bankruptcy. Western Air Express lost 80 percent of its value, falling from above 78 to 15; the giant United Aircraft sank from 162 to 31. By 1932 aviation stock values sank to five cents on every dollar invested, setting off a downward spiral of rate cutting that threatened to wipe out even relatively healthy companies. With expensive new planes flying half-empty and smaller companies clawing at the established firms, many feared a devastating round of cutthroat competition.[66]

Though Lindbergh was often up in the air he was not oblivious. His own investments declined in value and he stopped collecting retainer fees from the airlines. Anne's trust fund, a robust $715,000 when they first got married, had been reduced to $345,000 by January 1932. But even as the giant air companies struggled to avoid bankruptcy he remained convinced that the industry's future lay with the large cartels. They alone could afford the best and latest equipment while supporting research and development to compete for international leadership in the skies.[67]

Fundamentally in agreement with the Republican Party's support of the large air monopolies, he warmly endorsed Herbert Hoover for reelection in 1932, declaring, "Your experience, your courage and vision are . . . needed to pilot us safely out of the world-wide depression from which we are emerging." The Hoover plan for piloting out of the Depression took government support for the air cartels to new levels.[68]

Walter Folger Brown, Hoover's postmaster general, believed that government needed to nurture critical new industries like aviation to restore economic health. Certain that the established air monopolies were better equipped than their pesky competitors to ride out the economic crisis, he aimed to sustain them with government funds. Declaring, "[The] very life of the passenger transport industry is in the balance," Brown hammered out a four-point plan to reform existing policy regarding postal contracts.[69]

The bill he wrote, introduced in February 1930 by Laurence Watres, Republican of Pennsylvania, sought to give to the passenger lines on essential routes sufficient funds to keep them from going out of business and to maintain the investment that had gone into the aviation industry. Brown aimed to use the government's discretionary power to award million dollar mail contracts to bolster the monopolies while starving their smaller, undercapitalized competitors. "I do not believe in competition in public service," he later explained. "Monopoly in public service under very definite regulation is my idea."[70]

Passed on April 29, 1930, the Watres Act gave Brown broad authority to award franchises and to consolidate mail routes. The very next month Brown called together a conference of twenty-six prominent air industry leaders to apportion the airmail franchises that served as a critical lifeline for the air carriers. Smaller firms and recently organized airlines were not invited. "I am sure," one TAT official wrote, "that the P.M.G. [postmaster general] will go the full limit to avoid competitive bidding." "Lindbergh," he added, "has helped" smooth the way with Congress for the new policies.[71]

Working closely with former Assistant Postmaster General William P. MacCracken Jr. (now a lobbyist for the large airlines) and consulting Lindbergh, Brown rigged the bidding system to advantage a small circle of preferred air carriers. He went further, forging even larger conglomerates by forcing the larger firms he favored into mergers. For example, with Lindbergh's input he designed a plan to save struggling TAT from collapse by pressing the solid and profitable Western Air Express to merge with it, forming Transcontinental and Western Air (TWA). Then Brown rewarded the new company with a huge plum: the central transcontinental route, despite the fact that TWA's bid at 97.5 percent of the maximum rate was more than twice that offered by other competitors.[72]

In this way Brown used control over the airmail contracts to shape the industry. Out of this process emerged three colossal holding companies, which were awarded ten year franchises for more than 90 percent of the U.S. airmail business. The other airlines that submitted bids he simply ignored.[73]

Unfortunately for the devotees of big aviation, the American public voted Hoover out of office and his successor, Franklin Roosevelt, proved much less friendly toward monopolies and the unchecked accumulation of huge profits. In the 1920s the tale of Fred B. Rentschler's $253 investment in stock that turned into $35,000,000 stirred imaginations and envious admiration. In the 1930s Americans took this as evidence of an economy badly out of kilter. Congressional insurgents attacked Brown for "prostituting the Nation's air mail with monopolies," leading to a host of investigations into the airline industry and the airmail program.[74]

The 1933 Crane Commission disclosed that interlocking interests and directorates had manipulated the aviation market and bilked the government through inflated airmail contracts. Another investigation revealed that Postmaster Brown had openly favored the large holding companies over their smaller competitors. Other hearings reported on unseemly profits made off army and navy contracts. Taken together, the investigations unfolded a sordid narrative of greed and advantage taking by a small group of insiders.[75]

Beginning in the spring of 1933 Senator Hugo Black, an Alabama Democrat and future Supreme Court justice, led the most damaging of these investigations. Bristling at the notion that the few were better than the many and the rich somehow more capable than others, he exposed Brown's forced mergers, his open favoritism toward monopolies, and his "overpayments" for airmail contracts. In a Depression environment deeply suspicious of business, the notion of a government-orchestrated division of spoils that cheated taxpayers and undermined competition did not go over well.[76]

The new mood tarnished aviation's purest and most admired brand, tying Lindbergh to the loose atmosphere of questionable profits and collusive monopolists. For years now Americans had cherished their untainted air hero, who pursued progress for the common good. Their Lindbergh had held on to his innocence even as the philistines pushed to convert his pure accomplishment into sensational celluloid and filthy lucre; he was the Viking, praised by President Coolidge for refusing to "become commercialized." The hearings revealed that there was more to his reward than $10,000 retainers from TAT and Pan Am. In addition to his salary, there were insider options, unrevealed bonus payments, and some solid profit taking. It did not come close to the profits pulled in by Rentschler, but his *profit* (not counting the significant signing payments and bonus warrants) of more than $150,000 on Pan Am stock and another $195,000 on TAT did not strike a public devastated by Depression as Viking-like abnegation.[77]

The new skepticism had already stung Lindbergh. Led by chief counsel Ferdinand Pecora, the Senate Banking Committee issued a scorching report on the American financial community, uncovering much that was unsavory. The imperious J. P. Morgan Company proved a rather easy target, especially when the committee discovered that the fabled bank's head, J. P. Morgan Jr., had paid no taxes for three years running. Equally disturbing was the revelation that the Morgan Company maintained a favored list of insiders who were allowed to purchase new stock issues at below-market prices. Prominent among the preferred clients was Colonel Charles A. Lindbergh, the son of the old Morgan hater.[78]

Now, seven months later, on January 11, 1934, papers breathlessly headlined the news coming out of the Black investigations: Lindbergh had collected a secret gift of a quarter-million dollars for joining TAT. Try as they might to imply impropriety in the "gift," in the fact that TAT's stock "suddenly went up" when Lindbergh joined the company, that he had been instructed to be discreet in selling his warrants, and that he had also been given options to purchase an additional twenty-five thousand shares at below-market prices, it did not add up to much of a scandal. Still the headlines marred his image, especially coming in the course of hearings aimed at proving that the airlines had played with the people's money to benefit insiders. In high dudgeon Lindbergh handed over his business records to the committee to prove that he not only received no unreported gifts but that he had complied with all the laws and paid all the proper taxes, something the committee ultimately confirmed.[79]

More troubling to Lindbergh was the fact that his mission to build a powerful American aviation system stood impugned and his rationale that the ends of a powerful aviation industry justified monopolistic means was worn away by the acids of Depression bitterness. The New Deal changed the terms of debate from Brown's blueprint for a robust aviation industry to considerations of fairness, favoritism, and abuse of privilege that went into building this system.

On February 9, 1934, in light of the serious questions raised about the legality of Brown's contracts and Postmaster General James A. Farley's determination that Brown's noncompetitive awards had cost the nation more than $46,000,000 between 1930 and 1934 (TWA's bid alone exceeded the low bid by $5,000,000), President Franklin Roosevelt issued an executive order to take effect in ten days, canceling all existing airmail contracts and directing General Benjamin D. Foulois of the Army Air Corps to create a new airmail operation, using military planes and army pilots to fly the mail. Under the order existing contract holders would be cut off from the cash supports that sustained their operations.[80]

Frantic, TWA turned to Lindbergh to respond. This was the industry to which he had devoted a large part of this life. If he stood for anything it was for the existing American aviation system, which was now being smeared and undermined. The repudiation of the industry and of the people with whom he had labored to build so much of it was disturbing. After mulling over how to respond, Lindbergh went to his office and on Sunday afternoon, February 11, fired off a telegram to the president. This was no simple two-line wire. It was a long and indignant cry of anger and disapproval, declaring that FDR's new policy was unwise, unfair, a crushing blow to American aviation, and a violation of basic American justice. "Your action of yesterday," he began, condemned the "largest portion of our commercial aviation without trial." He had "devoted the last twelve years of [his] life" to this industry, which had become the best in the world. The president's action threatened irreparable harm. Angrily he released the telegram to the press even before it reached the White House. Papers reported Lindbergh's conviction that replacing the best aircraft in the world and their tested pilots with lesser equipment and air service pilots unfamiliar with the routes and unpracticed in night flying was an invitation to disaster.[81]

The president was not amused. The administration denounced the telegram as a publicity ploy by someone who had grown rich from the airlines and naturally towed their line. In Congress representatives exchanged sharp words; Hamilton Fish called Lindbergh "the greatest authority in the world on aviation" and asserted that "every word of his telegram rang true with sincere conviction." The *Washington Post*, *New York Times,* and many of the leading newspapers suggested that Lindbergh deserved a hearing and certainly deserved better than the White House's cavalier dismissal. Press lord William Randolph Hearst, whose tabloids Lindbergh had often denounced, defended the hero against charges that he had been bought by the airlines. Upon Lindbergh's return from Paris, Hearst wrote, he had "wanted to do something substantial for him" and had offered him a very attractive film contract. Young Lindbergh tore up the contract. "That young man," Hearst wrote, was not money hungry.[82]

Meanwhile the army's airmail deliveries met with disaster. Unfamiliar with the routes and hampered by freezing rains and unusual blizzards, the inexperienced pilots did not perform well. In the very first week of the new airmail flights five army pilots were killed in crashes, six were critically injured, and eight planes were smashed. The airmail had to be sharply curtailed and night flying stopped, but the devastating losses continued. By April there were forty-six forced landings and twelve U.S. Army Air Corps pilots killed, eight in training, leading the famed flight authority Eddie Rickenbacker to charge that the president's policy was no more than "legalized murder."[83]

Left with no other option, the president returned to the old carriers for three months in preparation for a new round of bidding, from which the companies that had participated in Brown's so-called Spoils Conference were barred from participating. As Lindbergh later observed, this was a face-saving measure, as it was not possible to set up new airline companies overnight. The old lines simply changed their names; United Aircraft became United Airlines, American Aircraft turned into American Airlines, Eastern Air Transport emerged as Eastern Airlines, and Transcontinental and Western Airlines became Trans World Airlines.[84]

Then, in what Lindbergh termed "one of the most unjust acts [he had] ever seen in American legislation," those airlines that had their contracts summarily canceled were barred from bringing suit for damages. The entire process, he bristled, was "un-American" and a terrible setback for American airmail. Furious with the Roosevelt administration, he declined the secretary of war's invitation to serve on a committee to study the Army Air Corps' experience with the airmail service.[85]

In the end the rates charged to the government came down; air policy was taken away from the Postal Department and placed with the Interstate Commerce Commission; individuals who had participated in the Spoils Conference were driven from the industry; and the new Air Mail Act of 1934 prohibited vertically integrated holding companies from holding mail contracts, effectively preventing airlines from owning aircraft manufacturers (to prevent a situation in which carriers had a vested interest in using their own manufactured planes even if they were not the safest). Also prohibited were interlocking directorates, overlapping interests, and certain mergers and consolidations. Four years later the Civil Aeronautics Act was passed, coordinating all regulation of the air industry in one office under the Civil Aeronautics Administration.[86]

The dispute had lasted for merely a month, but the Roosevelt scholar Arthur M. Schlesinger Jr. argues that it represented a turning point in New Deal history. It "dented the myth of Roosevelt's invulnerability" and solidified business's distrust of the New Deal. But, as the respected columnist Arthur Krock observed, Lindbergh too had been brought down a notch by the president's men, who had attacked him as a big business partisan out of tune with Depression America. There was too much money, too much involvement with the big capitalists for him to emerge with his innocence intact.[87]

The most pointed criticism came from the outspoken aviation gadfly Billy Mitchell. He had sacrificed his career in the name of American air readiness, and now he took Lindbergh to task for what had become of American aviation under his watch. The United States had poured hundreds of millions into aviation, and what did it have to show for it? In an emergency it had turned to its air force and found nothing but inferior machines, ill-trained pilots, and inadequate equipment: "If an Army aviator can't fly a mail route in any sort of weather, what would we do in a war?" Lindbergh, the voice of the air establishment, had advocated government support for large aviation in part as a way to build an air force that could defend the nation in an emergency. Only the most deluded would claim that the U.S. air fleet was prepared to do that. What had the aviator accomplished with his support for commercial aviation? A system where the air force remained inefficient and federal funds built up a handful of private companies at a very stiff price, while much of this money was drained off in private profits. The best aircraft, the most advanced equipment, and the most experienced hands were all in the private sector. Let us hope, Billy Mitchell added mordantly, that if the United States is attacked the enemy comes during daylight and in good weather, so that the air force is able to fly. Lindbergh could have promoted American readiness, but instead he had become a "front man of the Air Trust. . . . He is a commercial flyer. His motive is principally profit."[88]

Charles Lindbergh Sr. had railed against the money changers and would no doubt have supported the New Deal president's crusade against economic royalists, but for his son the charms of the common man, the ones who chased him down streets and intruded on his privacy and read the daily tabloids and resented those who, like himself and his wife, had put together substantial fortunes, proved elusive. Out of touch with the New Deal and Depression America, Lindbergh increasingly felt out of place and uncomfortable with the nation whose spirit he had once been said to have embodied.

EPILOGUE: THE END OF HEROES

ON MONDAY, DECEMBER 23, 1935, the *New York Times* ran a front-page article by Lauren "Deak" Lyman, the paper's veteran aviation reporter, "Lindbergh Family Sails for England to Seek a Safe Secluded Residence; Threats on Son's Life Force Decision." America's hero of the air, the celebrated Lone Eagle, and his family were already on their way to England as the papers came out.[1]

The previous Thursday, December 19, Charles Lindbergh had called Lyman, who was a friend. "I've got something I want to talk about, but not on the telephone," he told him mysteriously. Lindbergh had long before come to despise many in the press, viewing them as vultures, scavenging off the reputations of those who had achieved fame. But he trusted the *Times,* and he especially trusted Lyman, a Yale-educated patrician. The next day Lindbergh shocked Lyman, informing him that he was moving his family to England.[2]

Perhaps Lyman should have seen it coming. Lindbergh's run-ins with the press and his impatience with crowds had revealed a brittleness of spirit. His close embrace of the aviation lobby and its corporate monopolists; his marriage to the upper-crust daughter of a Morgan banker; and his bitter clash with President Roosevelt over aviation industry privileges, had all taken their toll, such that by 1935 Lindbergh was no longer the uncomplicated symbol he had once been.

He had been America's golden boy in good times, but the bottom had dropped out of Hoover's America. Unemployment, food scarcity, bankruptcies, dust bowls, and milk strikes had soured the national mood. The land of endless promise was now a place of bread lines and soup kitchens. Too many Americans were too busy picking through debris piles and cursing the earth to marvel at what was going on in the skies. An adventurous sensibility comports well with full stomachs and rosy cheeks; America's streets were filled with pinched men struggling to get by.

His son's kidnapping and murder had tested Lindbergh's own equanimity as well. Suffering sometimes makes heroes, challenging them to a new greatness of spirit. Part of Franklin Roosevelt's appeal to his Depression-plagued nation came from the example of how much he had overcome in his own life. But Lindbergh had drawn nothing from his ordeal to inspire his nation. Instead he retreated deeper into his own inner world, shielded by the isolation of Dr. Alexis Carrel's laboratory. His boyish charm curdled into racism, disillusionment with democracy, and an inclination toward Carrel's warped metaphysics. He made common cause with a powerful elite, opposing the New Deal and privately dismissing Roosevelt as "personally distasteful." He denounced American society as disorderly, blaming excessive freedom for the unbridled tabloids, attacking policies that allowed "inferior" immigrants to flood his land, and condemning the country's failure to take stronger steps to protect its citizens. The nation that had raised him to the heights of prominence he now reproved as "immoral."[3]

The idea of voluntary exile was not entirely new. Anne had raised it in a letter to her mother early in the marriage, while complaining about the pestering and ceaseless hounding that made normal life impossible. By June 1932 she and Charles were discussing it again: "Terrible argument about managing publicity. . . . C. arguing to live somewhere else for more peace." But when Anne wrote this they were living through the darkest moment of their lives and she concluded her letter saying, "We are too sore and hurt to argue on this subject. We quiver when we're touched."[4]

The Lindberghs had implored the press to honor their privacy. But the tragedy, followed by the sensational trial, would not allow it. The tabloids fed what had become a morbid preoccupation. During the trial, peddlers outside the courtroom hawked miniature models of the ladder used in the kidnapping. Editors rushed photographs of the second Lindbergh child into print without a second thought. Even as cranks and opportunists plagued the family with threats and extortionate demands, the furious competition for scoops continued, leading what had by now become the inevitable crackpots to come out of the woodwork: "Well, Lindy," read one anonymous letter, "here is hoping that when you and your China-faced wife go up in a plane you will both come down in flames." By the winter Lindbergh was writing to his mother that "between the politician [the issue of Hauptmann's guilt became a political football in New Jersey politics] the tabloid press and the criminal," life had become intolerable.[5]

The final straw came shortly before their departure. Jon Lindbergh was being driven home in a car with his nanny when they were forced off the road by another vehicle. Several men jumped out, rushing toward the child. For a fevered moment his guardian clutched Jon tightly, anticipating the worst. Then the men bared press cameras and began snapping pictures. The Lindberghs resolved to keep the child at home. Charles, meanwhile secured the necessary papers and made the arrangements for the trip, then came home one day and ordered Anne to pack up the family for their "Yuletide flight."[6]

Lyman knew that his article would land like a bombshell, but he pledged to hold it back until the family was out at sea. That Saturday night, with one eye on the ship-news ticker to check for any last-minute delays, Lyman sat down to write the story that would ultimately win him a Pulitzer Prize. He discarded thirteen different leads, finally settling on an understated opening, reporting that the Lindberghs were giving up residence in the United States: "And so the man who eight years ago was hailed as an international hero and a good-will ambassador between the peoples of the world is taking his wife and son to establish, if he can, a secure haven for them in a foreign land."[7]

On Monday, December 23, with Americans preparing for their Christmas celebrations, the *Times* waited until all other late city editions had appeared, then, at 2:30 a.m., began shipping the papers that broke the copyrighted story. The news further dampened the holiday season, already made grim by years of persistent economic crisis and the rise of European tyrants with bold ambitions. The yearning for resolute moral leadership was acute, but heroes were few, making Lindbergh's flight into exile even more disturbing. Only three generations before, the *Washington Post* wrote sadly, Lindbergh's grandfather had emigrated from Sweden to this country with his wife and son: "With what high hopes they must have set sail for the land of promise. And the promise was for a time fulfilled. That little boy became a member of Congress and father of the famous aviator. Now this Lindbergh in turn leads his small family back to the Old World, looking for privacy and peace. The cycle is complete; the moral for America is unmistakable."[8]

Column after anguished column complained of the hideous cultural rot that hectored "America's First Couple" from the land. American society, cried the *Herald Tribune*, had descended into "barbarism and cheapness." Its "press . . . respects no law and knows no decency," keened the *Christian Science Monitor*. "It was as though the Lindbergh family were living alone on a frontier," the *New York Times* added, "their home surrounded by savages." The *Los Angeles Times* described them as "refugees from the tyranny of yellow journalism," chased "by their tormentors," in the words of another melodramatic scribbler, to a forlorn Christmas upon the "tumbling Atlantic."[9]

Responding to the criticism of his tabloids, William Randolph Hearst blamed the departure on "cranks, criminals and Communists," conveniently ignoring the fact that the photographers who had terrified the young Jon Lindbergh just a few weeks before worked for him, not the Soviets or the criminal underworld.[10]

New York's feisty *Daily News* refused to join in the hand wringing, pointing out that Lindbergh was no simple innocent. He had pursued fame and exploited its privileges. With celebrity comes public attention. Shunning the press "after the manner of Greta Garbo" only provoked it to excess. Had Lindbergh behaved like "a popular hero is supposed to act," insisted the *News*, he could have avoided much unpleasantness.[11]

Walter Lippmann thought not. Yes, the "incomparable youth . . . who . . . conquered the imagination of mankind" might have been shrewder in dealing with the public. But, asked Lippmann, was it not enough to ask heroes to be daring and courageous; must they also become a genius in outwitting a crazed press? And failing that, must they suffer "ingenious, ruthless and unending inquisition which commercialize[s] pandering to the curiosity of the mob?" This endless prying by means both pitiless and frightening had caused tragic harm. "Nothing . . . was left undone which might dredge out of the slime of animal passion all imaginable varieties of lunatic envy and resentment and lust against their fame, their fortune, their happiness."[12]

Lindbergh's departure closed a chapter in his life and a critical page in American aviation history. Over the seven and a half years since his flight to Paris he had advanced American commercial aviation to international leadership, changing forever the interplay of time, distance, trade, travel, big business, diplomacy, and defense. Now the Lindbergh era was over.

But Lindbergh was still a young man in search of fresh challenges to stir his imagination. He carried with him to England a letter of introduction to the British medical community. Yet laboratory science, with all its exoticism for an airplane pilot, would not hold his interest for long. He craved an impact more significant in scope, and this brought him to a new involvement in war-time politics.[13]

Even without Carrel's social theories, Lindbergh's life-long regard for order, regimentation, and predictability made him uncomfortable with democracy's sloppy inefficiencies. The untidy passions of his parental home inclined him to favor processes that were reliable and unvarying, unlike the father who often disappeared and the mother who was so vulnerable and unstable. "Whatever the sincerity of Lindbergh's beliefs," writes Leo Braudy, "in the context of the 1930s and 1940s they easily shaded toward fascism."[14]

The "fascist temptation" proved particularly powerful for the pioneer generation of aggressive flyboys. "Every aviator," the Italian journalist Guido Mattioli observed in describing Benito Mussolini's early years as a pilot, "is a born fascist."

Flight involved the concentration of focus and will, and, Mattioli argued, every pilot knew well what it meant to "govern," to raise oneself by one's own pluck and audacity above the common grain. The early fliers saw themselves as members of a select brotherhood, with privileged access to a panoramic vision. They adopted an ascetic discipline, honored the charismatic figure, disdained the masses, and followed a cult of the hero who willingly chanced his life for a larger cause. Those who went down in the new machines they venerated as martyrs. We have seen the intense focus—whether planning his trip to Paris, searching for his abducted son, or perfecting a perfusion pump—that allowed Lindbergh to reduce to negligibility common needs like food, sleep, and human contact. This gave him the illusion of being in control of himself, his environment, and his fate.[15]

But, of course, he was in less control than he imagined. He had helped open the skies, but war twisted this breakthrough into a horror. In the shadow of massive air bombing in 1942 Elias Canetti wrote, "How quickly has flight, this age old and precious dream, lost every charm, lost every meaning, lost its soul. . . . One after another of our dreams is realized to death." Not only did air travel expand the killing theater; it dehumanized the process. Little wonder that in the light of the blitz, Pearl Harbor, Hiroshima and Nagasaki, and the firebombing of Dresden, Lindbergh's flight lost some of its luster. If the conquest of the heavens symbolized man's growing mastery it also fostered some of the twentieth century's most barbaric tendencies.[16]

Well before the outbreak of war, however, Lindbergh was once again capturing the headlines. In July 1936, on the first of several trips to Germany to study the Luftwaffe, he gave the first overtly political speech of his career. He spoke seriously about aviation's ambivalent legacy, acknowledging its terrifying underside and that it had changed forever the calculus of battle. The old fortresses and battlements could no more protect against attack from the sky than could a parasol. In a single day offensive aircraft threatened more damage "than could be replaced in a lifetime." Yet curiously, despite the open secret of Germany's metastasizing war arsenal, he said nothing about its open violation of treaties or its gathering threat to peace. In terms more than perfunctorily gracious he expressed his admiration for the advanced status of his host's air forces.[17]

Very much under her husband's influence, Anne Lindbergh went on to contrast the "neatness, order, trimness, and cleanliness" that they found in Germany with the pervasive shabbiness and destitution that they had encountered on an earlier visit to Soviet Russia. In Germany she found a festive air filled with tanned youth and a strong citizenry exuding "a spirit of hope, pride and self sacrifice," something that she missed in the United States, France, and England. Admittedly

Nazi Germany was not a democracy, but nevertheless she found much to admire.[18]

For his part, her husband called the German people "magnificent" and Hitler a visionary leader who wanted the best for his people, a leader of iron will and vision, not at all a madman. Anne wrote to her mother about the German dictator: "I am beginning to feel [Hitler] is a very great man, like an inspired religious leader." Perhaps he was fanatical, but "not selfish, not greedy for power," rather more like a mystic "who wants the best for his country." Both Lindberghs held on to this notion of the monstrous tyrant as a benign despot for a very long time.[19]

Lindbergh called for peace, but knew full well that war was coming. He visited the various world powers to assess their air capabilities. (In addition to Germany, Russia, England, and France welcomed a visit from the aviation icon.) He came away convinced that Germany's staggering arsenal assured its dominance over Europe. England and France, he declared, did not have the wherewithal to stand in its way. The best thing they could do was to accept this and allow Germany to arrange Western Europe as a bulwark against Soviet communism and the inferior Asian races.[20]

Harold Nicolson, the British Liberal MP who had been charmed by the Lindberghs and rented them his home in England, was now convinced that Lindbergh was sympathetic to "the Nazi theology, all tied up with his hatred of degeneracy and his hatred of democracy." In *Life* magazine Roger Butterfield came to similar conclusions. The great flier's disdain for the common folk and messy democracy inclined him to the swift, if ruthless, efficiencies of totalitarian regimes. With his friends among England's Clraveden circle, Lindbergh preferred Germany to the democracies. In a report he prepared for Joseph P. Kennedy, U.S. ambassador to the Court of St. James, Lindbergh wrote, "German air strength is greater than all other European nations combined, [making Germany] inseparable from the welfare of our[!] civilization"; it was the last best barrier to barbarism. Reassured in his own inclinations, Kennedy backed Neville Chamberlain's plan to appease Hitler at Munich.[21]

On repeated visits to Germany Lindbergh was treated with great deference and taken on private tours of secret munitions works. On two separate occasions the German air minister and chief of the Luftwaffe Hermann Göring entertained him and on October 18, 1938, awarded him the Service Cross of the Order of the German Eagle with Star, on orders from Hitler. "How," asked Eleanor Roosevelt, "could Lindbergh take that Hitler decoration?"[22]

After the coordinated attack on Germany's Jewish community on November 9, 1938, when shops were looted, homes burned to the ground, scores of synagogues torched, and dozens of Jews killed and tens of thousands carted off to camps and their belongings pilfered, the U.S. ambassador left and never returned to Nazi Berlin. The call for Lindbergh to return the medal became an insistent chorus among the press and public. But Lindbergh refused to abandon his willful naïveté about Germany.[23]

Lindbergh returned to the United States in 1939 and came out from behind the scrim of fame and celebrity to speak to his countrymen. Throughout his life he had prized his privacy, but now, he said, he had something too important to keep to himself. In an article entitled "Aviation, Geography, and Race" published in the November 1939 *Reader's Digest* he candidly shared his thoughts on race and *realpolitik*. Destiny, he began, had favored the West with leadership. Aviation was one of those privileged fields "specially shaped for Western hands," an essential barrier between Asia's teeming millions "and the Grecian inheritance of Europe—one of those priceless possessions which permit the White race to live at all in a pressing sea of Yellow, Black, and Brown." But despite the great hopes, aviation had failed to usher in everlasting peace. Instead it fueled a disastrous war among the "heirs of European culture . . . a war within our own family of nations," threatening "the White race . . . which may even lead to the end of our civilization."[24]

While the great Western nations busy themselves with killing each other, he continued, "Oriental guns are turning westward, Asia presses towards us on the Russian border, all foreign races stir restlessly." The nations of Europe must make common cause and "build our White ramparts again. . . . to guard our heritage from Mongol and Persian and Moor, before we become engulfed in a limitless foreign sea." In a new iteration of his famous *We*, he called on England, France, Germany, and the United States to form a "Western Wall of race and arms" to hold back "the infiltration of inferior blood." Differences between the Nazis and the Allies over freedom, democracy, and human rights paled before the larger goal of uniting behind Germany to defend "that most priceless . . . inheritance of European blood."[25]

Lindbergh had never written with such emotional force before. Anne may have helped with the prose, but the ideas were his, what Anne described as his "deepest best thinking." He went on to lead the forces opposed to American intervention in the war, touring the nation in 1940 and 1941 and becoming the most popular leader of the "America First" movement. Lindbergh had attacked Randolph Hearst's tabloid journalism in the past, but in 1941, persuaded that Hearst was "good on the war issue," he joined with the Hearst papers to beat the drums for leaving the Allies to Germany's tender mercy. By then Lindbergh's phone was being tapped by the FBI. As for Europe's Jews, he told the poet and journal editor Selden Rodman, "I shall certainly not take it upon myself to defend them."[26]

Lindbergh's thinking alienated his closest supporters, including Harry Guggenheim. No one had a more intimate knowledge of his affairs than his long-time aide and adviser Henry Breckinridge, whom Lindbergh entrusted with his reputation. Breckinridge was his rock during the kidnapping. He hardly slept and seldom left Lindbergh's side throughout the ordeal. Yet Breckinridge too peeled away in sorrow at what had become of the man he had once admired. It is striking how Breckenridge's 348-page unpublished memoir contains not a word about the man he served like a brother for years. Russell Owen, the friendly *New York Times* reporter who defended Lindbergh against the tabloids, concluded sadly that Lindbergh's pro-Nazi leanings "caused infinite harm up to Pearl harbor." Lindbergh broke with his own firmly pro-Ally mother, and the resolutely pro-British Morrow family also was riven by his stance. Walter Lippmann now referred to the fallen hero as a "Nazi lover."[27]

Harold Nicolson had once described Charles Lindbergh in warm and affectionate terms. In an eviscerating magazine profile Nicolson now recast his appraisal of Lindbergh. Following the Paris flight, he wrote, Lindbergh had struggled "almost with ferocity" to remain himself. In the process of "that arduous struggle his simplicity became muscle bound; his virility ideal became not merely inflexible, but actually rigid; his self control thickened into arrogance, and his convictions hardened into granite." When that armor failed to defend him against the terrible ordeal of the kidnapping and murder he emerged with "a loathing for publicity that was almost pathological." His outrage at the press led him to a "loathing" of democracy and an attraction for Nazi Germany, especially the tough efficiency of the state and the hardening of a young generation to harsh sacrifice in the name of national honor. The "schoolboy hero," Nicolson concluded, remained "a schoolboy."[28]

Schoolboy or not, Lindbergh had become a formidable political figure. As early as 1937 the *Washington Post* reported that many in Berlin were convinced that in the next presidential election, when presumably FDR would not run for a third term, the contest would be between New York City's progressive mayor, Fiorello H. La Guardia, and Charles A. Lindbergh. The newspaper *der Arbeitsmann* ran pictures of the two men with a Star of David above the fireplug-shaped mayor and a heroic photo of the Lone Eagle. Lindbergh proceeded to galvanize an impossibly fragmented neutrality movement, persuading millions with his legendary magnetism and new forcefulness. Those close to him in America First marveled at the cheers and almost hysterical response to his appearances. "Lindbergh evokes a fervor," one comrade exclaimed in admiration. "Hitler has the same thing; Roosevelt has it sometimes, Huey Long used to get it, and [Father Charles] Coughlin occasionally." Audiences regularly greeted him with shouts of "Lindy for President."[29]

In rallies in St. Louis, Minneapolis, New York, Philadelphia, Hollywood, and San Francisco, Lindbergh took the lead in denouncing FDR's foreign policy. Followers thronged to see him, crowding his rallies. After war broke out in Europe, in the fall of 1939, he delivered more than fifteen increasingly strident major addresses. By June 1940 he was attacking "the interests"—the press, Anglophiles, the Jews and propagandists—as "an organized minority," who along with refugees, college presidents, idealists, and "war agitators" were pushing the United States into war. Denouncing the democracies, he charged Roosevelt with "government by subterfuge."[30]

He continued to avoid criticizing Germany. Asked why, he set his jaw and answered that he intended to remain neutral. Some took to calling the still imposing hero a "sulking knight in shining pewter." In Kansas City, TWA removed its tag slogan, "the Lindbergh Line," from its promotions and never used it again. Monuments honoring his earlier feats were toppled. Streets bearing his name were changed. In Chicago the "Lindbergh Beacon" topping one of the city skyscrapers was renamed "the Palmolive Beacon."[31]

Privately President Roosevelt told Treasury Secretary Henry Morgenthau that Lindbergh was a Nazi. In April 1941 the president publicly compared him to a Copperhead (the name for Northerners who supported the South during the Civil War), leading Lindbergh to resign his air force commission. The Lone Eagle, wrote Walter Winchell, had become the "lone Ostrich." The FBI reactivated the Lindbergh file that was opened during the kidnapping, except that now he was the subject. Famed anti-Nazi journalist Dorothy Thompson called him a "somber cretin." To Lindbergh, who never feared being alone in a cause he believed in, the furor reinforced his belief that a small minority was twisting U.S. policy and opinion to inveigle the country into joining a bad war.[32]

The curmudgeonly interior secretary Harold Ickes hit him hardest: "I have never heard this Knight of the German Eagle denounce Hitler or Nazism or Mussolini or Fascism," nor had he heard him "utter a word of pity" for the nations overrun by Germany, nor for the Poles or the Jews "who have been slaughtered by the hundreds of thousands by Hitler's savages." Lindbergh demanded an apology. He got back a suggestion that now that Hitler's true colors were abundantly clear he send back his "Nazi medal."[33]

On January 23, 1941, Lindbergh testified before the congressional Committee on Foreign Affairs. Pressed by Congressman Luther Johnson of Texas about which of the two sides at war it would be in our interest to see victorious, he responded, "Neither." The respected Christian theologian Reinhold Niebuhr called upon Americans to separate themselves from Lindbergh's stand and clean their "ranks of those who would incite to racial and religious strife." Lindbergh's celebrity was turned upside down. "In just fifteen years," Anne's sister Constance exclaimed, "he has gone from Jesus to Judas." The flier whom fame had lifted high above his competence, the beloved golden boy of the twenties, had by the forties become a detested apologist for fascism and the most virulent strain of racism of modern times.[34]

One of the lessons of the celebrity age is that reputations are always a work in progress. Second thoughts are very much a part of a process that is quick to praise, even quicker to damn, and leaves ample room for repair. Rehabilitation is not only possible; it often has its own redemptive script. Lindbergh, who had always been the single best and shrewdest guardian of his own eminence, began fashioning a vital third act for his life even before the war was over.

Following Pearl Harbor, which made the issue of neutrality moot (and focused Lindbergh's furor on an Asian enemy), he sought reinstatement in the Army Air Corps. This did not go over well. Harold Ickes argued that restoring this "ruthless and conscious fascist motivated by . . . a contempt for democracy" would be a "tragic disservice to American democracy." Ickes advised burying Lindbergh "in merciful oblivion." FDR's war cabinet agreed. The administration managed to keep him out of the military for the time being and also prevented him from returning to the aviation industry, until Henry Ford, himself an America Firster and not unsympathetic to Lindbergh's broader outlook, hired him to help the Ford Motor Company transition from manufacturing automobiles to making B-24 Liberator bombers.[35]

More than a job, Lindbergh wanted to demonstrate his loyalty and prove himself in combat. At the beginning of 1944 he met with U.S. Marine officials, offering to help in the South Pacific. By April he was ordering a uniform. Allowed by local officers to assume an unofficial role, he joined dawn patrols and rescue operations, and while they looked the other way, the forty-two-year-old pilot participated in air combat, strafing, dive bombing, and logging tens of combat missions over New Guinea. Much later Anne would argue that he opposed war on moral grounds, appalled by the destruction it wrought, but that is not quite accurate. He was thrilled to volunteer for dangerous bombing missions, and for all his angst about the offensive role of airplanes he killed from the sky with great panache.[36]

After the war Lindbergh rejoined Pan Am as a director and a consultant. He worked again with Juan Trippe and resumed his worldwide travels, this time usually without Anne, who remained home to care for their five children and to write. He never felt comfortable being tied down and much preferred living out of a suitcase, flitting from country to country like a free bird.[37]

Lindbergh remained very much a man alone. Michael Collins, the first American to walk in space, received a note from him in 1974, only a few months before

Lindbergh's death. It reaffirmed a persistent theme through his life, his reveling in isolation. It was a feeling he had cultivated since he was a little boy in a conflicted home who would wander the woods and contemplate the sky: "There is a quality of aloneness that those who have not experienced it cannot know."[38]

But it was a crippling aloneness. Although his letters to Anne never failed to mention how much he missed her, as soon as he returned home he was itching to leave again. His children recalled that they never knew when their father would be home. When he was home he kept them secluded and guarded, taught them to shade their identity by mumbling their names when asked, to avoid giving their names when answering the telephone, and never to speak to reporters. He held them to an exacting discipline, not only to behave but to account for every penny spent, for every minute wasted. Lindbergh accepted no excuses for work not done, for challenges avoided. He was endlessly demanding, with his lists of rules, assignments and chores, and house inventories. But he offered little compensating warmth. Before long the children did not so much mind his absences as dread his return home. Reeve Lindbergh, the youngest, recalled that her stern father seemed to suck up all the oxygen when he entered a room.[39]

Anne too was torn between missing him when he was away and resenting the unrelenting control and blizzard of demands he issued when he returned, only to leave on the spur of the moment when the mood caught him. She spent entire days crying and gradually turned to others who were more understanding and less demanding. In the mid-1950s he began a long-term secret affair in Germany with Brigitte Hesshaimer that resulted in three children. It was one of several surreptitious overseas relationships that produced at least three Lindbergh families and seven children. These were serious relationships. He visited Hesshaimer several times a year and exchanged more than 150 letters with her, while he also carried on an affair with her sister, Marietta, who bore him two more children.[40]

Following the war the critic Bernard de Voto wrote a long article condemning Lindbergh. It had not mattered to Lindbergh that the Jews were exterminated, nor the Poles, the Greeks, or the Czechs: "The destruction of France did not matter, nor the invasion of Russia, nor Holland, Belgium, Norway, Denmark." The bombings, massacres, "the enslavement of millions, the starvation of millions, the slaughter of millions": these were unimportant to him. What mattered to Lindbergh, de Voto wrote, was "to get along with the Germans." But by the mid-1950s the Germans were American allies, Werner von Braun was building America's missile defenses, and in light of the cold war Lindbergh's hatred of Soviet Russia seemed prescient. A fellow warrior and now president Dwight David Eisenhower welcomed him back to the pantheon by nominating him to the rank of brigadier general, and on April 7, 1954, he was duly promoted.[41]

Shortly before, Lindbergh published *The Spirit of St. Louis*, in which he retold the story of his flight, this time with novelistic techniques and leaving in all the scary parts. He had been working on this project since 1938, laboring through countless drafts with help from his ever-supportive wife (to whom he warmly dedicated the book). They managed to give the well-known story a new excitement and a reflective texture that was missing from *We*. In September 1953 the volume was made a Book-of-the-Month Club main selection. The *Saturday Evening Post* paid $100,000 to serialize a condensed version in ten installments, and *The Spirit of St. Louis* went on to become a best-seller and to win the Pulitzer Prize. Sales garnered $1.5 million in royalties and, more important for him, restored Lindbergh to national honor after more than a decade of disfavor. Hollywood made a popular film version of the book starring Jimmy Stewart.[42]

His book's success gave Lindbergh the confidence to work on his magnum opus, a meditation on his own past and the deeper meaning of life. Published posthumously as *Autobiography of Values*, it is a messy mélange with shafts of insight and wisdom but much that draws him down into obscure metaphysics. Interestingly, this manuscript, representing his fiercest struggle to make sense of life and its larger meaning, he did not entrust to his celebrated writer-spouse. Instead, shortly before his death from lymphoma on August 26, 1974, at seventy-two, he called his friend, the publisher William Jovanovich, and asked him to work the many hundreds of pages that he had assembled over the years into a memoir. Front and center in this meditation is his regretful recognition that his early enthusiasms were misguided.[43]

Lindbergh had begun this process of rethinking flight and aviation years before. In 1948, after the war, he published his pensive *On Flight and Life*. In this slim volume of less than sixty pages he reconsidered his own values: "Like most modern youth, I worshipped science. I was awed by its knowledge." But he had seen the science he "had worshipped, and the aircraft [he] loved, destroying the civilization [he] expected them to serve, and which [he] thought as permanent as earth itself." He was mistaken to think that opening the skies, hurtling over borders, and building new technology meant progress and great things. He had not counted, as he now saw, on the perversity of human nature. Making it possible to enter new spaces or do things faster or more efficiently brought no assurance that such "progress" would redound to anyone's benefit or prevent cruelty and destruction. World War II had proven, if such proof was necessary, that knowledge could be used for ill, that progress could lead to a better bomb. Years before, Raymond Orteig (whose prize had inspired Lindbergh) had complained that trench warfare had stripped war of its romance, that the air was the last refuge of the gentleman warrior. But the air had become a place from which to rain down mass destruction without witnessing the pain.[44]

Lindbergh considered his own bombing experience during the war. For all the rhetoric about the clarifying benefits of the heavenly perspective, being removed from the world of men meant you lost connection with life on earth. The separation from the quotidian that he had celebrated earlier—"the limitless future of the sky"—became an anodyne buffer, creating a psychic distance from the agony, the brutality, the gore of war. This was the other side of the romance of the air, the danger of viewing the earth from too great a height, the distortion brought on by detachment.[45]

War had made his aviation work and his biological researches seem trivial compared with cosmic forces. On December 21, 1968, witnessing the launch of the Apollo 8 manned lunar orbiter, Lindbergh felt an "almost overwhelming desire" to join the astronauts, but decades of work in science, he wrote, thrust his "mind and senses to . . . mysteries beyond scientific research. In these vaguely appreciated azimuths . . . the great adventures of the future lie in voyages inconceivable by our twentieth century rationality." On reflection he realized that it was not the science of flight that had attracted him many years before, but rather the art of flying, and as that art had given way to more and more mechanization, uniformity, and convention his interest had waned. For the last third of his life he turned his attention from "technological progress to life, from the civilized world to the wild."[46]

Lindbergh came to value the simple and primitive elements of those societies that had avoided the march of civilization, the complexities of technology, and the hemlock of conspicuous consumption. He had changed in other ways as well. "Who could say with certainty," he wrote, "that black men are not the future carriers of human evolution, and that we whites are not so overspecialized a branch that we will rot away with time [and] nuclear warfare?" He was especially concerned that if society separated itself too much from nature it might lose its vitality. No longer awed by the laboratory, he now celebrated wisdom "born of instinct, intuition and genetic memory, held by the subconscious rather than the conscious mind."[47]

He contemplated "life streams" and other mystical notions, writing, "I am at once my past, my present, and my future. . . . I am billions of years old, [having] . . . existed through past eons with unbroken continuity." As early as 1937 he had become interested in the occult, flying in March of that year to India for a conference of the World Fellowship of Religions. When Anne described the conference to her mother she admitted to struggling to keep a straight face while her celebrated husband occupied a front-row seat facing a "large sugary picture of

Ramakrishna," the walls decked with banners declaring "Blessed is he who is free from thoughts of I-Am" and surrounded by barefoot holy men, fakirs, "and a few stray wispy people from Pasadena, London, Boston, following an Indian swami in an orange turban."[48]

Now Lindbergh wrote about withdrawing "to his core," stripping away the accoutrements of civilization, the possessions, connections, obligations, and clothes. As a young man drawn to research he had sought the secret of immortality; as an older man "lying naked in the sun in a hollow in the rocks" he wrote, "I had little concern about death," which he defined as "no more than the stuff of substance transported to the stuff of dream." The answers to his mysteries did not lie in the laboratory: They were to be found "beyond the solar system, through distant galaxies, possibly through peripheries untouched by time and space." It is rhetoric in search of a firm idea, but these are also the words of a man at the end of his life wrestling with its meaning, confronting his massive misreading of progress and the power of reason, trying now to reset the process of his thought.[49]

Lindbergh's thinking was neither elegant nor precise, and certainly not systematic, but in its way it was consistent. Years before a reviewer of his *Wartime Journals* wrote, "Lindbergh has a genuine feeling for nature—preferably without people in it—and when he is communing with the wind, waves, and the sky above, he approaches genuine eloquence." He continued to avoid the large moral issues. While struggling to make sense of the world he failed to ask what is good and what is right. Alongside his mystical assertions and abstract speculations in *Autobiography of Values*, he continued to make shambling excuses and withhold any apologies for flirting with Hitler's totalitarianism, equating the American treatment of the Japanese with the Nazi depredations.[50]

It was in Africa that Lindbergh experienced a new epiphany, bringing together "the sensate, intuitive, and intellectual" faculties in "a supernatural awareness": "I took the form of my environment as my own." He devoted his remaining energies to the cause of conservation, traveling the globe to meet once again with world leaders and opinion makers. Much as he had used his celebrity to publicize aviation, he now used it to raise awareness about the need to protect wildlife species from extinction and to protect the environment. He visited and lived with primitive tribes, lauding their values and lifestyle, voicing a profound disappointment with modern civilization. Like his earlier uncomplicated embrace of technology, this simplistic turn to the opposite illustrated one of the constants of his rather inconstant life: a world of absolutes, lacking grays.[51]

This quest for new meaning, for a world remade, was one he had pursued from early on. Standing before his new plane in San Diego in April 1927, before the world knew his name, he marveled at the machine that would transport him to glory, "trim and slender, gleaming in its silver coat!" He was awestruck: "All our ideas, all our calculations, all our hopes lie there before me waiting to undergo the acid test of flight. For me it seems to contain the whole future of aviation. When such planes can be built there is no limitation to the air."[52]

Less than a year before his death, Lindbergh went back to Minnesota, to the home where he spent the happiest days of his childhood, to deliver an address that praised parks rather than spacecraft: "In establishing parks and nature preserves, man reaches beyond the material values of science and technology. He recognizes the essential value of life itself." For all his new thinking, he fell prey to the old trap, seeking some *thing* that represented the hope of humanity, this time a reverence for the natural environment. It was the same thinking that bade him to revere airplanes and science laboratories, to read big things into external realities rather than into internal human values.[53]

Charles Lindbergh was an American innocent who was thrown into the spotlight and persistently—sometimes vainly, sometimes poignantly—tried to develop a level of sophistication appropriate to his new status. But the race always stayed ahead of him. For all his efforts he was never able to free his thinking from the thick harness of his early certainties, until finally he turned his back on aviation, Western civilization, and the idea of progress itself. He escaped urbane adulthood to return to the farm and his provincial boyhood, where life was simple and pure among the elements.

He was a man of outsized gifts who had given his nation an extended moment of greatness without asking for much in return. But what he did ask for was beyond its capacity to award him. America could not give him privacy; later it would not listen to his prescriptions for world peace and security. And great though his gifts of will, precision, and daring were, important lacunae remained. He lacked enough of the softer human qualities of kindness, compassion, and empathy, which made it hard for him to feel the pain of his fellow Americans during the Depression and to react with outrage at genocide. Unable to feel the pain, he made dispassionate reckonings, equating different sufferings as if they were so many trading cards.

The restless engine of his youth (Anne attributed his "chronic restlessness" to a fear of facing his own emotions "reaching all the way back to childhood") remained with him throughout his life, urging him on to new pursuits, new challenges. His focus remained always on the big picture. He never tired of asking fundamental questions about life, technology, the environment, and race. His curiosity was boundless and he had the energy to pursue it. He had tinkered in his youth and he remained a tinkerer throughout life, dabbling in engineering, biology, conservation, and philosophy. He exhausted others around him, drove his wife to distraction and even depression; he hounded his children to excel and demanded of his own rather pedestrian mind that it stretch to the challenges of some of the largest and most meaningful questions of his time.[54]

Lindbergh had traveled a long way from the callow, bold flier who brought glory to his country and helped push off the Aviation Age. Endless speeches and columns were devoted to analyzing what particular nerve he touched to set off so resonant a response. If in large measure he projected the good American—the country's innocent individualism, its daring and raw energy, its penchant for asking simple questions and its naïve belief that every man had a right to be a hero—he also demonstrated the shortcomings of such populism by using the hero's platform to speak of things he understood imperfectly, blatantly ignoring the evils of totalitarianism and genocide. He led a political movement, carried out advanced scientific research, and mused on the philosophy of life. Other nations had their idiots savants; he represented the everyman savant, not always right or even good, but undaunted before those smarter and better prepared, insisting on the right to see the world fresh, to seek out some better model and to be heard.

If there is one steadfast thread throughout Lindbergh's long, uneven history it is his ability to discard old truths, certainties, and loyalties and transfer them to some new optimism, some new hope for unifying the world and leading it toward salvation with freshness, credulity, and commitment. He moved serially through aviation, science, race, the environment, but all the while he failed to confront the core issue: it was not that technology could facilitate evil, but rather that unless human society made commensurate progress in civility, humanity, and decency, all the advances of modern life in technology, medicine, and communication could offer no assurances of real progress. In the face of this challenge he gave up and escaped back to primitive society, hoping to start all over. It was not that these non-Western men and women exhibited less evil inclinations; it was the primitivism itself, the closeness to earth, the negation of modernity, the absence of advanced weaponry that gave him hope in the American ideal of starting again, that a new frontier might yield different results.

Late in life, after he had examined his own life several times at different depths in a series of biographies, after he had experienced tragedy and witnessed war, an atom bomb and space flight, he thought anew about the meaning of his first transatlantic flight to Paris. Falling into a rhetorical convention he contrasted the image of the painted Maasai warriors he saw in Africa with the soldiers who had dropped the atom bomb and wondered if the evolution from poisoned arrows to spectacular weapons of mass destruction really meant that the world was moving forward. Lying under an acacia tree one early morning in Kenya, he decided that he was less certain than ever about the benefits of "progress." Given the choice between birds and airplanes, the great flier decided he would rather have birds.[55]

He was buried in Maui on August 26, 1974, in a grave he helped design in the traditional Hawaiian style.

ACKNOWLEDGMENTS

I AM INDEBTED to a great many people whose contributions have enriched this book and my experience in writing it. Those whose work bears directly on my themes are cited in the notes. Many more individuals have shaped my thinking, and while I cannot thank them all here, I do want to mention Kenneth T. Jackson, whose thinking and research has been an ongoing influence.

I have also benefited from colleagues whose generosity of spirit and willingness to share are part of the joys of academic life. The president of the CUNY Graduate Center, Bill Kelly, and my colleagues in the History program have made the GC an exciting and intellectually challenging environment. I especially want to thank Joshua Freeman, Dagmar Herzog, David Nasaw, James Oakes, and Helena Rosenblatt for their advice and stimulating suggestions. The late Jack Diggins, a cherished colleague, encouraged me in this project and would drop books on my desk to help with the research. I am indebted to Reeve Lindbergh for granting me unrestricted access to the Charles A. Lindbergh Papers at the Yale University Libraries, and I am grateful to Judith Ann Schiff, the Chief Research Archivist/Manuscripts and Archives at Yale and the foremost expert on the Lindbergh Papers, for her help. I also want to thank staffs at the Amherst College Archives Libraries and Special Collections, the Herbert Hoover Presidential Library, Library of Congress, and the National Archives

It is also a pleasure to thank a number of wonderful history students from the City University of New York Graduate School, Michelle Chen, Jeannette Gabriel, Lindsay Krasnoff, Daniel London, Paul Naish, and Alisa Stern for their assistance with this project. Renee Epstein commented on early versions of several chapters. I am grateful to Matt Magida for his help with copying massive amounts of research material.

Dan Green, my agent, suggested this topic to me and was a source of boundless encouragement and good cheer throughout. It is very much a part of the craft of my editor at Oxford University Press, Tim Bent, that the extent of his contribution is evident to me alone. He was a joy to work with. Dayne Poshusta, also of Oxford, was unfailingly helpful and gracious.

To my wife, Rachel, and to my family, who contribute to my work in so many important ways, I owe a special debt.

NOTES

Abbreviations

AML: Anne Morrow Lindbergh

Berg: A. Scott Berg, *Lindbergh*

CAL: Charles A. Lindbergh

CALP: Charles Augustus Lindbergh Papers, Manuscripts and Archives, Yale University Library

CSM: Christian Science Monitor

DWM: Dwight W. Morrow Papers, Amherst College Archives and Special Collections

LAT: Los Angeles Times

NYT: New York Times

OHCCU: Oral History Collection, Columbia University

WP: Washington Post

WSJ: Wall Street Journal

Introduction

1. "How did he make it in that thing?" Senator Barry Goldwater, a flier himself, asked himself when he looked at the *Spirit* on display at the Smithsonian. The plane weighed less than a ton. David Courtwright, *Sky as Frontier: Adventure, Aviation, and Empire* (College Station: Texas A&M University Press, 2005), 70.

2. Charles A. Lindbergh, *Autobiography of Values*, ed. William Jovanovich and Judith A. Schiff (New York: Harcourt Brace Jovanovich, 1978), 394.

3. A. Scott Berg, *Lindbergh* (New York: G. P. Putnam, 1998), 6.

4. "divine genius," Modris Eksteins, *Rites of Spring: The Great War and the Birth of the Modern Age*, (New York: Anchor Books, 1990), 248; "greatest," Review of Berg, *Lindbergh*, in *The Economist*, 14 November 1998, S6–S7.

5. William F. Buckley, Jr., "Charles Lindbergh, Unexplained," *New York Times Book Review*, 24 April 1977, BR3. A valuable, if dated, review of a wide range of Lindbergh material can be found in Perry D. Luckett, *Charles A. Lindbergh, A Bio-Bibliography* (Westport, CT: Greenwood Press, 1986); Joyce Milton, *Loss of Eden: A Biography of Charles and Anne Morrow Lindbergh* (New York: HarperCollins, 1993); Walter L. Hixson, *Charles A. Lindbergh, Lone*

Eagle (New York: HarperCollins, 1996); and Berg were all published subsequently. Among biographies and monographs the following remain useful: Brendan Gill, *Lindbergh Alone* (New York: Harcourt Brace Jovanovich, 1977); Leonard Mosley, *Lindbergh: A Biography* (Garden City, NY: Doubleday, 1976); Walter S. Ross, *The Last Hero: Charles A. Lindbergh* (New York: Harper & Row, 1968); Kenneth Sydney Davis, *The Hero: Charles A. Lindbergh and the American Dream* (Garden City, N.Y.: Doubleday, 1959); Dominick A. Pisano and F. Robert van der Linden, *Charles Lindbergh and the Spirit of St. Louis* (New York: Harry N. Abrams, 2002). Lindbergh's own writings can be read to trace the flier's own changing attitudes and outlooks. They include *We: The Famous Flier's Own Story of His Life and His Transatlantic Flight* (New York: G. P. Putnam's Sons, 1928); *The Spirit of St. Louis* (New York, Scribner, 1953); *The Wartime Journals of Charles A. Lindbergh* (New York: Harcourt Brace Jovanovich, 1970); and *Autobiography of Values*. More than a dozen works by his wife Anne Morrow Lindbergh and memoirs by his youngest daughter, Reeve Lindbergh, help fill out the historical picture.

6. Paul A. Carter, *The Twenties in America*, 2nd ed. (New York: Thomas Y. Crowell, 1975), 67.

7. Eksteins, *Rites of Spring*, 248.

8. *NYT*, 24 May 1927, 3.

9. Courtwright, *Sky as Frontier*, 35.

10. CAL, *Autobiography of Values*, 3

Chapter 1

1. Bruce L. Larson, *Lindbergh of Minnesota: A Political Biography* (New York: Harcourt Brace Jovanovich, 1973), 18–30; CAL, *Autobiography of Values*, 50.

2. CAL, *Autobiography of Values*, 50–52; quote, Davis, *Hero*, 19; CAL, "Comments on Kenneth Davis, *The Hero*," 4 August 1969, box 450, folder 4, p. 3, CALP; Berg, 25.

3. Davis, *Hero*, 32; Larson, *Lindbergh of Minnesota*, 4; Milton, *Loss of Eden*, 5; Berg, 11.

4. Milton, *Loss of Eden*, 6; Berg, 11–13.

5. Berg, 13.

6. Larson, *Lindbergh of Minnesota*, 16–17; Berg, 15–16; Milton, *Loss of Eden*, 7.

7. CAL to Bruce Larson, "Comments for his biography of Charles Lindbergh, Sr.," 7 April 1967, box 450, folder 11, quote on 8, 18–26, CALP.

8. Berg, 29.

9. Larson, *Lindbergh of Minnesota*, 20, 28; Berg, 16–18.

10. CAL to Larson, "Comments for his biography of Charles Lindbergh, Sr.," quote on 15; Berg, 22; Milton, *Loss of Eden*, 1.

11. CAL to Larson, "Comments for his biography of Charles Lindbergh, Sr.," quote on 16; Berg, 18–23.

12. CAL to Larson, "Comments for his biography of Charles Lindbergh, Sr.," 16; Larson, *Lindbergh of Minnesota*, 29; both quotes in Berg, 23.

13. CAL, "Comments on Davis," 2; CAL, *Autobiography of Values*, 50; Davis, *Hero*, 18–19; Berg, 24.

14. CAL, *Autobiography of Values*, 50; Berg, 31; CAL, "Comments on Davis," "rippling" quote on 1; CAL to Larson, "Comments for his biography of Charles Lindbergh, Sr.," "most handsome," 9, 28, 31.

15. Berg, 25–28.

16. CAL, "Comments on Ross, *Last Hero*," 1 August 1968, box 450, folder 14, p. 12, CALP; CAL, *We*, 19; CAL, "Comments on Associated Press biographical sketch issued 1 April 1954," 6 May 1969, box 450, folder 1, pp. 1–3, CALP; Larson, *Lindbergh of Minnesota*, 30.

17. CAL, *Autobiography of Values*, 50–51; CAL to Larson, "Comments for his biography of Charles Lindbergh, Sr.," 10; Berg, 28–29.

18. CAL, *Spirit of St. Louis*, 373.

19. Larson, *Lindbergh of Minnesota*, 35.

20. Milton, *Loss of Eden*, 8.

21. CAL, "Comments on Davis," 1, "experience" quote on 3; CAL to Bruce Larson, "Comments for his biography of Charles Lindbergh, Sr.," "protected family life" quote on 16; CAL, "Comments on Associated Press"; CAL, *We*, 19; Larson, *Lindbergh of Minnesota*, 30–31; Berg, 24.

22. Larson, *Lindbergh of Minnesota*, 31.

23. Berg, 30–31, 37; Larson, *Lindbergh of Minnesota*, quote on 31.

24. CAL, *Spirit of St. Louis*, 392.

25. CAL to Larson, "Comments for his biography of Charles Lindbergh, Sr.," "loved the farm" quote on 3, 32; Berg, 32; CAL, *Spirit of St. Louis*, "Wall Street interests" quote on 392.

26. Berg, 32; CAL, *Spirit of St. Louis*, quote on 392; John Lardner, "The Lindbergh Legends," in Isabel Leighton, ed., *The Aspirin Age* (New York: Simon and Schuster, 1949), 193.

27. CAL to Larson, "Comments for his biography of Charles Lindbergh, Sr.," 9; Luckett, *Charles A. Lindbergh*, 2–4; CAL, "Comments on Associated Press," 4; Berg, 32, quotes on 37, 39, 42.

28. CAL to Larson, "Comments for his biography of Charles Lindbergh, Sr.," 9, 16; Berg, "bloodsucker" quote on 39, "awfully sorry" quote on 47.

29. Larson, *Lindbergh of Minnesota*, 32; CAL, "Comments on Davis," 7; Davis, *Hero*, 46; CAL, "Comments on Ross," 12.

30. CAL, *Spirit of St. Louis*, 310–12; Berg, 43.

31. Berg, 38; CAL, *Spirit of St. Louis*, 310–13, quote on 312–13.

32. CAL, *Spirit of St. Louis*, 310–13.

33. Ibid., 310–11, "feel of " quote on 313; CAL, "Comments on Davis," 1.

34. CAL, *Spirit of St. Louis*, 311–12, 334; CAL, "Comments on Davis," quotes on 1.

35. CAL, *Autobiography of Values*, 51; CAL, *Spirit of St. Louis*, 290, 336; CAL, "Comments on Davis," quote on 7.

36. CAL to Larson, "Comments for his biography of Charles Lindbergh, Sr.," 9, 24; Berg, quote on 41.

37. CAL to Larson, "Comments for his biography of Charles Lindbergh, Sr.," 1–2; CAL, *Spirit of St. Louis*, quotes on 377. "Guns played a big part in the values of my boyhood" (CAL, *Autobiography of Values*, 4).

38. CAL, "Comments on Ross," 13; CAL, *Spirit of St. Louis*, quotes on 376, 391; Milton, *Loss of Eden*, 29.

39. CAL, "Comments on Davis," "You and I" quote on 2, "I was proud" quote on 7, "the deepest" quote on 2; Berg, "We'll get along" quote on 42; CAL to Larson, "Comments for his biography of Charles Lindbergh, Sr.," 27; Larson, *Lindbergh of Minnesota*, 32; CAL, "Comments on Ross," 13.

40. CAL, "Comments on Davis," 4–5, "zone of gloom" quote on 10; CAL, "Comments on Dale Van Every, *Charles Lindbergh: His Life*," 29 November 1968, box 450, folder 15, "I loved" quote on 1, 9, CALP; Davis, *Hero*, 25; Lardner, "Lindbergh Legends," 197; CAL, *Autobiography of Values*, 58; Berg, 33; CAL, *Spirit of St. Louis*, "if I had" quote on 244.

41. CAL, *Spirit of St. Louis*, "secret" quote on 376; Berg, "the value" quote on 34.

42. CAL, *Spirit of St. Louis*, 245, 339; CAL, *Autobiography of Values*, 58–59.

43. CAL to Larson, "Comments for his biography of Charles Lindbergh, Sr.," 9; CAL, *Spirit of St. Louis*, 316–18, "face beaming" quote on 317; Davis, *Hero*, 55–57.

44. CAL, *Spirit of St. Louis*, 317, 376–77; CAL, "Comments on Ross," 13; Milton, *Loss of Eden*, 15.

45. CAL, *Spirit of St. Louis,* 318; Milton, *Loss of Eden,* 16–17; Davis, *Hero,* 57; Berg, 39–40.

46. CAL, *Spirit of St. Louis,* 318–19.

47. Milton, *Loss of Eden,* 17; CAL, *Spirit of St. Louis,* 319–20.

48. Berg, 32, quote on 4; CAL, "Comments on Van Every," 6; CAL, *We,* 22; Luckett, *Charles A. Lindbergh,* 2–4; CAL, *Spirit of St. Louis,* 320.

49. CAL, *We,* 22; CAL, "Comments on Davis," 11.

50. *WP,* 22 May 1927, "while not" quote on 4; Berg, 42; CAL, "Comments on Davis," 12; CAL, "Comments on Van Every," "Limburger" quote on 5; CAL, *We,* 22.

51. CAL, "Comments on Davis," "preferred few" quote on 12; CAL to Larson, "Comments for his biography of Charles Lindbergh, Sr.," 25; Davis, *Hero,* 58–59; Berg, 21–22, "only insanity" quote on 47.

52. CAL, *Autobiography of Values,* 55–57, quote on 57.

53. Ibid., 59; CAL to Larson, "Comments for his biography of Charles Lindbergh, Sr.," 28.

54. Larson, *Lindbergh of Minnesota,* 179–81, 191, 206, 213, 285, "We must" quote on 288; CAL to Larson, "Comments for his biography of Charles Lindbergh, Sr.," 2–3; CAL, *Spirit of St. Louis,* 392.

55. Larson, *Lindbergh of Minnesota,* 37, "true and impartial" quote on 207; Davis, *Hero,* 48–51. Charles would later write with a firm sense of racial identity, suggesting that the United States must try to keep itself from "mongrelization." This is discussed in the epilogue.

56. Berg, 45; Larson, *Lindbergh of Minnesota,* 186–90, quotes on 189–90; Lardner, "Lindbergh Legends," 193.

57. CAL, *Autobiography of Values,* quotes on 7, 61; CAL to Larson, "Comments for his biography of Charles Lindbergh, Sr.," 2–3; Larson, *Lindbergh of Minnesota,* 192–96.

58. Davis, *Hero,* 42, 446; Berg, 48.

59. CAL, "Comments on Associated Press," 4; CAL to Larson, "Comments for his biography of Charles Lindbergh, Sr.," 6; CAL, "Comments on Van Every," 6–7; CAL, *Autobiography of Values,* 7; Berg, 46–47.

60. Larson, *Lindbergh of Minnesota,* 210; Berg, quotes on 46–47.

61. CAL to Larson, "Comments for his biography of Charles Lindbergh, Sr.," 2, 30; Milton, *Loss of Eden,* 24, 30; Berg, 48–52.

62. CAL to Larson, "Comments for his biography of Charles Lindbergh, Sr.," 6; Berg, 48–50.

63. Davis, *Hero,* 62; CAL, "Comments on Davis," 13; CAL, *Autobiography of Values,* 62.

64. CAL to Larson, "Comments for his biography of Charles Lindbergh, Sr.," 6; CAL, *Autobiography of Values,* 62–63; Berg, 50; Milton, *Loss of Eden,* 36.

65. CAL, *Autobiography of Values,* "I was among" quote on 8; Davis, *Hero,* "I guess I knew" quote on 60–61; Berg, 50–52, "to buck" quote on 50; Milton, *Loss of Eden,* 37–38.

66. CAL, "Comments on Davis," 9.

67. Lardner, "Lindbergh Legends," 193; AML, "The Changing Concept of Heroes," *Minnesota History,* Winter 1979, 307; Davis, *Hero,* 53; Berg, 49; Milton, *Loss of Eden,* 34–35.

68. CAL, *Spirit of St. Louis,* "spend too much" quote on 392; CAL to Larson, "Comments for his biography of Charles Lindbergh, Sr.," "He himself" quote on 17.

69. CAL to Larson, "Comments for his biography of Charles Lindbergh, Sr.," 17.

70. CAL, "Comments on Davis," 20; CAL to Larson, "Comments for his biography of Charles Lindbergh, Sr.," 8; CAL, *Spirit of St. Louis,* 245; CAL, *Autobiography of Values,* 8, 63.

71. Davis, *Hero,* 65–66; CAL, "Comments on Davis," 14–15.

72. CAL to Larson, "Comments for his biography of Charles Lindbergh, Sr.," 11–13; Davis, *Hero,* "After leaving" quote on 15; Berg, 53, 59.

73. CAL, "Comments on Davis," 20; CAL to Larson, "Comments for his biography of Charles Lindbergh, Sr.," 3; Berg, 57; Milton, *Loss of Eden,* 43.

74. CAL, *Spirit of St. Louis,* 384.

75. CAL, *Autobiography of Values,* 6; Luckett, *Charles A. Lindbergh,* 5; Davis, *Hero,* 63; Berg, 36, 34, 45; Robert A. Rosenbaum, *The Aviators* (New York: Facts on File, 1992), 44; Lardner, "Lindbergh Legends," 197; Milton, *Loss of Eden,* 27.

76. CAL, *Autobiography of Values,* 57.

77. CAL, "Comments on Van Every," quote on 6; CAL to Larson, "Comments for his biography of Charles Lindbergh, Sr.," 6.

78. CAL, *Spirit of St. Louis,* quote on 403; Berg, 55; Davis, *Hero,* 67.

79. CAL, "Comments on Ross," 17; CAL, "Comments on Davis," quote on 15.

80. Davis, *Hero,* 69–70; Berg, 53–54.

81. CAL, *Spirit of St. Louis,* quotes on 403–4; Berg, 55.

82. Brian Horrigan, "My Own Mind and Pen: Charles Lindbergh, Autobiography and Memory," *Minnesota History,* Spring 2002, 4; CAL, "Comments on Davis," 18; CAL, "Comments on Ross," 16; CAL, *We,* "the long hours" quote on 23; CAL, *Spirit of St. Louis,* 404; CAL, "Comments on Van Every," "I thoroughly disapproved" quote on 7.

83. CAL, "Comments on Van Every," "rifle team" quote on 9; CAL, "Comments on Raymond H. Fredette, Notes," 19 May 1973, box 450, folder 9, 1, CALP; CAL, *We,* "every minute" quote on 24.

84. Berg, quotes on 56, 58; CAL, *Spirit of St. Louis,* 247; CAL, "Comments on Van Every," 9; CAL, "Comments on Davis," 6.

85. Berg, 56–58.

86. P. H. Hye(?) approved by F. E. Turneaure to Mrs. Charles Lindbergh, 7 February 1922, box 325, folder 1, CALP.

87. CAL, *Autobiography of Values,* 9; CAL, *Spirit of St. Louis,* quote on 404.

88. CAL, "Comments on Van Every," "to enter" quote on 1; CAL, *Spirit of St. Louis,* "Science, freedom" quote on 261.

89. CAL, *Spirit of St. Louis,* "wild with" quote on 252, 385; CAL, "Comments on Davis," "You're your own" quote on 20.

Chapter 2

1. I have borrowed this idea from Richard C. Wade's treatment of the omnibus, "Urbanization," in C. Vann Woodward, ed., *The Comparative Approach to American History* (New York: Oxford University Press, 1968), 191–92.

2. Robert M. Kane and Allan Vose, *Air Transportation,* 8th ed. (Dubuque, Iowa: Kendall/Hunt, 1982), 2.1–2.5.

3. Roger E. Bilstein, *Flight in America 1900–1983: From the Wrights to the Astronauts* (Baltimore: Johns Hopkins University Press, 1984), 9–10; Carl Solberg, *Conquest of the Skies: A History of Commercial Aviation in America* (Boston: Little, Brown, 1979), quote on 4–5.

4. Robert Wohl, *A Passion for Wings: Aviation and the Western Imagination, 1908–1918* (New Haven: Yale University Press, 1994), 9–10; Tom D. Crouch on Wright in Eric Foner and John A. Garraty, eds., *The Reader's Companion to American History* (Boston: Houghton Mifflin, 1991), 1183.

5. Foner and Garraty, *Reader's Companion,* 1183; Bilstein, *Flight in America,* 8–10.

6. Joseph J. Corn, *The Winged Gospel: America's Romance with Aviation, 1900–1950* (New York: Oxford University Press, 1983), 5; Foner and Garraty, *Reader's Companion,* 1183; Kane and Vose, *Air Transportation,* 3.16–17.

7. Solberg, *Conquest of the Skies,* 6; Bilstein, *Flight in America,* 3; Kane and Vose, *Air Transportation,* 3.17–19.

8. Kane and Vose, *Air Transportation,* 3.15; Corn, *Winged Gospel,* 5.

9. Berg, 60–61; Wohl, *Passion for Wings,* quote on 2; William J. Claxton, *Mastery of the Air,* 2nd ed. (London: Blackie and Sons, 1915).

10. Corn, *Winged Gospel,* 6–7; Bilstein, *Flight in America,* 12–15; G. R. Simonson, "The Demand for Aircraft and the Aircraft Industry, 1907–1958," *Journal of Economic History* 20, no. 3 (1960): 361; Berg, 61.

11. Corn, *Winged Gospel,* 7–9, "air ships" quote on 8; Bilstein, *Flight in America,* 15–17, "age of flight" quote on 17.

12. Solberg, *Conquest of the Skies,* 8; Claxton, *Mastery of the Air,* 143.

13. The search for a way to measure longitude was furthered by the offer of prizes. Prizes were commonly offered to patronize basic research in the eighteenth century. Dava Sobel, *Longitude: The True Story of a Lone Genius Who Solved the Greatest Scientific Problem of His Time* (New York: Walker, 1995); Michael Schrage, "Use Ingenious Prizes to Capture Ingeniousness of Inventors," *WP,* 20 July 1990, F3; Joel Mokyr, *The Lever of Riches: Technological Creativity and Economic Progress* (New York: Oxford University Press, 1990); Robin Hanson, "Patterns of Patronage: Why Grants Won Over Prizes in Science," University of California, Berkeley, 28 July 1998, http://www.hanson.gmu.edu/whygrant.pdf+robin+hanson,+Prizes& hl=en&ct-clnk&cd=1&gl=us; Edward Jablonski, *Atlantic Fever* (New York: Macmillan, 1972), 6.

14. *NYT,* 19 April 1911, 12; "Aviation Prizes at Home and Abroad," *Scientific American* 104 (13 May 1911): 475; "Aeronautic Apathy in This Country," *NYT,* 1 June 1911, 9.

15. http://www.spartacus.schoolnet.co.uk/BUharmsworth.htm; Claxton, *Mastery of the Air,* 157–60; Jablonski, *Atlantic Fever,* 2.

16. *NYT,* 2 October 1910, 1, 11 October 1910, 2, 30 October 1910, 1; "Prizes at the International Aviation Meeting," *Scientific American* 103 (8 October 1910): 274; "Aviation Prizes at Home and Abroad," *Scientific American* 104 (13 May 1911), quote on 475; "Failure of the Military Aeroplane Competition," *Scientific American* 111 (7 November 1914): 397; Earle L. Ovington, "Gordon Bennett International Aviation Trophy," *Scientific American* 104 (22 April 1911): 407–8; "James Gordon Bennett Aviation Contest of 1912," *Scientific American* 107 (21 September 1912): 245–46; Coverage of Curtiss in *NYT,* 30 May 1910, 1–6; Corn, *Winged Gospel,* 8; Solberg, *Conquest of the Skies,* 8.

17. *NYT,* 21 November 1910, 7, 21 August 1911, 2.

18. French Strother, "Flying across the Continent," *World's Work,* part 1, 23 January 1912, 339, part 2, 2 February 1912, 399–408; "First Transcontinental Aeroplane Flight by Calbraith P. Rodgers on a Wright Aeroplane," *Scientific American* 105 (18 November 1911): 449.

19. *NYT,* 6 April 1912, 5; Corn, *Winged Gospel,* 10–11; "Fatal Accident to Rodgers," *Scientific American* 106 (20 April 1912): 356.

20. Marius Krarup, "The Coroner's Inquest: Why Men Are Killed in Airplanes," *Scientific American* 104 (13 May 1911): 464–65.

21. "Death Roll of the Aeroplane," *Scientific American* 104 (14 January 1911), quote on 28; Courtwright, *Sky as Frontier,* 34; Bilstein, *Flight in America,* 17, 25; Corn, *Winged Gospel,* 9.

22. *NYT,* 19 November 1911, "useless" quote on C8; 21 August 1911, 2, 6 April 1912, 5, 27 November 1910, C4; Patricia Kerwin and Bradley Germand, "Aero Club of America Scrap Books: A Finding Aid," Library of Congress, http://www.loc.gov/rr/mss/text/aero.html; Krarup, "Coroner's Inquest," "death trap" quote on 464; Bilstein, *Flight in America,* 17, 26; Corn, *Winged Gospel,* 9; *NYT,* 3 January 1911, "means of display" quote on 6.

23. Richard P. Hallion, *Legacy of Flight: The Guggenheim Contribution to American Aviation* (Seattle: University of Washington Press, 1977), "rambunctious" quote on 3; Bilstein, *Flight in America*, 31; Eksteins, *Rites of Spring*, "vitalism" quote on xv.

24. Corn, *Winged Gospel*, 11; Bilstein, *Flight in America*, 32.

25. The Wrights held a very broad patent for controlling flight and demanded licensing fees. They fiercely defended their patents in the courts. For more than a decade both the Wright and Curtiss companies were locked in court battles that blocked new construction of airplanes, until the U.S. government pressed them to arrive at a cross-licensing agreement. *NYT,* 7 August 1917, 5; Bilstein, *Flight in America*, 36; Donald M. Pattillo, *Pushing the Envelope: The American Aircraft Industry* (Ann Arbor: University of Michigan Press, 1998), 32.

26. John B. Rae, *Climb to Greatness: The American Aircraft Industry 1920–1960* (Cambridge, MA: MIT Press, 1968), 2; Bilstein, *Flight in America*, 36; National Academy of Engineering website, Great Achievements, http://www.greatachievements.org/?id+2951, 1–2; Davis, *Hero*, 125; Elsbeth Freudenthal, *The Aviation Business: From Kitty Hawk to Wall Street* (New York: Vanguard Press, 1940), "flaming coffins" quote on 35–36; Simonson, "Demand for Aircraft," 364.

27. Bilstein, *Flight in America*, 36–37; National Academy of Engineering website, 2.

28. Bilstein, *Flight in America*, 37, quote on 39.

29. Henry Ladd Smith, *Airways: The History of Commercial Aviation in the United States* (New York: Knopf, 1942), 88.

30. Pattillo, *Pushing the Envelope*, 57; Rae, *Climb to Greatness*, 2; Simonson, "Demand for Aircraft," 365; Smith, *Airways*, 88.

31. Bilstein, *Flight in America*, 42.

32. *NYT,* 29 August 1920, quote on 6; Roger Bilstein, *Flight Patterns: Trends of Aeronautical Development in the United States, 1918–1929* (Athens: University of Georgia Press, 1983), 12; Bilstein, *Flight in America*, 43.

33. *NYT,* 29 August 1920, 6, editorial, 15 November 1921, 15, 12 June 21, 81; Simonson, "Demand for Aircraft," 365.

34. The term *barnstorming* comes from the practice of flying in and out of barns; National Academy of Engineering website, 1–2; Hallion, *Legacy of Flight*, 6. Between 1921 and 1924 the *Yearbook* published by the Aeronautical Chamber of Commerce reported 470 accidents, resulting in 221 deaths, most caused by gypsy fliers. Bruce Larson, "Barnstorming with Lindbergh," *Minnesota History*, Summer 1991, 237; Bilstein, *Flight in America*, 21–25.

35. Courtwright, *Sky as Frontier*, "aeronauts" quote on 48; Bilstein, *Flight Patterns*, 60–61, 62, "lively example" quote on 60; Hallion, *Legacy of Flight*, 6; Corn, *Winged Gospel*, "flying gypsies" quote on 12–13.

36. Bilstein, *Flight Patterns*, 156; Wohl, *Passion for Wings*, 292.

37. Quoted in Corn, *Winged Gospel*, 39, 30.

38. All quotes in ibid., 30–31, 135, 27, 47–48, x, 35.

39. Wohl, *Passion for Wings*, "heroic brotherhood" quote on 3, 282, 312, n. 91; Raymond H. Fredette, "Cadet Days and Flight Training," box 450, folder 7, p. 1, CALP; CAL, *Spirit of St. Louis*, 312; CAL, *Autobiography of Values*, "intense and fascinating" quote on 55, 63; CAL, *We*, 23, "study aeronautics" quote on 24–25.

40. Milton, *Loss of Eden*, "flying gypsies" quote on 43; CAL, *Autobiography of Values*, "life of the aviator" and "Look down" quotes on 63–64.

41. CAL, *We*, 25; CAL, *Autobiography of Values*, "the name 'Nebraska'" quote on 9; Davis, *Hero*, 77; Berg, 63.

42. CAL to R. H. Fredette, 15 July 1971, box 450, folder 7, p. 1, CALP.

43. Berg, 64; Milton, *Loss of Eden*, 44; CAL, *We*, "How clearly" quote on 25; CAL, *Spirit of St. Louis*, "resting on" quote on 249–51; Davis, *Hero*, 79–80.

44. CAL, *Autobiography of Values*, 64; CAL, *Spirit of St. Louis*, "Behind every" quote on 247–48, "immortality is" quote on 255; CAL, "Comments on Davis," 13.

45. CAL, *We*, 26–29; CAL, *Spirit of St. Louis*, 250–51, "branches of" quote on 264; Raymond H. Fredette, Notes for a ms. on Lindbergh and the army, box 450, folder 9, p. 2, CALP; CAL, "Comments on Davis," 17–18.

46. CAL, *We*, 29, "exhilarated calmness" quote on 30–31; CAL, *Spirit of St. Louis*, 254–61.

47. CAL, *Spirit of St. Louis*, "stepped suddenly" quote on 260–61; Davis, *Hero*, 87; CAL, *We*, 31–34; Milton, *Loss of Eden*, 48.

48. Larson, "Barnstorming with Lindbergh," 234; CAL, *Spirit of St. Louis*, 265–68; Davis, *Hero*, 91; Berg, "great life" quote on 67.

49. CAL, *Spirit of St. Louis*, "take me" quote on 431; Berg, 82.

50. CAL, *We*, 30–39, "own ship" on 39; Milton, *Loss of Eden*, 51; Berg, "You know" quote on 68. Bud Gurney, who flew with Lindbergh, later characterized the Jenny as, next to the B-24, "the worst airplane ever put in the air": Larson, "Barnstorming with Lindbergh," 231.

51. CAL, *We*, 42; CAL, "Comments on Davis," 20–21; CAL, *Spirit of St. Louis*, "Nothing broke" quote on 438–39; Davis, *Hero*, 94.

52. CAL, *Spirit of St. Louis*, 38–39, 439–41; CAL, *We*, 42–43, "worst flying country" quote on 44.

53. Davis, *Hero*, 96; CAL, *We*, 49–53; CAL, *Spirit of St. Louis*, 441–43.

54. CAL, *We*, 56–60; CAL, *Spirit of St. Louis*, 447.

55. CAL, *Spirit of St. Louis*, 447–48.

56. R. F. Fredette to CAL, 12 December 1973, box 450, folder 9, p. 1; *NYT*, 26 December 1927, 4; CAL, *We*, 41; Davis, *Hero*, 459.

57. Milton, *Loss of Eden*, 57; John G. Magee quoted in Wohl, *Passion for Wings*, 281.

58. CAL to R. H. Fredette, 15 July 1971, box 450, folder 7, p. 1, CALP; CAL, *Spirit of St. Louis*, 406–9, "four hundred" quote on 400; CAL, *We*, 78–81; CAL, *Autobiography of Values*, 10, 64.

59. CAL, *We*, 91, 97, 104.

60. CAL, *Spirit of St. Louis*, 417–19, "silver passport" quote on 405; CAL, *Autobiography of Values*, 10; Berg, 74.

61. Berg, "I may be" quote on 74–75; CAL, *Autobiography of Values*, "spread to" quote on 389; CAL to Bruce Larson, "Comments for his biography of Charles Lindbergh, Sr.," 32; CAL, "Comments on Davis," 24; CAL, "Comments on Ross," 11–12.

62. CAL, *Spirit of St. Louis*, 418–20.

63. Milton, *Loss of Eden*, 61; CAL, "Comments on Van Every," "full part" quote on 20; Berg, 78, 86; CAL, "Comments on Davis," "When the powder" quote on 35; *NYT*, 22 May 1928, 14; Davis, *Hero*, 488.

64. CAL, *Spirit of St. Louis*, 406–8, 421; Davis, *Hero*, 112; CAL, *We*, 140; CAL, "Comments on Davis," 24.

65. CAL, *We*, 128.

66. Ibid., 144–46.

67. Ibid., 144–45, 150–52; CAL, *Spirit of St. Louis*, 216; Davis, *Hero*, 115; CAL, "Comments on Davis," "I accepted danger" quote on 24. "Lt. McAlister had grown sore about our collision at Kelly and made a number of uncalled for remarks": CAL, "Dear Gang," January 1926, box 34, folder 16, CALP.

68. Davis, *Hero*, 115; Berg, 79, "any future" quote on 68; CAL, "Comments on Davis," "any acrobatic" quote on 26; "money to be made" quote in CAL to Hoag, 12 May 1925, box 1, folder 15, CALP; CAL to R. H. Fredette, 15 July 1971, box 450, folder 7, p. 1, CALP.

69. CAL, "Comments on Davis," "in-betweenness" quote on 25; Berg, "real stuff" quote on 72.

70. Berg, 84–85; Carl B. Fritsche to Lindbergh, 7 January 1925 (corrected to 1926 by curator), box 1, folder 7, CALP; Davis, *Hero*, 127; Fredette, Notes for a ms. on Lindbergh and the army, "maneuvers" and "He will successfully" quotes on 5.

71. CAL, *Autobiography of Values*, 66.

72. Bilstein, *Flight in America*, 50; Pisano and van der Linden, *Charles Lindbergh*, 95.

73. Davis, *Hero*, 124; Bilstein, *Flight Patterns*, 33, 41.

74. Davis, *Hero*, 130; CAL, "Dear Gang"; CAL, *Spirit of St. Louis*, 281; CAL to R. H. Fredette, 15 July 1971, box 450, folder 7, pp. 1–2.

75. CAL, "Comments on Harry Bruno, *Wings over America*," July 1971, box 450, folder 2, pp. 1–2, CALP; CAL, *We*, "saved his life" quote on 153–55; CAL to "Dear Gang"; Davis, *Hero*, 126–27; "first case" quote in George Polk Jr. to CAL, 20 June 1925, box 1, folder 4, CALP; "My gosh" quote in H. Bidd to Lindbergh, 29 June 1925, box 1, folder 4, CALP.

76. "COME IMMEDIATELY" quote in J. B. Wray Vaughan to CAL, 9 August 1925, box 1, folder 5, CALP; CAL, *Spirit of St. Louis*, 281; Davis, *Hero*, "giant hands" quote on 127, "tall gangling" quote on 128.

77. CAL, *We*, 159, 165–69; CAL, *Spirit of St. Louis*, 286–87; CAL to R. H. Fredette, 15 July 1971, box 450, folder 7, p. 1, CALP; CAL to "Dear Gang"; M. J. McInaney to CAL, 17 July 1926, box 1, folder 9, CALP; Clarence Young to CAL, 22 July 1926, box 1, folder 9, CALP; O. P. Austin to CAL, 18 October 1926, box 1, folder 10, CALP.

78. CAL, *We*, 158; CAL to "Dear Gang"; CAL to Hoag, 12 May 1925, box 34, folder 15, CALP.

79. Solberg, *Conquest of the Skies*, 25.

80. *NYT*, 16 January 1921, BR4; Pattillo, *Pushing the Envelope*, 37; Solberg, *Conquest of the Skies*, "Fly by compass" quote on 19.

81. Bilstein, *Flight in America*, 50; Pisano and van der Linden, *Charles Lindbergh*, 95; Freudenthal, *Aviation Business*, 75; Smith, *Airways*, 117; Davis, *Hero*, 125; Bilstein, *Flight Patterns*, 35.

82. CAL, *Autobiography of Values*, 66; Rosenbaum, *Aviators*, 47; CAL, "Comments on Bruno," 1, 2; Luckett, *Charles A. Lindbergh*, 6; CAL, *We*, 176.

83. Hallion, *Legacy of Flight*, 12.

84. Bilstein, *Flight Patterns*, 44; CAL, *We*, 176.

85. Davis, *Hero*, 134; Solberg, *Conquest of the Skies*, "normal thing" quote on 28; Corky Meyer, "Lindbergh before Paris," *Flight Journal*, February 2004, 62.

86. CAL, *Spirit of St. Louis*, "the [four] DH-4s" quote on 13; CAL, *Autobiography of Values*, "pile of refuse" quote on 67.

87. CAL, *We*, 175; Fredette, Notes for a ms. on Lindbergh and the army, 5.

88. Bilstein, *Flight Patterns*, 44–45.

89. CAL, *We*, "Practically everyone" quote on 176–77; Solberg, *Conquest of the Skies*, "The forced landing" quote on 22; Hallion, *Legacy of Flight*, "Flying low" quote on 12.

90. Solberg, *Conquest of the Skies*, "I knew that" quote on 28; CAL, *Spirit of St. Louis*, "could look forward" quote on 251–52; Berg, 83–84.

91. "Gathercoal" quote in CAL to "Dear Gang"; Hallion, *Legacy of Flight*, 12; CAL, *Spirit of St. Louis*, 243–44.

92. CAL, *We*, 179–81; CAL, *Spirit of St. Louis*, 324.

93. CAL, *Spirit of St. Louis*, 5–11; CAL, *We*, 179–86; Davis, *Hero*, 131.

94. August Thiemann to CAL, 18 September 1926, box 1, folder 10, CALP; Davis, *Hero*, 132–33; "He Does It Again: Pilot Lindbergh's Parachute Jumps Have Become a Monthly Affair," *Aeronautic Review*, November 1926, 174–75; Davis, *Hero*, 132–33; "It appears" quote

in Thiemann to CAL, 27 November 1926, box 1, folder 10, CALP; CAL, *Spirit of St. Louis*, 468. "In our October issue we published a report by Pilot Lindbergh of his parachute jump in the fog on the night of September 16th. On November 3rd Mr. Lindbergh was forced to make a second jump under almost identical circumstances and his account of this is, if possible, even more thrilling than the first one. The *Review* editor is wondering whether or not to save a page for Mr. Lindbergh in every issue" ("He Does It Again," 174–75).

95. All quotes in Davis, *Hero*, 134–35; Bilstein, *Flight Patterns*, 44–45.

96. CAL, *Spirit of St. Louis*, 261–62.

97. Ibid., 288–89.

98. Milton, *Loss of Eden*, 71.

Chapter 3

1. Mark Sullivan, *Our Times: The United States 1900–1935. Part IV, The War Begins* (New York: Scribner, 1932), 215–16, quoted in Bilstein, *Flight Patterns*, 2.

2. *WP*, 10 December 1920, 5; *NYT*, 12 December 1921, 3, 15 January 1925, "behind" quote on 20; Earl S. Findley, "Twenty Months of Commercial Aeronautics," *NYT*, 16 January 1921, BR3; "The Thing," *WSJ*, 28 October 1921, 11.

3. *NYT*, 2 June 1922, "Anybody" quote on 8; *CSM*, 20 April 1921, "whole course" quote on 2.

4. Editorial, *WP*, 14 March 1921, 6; *NYT*, 24 February 1924 XX9; Editorial, *LAT*, 19 November 1922, X17; Editorial, *NYT*, 26 March 1922; *WP*, 16 October 1921, 29.

5. *NYT*, 7 November 1926, 17, "future," "passengers whirring," and "unchallenged" quotes on 26, 19 December 1926, SM4, 24 February 1924, XX9, 24 August 1924, E5, 8 July 1923, 1; *CSM*, 17 October, 1927, 9; *WSJ*, 8 April 1925, 13, 10 July 1923, 11; editorial, *WP*, 14 April 1926, 6; Bilstein, *Flight Patterns*, 46. See also Hallion, *Legacy of Flight*, 7.

6. *WP*, 6 July 1921, 6, 29 December 1924, 2, 24 February 1927, 6; *NYT*, 18 December 1922, 26, 31 August 1924, XX7, 24 September 1925, 1, 21 October 1924, "We who gave" quote on 16, editorial, 23 November 1926, 47, 30 November 1926, 23, 19 December 1926, SM4; Col. Paul Henderson, "U.S. Aviation Depends on Air-mail's Success," *NYT*, 7 December 1924, XX9; *CSM*, 29 January 1927, 5A; Bilstein, *Flight Patterns*, 48.

7. *NYT*, 11 August 1926, "aeronautical conscience" quote on 20, 28 December 1925, 27, editorial, 16 May 1923; "All Nations but U.S. in Race for Air Supremacy," *NYT*, 24 February 1924, "only large nation" quote on XX9; more such references in *NYT*, 31 December 1923, 6, 7 July 1922, 4, 22 August 1922, 30, editorial, 18 September 1924, 20, 19 December 1926, SM4. *NYT*, 6 January 1925, "tell me" quote on 8; *WP*, 29 August 1924, "unspeakable" quote on 6; *WSJ*, 29 November 1923, 10; *LAT*, 10 June 1924, 5.

8. Findley, "Twenty Months of Commercial Aeronautics," BR3; *NYT*, 31 August 1924, SM4, XX7, E1; Smith, *Airways*, 117–25.

9. *NYT*, 24 September 1925, "to encourage" quote on 1, 10, editorial, 1 April 1925, 22; Smith, *Airways*, 117–25. The first airmail stamp cost twenty-four cents and featured the "Jenny" mail plane. A small number of this original issue were printed with the Jenny upside down, and the "inverted Jenny" stamps became highly valued collector's items: http://www.1847usa.com/identify/YearSets/1918.htm; *NYT*, 2 November 2005, A19; Solberg, *Conquest of the Skies*, 18.

10. Bilstein, *Flight Patterns*, 150; Robert Wohl, *The Spectacle of Flight: Aviation and the Western Imagination, 1920–1950* (New Haven: Yale University Press, 2005), 49, 113.

11. G. Douglas Wardrop, "War, Aviation in Retrospect: Commercial Aviation in Prospect," *Journal of the Engineers Club*, 36 (April 1919): 147–49, quoted in Bilstein, *Flight Patterns*, "the aeroplane"

quote on 164; *Harper's Weekly,* November 1926, 153, quoted in Bilstein, *Flight Patterns,* "long chained" and "Is Progress a Delusion" quotes on 160, "something better" quote on 161.

12. *NYT,* 7 February 1925, 1, 23 August 1925, XX5, 22 September 1925, 1; Bilstein, *Flight Patterns,* "incompetency" quote on 13–15.

13. *NYT,* 14 April 1927, 1; Ev Cassagneres, *The Spirit of Ryan* (New York: McGraw-Hill, 1982), 3; Jablonski, *Atlantic Fever,* 75; *CSM,* 15 October 1924, 18.

14. Alexander Klemin, "Learning to Use Our Wings," *Scientific American,* August 1927, 167; *NYT,* 26 June 1927, 1.

15. Russell Owen, "Flight to Paris Lures Noted Pilots of Air," *NYT,* 20 March 1927, XX5.

16. "Transport by Air Enters a New Stage," *NYT,* 29 August 1926, "cannily allowed" quote on XXI; *NYT,* 15 December 1925, "well known" quote on 14; *LAT,* 3 November 1925, 12; Smith, *Airways,* 104–6; Bilstein, *Flight Patterns,* 37; Bilstein, *Flight in America,* 52; Rae, *Climb to Greatness,* 15.

17. *NYT,* 19 April 1925, XX1; *CSM,* 16 July 1920, 7; Rae, *Climb to Greatness,* 14; Corn, *Winged Gospel,* 94; Douglas J. Ingells, *Tin Goose: The Fabulous Ford Trimotor* (Fallbrook, CA: Aero Publishers, 1968), 13–23.

18. *LAT,* 3 November 1925, 12; editorial, *WP,* 15 April 1925, 6; *NYT,* 27 July 1926, "comparatively cheap" quote on 16; editorial, *NYT,* 29 July 1926, 1; editorial, *CSM,* 24 January 1927, 14; *LAT,* 7 January 1925, "the U.S." quote on 2.

19. *WP,* 29 July 1926, "Putting flying" quote on 1, 28 February 1927, 1, 24 February 1927, "It is predicted" quote on 6; *NYT,* 29 August 1926, "put [America]" quote on XXI.

20. *CSM,* 27 August 1926, 1; *NYT,* 26 June 1927, 13, 16 September 1925, 3, 8 August 1926, E13, 20 August 1926, 11, 18 December 1925, 2; "Ford's Airliners Run Like Scheduled Trains," *NYT,* 14 November 1926, "Flying" quote on XX6; Hallion, *Legacy of Flight,* 18–19; *WP,* 14 April 1925, 1; Corn, *Winged Gospel,* 96; Harry Guggenheim, *The Seven Skies* (New York: G. P. Putnam's Sons, 1930), 110–12.

21. Von Hardesty, *Lindbergh, Flight's Enigmatic Hero* (New York: Harcourt, 2002), 112; *NYT,* 15 January 1925, 20.

22. Smith, *Airways,* 98–101; Hallion, *Legacy of Flight,* 14; Simonson, "Demand for Aircraft," 365; Pattillo, *Pushing the Envelope,* 58–59; *NYT,* 17 January 1926, XX6, 18 September 1925, 1, 17 January 1926, XX6, 26 June 1927, 1, 15, 6 November 1925, 25; *WP,* editorial, 14 April 1926, 6; http://www.stormingmedia.us/authors/Tate_James_P_html, *The Army and Its Air Corps: Army Policy toward Aviation, 1919–1941* (Maxwell Air Force Base, AL: http://www.stormingmedia.us/corpauthors/AIR_UNIV_MAXWELL_AFB_AL.html, 1998, 81; Charles F. Downs II, "Calvin Coolidge, Dwight Morrow and the Commerce Act of 1926," http://www.calvin-coolidge.org/htmlair_commerce_act_of1926.html.

23. Rae, *Climb to Greatness,* 123; Freudenthal, *Aviation Business,* 83; Hallion, *Legacy of Flight,* 13; Bilstein, *Flight in America,* 71, 75; Bilstein, *Flight Patterns,* 101, 127–28; "Transport by Air Enters a New Stage," *NYT,* 29 August 1926, "You may" quote on XXI.

24. Hallion, *Legacy of Flight,* 20- 26, "well being," quote on 19, "greatest road," quote on 30; Guggenheim, *Seven Skies,* 12.

25. Guggenheim *Seven Skies,* 96; Milton Lomask, *Seed Money:The Guggenheim Story* (New York: Farrar Straus, 1964), 84–85; Hallion, *Legacy of Flight,* "What" quote on 32.

26. Hallion, *Legacy of Flight,* 34–44, "actual demonstration" quote on 44.

27. *WP,* 9 January 1926, 3, 19 June 1926, "the single obstacle" quote on 5; 30 April 1927, 3; Hallion, *Legacy of Flight,* 43–44, 153.

28. http://www.aviation-history.com/navy/nc4.html, 1.

29. Robert de la Croix, *They Flew the Atlantic,* trans. Edward Fitzgerald (New York: Norton, 1959), 7–18; James V. Martin, "Across the Atlantic by Aeroplane: The Problem and Suggestion for Its Solution," *Scientific American,* 3 February 1912, quote on 106, 116.

30. Martin, "Across the Atlantic by Aeroplane," 106, 116.

31. *NYT*, 5 February 1914, 1, 21 June 1914, 3.

32. Jablonski, *Atlantic Fever*, 2; Cassagneres, *Spirit of Ryan*, 2–3; http://www.aviation-history.com/navy/nc4.html, 1; http://www.aviation-history.com/navy/nc4.html, 1–2.

33. Harry Bruno, *Wings over America: The Inside Story of American Aviation* (Garden City, NY: Halcyon House, 1944), 98; *NYT*, 9 May 1927, 2, 23 May 1927, 5; Jablonski, *Atlantic Fever*, 29–30, 33; de la Croix, *They Flew the Atlantic*, 22, 26; http://www.aviation-history.com/navy/nc4.html, 2. From Lisbon Read flew on to Plymouth, England, landing on May 31, 1919.

34. Ross, *Last Hero*, 79; *NYT*, 9 May 1927, "Cook's tour" quote on 2; http://www.aviation-history.com/navy/nc4.html, 2;; Jablonski, *Atlantic Fever*, 8, 13, 15; de la Croix, *They Flew the Atlantic*, 21. "There were emergencies, forced landings, and engine trouble all along the route": CAL, *Spirit of St. Louis*, 294–95.

35. Smith, *Airways*, 122–23; Jablonski, *Atlantic Fever*, 35–48; de la Croix, *They Flew the Atlantic*, 26; CAL, *Spirit of St. Louis*, 295.

36. *NYT*, 9 May 1927, 2; Jablonski; *Atlantic Fever*, 48–52; de la Croix, *They Flew the Atlantic*, 28.

37. Jablonski, *Atlantic Fever*, 67.

38. Davis, *Hero*, 140–41.

39. Hardesty, *Lindbergh, Flight's Enigmatic Hero*, 20; Davis, *Hero*, 141; Wohl, *Spectacle of Flight*, 14.

40. Davis, *Hero*, "the sleet" quote on 140–42; Frank P. Stockridge, *Popular Science Monthly*, August, quoted in *Literary Digest* (27 July 1926), 18; *CSM*, 28 June 1926, 1, 11 May 1926, "Having devoted" quote on 1; *NYT*, 20 August 1926, 28.

41. Davis, *Hero*, 143; Cassagneres, *Spirit of Ryan*, 3; Jablonski, *Atlantic Fever*, 75; Rae, *Climb to Greatness*, 16; *NYT*, 2 September 1926, "unsurpassed" quote on 20, 16 September 1926, 1; Wohl, *Spectacle of Flight*, 15.

42. *NYT*, 2 September 1926, 20; Davis, *Hero*, 142–43; *WP*, 4 August 1926, 3.

43. Cassagneres, *Spirit of Ryan*, 3; Jablonski, *Atlantic Fever*, 75; Rae, *Climb to Greatness*, 16; Wohl, *Spectacle of Flight*, 15; *NYT*, 16 September 1926, 1, 9, 22 September 1926, "everything" quote on 3.

44. *NYT*, 25 September 1926, 19; Stockridge, *Popular Science Monthly*, 18.

45. *NYT*, 16 September 1926, "courageous adventure" quote on 1; de la Croix, *They Flew the Atlantic*, 57.

46. *NYT*, 23 September 1926, 5, 22 September 1926, "Dinner" quote on 3.

47. *NYT*, 22 September 1926, 1, 3, 23 September 1926, 5, 24 September 1926, 23; de la Croix, *They Flew the Atlantic*, 58; Jablonski, *Atlantic Fever*, 78–81.

48. *NYT*, 22 September 1926, 3.

49. *NYT*, 22 September 1926, "We will" and "the fortune" quotes on 3, editorial, *NYT*, 22 September 1926, 26.

50. *NYT*, 22 September 1926, 4, 5, editorial, 22 September 1926, 26, 23 September 1926, "Probably Islamoff" quote on 5, 24 September 1926, 23, 25 September 1926, 19; Jablonski, *Atlantic Fever*, 80–81.

51. CAL, *Spirit of St. Louis*, 9.

52. Ibid., 4–8, 10–11, 43–45; CAL, "Comments on Associated Press," 4.

53. Berg, "I am working" quote on 93; CAL, "Comments on Davis," 30.

54. CAL, *Autobiography of Values*, 70; CAL, *Spirit of St. Louis*, quote on 15.

55. Bruno, *Wings over America*, 176; CAL, "Comments on Bruno," "No pilot" and "stature" quotes on 2; CAL, "Comments on Davis,""well satisfied" quote on 25.

56. CAL, *Spirit of St. Louis*, 15–16; CAL, *Autobiography of Values*, quote on 71.

57. CAL, *Spirit of St. Louis*, "A plane" quote on 18, "it certainly" quote on 17.

58. Ibid., 191–92.

Chapter 4

1. CAL, *Spirit of St. Louis*, 15, 19.

2. William Cronon, *Nature's Metropolis: Chicago and the Great West* (New York: W. W. Norton, 1991), 296.

3. Ibid, 297–99.

4. *NYT*, 10 July 1927, E8, 13 June 1927, 7, 26 August 1937, 21, 20 November 1965, 35; CAL, *Spirit of St. Louis*, 22.

5. *NYT*, 13 June 1927, 7; *WP*, 25 May 1927, 3.

6. CAL, "Comments on Davis," 25.

7. CAL, *Spirit of St. Louis*, "propaganda" quote on 22, "aid in making" quote on 23, "a hub" quote on 24; *NYT*, 18 March 1927, "biggest thing" quote on 9.

8. Davis, *Hero*, 149.

9. CAL, *Spirit of St. Louis*, "Besides" quote on 24–25, "trump card" quote on 26, 59.

10. Ibid., 30–31.

11. Ibid., 27–29.

12. J. S. Butz, "New York to Paris . . . How Lindbergh Did It," *Aerospace International*, May–June 1967, 25–26. In the 1925 National Air Races the Wright J-5C's forerunner scored 58 percent higher efficiency than its nearest rival and demonstrated the endurance for a cross-Atlantic trip. Milton, *Loss of Eden*, 102; Lela Warren, "Before the Flight," *Collier's*, 18 July 1931, 18; CAL, *Spirit of St. Louis*, 14.

13. CAL, "Comments on Van Every," 27; CAL, *Spirit of St. Louis*, 36–38, 45–46.

14. CAL, *Spirit of St. Louis*, 51–52.

15. Ibid., 53–55.

16. Ibid., "exceptionally" quote on 55–57; Davis, *Hero*, 470–71; Warren, "Before the Flight," 18, 19; Butz, "New York to Paris," 26.

17. CAL, *Autobiography of Values*, 72; CAL, *Spirit of St. Louis*, "We couldn't" quote on 31–32, 57; *St. Louis Post Dispatch*, 25 May 1927, quoted in in Davis, *Hero*, 468; *NYT*, 10 July 1927, E8; CAL, "Comments on Ross," 23.

18. CAL, *Spirit of St. Louis*, "worry" quote on 58; CAL, *Autobiography of Values*, 72; *NYT*, 20 November 1965, "all of" quote on 35; Reminiscences of Harold Bixby, OHCCU, 9 April 1960, "Lindbergh was" quote on 24, "even then" quote on 27.

19. CAL, *Spirit of St. Louis*, 61; *NYT*, 20 November 1965, 35, 13 June 1927, "urge to" quote on 7; Davis, *Hero*, "Charles A. Lindbergh" quote on 468–69.

20. Harold Bixby, OHCCU, 9 April 1960, quotes on 24; CAL, *Spirit of St. Louis*, 66–68.

21. CAL, *Spirit of St. Louis*, quotes on 67, 69, 70.

22. CAL, "Lindbergh Notes That Flight Today Marks Year Since He Quit Air Mail," *NYT*, 13 February 1928, 3; CAL, *Spirit of St. Louis*, quotes on 71, 72.

23. CAL, *Spirit of St. Louis*, 73–74; Berg, 96.

24. CAL, *Spirit of St. Louis*, 74–76.

25. Harold Bixby, OHCCU, 9 April 1960, 27–28; CAL, *Spirit of St. Louis*, 77.

26. Owen, "Flight to Paris," XX5; *NYT*, 17 April 1927, 22; *WP*, 24 February 1927, 6, 17 April 1927, 1, C4, 21 April 1927, "AMERICAN AIRMEN" quote on 1; Jablonski, *Atlantic Fever*, 82–84.

27. CAL, *Spirit of St. Louis*, 76–77; Owen, "Flight to Paris," XX5; *WP*, 20 April 1927, 4.

28. *NYT*, 9 February 1927, "one of the" quote on 1, 17 April 1927, 1, 22, 13 May 27, 3; Owen, "Flight to Paris," XX5; *WP*, 10 February 1927, 6, 17 April 1927, 7; Wohl, *Spectacle of Flight*, 17; Jablonski, *Atlantic Fever*, 85–87; Berg, 97, 100; CAL, *Spirit of St. Louis*, 33; http://www.check-six.com/Crash_Sites/America-NX206.htm (accessed 27 November 2007).

29. *NYT*, 17 April 1927, 1, 22; *WP*, 17 April 1927, 1; Jablonski, *Atlantic Fever*, 89–90.

30. *NYT,* 14 March 1927, 1, 24 March 1927, 12; Davis, *Hero,* 162.

31. *NYT,* 14 March 1927, "all-American" and "a French Pilot" quotes on 1, 8 May 1927, E1; *WP,* 22 April 1927, "a French plane" quote on 2, 21 April 1927, 1.

32. Jablonski, *Atlantic Fever,* 136; *WP,* 25 April 1927, 1.

33. *NYT,* 27 April 1927, "perfectly safe" quote on 3; Davis, *Hero,* 164; Jablonski, 90–91; *WP,* 27 April 1927, 3. Upon delivery Davis found that the *American Legion* actually weighed 1,150 pounds more than the design called for, throwing many of his calculations off and requiring more testing.

34. Marius Krarup, "The Coroner's Inquest: Why Men Are Killed in Airplanes," *Scientific American,* 13 May 1911, 464–65.

35. *WP,* 5 May 1927, 5; Berg, "Seems to me" quote on 104.

36. *NYT,* 8 May 1927, 1, 9 May 1927, 3; de la Croix, *They Flew the Atlantic,* "often" quote on 56–57.

37. *NYT,* 8 May 1927, 1; *WP,* 9 May 1927, 3.

38. *NYT,* 20 April 1927, 1, 26 April 1927, "willing to" quote on 3, 8 May 1927, "20 per cent" quote on E1; Jablonski, *Atlantic Fever,* 93–94.

39. *NYT,* 26 April 1927, 3, 30 April 1927, 2, 1 May 1927, 29, 3 May 1927, "Every American" quote on 10.

40. *Le Matin,* 26 May 1927,1, 9 May 1927, 1; *l'Humanité,* 9 May 1927,1; *NYT,* 3 May 1927, 10, 7 May 1927, 1, 6; Davis, *Hero,* 166.

41. *NYT,* 8 May 1927, E1.

42. *NYT,* 7 May 1927, 1, 6, 8 May 1927, "Never" quote on E1.

43. Jablonski, *Atlantic Fever,* 94; *NYT,* 7 May 1927, 1, 6; *WP,* 9 May 1927, 3; de la Croix, *They Flew the Atlantic,* 72–73; Wohl, *Spectacle of Flight,* "A strong heart" quote on 16.

44. *NYT,* 8 May 1927, "The most pathetic" quote on 1; *WP,* 9 May 1927, 3; Wohl, *Spectacle of Flight,* "the total" quote on 17.

45. Jablonski, *Atlantic Fever,* 95; Davis, *Hero,* 166; *NYT,* 9 May 1927, 1, 3.

46. Davis, *Hero,* 166; *WP,* 9 May 1927, 3, 8 May 1927, "greatest of" quote on 1, 11 May 1927, 1; de la Croix, *They Flew the Atlantic,* 78; *NYT,* 9 May 1927, 2, 30 April 1921, "Ice formation" quote on 1, 10 May 1927, "secret" quote on 1.

47. *NYT,* 11 May 27, 1; Davis, *Hero,* 167; *WP,* 11 May 1927, "misunderstood," quote on 1–2; Jablonski, *Atlantic Fever,* 98.

48. *NYT,* 9 May 1927, 2, 10 May 1927, 1, "Grave Anxiety" quote on 4, 11 May 1927, "They hoped" quote on 1.

49. *NYT,* 6 February 1927, E9, 17 April 1927, 22, 11 April 1927, 3; *WP,* 20 April 1927, 6.

50. Jablonski, *Atlantic Fever,* "character" quote on 105; Davis, *Hero,* 152.

51. Cassagneres, *Spirit of Ryan,* 1; CAL, *Spirit of St. Louis,* 80–82; Davis, *Hero,* 154.

52. CAL, *Spirit of St. Louis,* "I believe" quote on 85, 86.

53. Davis, *Hero,* 164; CAL, *Spirit of St. Louis,* "I can inspect" quote on 86; Butz, "New York to Paris," 22.

54. Fredette, Notes for a ms. on Lindbergh and the army, 6; CAL, *Autobiography of Values,* 72; CAL, *Spirit of St. Louis,* 88; Cassagneres, *Spirit of Ryan,* 52.

55. Cassagneres, *Spirit of Ryan,* 51–52; Donald Hall, "Technical Preparation of the Airplane 'Spirit of St. Louis' Technical Notes, National Advisory Committee for Aeronautics," no. 257 (Washington, 1927), 84; CAL, *Spirit of St. Louis,* 87;Fredette, Notes for a ms. on Lindbergh and the army, 6; CAL, "Comments on Fredette," 1.

56. Cassagneres, *Spirit of Ryan,* 52–54.

57. Ibid., "I'd rather" quote on 82–83, "every part" quote on 86; CAL, "Comments on Davis," 304; Hall, "Technical Preparation of the Airplane," 84–86, "practically" quote on 85;

Berg, 95, 98–100; Cassagneres, *Spirit of Ryan*, 51. Specifications for this engine are in CAL, *Spirit of St. Louis*, 545.

58. CAL, *Spirit of St. Louis*, 88–91, 96, 100, 107.

59. Cassagneres, *Spirit of Ryan*, 60; Hall, "Technical Preparation of the Airplane," 84; CAL, "Comments on notes sent by Col. Fredette," box 450, folder 9, p. 3, CALP.

60. J. T. Hartson to Mr. Petersen, 1 March 1927, reprinted in Warren, "Before the Flight," 19.

61. Davis, *Hero*, "fuss" quote on 470–71; Cassagneres, *Spirit of Ryan*, "Here" quote on 55; Berg, 102; CAL, *Spirit of St. Louis*, 102.

62. Cassagneres, *Spirit of Ryan*, "This young" quote on 45; www.Charleslindbergh.com/hall/spirit.asp, 28 July 2005, 2; *St. Louis Globe Democrat*, 23 May 1927, "and he" quote on 3, quoted in Davis, *Hero*, 469.

63. Cassagneres, *Spirit of Ryan*, "vibrations" quote on 48–49, 60; CAL, *Spirit of St. Louis*, 103–5.

64. Cassagneres, *Spirit of Ryan*, 48–49; CAL, *Spirit of St. Louis*, 99–105, 539–40; www. Charleslindbergh.com/hall/spirit.asp, 28 July 2005, 2.

65. CAL, *Spirit of St. Louis*, "with odds" quote on 99, 102, 104.

66. Wohl, *Spectacle of Flight*, 17; Davis, *Hero*, 178; Hall, "Technical Preparation of the Airplane," 85; Cassagneres, *Spirit of Ryan*, 56–57; CAL, *Spirit of St. Louis*, 92–95. This route between New York and Paris was called the Great Circle because on flat maps formed by Mercator projection the route forms a semicircle, though when observed on a globe it forms the shortest route between the two cities (Davis, *Hero*, 155).

67. Owen, "Flight to Paris," "venture" quote on XX5; CAL, *Spirit of St. Louis*, 103, 106, "almost everyone" quote on 107; *WP*, 15 April 1927, 6.

68. Cassagneres, *Spirit of Ryan*, 61; CAL, *Spirit of St. Louis*, 118–19; *NYT*, 14 May 1927, "for luck" quote on 1.

69. Davis, *Hero*, 156–57; CAL, *Spirit of St. Louis*, 531–35, "On this" quote on 102; Berg, 103.

70. CAL, "Comments on Fredette," "not much worse" quote on 3; CAL, "Comments on Davis," 30; Davis, *Hero*, 472; CAL, *Spirit of St. Louis*, 122, 504; Hall, "Technical Preparation of the Airplane," 85; Cassagneres, *Spirit of Ryan*, 64–65.

71. Hall, "Technical Preparation of the Airplane," 85; Fredette, Notes for a ms. on Lindbergh and the army, 1; CAL, *Spirit of St. Louis*, 128; Davis, *Hero*, 160.

72. CAL, *Spirit of St. Louis*, "What freedom" quote on 94, 112, "My bills" quote on 129; Fredette, Notes for a ms. on Lindbergh and the army, 6; *WP*, 29 April 1927, 7; *NYT*, 30 April 1927, 1; Davis *Hero*, 470.

73. CAL, *Spirit of St. Louis*, 128–30.

74. Ibid., 113, 132–35; *WP*, 25 May 1927, 3; Davis, *Hero*, 168, 260.

75. CAL, *Spirit of St. Louis*, "one of" quote on 138, 139–42.

76. *NYT*, 12 May 1927, 2, 28 May 1927, 3; Russell Owen, "Lindbergh Adds a New Chapter to His Saga," *NYT*, 19 February 1928, 133; Davis, *Hero*, 169; CAL, *Spirit of St. Louis*, "Right side" quote on 145.

77. CAL, *Spirit of St. Louis*, 145, "It looks" quote on 134–35, 97–98, 516; Davis, *Hero*, 479; CAL, "Cap't Lindbergh Begins Own Story of Flight," *LAT*, 28 May 1927, 1.

78. CAL, *Spirit of St. Louis*, quote on 98, 167.

79. Davis, *Hero*, 170; CAL, *Spirit of St. Louis*, 146–47, "I feel" quote on 149–50; *WP*, 13 May 1927, 1; *LAT*, 13 May 1927, 1.

80. Corn, *Winged Gospel*, "Dramatically" quote on 18; CAL, *Spirit of St. Louis*, "I've never" quote on 150; Cassagneres, *Spirit of Ryan*, "Flying" quote on 70–71; *NYT*, 13 May 1927, "sheer" quote on 1.

81. *WP*, 11 June 1927, 1; *NYT*, 13 May 1927, 1, 3, 14 May 1927, "throngs" quote on 1, 15 May 1927, "No one" and "He is" quotes on 3, 16 May 1927, 1. "Even his collar was spotless and his flying suit was immaculate" (*NYT*, 13 May 1927, 2).

82. Davis, *Hero*, 173, 179; CAL, *Spirit of St. Louis*, 169; *WP*, 16 May 1927, 1.

83. CAL, *Spirit of St. Louis*, "To hell" quote on 169; *NYT*, 15 May 1927, 2.

84. *NYT*, 14 May 1927, "would get" quote on 1; *LAT*, 13 May 1927, "remarkable" quote on 1; Berg, "for the" quote on 101; CAL, *Spirit of St. Louis*, "ARRIVE" quote on 162–64.

85. Davis, *Hero*, 176; *NYT*, 14 May 1927, 1, 15 May 1927, "I wouldn't" quote on 2; CAL, *Spirit of St. Louis*, 162, 166.

86. *NYT*, 15 May 1927, 1, 2; CAL, *Spirit of St. Louis*, 161–62, "Undismayed" quote on 166.

87. CAL, *Spirit of St. Louis*, "Accuracy" quote on 166–67, "I wanted" quote on 176, "There's never" quote on 163, 161–64; *WP*, 16 May 1927, 1; *NYT*, 21 May 1927, 2.

88. Bruno, *Wings over America*, "protect," quote on 172; Warren, "Before the Flight," "Joe" quote on 42, 43; CAL, *Spirit of St. Louis*, 225–26, 160; *NYT*, 8 March 1935, 21; CAL, "Comments on Fredette," 6. He tells a different story in "Lindbergh's Own Story: The History of the Atlantic Flight as Told by Himself," *Current History Magazine*, July 1927, 26. The Pioneer company installed an earth inductor compass for Lindbergh. It was only sporadically reliable, and Lindbergh writes, "Had I known, I would have saved weight by not installing it in the first place" (CAL, "Comments on Van Every," 23).

89. Bruno, *Wings over America*, 173; CAL, "Comments on Bruno," "I liked him" quote on 1; Davis, *Hero*, 180; CAL, "Comments on Davis," 33.

90. CAL, "Comments on *Harry A. Bruno* by Princine M. Calitri," July 1971, box 450, folder 2, "taken" quote on 1, CALP; CAL, *Spirit of St. Louis*, 156–57, 166, "several" quote on 155. Harry Knight negotiated the deal for syndication rights with the *New York Times* totaling $5,000 for world rights if the flight succeeded. See W. S. Ross, *Last Hero* (1968), 102–3.

91. CAL, *Spirit of St. Louis*, 155, 160, 166; *NYT*, 14 May 1927, 1; Berg, 107; CAL, "Comments on *Harry A. Bruno* by Princine M. Calitri," 1; CAL, "Comments on Van Every," "most courteous" quote on 21.

92. Cassagneres, *Spirit of Ryan*, 73; *NYT*, 13 May 1927, "the most" quote on 2, 1 May 1927, 1; Davis, *Hero*, 172.

93. CAL, *Spirit of St. Louis*, 168–69; Guggenheim, *Seven Skies*, "great dignity" quote on 69; Hallion, *Legacy of Flight*, "sitting" quote on 154.

94. Hallion, *Legacy of Flight*, 154; *NYT*, 14 May 1927, 1; *WP*, 14 May 1927, 1; CAL, *Spirit of St. Louis*, 164, 166–67.

95. Cassagneres, *Spirit of Ryan*, 70–71; CAL, "Comments on Ross," 25; W. S. Ross, *Last Hero*, (1968), 104; CAL, "Comments on Van Every," 21; CAL, "Comments on *Harry A. Bruno* by Princine M. Calitri," 1.

96. CAL, "Lindbergh's Own Story," 513; *NYT*, 21 May 1927, 2; CAL, *Spirit of St. Louis*, 171–73; Davis, *Hero*, 180.

97. Cassagneres, *Spirit of Ryan*, 75; CAL, *Spirit of St. Louis*, 171–72; Davis, *Hero*, 181.

98. CAL, *Spirit of St. Louis*, 172–73.

99. Cassagneres, *Spirit of Ryan*, 58.

100. *NYT*, 21 May 1927, 2; CAL, *Spirit of St. Louis*, 174–75.

101. Some reported that Lindbergh had practiced staying awake in long walks, sleepless nights, and flying jaunts, but he himself denied all this: "I made a point of averaging plenty of sleep at might. I did not practice staying awake and saw no point in doing so. I knew from

flying the mail that I could stay awake for more hours than would be required for the Paris flight." What he had not considered, he writes, was "that [he] would have to take off for the flight after almost 24 hours without sleep." This did come to haunt him. CAL, "Comments on George Fife, *Lindbergh, the Lone Eagle,*" 11 December 1968, box 450, folder 5, p. 15, CALP; CAL, "Lindbergh's Own Story," 514; CAL, *Spirit of St. Louis,* 173–77; CAL, "Comments on Davis,""Slim" quote on 34; CAL to Bruce Larson, "Comments for his biography of Charles Lindbergh, Sr.," 25.

102. CAL, "Cap't Lindbergh Begins Own Story of Flight," *LAT,* 28 May 1927, 1.

Chapter 5

1. Davis, *Hero,* 186; Cassagneres, *Spirit of Ryan,* 77; CAL, *Spirit of St. Louis,* "to slip" quote on 178.

2. *NYT,* 21 May 1927, "all the" quote on 2; *LAT,* 21 May 1927, 2; CAL, *Spirit of St. Louis,* "more like" quote on 178; Robert J. Serling, "Flying into History," *Airline Pilot,* August 1987, 24; L. E. Leipold, *Charles A Lindbergh, Aviation Pioneer* (Minneapolis: Denison, 1972), 122.

3. Warren, "Before the Flight," 44; CAL, *Spirit of St. Louis,* 182–83; Rosenbaum, *Aviators,* 41–42, 49; *LAT,* 21 May 1927, "Good luck" quote on 2; *NYT,* 21 May 1927, "If I" quote on 2.

4. His flying suit, ordered from A. G. Spalding & Bros., cost $50. "Flight Suit Worn by Charles Lindbergh," http://www.flickr.com/photos/mohitory/3462076961/ (accessed 7 December 2009); *LAT,* 21 May 1927, 2; CAL, *Spirit of St. Louis,* 184–85; Stockridge, *Popular Science Monthly,* 19; Berg, 104. Cassagneres reports that he dressed in wool, not cotton or leather, so that if he landed in water he would stay as warm as possible in wet clothing (*Spirit of Ryan,* 59).

5. CAL, *Spirit of St. Louis,* 182–83.

6. Warren, "Before the Flight," 44; Berg, "What do" quote on 115; CAL, *Spirit of St. Louis,* "Nothing" quote on 186, 538.

7. *NYT,* 21 May 1927, "Men watched" quote on 2; Warren, "Before the Flight," "died" quote on 44; Owen, "Lindbergh Adds a New Chapter," 133.

8. Lindbergh, *Spirit of St. Louis,* 186–87.

9. Ibid., "last bow" quote on 187; Warren, "Before the Flight," "5000" quote on 44; Rosenbaum, *Aviators,* 43; *NYT,* 21 May 1927, "The spirit" quote on 1.

10. *NYT,* 21 May 1927, 4.

11. Davis, *Hero,* 192.

12. CAL, *Spirit of St. Louis,* 189.

13. Ibid., 189–90, "a suit" quote on 190–91.

14. Ibid., 191–92, 195; Davis, *Hero,* 193.

15. Davis, *Hero,* 194.

16. CAL, *Spirit of St. Louis,* 196–99.

17. CAL, "Comments on Van Every," 20.

18. CAL, *Spirit of St. Louis,* 200–203.

19. Ibid., 203.

20. Ibid., 206.

21. Ibid., 209–10; CAL, "Comments on Ross," 26.

22. CAL, *Spirit of St. Louis,* "sheet of" and "I don't" quotes on 224, 225, "What justifies" quote on 269, 229.

23. Ibid., 230–32.

24. *NYT,* 21 May 1927, 2–3, quote on 3; *WP,* 21 May 1927, 1–2, quote on 2; *LAT,* 21 May 1927, 1.

25. Solberg, *Conquest of the Skies,* 71; *NYT,* 21 May 1927, "I want" quote on 6, 22 May 1927, 1; Davis, *Hero,* 195; *LAT,* 21 May 1927, "No jokes" quote on 1.

26. *LAT,* 21 May 1927, 1, 22 May 1927, B10; *NYT,* 22 May 1927, 2.

27. CAL, *Spirit of St. Louis,* "expanse" quote on 296–97, "feel dry" quote on 233, 234; *NYT,* 21 May 1927, 2.

28. CAL, *Spirit of St. Louis,* "sentries" quote on 301; CAL, "Cap't Lindbergh Begins Own Story of Flight," 1.

29. CAL, *Spirit of St. Louis,* 303.

30. Ibid., 323–25.

31. Ibid., 322, quotes on 330; CAL, "Lindbergh's Own Story," 513. *NYT,* 22 May 1927, 4, shows and describes all the instruments on his panel.

32. CAL, *Spirit of St. Louis,* 326–27, 330–31; CAL, "Lindbergh's Own Story," 513. He mentions the effect sleet had on making him consider turning back as early as 5 June 1927 in his by-line article in the *New York Times* of that day.

33. CAL, *Spirit of St. Louis,* 349, 328–29.

34. Ibid., 344, "I've lost" quote on 355.

35. Wohl, *Spectacle of Flight,* 34; CAL, *Spirit of St. Louis,* 355, "I'm asleep" quote on 362, 365.

36. CAL, *Spirit of St. Louis,* 369.

37. Ibid., 389–90.

38. Ibid., 405–6, 423, 425; CAL, "Comments on Davis," 44.

39. CAL, *Spirit of St. Louis,* 434, 452–53, 457.

40. Ibid., "Which way" quote on 459, "I want" quote on 60 ; CAL, "Lindbergh's Own Story," 515.

41. CAL, *Spirit of St. Louis,* 463, "I've never" quote on 463–64, 466.

42. Ibid., 464, 467.

43. Ibid., 471; Davis, *Hero,* 203.

44. CAL, *Spirit of St. Louis,* "A hundred" quote on 475–76, "a child" quote on 476, "All England" quote on 478.

45. *NYT,* 22 May 1927, 3, S1; Wohl, *Spectacle of Flight,* 9.

46. CAL, *Spirit of St. Louis,* "a magic carpet" quote on 480, "We" quote on 486.

47. CAL, *Autobiography of Values,* "I struck" quote on 79; CAL, *Spirit of St. Louis,* 487.

48. CAL, *Spirit of St. Louis,* 486.

49. *NYT,* 23 May 1927, 1–2.

50. CAL, *Spirit of St. Louis,* 481–82.

51. Ibid., 513, 539, "uncoordinated" quote on 490.

52. Ibid., 488–89; *NYT,* 22 May 1927, 2; *New York Herald Tribune,* international edition, 22 May 1927, 1. *Le Matin* reported 100,000 (22 May 1927, 1).

53. CAL, *Spirit of St. Louis,* 491–92; Waverly Root, *The Paris Edition: The Autobiography of Waverly Root* (San Francisco: North Point Press, 1987), "mowing" quote on 31.

54. CAL, *Spirit of St. Louis,* "of killing" quote on 326–27, 495; CAL, "Lindbergh's Own Story, 516; Berg, "as if" quote on 6; Cassagneres, *Spirit of Ryan,* 82.

55. CAL, "Lindbergh's Own Story," "The reception" quote on 516; CAL, *Spirit of St. Louis,* 495–97.

56. CAL, *Spirit of St. Louis,* 497–99; "Lindbergh entre dans L'Histoire," *Equipe,* 21 May 1927, 5.

Chapter 6

1. Henry Wales offers a firsthand but surprisingly sloppy recording of events in "Formidable," *Atlantic Monthly,* June 1937, 668. Root is generally skeptical about the account that

Lindbergh gives in *The Spirit of St. Louis* and questions Lindbergh's account of being tossed about by the crowd (*The Paris Edition*, 28–29).

2. *NYT*, 22 May 1927, 2.

3. Wohl, *Passion for Wings*, quotes on 2; Wohl, *Spectacle of Flight*, 205.

4. *NYT*, 22 May 1927, quotes on 2. Orteig was much relieved by Lindbergh's safe landing: "The thought that many men might lose their lives . . . he said, had been a severe strain on his conscience" (*WP*, 11 July 1927, LS11).

5. *NYT*, 22 May 1927, quotes on 2.

6. Root, *Paris Edition*, 30–31; T. Bentley Mott, *Myron Herrick, Friend of France: An Autobiographical Biography* (New York: Doubleday, 1929), "But" quote on *347*.

7. Raymond H. Fredette worked for many years on a book about Lindbergh. He was given unrestricted access to the Lindbergh papers, and Lindbergh read and extensively critiqued much of the working manuscript, but in the end Fredette and the publisher William Jovanovich of Harcourt Brace Jovanovich could not come to terms, and the book was never completed. While other accounts treat Lindbergh's extraordinary tour de force in France as a natural extension of his flight, Fredette offers a more plausible account of how Lindbergh, with scant preparation for diplomacy, made such a powerful impact. Fredette explains Herrick's role and argues that Lindbergh essentially became a product of his State Department handlers. Raymond H. Fredette, "The Making of a Hero: What Really Happened after Lindbergh Landed at Le Bourget," *Air Power History*, Summer 2002, 6–19; Mott, *Myron Herrick*, 341–43. *NYT*, 12 June 1927, XX15, talks of Herrick's influence; see also the extensive Herrick obituary in *NYT*, 5 April, 1929, 1, 16.

8. Captain Charles A. Lindbergh, "Lindbergh Calls London 'Bully,'" *NYT*, 2 June 1927, 2.

9. Fredette, "Making of a Hero," 6.

10. "Mott, *Myron Herrick*, such" quote on 259, "the orphans" quote on 261, "Germany's" quote on 277.

11. Philippe Roger, *The American Enemy: The History of French anti-Americanism*, trans. Sharon Bowman (Chicago: University of Chicago Press, 2006), 304, 315–17, "Of one" quote from André Siegfried, *America*, on 306, "Everything" quote from André *Tardieu*, *France and America: Some Experiences in Cooperation*, on 285–86; Mott, *Myron Herrick*, 278–79.

12. Mott, *Myron Herrick*, 271–72.

13. *WP*, 11 May 1927, 1–2; *NYT*, 11 May 1927, 1; Fredette, "Making of a Hero," 6.

14. Lisa McGerr, "The Passion of Sacco and Vanzetti: A Global History," *Journal of American History* 93, no. 4 (2007): 1091, 1105, 1109; Fredette, "Making of a Hero," 6.

15. Mott, *Myron Herrick*, quotes on 340; *NYT*, 22 May 1827, S1.

16. Fredette, "Making of a Hero," "a situation" quote on 7. These are not Herrick's words but those of someone described as being familiar with his thinking.

17. Edwin L. James, "When Lindbergh Reached Paris: A Tale of Newspaper Hardships," *NYT*, 27 May 1927, "isolate" quote on 1.

18. Wales "Formidable," "milk" quote on 670; Fredette, "Making of a Hero," 7–8. Fredette relies on some of Henry Wales's recollections, but Wales seems not to have hesitated to make up quotes and even scenes. See his "Lindy and the French," *Liberty Magazine*, 10 September 1927, 71–74. Waverly Root, who worked with him, writes that Wales would write an article describing events before they occurred and that he relied on his imagination for the Lindbergh story (*Paris Edition*, 35). Wales claims in this article that the State Department cabled Herrick "in secret code to exploit the hero to the utmost," to strengthen relations with France ("Lindy and the French," 73).

19. Fredette, "Making of a Hero," 7–8; James, "When Lindbergh Reached Paris," 1–2; *New York Herald Tribune*, 20 May 1928, II 4; *NYT*, 27 May 1927, 1.

20. Wales "Formidable," 672; James, "When Lindbergh Reached Paris," 2; Mott, *Myron Herrick*, "Pandemonium" quote on 341.

21. CAL, *Spirit of St. Louis*, "Are there" quote on 495; Wales, "Formidable," "Careful" quote on 674; Fredette, "Making of a Hero," 9.

22. Fredette, "Making of a Hero," 9; James, "When Lindbergh Reached Paris," "the men" and "the very" quotes on 1–2; CAL, *Spirit of St. Louis*, "Two French" quote on 497; *New York Herald Tribune*, 20 May 1928, II, 4; Wales, "Formidable," 670–72; Mott, *Myron Herrick*, 342.

23. James, "When Lindbergh Reached Paris," quotes on 2.

24. Fredette, "Making of a Hero," 11; James, "When Lindbergh Reached Paris," "wormed him" quote on 2; *New York Herald Tribune*, 20 May 1928, II, 4; Russell Owen, "Lindbergh's Epoch Making Flight from New York to Paris," *Current History* 26 (July 1927), "hidden" quote on 512.

25. Mott, *Myron Herrick*, "half torn" quote on 341, "This" quote on 342; *New York Herald Tribune*, 20 May 1928, II, 4; Fredette, "Making of a Hero," 12; CAL, *Spirit of St. Louis*, "in the midst" quote on 498.

26. Mott, *Myron Herrick*, "I have" quote on 342–43; Myron Herrick's article in the *Daily Northwestern* (Oshkosh, Wisconsin), 22 May 1928, in Fredette, "Making of a Hero," "My boy" quote on 12; J. C. d'Ahetze, letter to the editor, *NYT*, 13 July 1930, 48.

27. Fredette dramatizes this event, arguing that "his whole life would be changed" as a result of accepting the invitation ("Making of a Hero," 12).

28. CAL, *Spirit of St. Louis*, 499–500; Mott, *Myron Herrick*, 343; Fredette, "Making of a Hero," 13.

29. *New York Herald Tribune*, 20 May 1928, II, 4; Fredette, "Making of a Hero," 13.

30. CAL, *Spirit of St. Louis*, "*They*" quote on 500, italics added; *New York Herald Tribune*, 20 May 1928, "walked to" and "That night" quotes on II, 4 ; Mott, *Myron Herrick*, 343.

31. CAL, *Spirit of St. Louis*, 500; Mott, *Myron Herrick*, 343–45; *NYT*, 22 May 1927, 1; Root, *Paris Edition*, "great sorrow" quote on 35–36.

32. Calvin Coolidge [Kellogg] to American Embassy for delivery to Captain Lindbergh immediately upon his arrival, *The Flight of Charles A. Lindbergh from New York to Paris, May 20–21, 1927, as compiled from the Official Records of the Department of State,* (Washington, DC: Government Printing Office, 1927), "the brilliant" quote on 6; *NYT*, 22 May 1927, 1; *LAT*, 22 May 1927, 1.

33. Myron Herrick to Secretary of State, *Flight of Charles A. Lindbergh*, "deliberately" quote on 7.

34. Ibid., "YOUR" quote on 7; Fredette, "Making of a Hero," 15.

35. *NYT*, 23 May 1927, 4.

36. *NYT,* 23 May 1927, 1; CAL, "Comments on Fife," 5.

37. *NYT,* 24 May 1927, 2, 23 May 1927, "Vive la" quote on 2; *l'Humanité*, 22–29 May 1927, 28 May 1927, "cher enfant" quote on 4; *WP,* 27 May 1927, "Mr. Lindbergh" quote on 4. The *New York Times* described Lindbergh in Paris as "always accompanied by the indefatigable Ambassador Herrick" (28 May 1927, 2).

38. *NYT,* 23 May 1927, 2.

39. CAL, "Comments on Fredette," "The phraseology" quote on 1, 2. Lindbergh claimed that these articles were "often inaccurate." His version of the way it happened: "At the . . . Embassy in Paris, late in the night of May 21–22, I talked about my flight to the *Times* representative for roughly twenty minutes. I did not realize that he intended to ghost write the story, and [was] shocked when I saw the result a day or two later. However, there was simply not enough time in my schedule for me to write the stories myself, and as a result, those ghost-written accounts continued in The *Times* during the days I spent in Europe and for a short period after my return to the U.S. As soon as I could find enough time, I began writing the

stories for the *Times* myself and never permitted ghost-writing under my name thereafter" (CAL, "Comments on Fredette," 1). In CAL, "Comments on Ross," 14, 54, he adds that some later pieces written during his Caribbean tour were also ghosted.

40. *LAT,* 23 May 1927, "I am a flier" quote on 1. His first bylined *Times* account refers to "we" ("that's my ship and I"): *NYT,* 23 May 1927, 1. Herrick was struck by Lindbergh's use of the term "we" in referring to his flight and asked him what he meant by it. "Why, my ship, and me, Lindbergh replied" (Mott, *Myron Herrick,* 345).

41. *NYT,* 23 May 1927, "private visit" quote on 1; Mott, *Myron Herrick,* "scared" and "brave" quotes on 345. *Le Courier,* 23 May 1927, 1, and other accounts tell of his reassuring her that her son would be found. He later denied this: "I did not believe in raising false hopes under such circumstances" (CAL, "Comments on Ross," 27.) See also Mark Helbling, "The Meaning of Lindbergh's Flight in France," *Research Studies* 50, no. 2 (1982): 92.

42. Eksteins, *Rites of Spring,* "In Lindbergh" quote on 249; *CSM,* 23 May 1927, "intellectuals" quote on 4.

43. *CSM,* 23 May 1927, "most audacious" quote on 4; *NYT,* 26 May 1927, "Gentlemen" quote on 1.

44. Mott, *Myron Herrick,* "Benjamin Franklin" quote on 349; *NYT,* 26 May 1927, "the forerunner" quote on 1.

45. *WP,* 24 May 1927, 3; *NYT,* 24 May 1927, "Oh" quote on 2; *CSM,* 24 May 1927, 1.

46. *NYT,* 24 May 1927, 1, quotes on 2; *WP,* 24 May 1927, 3.

47. *NYT,* 24 May 1927, 3, 26 May 1927, "I could not" quote on 1; *WP,* 26 May 1927, 2.

48. *Le Matin,* 27 May 1927, "the world" quote on 1; *NYT,* 26 May 1927, "I shall" quote on 1, 27 May 1927, 1; Owen, "Lindbergh's Epoch Making Flight," 608.

49. CAL, "Lindbergh Says Sea Flying Aids Distance Flying," *LAT,* 29 May 1927, 2; *NYT,* 28 May 1927, 2.

50. Root, *Paris Edition,* quotes on 36.

51. *WP,* 24 May 1927, "the greatest" quote on 2, 29 May 1927, 1; Helbling, "Meaning of Lindbergh's Flight in France," 95; Wohl, *Spectacle of Flight,* 21; *NYT,* 24 May 1927, "the people" quote on 2, 26 May 1927, "unofficial diplomat" quote on 2; *London Times,* 27 May 1927, "Royalty" quote on 16.

52. *Le Matin,* 4 June 1927, 1, 15 June 1927, 1.

53. *NYT,* 29 May 1927, E2.

54. *NYT,* 27 May 1927, "He brought" quote on 2, 23 May 1927, "Rupert" quote on 4, "immortal" quote on 20.

55. Helbling, "Meaning of Lindbergh's Flight in France," "his personal" quote on 90; *NYT,* 29 May 1927, "Everyone" quote on E2, 23 May 1927, 4, 25 May 1927, 1, 26 May 1927, 2; *CSM,* 26 May 1927, 1.

56. *NYT,* editorial, 1 June 1927, quotes on 26; CAL, "Cap't Lindbergh Begins Own Story of Flight," *LAT,* 28 May 1927, "I would" quote on 1; CAL, "Lindbergh Says Sea Flying Aids Distance Flying," *LAT,* 29 May 1927, 1.

57. *NYT,* 29 May 1927, 1–2.

58. *NYT,* 30 May 1927, "I have met" quote on 3; CAL, "God Bless You All, Lindbergh Farewell," 5 June 1927, "changed all" quote on 1; CAL, "Belgian Ruler Knows a Lot about Flying," 30 May 1927, "more democratic" quote on 1. His articles appeared in both LAT and NYT and in this case I am quoting NYT.

59. *WP,* 29 May 1927, 1; CAL, "Comments on Fredette," 13–14; *WP,* 29 May 1927, 2; *NYT,* 30 May 1927, "I salute" quote on 3.

60. Wales, "Lindy and the French," "We must" quote on 74; Mott, *Myron Herrick,* 350; *NYT,* 26 May 1927, 2.

61. *Times* (London), 30 May 1927, "Every" quote on 14; *WP,* 30 May 1927, "worse" quote on 2; CAL, "Lindbergh Calls London 'Bully,'" 1.

62. *WP,* 30 May 1927, 1; *NYT,* 5 June 1927, "semi-hysterical" quote on E1; CAL, "Lindbergh Explains Early Return," *NYT,* 31 May 1927, 1.

63. CAL, "King George Makes Good with Capt. Lindbergh," *LAT,* 31 May 1927, "Interestingly" quote on 1; Milton, *Loss of Eden,* "How do" quote on 122; Berg, 148, 149; Leonard Mosely, *Lindbergh, a Biography* (New York: Doubleday, 1976), 116, 406; Davis, *Hero,* "he represents" quote on 225; *WP,* 1 June 1927, 1, "Absolutely" quote on 2, 31 May 1927, 2; CAL, "Comments on Fredette," "the first" quote on 16; *NYT,* 31 May 1927, 2. The answer to King George's query is that he used a container that he discarded over the ocean. He apparently violated a bit of protocol by repeating this conversation (Milton, *Loss of Eden,* 491).

64. CAL, "Lindbergh Calls London 'Bully,'" 1; Ernest Marshall, "Lindbergh's Exploit Wins British Heart; London Warms to Flight Itself More Than to His Mission as 'Ambassador,'" *NYT,* 5 June 1927, "remain[ed]" quote on E1.

65. *CSM,* 3 June 1927, 1; *NYT,* 4 June 1927, 1; *WP,* 22 May 1927, 3.

66. *NYT,* 6 June 1927, 1–2; Davis, *Hero,* 226.

67. *NYT,* 29 June 1927, 1, 2 July 1927, "hopelessly lost" quote on 1, 3; "Fliers First Story of Trip to Germany; Compass Fails, Fog and Wind Add to Peril Lost All Night 20,000 Feet Up Over Europe," *NYT,* 9 June 1927, "like riding" quote on 1.

68. *WP,* 24 May 1927, "an aesthetic" quote on 3; CAL, "Comments on Bruno," 5; Edwin L. James, "What Lindbergh Has Achieved in Europe," *NYT,* 5 June 1927, XX1.

69. *NYT,* 24 May 1927, 3.

70. *WP,* 22 May 1927, 5; *NYT,* 23 May 1927, 4, 24 May 1927, "decisively" quote on 3, 26 May 1927, "London" quote on 2; *Le Matin,* 25 May 1927, 1; *LAT,* 23 May 1927, 2. The largest single offer was for $700,000, as reported in *NYT,* 30 May 1927, 1.

71. *NYT,* 26 May 1927, "a little" quote on 2, 9 June 1927, 4; CAL, "Comments on Fredette ms. on Lindbergh and the army," 27 December 1973, box 450, folder 9, "a Franklin" quote on 3, CALP.

72. *LAT,* 25 May 1927, 1.

73. *NYT,* 9 June 1927, 4; CAL, "Lindbergh Explains Early Return," *NYT,* 31 May 1927, "What sort" quote on 1–2; *NYT,* 24 May 1927, "I made" quote on 2; CAL, "Belgian Ruler Knows a Lot about Flying," "There has" quote on 1. These articles under his byline were based on a bit of his own thinking and a lot culled from responses he gave to press queries, pulled together in a first-person voice by ghost writers.

74. *NYT,* 24 May 1927, "a big businessman" quote on 2, 25 May 1927, 1.

75. *NYT,* 30 May 1927, 1; CAL, "Comments on Davis," 38; CAL, "Cap't Lindbergh Begins Own Story of Flight," 1; CAL, *Spirit of Saint Louis,* "I can . . . fly" quote on 482.

76. Wales, "Lindy and the French," 71–74; *WP,* 27 May 1927, "I see" quote on 4; *NYT,* letters to the editor, 27 May 1927, 25.

77. *NYT,* 24 May 1927, 2, 25 May 1927, 1, 1 June 1927, "deplored" quote on 3; *WP,* 31 May 1927, 1. On Coolidge vacation plans, see Davis, *Hero,* 224.

78. *NYT,* 30 May 1927, "see many" quote on 1; James, "What Lindbergh Has Achieved in Europe," "across" quote on XX1.

79. Davis, *Hero,* 224; CAL, *Spirit of Saint Louis,* 482–83; CAL, "Comments on Fredette ms. on Lindbergh and the army," "the wish" quote on 25–26; CAL, "Lindbergh Explains Early Return," 1; CAL, "Comments on Fife," 20.

80. CAL, "Comments on Fredette ms. on Lindbergh and the army," 20, 26–27; CAL, "God Bless You All, Lindbergh Farewell," *NYT,* 5 June 1927, "lies" quote on 1; *NYT,* 5 June 1927, 1.

81. *LAT,* 23 May 1927, 3.

82. Reminiscences of Gregory Brandewiede, 1960, 41, OHCCU.

83. "The Fortnightly Field Letter," Bureau of Foreign and Domestic Commerce, Department of Commerce, July 1, 1927, no. 8, p. 3, Commerce papers, File: Lindbergh, Charles A., 1927, July–December, Herbert Hoover Papers, West Branch, Iowa.

84. Quoted in *NYT*, 6 June 1927, 2.

85. Roger, *American Enemy*, quote on 309.

86. *LAT*, 20 September, 1927, A4; Eksteins, *Rites of Spring*, "scaffolding" quote on 269, 268.

87. CAL, "Lindbergh 'Ready for Anything,'" *NYT*, 11 June 1927, "I want" quote on 1; *NYT*, 22 May 1927, 4, 7 June 1927, "American pilots" quote on 3; CAL, "Comments on Fredette ms. on Lindbergh and the army," 15–18; CAL, "Cap't Lindbergh Begins Own Story of Flight," "Flying is" quote on 1.

88. CAL, "Behind Europe in Flying Matters, Lindbergh's View of Our Status," *NYT*, 2 June 1927, 1; "Lindbergh Says Flying Boats Will Come in 5 to 10 Years," *NYT*, 9 June 1927, 1, 4.

89. *WP*, 26 May 1927, 3.

Chapter 7

1. Berg, 152.

2. Milton, *Loss of Eden*, 127; Berg, 153.

3. *LAT*, 20 September, 1927, "the accepted" quote on A4; *NYT*, 22 May 1927, 4.

4. John W. Ward, "The Meaning of Lindbergh's Flight," *American Quarterly* 10 (Spring 1958): 3–16; *NYT*, 22 May 1927, "one of" quote on 5; Walter Hinton, "What Lindbergh Is Doing for Aviation," *The Outlook* 146, no. 8 (1927), "turn of" quote on 246; Lindbergh's Leap to Paris and Fame," *Literary Digest* 93, no. 10 (1927), "the spearhead" quote on 7.

5. *NYT*, 22 May 1927, 23 May 1927, 24 May 1927, 3. The *Times* calculated that twenty-five tons of newsprint went to covering the Lindbergh story (18 June 1927, 2).

6. "UPI's 20th Century Top Stories," 23 May, 1927, UPI article A132088901; *CSM*, letter to the editor, 10 June 1927, 22; *LAT*, 23 May 1927, "was to" quote on 1.

7. "Why the World Makes Lindbergh Its Hero," *Literary Digest* 93, no. 13 (1927), "a work" quote on 8; "Lindbergh's Leap to Paris and Fame," "Nature" quote on 5–6; Solberg, *Conquest of the Skies*, "touched off" quote on 71.

8. Frederick Lewis Allen, *Only Yesterday: An Informal History of the 1920s* (New York: Harper & Bros., 1931), 183.

9. *NYT*, 11 June 1927, 1–2; *WP*, 11 June 1927, 1.

10. *NYT*, 11 June 1927, 2. Harry Bruno claimed that Richard Blythe was the one who scampered aboard to deliver the army uniform and that Blythe told Lindbergh, "Look dumbbell. . . . You were identified with no movements or causes. You were young, healthy, good looking and single—a possible future husband for every American girl. And you weren't an Army man or a Navy man but a plain civilian with a job. . . . Nobody could claim you and nobody could be against you. This Army uniform would spoil that picture" (Bruno, *Wings over America*, 183). The papers took notice. "LINDBERGH . . . WEARS PLAIN BLUE SUIT" ran the headline in *NYT*, 12 June 1927, 1; Davis, *Hero*, 227. Lindbergh disputes this version; see CAL, "Comments on Bruno," 3; "I made my flight as a civilian. Why should I not finish it as such? The suit was dark but, he recalled, not as the papers reported 'blue serge.'" See also CAL, "Comments on Davis," 39.

11. *NYT*, 12 June 1927, 1; Berg, 152–53.

12. *NYT*, 12 June 1927, 1; Davis, *Hero*, 231–32; Berg, 153.

13. *NYT*, 12 June 1927, 1, full text of speech on 2; *LAT*, 12 June 1927, 1; Davis, *Hero*, 229; Berg, 154.

14. *NYT,* 12 June 1927, 1; "It's as" quoted in Eksteins, *Rites of Spring,* 248.

15. *NYT,* 12 June 1927, "We of" and "No act" quotes on 7; "worthily won" quote on 16; Davis, *Hero,* 229–30.

16. Fredette, Notes for a ms on Lindbergh and the army, 37; Davis, *Hero,* 230; *NYT,* 13 June 1927, 2, 14 June 1927, 4; Berg, 155; Davis, *Hero,* 231.

17. CAL, Notes on R. H. Fredette, July 1971, box 450, folder 9, p. 2, CALP; *NYT,* 10 June 1927, 1; "My heart" quote in Fredette, "N[ational] G[uard]," box 450, folder 9, CALP.

18. *NYT,* 14 June 1927, "make it talk" quote on 1. "The War Dept . . . issued [an] order that he be allowed to use a plane whenever he wishes" (*WP,* 26 June 1927, 3).

19. Owen, "Lindbergh's Epoch Making Flight," 506–12, 608–11; *NYT,* 14 June 1927, 1, "What is" quote on 1–2.

20. *NYT,* 14 June 1927, 1.

21. Ibid.;"I do" ; Berg, 156.

22. *NYT,* 14 June 1927, 1, 2, 8; Fredette, Notes for a ms on Lindbergh and the army, 67.

23. Berg, "I greet" quote on 15; *NYT,* 14 June 1927, "an example" quote on 1–2, 15 June 1927, 2.

24. *NYT,* 15 June 1927, 1, 2.

25. *NYT,* 15 June 1927, 2.

26. Davis, *Hero,* "There is" quote on 233; *NYT,* 15 June 1927, 2.

27. *NYT,* 17 June 1927, 3.

28. Davis, *Hero,* 232; *LAT,* 14 June 1927, 1; *NYT* 14 June 1927, 1, 2.

29. *NYT,* 17 June 1927, "Through you" quote on 1; Berg, "I do" quote on 159.

30. *NYT,* 17 June 1927, 17.

31. *NYT,* 15 June 1927, 1, 3.

32. *NYT,* 17 June 1927, 1, 2; Berg, 122. The full text of the editorial "Lindbergh Rides Alone" (*New York Sun,* 22 May 1927) follows:

> Alone? Is he alone, at whose right side rides courage, with Skill within the cockpit and Faith upon the left? Does solitude surround the brave when Adventure leads the way and Ambition reads the dials? Is there no company for him for whom the air is cleft by Daring and the darkness is made light by Emprise?
>
> True, the fragile bodies of his fellows do not weigh down his plane; true the fretful minds of weaker men are lacking from his crowded cabin; but as his airship keeps her course he holds communion with those rarer spirits that inspire to intrepidity and by their sustaining potency give strength to arm, resource to mind, content to soul.
>
> Alone? With what other companions would that man fly to whom the choice were given? (Quoted in "Lindbergh's Leap to Paris and Fame," 7)

33. *NYT,* 19 June 1927, "its mystery" quote on 1–2; Wohl, *Spectacle of Flight,* "new Columbus" quote on 29–30.

34. Orville Wright, letter to John F. Ahlers [with message for Lindbergh], 10 June 1927, mwwright-03161, Wilbur and Orville Wright Papers, General Correspondence, Library of Congress; Marvin W. McFarland, ed., *The Papers of Wilbur and Orville Wright* (New York: McGraw-Hill, 1953), 2:1140–43; W. S. Ross, *Last Hero* (1968), 138.

35. *NYT,* 17 September 1927, 2, 15 June 1927, 5, 18 June 1927, 1; Davis, *Hero,* 237–38.

36. Berg, 158; "Why the World Makes Lindbergh Its Hero," "Women" quote on 1.

37. *NYT,* 18 June 1927, 7; CAL letter to William R. Hearst, April 1929(?), box 34, folder 1021, CALP.

38. Davis, *Hero*, "a rocket" quote on 238; *NYT*, 16 June 1927, 1–2; *WP*, 19 June 1927, 1; John S. Gregory, "What's Wrong with Lindbergh?" *Outlook*, 3 December 1930, 532–34, 556; W. S. Ross, *Last Hero* (1968), 148–49; Lindbergh, "Comments on Ross," "so she" quote on 30. *NYT*, 23 June 1927, 3, details some of the gifts, including two automobiles, wristwatches, medals, diamonds (one in the shape of an airplane), rare silver globes, and countless knickknacks. See also *NYT*, 18, December 1927, 30, by which time the number of gifts had grown and were deposited with the Missouri Historical Society. CAL, *Spirit of St. Louis*, 517–26, lists nine printed pages of gifts, awards, and decorations.

39. *NYT*, 2 July 1927, "to induce" and "the great" quotes on 6, *CSM*, 7 July 1927, 3. Tony Fokker rejected the idea of using amphibian craft to cross the ocean. They were too heavy: "The problem in transatlantic flying is not to build a boat which can land on the sea in an emergency, but to build a plane which will not come down at all" (quoted in *NYT*, 31 July 1927, XX12).

40. *NYT*, 14 June 1927, "There is" quote on 1, 13 June 1927, "Well" quote on 9.

41. Fredette, Notes for a ms. on Lindbergh and the army, 1; *NYT*, 2 July 1927, 4, 3 July 1927, 5.

42. W. S. Ross, *Last Hero* (1968), 144; "Will Hays" quote in Maurice Howland letter to Wm. J. MacCracken Jr., 14 June 1927, Commerce Papers, Lindbergh, Charles A., Herbert Hoover Papers, West Branch, Iowa.

43. Irwin H. "Ike" Hoover, "A Queen and Lindy," *Saturday Evening Post*, 11 August 1934, 49, 53.

44. Bruno, *Wings over America*, 85–125; Davis, *Hero*, "the route" quote on 218, "they are" quote on 218–19; CAL letter to H. Breckinridge, 18 September 1927, box 34, folder 1016, CALP. W. S. Ross, *Last Hero* (1968), 143, reports that Lindbergh received $25,000 from Socony Vacuum Oil Company for endorsing their oil, but this is wrong. He collected $10,000 (CAL, "Comments on Bruno," 4). Bruno also cites the figure of $10,000 (*Wings over America*, 186). "I knew I would need considerable money soon after landing in Europe, and saw no reason why I should not compliment companies whose products had contributed to the success of my flight" (CAL, "Comments on Davis," 38).

45. Bruno, *Wings over America*, 119, 134–37, "twenty" quote on 185–86; CAL, *Spirit of St. Louis*, "With a lot" quote on 547.

46. Wohl, *Spectacle of Flight*, "commercialize" quote on 49; Davis," *Hero*, "had better" and "a great" quotes on 219.

47. Reminiscences of Harold Bixby, 1960, "to take" quote on 37–38, OHCCU; CAL, "Comments on Davis," 38; CAL, "Comments on Bruno," 4, 5, 6; Lindbergh, "Comments on Ross," "buxom" quote on 7–8; CAL, "Comments on *Harry A. Bruno* by Princine M. Calitri," 2.

48. *NYT*, 15 June 1927, 1, 7, 10 July 1927, E8, 20 June 1927, "at the" quote on 2; *WP*, 22 June 1927, 1–3, 3 June 27, "to promote" quote on 6. He had already collected about $100,000, including $42,000 from his contract with the *New York Times* (Harold Bixby to CAL, "Dear Slim," 16 July 1927, box 15, folder 116, CALP).

49. Bixby reminiscences, "You do" quote on 31–32, "didn't have" quote on 33; Richard Melzer, "Dwight Morrow's Role in the Mexican Revolution: Good Neighbor or Meddling Yankee" (PhD diss., University of New Mexico, 1979), 1:215.

50. Bixby reminiscences, "the biggest" quote on 30–31, "that sort" quote on 34, "to write" quote on 31–33, 37–38; H. H. Knight to D. W. Morrow, 29 June 1927, series I, box 31, folder 47, DWM. Bixby wrote to H. Breckinridge on March 2, 1929, that he and the St. Louis backers had in fact argued with Lindbergh to take the award, which he initially refused to claim for himself (box 15, folder 116, CALP). See also Harold Bixby letter to CAL, "Dear Slim," 16 July 1927, box 15, folder 116, CALP.

51. *Guggenheim, Seven Skies,* "almost" quote on 61, "The world" quote on 75; Lomask, *Seed Money,* 92.

52. *NYT,* 28 June 1927, 3.

53. CAL, *Autobiography of Values,* 81; *NYT,* 29 June 1927, 4, 12 July 1927, 5; *WP,* 29 June 1927, 3; *CSM,* 12 July 1927, 3; CAL, *Spirit of St. Louis,* 547.

54. "Good enough" quote in H. F. Guggenheim letter to D. W. Morrow, 5 July 1927, series I, box 31, folder 47, DWM; "normal flyer" quote in D. W. Morrow letter to H. F. Guggenheim, 8 July 1927, series I, box 31, folder 47, DWM.

55. CAL, "Comments on Ross," 29; Hardesty, *Lindbergh, Flight's Enigmatic Hero,* 122; Hallion, *Legacy of Flight,* 155; Henry Breckinridge reminiscences, 1951–52, 168–69, 296, OHCCU.

56. *NYT,* 15 June 1927, 5; CAL, *Spirit of St. Louis,* 547.

57. This account is from Lindbergh, "Comments on *We* and *Spirit of St. Louis,*" 24 October 1971, box 450, folder 13, p. 1, CALP. CAL, "Lindbergh Says Flying Boats Will Come in 5 to 10 Years," *NYT,* 9 June 1927, "a true" quote on 4. There is disagreement between Lindbergh and the publisher about who hired MacDonald. Putnam said it was Lindbergh's decision. Lindbergh claimed that the publisher assigned him his ghost. See George Palmer Putnam, *Wide Margins: A Publisher's Autobiography* (New York: Harcourt Brace, 1942), 233–35.

58. Putnam, *Wide Margins,* 233–35, "hot from" quote on 235.

59. *NYT,* 2 July 1927, all quotes on 14; Fitzhugh Green letter to Harry H. Knight, 18 June 1927, box 11, folder 341, CALP; see subsequent correspondence with Fitzhugh Green with Breckinridge, same folder and file.

60. Putnam, *Wide Margins,* 233–35; CAL, "Comments on *We* and *Spirit of St. Louis,*" "a poor job" quote on 1. "The MacDonald galleys submitted to me . . . were in the first person, were highly inaccurate and out of character." As the years went by Lindbergh developed an ever stronger distaste for this manuscript and for the early articles in the *Times* that were ghost-written for him. Only forty years after the flight did he describe being "angry . . . and shocked" at seeing the early ghost-written pieces (CAL, "Comment on Ross," 28). It is unlikely, though, that he would have continued to work with MacDonald if his style were so distasteful. See also CAL, "Comments on Davis," 32.

61. Fitzhugh Green letter to CAL, 28 June 1927, box 11, folder 341, p. 2, CALP; CAL, "Comments on *We* and *Spirit of St. Louis,*" 1. Later he complained that he did not choose the title *We* and that he did not like it. He protested that the title was foisted upon him by the publisher. This is unlikely because he was not shy or reticent about disagreeing with his publisher; he could have insisted on changing the title and gotten his way. Many assumed that his use of "we" was his demonstration of regard for his plane, and from his very first days in Paris that is the way almost everyone understood it. Ambassador Herrick and the press explained it that way and in many of his speeches it came across that way. Moreover in his articles and in his repeated insistence on anthropomorphizing his "partner" and complaining about the sad treatment she was forced to endure, he did nothing to disabuse the public of that interpretation. In any event later in life he described this interpretation as "another newspaper concoction" (CAL, "Comments on *We* and *Spirit of St. Louis,*" 2). "I used the term 'we' to refer to the members of The Spirit of St. Louis Organization and myself," he insisted (CAL, "Comments on Associated Press," 1; Fredette, 19 May 1973, box 450, folder 9, p. 8, CALP). In his award-winning autobiography published in 1953 he wrote, "We have made this flight across the ocean, not I or it" (*Spirit of St. Louis,* 486). See also CAL to Bruce Larson, "Comments for his biography of Charles Lindbergh, Sr.," 21.

62. W. S. Ross, *Last Hero* (1968), 141; CAL, "Comments on Bruno," 5; Putnam, *Wide Margins*, 235; Fitzhugh Green letter to H. Breckinridge, 11 October 1927, box 11, folder 341, p. 2, CALP; "personal" quote in Fitzhugh Green letter to CAL, 28 June 1927, box 11, folder 341, p. 2, CALP; "quietly" quote in H. F. Guggenheim letter to D. W. Morrow, 5 July 1927, series I, box 31, folder 47, DWM; Berg, 166.

63. Fitzhugh Green letter to H. Breckinridge, 11 October 1927, box 11, folder 341, p. 2, CALP.

64. CAL, "Comments on *We* and *Spirit of St. Louis*," 1; CAL, *Spirit of St. Louis*, 547.

65. CAL, *Spirit of St. Louis*, "Being" quote on 547. "For reasons such as these, I left out of my story much of greatest interest—which I am now, twenty-five years later, attempting to portray in *The Spirit of St. Louis*" (547). CAL, *We: The Famous Flier's Own Story of His Life and His Transatlantic Flight* (New York: G. P. Putnam's Sons, 1928), 26.

66. "Lindbergh's Own Story," "This compass" quote on 514, 515; Lindbergh, "Comments on Van Every," "unreliable" quote on 23; Lindbergh, "Comments on Fredette," 6. "[Having seen] the aircraft to which we devoted our lives, destroying the civilization that created them, we realize that the very efficiency of our machines threatens the character of the men who build and operate them" (CAL, *Spirit of St. Louis*, xi). In the immediate post-flight interviews Lindbergh describes the compass as critically helpful; see *CSM*, 24 May 1927, 2.

67. Earl Reeves, "Lindbergh: A Hero's Boyhood," *Youth Companion* 102, no. 2, 1928, "bald" quote on 99; Leon Whipple, "Lindbergh Writes His Log," *The Survey*, 1 October 1927, "As an author" quote on 50, quoted in Horrigan, "My Own Mind," 7.

68. H. Breckinridge letter to CAL, 29 August 1927, box 5, folder 135, CALP; W. S. Ross, *Last Hero* (1968), 141–42; CAL, "Comments on Ross," 28; G. P. Putnam letter to CAL [perhaps written by Irving Putnam; see subsequent letter from Green to Breckinridge, 11 October 27, same file], 16 September 1927, box 11, folder 341, p. 2, CALP; "curt dismissal" quote in Fitzhugh Green letter to H. Breckinridge, 11 October 1927, 325/I, box 11/341, p. 2, CALP.

69. H. Breckinridge letter to Fitzhugh Green, 12 March 1928, box 11, folder 341, CALP.

70. Putnam, *Wide Margins*, 235–36, quote on 236. Putnam added that he viewed Lindbergh as a "very dull demigod indeed, but neither a fool nor a knave" (237).

71. Ibid., 235–39, quote on 236.

72. Wohl, *Spectacle of Flight*, 35; Dinah Livingston, "The Many Faces of Charles Lindbergh," *Minnesota Monthly*, May 1987, 29; Putnam, *Wide Margins*, 232–33.

73. Lomask, *Seed Money*, 92; CAL, *Autobiography of Values*, 80–81.

74. *NYT*, 29 June 1927, 4.

75. Hallion, *Legacy of Flight*, 155. See, for example, Lomask, *Seed Money*, 95, where Guggenheim tries to keep the tour focused on the message and not the messenger.

76. *NYT*, 31 July 1927, XX12, 29 June 1927, 4.

77. Casey Jones, "Lindbergh Flies On," *Youth Companion* 103, no. 1 (1929): 10.

78. *CSM*, 20 July 1927, 2, 21 July 1927, 3; *NYT*, 21 July 1927, 5.

79. Kenneth T. Jackson, "The Dozen Decisions That Changed New York," in *The Great Metropolis: Poverty and Progress in New York City* (New York: American Heritage, 1993), 233–34; *WP*, 21 July 1927, 2, 23 July 1927, M3; Donald E. Keyhoe, "Seeing America with Lindbergh," *National Geographic Magazine* 53, no. 1 (1928): 1–46; *LAT*, 21 July 1927, 2.

80. Keyhoe, "Seeing America with Lindbergh," 3, 8, 37; *NYT*, 23 July 1927, 5.

81. Keyhoe, "Seeing America with Lindbergh," 4, 7.

82. Ibid., 3; Hallion, *Legacy of Flight*, "Do you" quote on 157; *WP*, 3 June 1928, 12.

83. CAL, *Autobiography of Values*, 83, 99; "happy" quote in CAL letter to R. H. Fredette, 8 September 1973, box 450, folder 9, p. 2, CALP; *NYT*, 12 August 1927, 1, 4; *LAT*, 15 August 1927, 1.

84. *LAT*, 1 September 1927, A4, 18 September 1927, B1, 21 September 1927, A9, 23 September 1927, 1; *WP*, 23 October 1927, "That" quote on SM8.

85. Keyhoe, "Seeing America with Lindbergh," 1, 14; *WP*, 21 July 1927, 2; *NYT*, 20 June 1927, 1–2; *LAT*, 17 August 1927, 5, 21 September 1927, A9, 25 March 1928, 1, 12; R. H. Fredette, ms. on Lindbergh flight to Mexico and Central America, box 450, folder 10, p. 19, CALP.

86. CAL, *Autobiography of Values*, quotes on 81–82; Keyhoe, "Seeing America with Lindbergh," 19.

87. *NYT*, 30 August 1927, quote on 22; *WP*, 21 July 1927, 2.

88. Lomask, *Seed Money*, "I am" quote on 95. Fredette call these rumors "a newspaper bogy something with which to fill the columns" (CAL letter to R. H. Fredette, 27 December 1973, box 450, folder 9, CALP).

89. *NYT*, 27 September 1927, 2, 7 October 1927; *New York World* quotes in "Lindy Back Looking for a Job," *Literary Digest*, 12 November 1927, 62, 68; *WP*, 23 October 1927, M3, 21 July 1927, 2; *LAT*, 21 July 1927, 2; *NYT*, 23 July 1927, 1; CAL, "Main Needs That Must be Met in Selecting Airport Sites," *NYT*, 11 November 1928, "spreading" quote on 168; Hallion, *Legacy of Flight*, 156; Milburn Kusterer, "Colonel Lindbergh Sells Aviation," *The Outlook*, 7 December 1927, 439.

90. *NYT*, 25 September 1927, "there is" quote on XX13; Owen, "Lindbergh Adds a New Chapter," 133; *NYT*, editorial, 29 August 1927, 16; *LAT*, 29 June 1927, "directly responsible" quote on A4; *CSM*, 20 February 1928, 5, 6 August 1927, 5A.

91. Guggenheim, *Seven Skies*, 110–12.

92. Kusterer, "Colonel Lindbergh Sells Aviation," quote on 431; *NYT*, 24 October 1927, 3. Airmail poundage increased by 50 percent (*LAT*, 3 November 1927, 7).

93. *NYT*, 22 June 1927, 5, 26 June 1927, 3; *CSM*, 18 October 1927, "unannounced visits" quote on 2; R. H. Fredette, "U.S. Tour," box 450, folder 9, p. 8, CALP.

94. CAL, "Comments on Ross," "I have" quote on 30; *WP*, 24 October 1927, "my present" quote on 3.

Chapter 8

1. CAL, *Autobiography of Values*, "filmed with" quote on 317; "aeronautical picture" quote in CAL letter to H. Breckinridge, 2 October 1927, box 34, folder 1016, CALP; "neither break" quote in H. Breckinridge letter to CAL, 5 October 1927, box 5, folder 135, CALP; H. Breckinridge letter to no specified recipient, 3 November 1927, box 34, folder 1016, CALP.

2. Berg, 162; CAL, *Autobiography of Values*, quotes on 318. The value of the globes is based on inventory of Lindbergh Exhibit, 1942, ibid., p. 318; Lomask, *Seed Money*, 94.

3. CAL, "Comments on Davis," "Where I" and "on the highest" quotes on 46; Davis, *Hero*, 268–69; "Charlie Lindbergh Gets a Job," *Literary Digest*, 9 June 1928, 34–36; Russell Owen, "Lindbergh Gets a Job," *Current History* 28 (April 1928): 89–96. Lindbergh commented on various estimations of his wealth in CAL, "Comments on Bruno," 5; CAL, "Comments on *Harry A. Bruno* by Princine M. Calitri," 4; CAL, "Comments on Ross," 4.

4. *NYT*, 26 February 1928, 2.

5. At first Bixby reviews proposals (Harold Bixby letter to CAL, 16 July 1927, box 15, folder 116, CALP), but soon it is Guggenheim (John E. Watkins letter to H. Guggenheim, 26 September 1927, box 13, folder 366, CALP). Edward Streeter letter to CAL, 16 December and 18 October 1927, box 13, folder 366, CALP; *NYT*, 1 November 1927, 1, "His popularity" quote on 26.

6. *LAT*, 14 November 1927, 1; Davis, *Hero*, 252; *NYT*, 14 November 1927, "apostle of" quote on 1.

7. *NYT,* 15 November 1927, 1, 11 December 1927, "I have" quote on 1; Davis, *Hero,* 256; Raymond H. Fredette, ms. on Lindbergh, U.S. Decorations, box 450, folder 9, pp. 4–6, CALP.

8. Harold Nicolson, *Dwight Morrow* (New York: Harcourt Brace, 1935), 289–91; "absolute security" quote in H. Breckinridge letter to CAL, 26 September 1927, box 5, folder 135, CALP; *NYT,* 25 May 1933, 1, 26 May 1933, 14, 15, 1 June 1933, 1, 10.

9. Quotes in D. Morrow letter to Harry F. Guggenheim, 18 November 1927, Series I, box 24, folder 104, DWM.

10. L. Mosely, *Lindbergh,* "concealed" quote on 180; Ron Chernow, *The House of Morgan* (New York: Simon & Schuster, 1970), 288–89; Hewitt H. Howland *Dwight Whitney Morrow: A Sketch in Admiration,* introduction by Calvin Coolidge (New York: Century, 1930), "gifted" quote on v, vii; Nicolson, *Dwight Morrow,* 34.

11. Howland, *Dwight Whitney Morrow,* "not merely" quote on viii; Chernow, *House of Morgan,* "Morganizing" quote on 289, 287.

12. Chernow, *House of Morgan,* "philosopher king" quote on 213, 290–92.

13. Nicolson, *Dwight Morrow,* "Look" quote on 281, 135, 251–52, 268.

14. Ibid., 288, "a Bolshevik" quote on 303–4, 307; Howland, *Dwight Whitney Morrow,* "The situation" quote on x; Wesley Phillips Newton, *The Perilous Sky: U.S. Aviation Diplomacy and Latin America, 1919–1931* (Coral Gables, FL: University of Miami Press, 1978), 126; John Mason Hat, *Empire and Revolution: The Americans in Mexico Since the Civil War* (Berkeley: University of California Press, 2002), 260; Evans Clark, "The Two Americas Tied by Bonds of Gold," *NYT,* 15 January 1928, 123; Stanley R. Ross, "Dwight Morrow and the Mexican Revolution," *Hispanic American Historical Review* 38, no. 4 (1959): 506–28, 513; Davis, *Hero,* 253; Chernow, *House of Morgan,* 292.

15. Nicolson, *Dwight Morrow,* "I wish" quote on 290, 291–92, "My only" quote on 314; Chernow, *House of Morgan,* 296.

16. Nicolson, *Dwight Morrow,* "After Morrow" quote on 309; Chernow, *House of Morgan,* "Is there" quote on 292.

17. S. R. Ross, "Dwight Morrow and the Mexican Revolution," 525, 527; Melzer, "Dwight Morrow's Role in the Mexican Revolution," "American" quote on 2:205; *NYT,* 19 December 1927, 6.

18. S. R. Ross, "Dwight Morrow and the Mexican Revolution," 527; Stanley R. Ross, "Dwight Morrow, Ambassador to Mexico," *The Americas* 14, no. 3 (1958): 273–89, 286–87; Chernow, *House of Morgan,* "blistering" quote on 297, 298–300.

19. S. R. Ross, "Dwight Morrow and the Mexican Revolution," 508–10, 521; Melzer, "Dwight Morrow's Role in the Mexican Revolution," 2:88–105. A more recent text is Maria del Carmen Collado Herrera's *Dwight W. Morrow: Reencuentro y revolución en las relaciones entre México y Estados Unidos, 1927–1930* (Mexico City: Instituto Mora, 2005); Newton, *Perilous Sky,* 126.

20. Nicolson, *Dwight Morrow,* 297–98, 310; Melzer, "Dwight Morrow's Role in the Mexican Revolution," "than all" quote on 1:206, 209.

21. Nicolson, *Dwight Morrow,* 297–98; Melzer, "Dwight Morrow's Role in the Mexican Revolution," "a little" quote on 1:216, quoting CAL letter to D. W. Morrow, 29 September 1927, and Morrow letter to CAL, 4 October 1927; CAL, "Comments on Ross," 31; CAL, *Autobiography of Values,* 83.

22. Raymond H. Fredette, ms. on Lindbergh flight to Mexico and Central America, box 540, folder 10, pp. 1–3, CALP; Newton, *Perilous Sky,* 123, 126–27; Clark, "Two Americas Tied by Bonds of Gold," 123; "U.S. Intervention in Central America," Memorandum submitted 12 January 1927 to the U.S. Senate Foreign Relations Committee, http://historymatters.gmu.edu/d/4987/; William Kamman, *A Search for Stability: United States Diplomacy toward Nicaragua, 1925–1933* (Notre Dame, IN: University of Notre Dame Press, 1968).

23. Newton, *Perilous Sky*, 132; *WP*, 4 May 1927, quotes on 1; Melzer, "Dwight Morrow's Role in the Mexican Revolution," 1:225.

24. William A. M. Burden, *Struggle for Airways in Latin America* (New York: Council on Foreign Relations, 1943), 13–15; Lauren D. Lyman, "United States in Drive for South American Air," *NYT*, 31 March, 1929, 136.

25. *NYT*, 30 October 1927, N1; Newton, *Perilous Sky*, 114–27; Bilstein, *Flight Patterns*, 170, 214.

26. *NYT*, 2 July 1927, "to induce" quote on 6, 18 November 1927, 1; *CSM*, 7 July 1927, 3; Newton, *Perilous Sky*, 121–23, 127.

27. Melzer, "Dwight Morrow's Role in the Mexican Revolution," 1:216; CAL, "Comments on Ross," 31; "You get" quote in Adolph Ochs letter to Dwight W. Morrow, 20 December 1927, and reply, 24 December 1927, Series X, box 3, folder 19, DWM; slightly different version in Melzer, "Dwight Morrow's Role in the Mexican Revolution," 1:216; Nicolson, *Dwight Morrow*, 312; CAL, *Autobiography of Values*, 84; Newton, *Perilous Sky*, 127.

28. Melzer, "Dwight Morrow's Role in the Mexican Revolution," 1:214, 216, 220; *NYT*, 9 December 1927, "on the" quote on 1.

29. Newton, *Perilous Sky*, "We are" quote on 133; Burden, *Struggle for Airways in Latin America*, 24; Fredette, ms. on Lindbergh flight to Mexico and Central America, 27; Newton, *Perilous Sky*, 123, 128.

30. *NYT*, 10 December 1927, 16; "Everyone" quote in Adolph Ochs letter to Dwight W. Morrow, 20 December 1927, and reply, 24 December 1927, Series X, box 3, folder 19, DWM; Fredette, ms. on Lindbergh flight to Mexico and Central America, 20A, 27, 30.

31. *NYT*, 16 February 1928, "as can" quote on 3; CAL, "Lindbergh Writes for the Times While He Is Flying to Mexico City," *NYT*, 14 December 1927, "Aviation" quote on 1.

32. *NYT*, 15 December 1927, "the most" quote on 1, 11 December 1927, 2; *WP*, 14 December 1927, 1.

33. CAL, *Autobiography of Values*, 84; Fredette, ms. on Lindbergh flight to Mexico and Central America, "in charge" quote on 7.

34. *NYT*, 9 December 1927, 1; CAL, *Autobiography of Values*, 83–84; CAL, "To Bogota and Back: The Narrative of a 9,500-Mile Flight from Washington, over Thirteen Latin-American Countries and Return, in the Single Seater Airplane *Spirit of St. Louis*," *National Geographic* 53, no. 5 (1928): 530.

35. CAL, "Lindbergh Writes for the Times While He Is Flying to Mexico City," "VIKING" quote on 1; Fredette, ms. on Lindbergh flight to Mexico and Central America, 7–10.

36. CAL, *Autobiography of Values*, 85, 87–88; Fredette, ms. on Lindbergh flight to Mexico and Central America, 12–13; CAL, "To Bogota and Back," 530; CAL, "Comments on Davis," 41–43; Davis, *Hero*, 257–60; CAL, "Completely Lost in Fog Over Mexico," *NYT*, 15 December 1927, 1.

37. *NYT*, 15 December 1927, 41; Davis, *Hero*, 259–60; Fredette, ms. on Lindbergh flight to Mexico and Central America, "too great" quote on 12.

38. Fredette, ms. on Lindbergh flight to Mexico and Central America, 13; Davis, *Hero*, 257–60; CAL, *Autobiography of Values*, 87; CAL, "Lost in Fog," 1.

39. Davis, *Hero*, "Something" quote on 257–60; Fredette, ms. on Lindbergh flight to Mexico and Central America, 13; CAL, *Autobiography of Values*, 87.

40. *NYT*, 15 December 1927, "happy" quote on 2, "Wonderful!" quote on 1, 16 December 1927, 2; *LAT*, 25 December 1927, 3.

41. *WP*, 15 December 1927, 1; *NYT*, 15 December 1927, "a priceless" quote on 3, 1, 2.

42. *NYT*, 24 December 1927, 3, 27 December 1927, 1, 19 December 1927; CAL, "Lindbergh Maps Route for Flights to Six Central American Republics," *NYT*, 17 December 1927, 1; CAL,

Autobiography of Values, 83–88; Davis, *Hero*, 260; *WP*, 19 December 1927, "a guest" quote on 1; *LAT*, 19 December 1927, 1. This Lindbergh is markedly different from the opinionated and decidedly unrelativistic racist of the later 1930s. *Literary Digest*, 7 January 1928, 39–42, contains a range of opinions regarding the propriety of Lindbergh's attendance at the bullfight.

43. *NYT*, 21 December 1927, 1, 14, 18 December 1927, 1, 16 December 1927, 2, 19 December 1927, 1, 26 December 1927, 1, 15 December 1927, "dispelled" quote on 3; *LAT*, 16 December 1927, 2; Davis, *Hero*, "deplorable" quote on 253, 261; Melzer, "Dwight Morrow's Role in the Mexican Revolution," 1:227.

44. *NYT*, 19 December 1927, 6, 18 December 1927, "swept" quote on 1, 21 December 1927, 1, 14; Fredette, ms. on Lindbergh flight to Mexico and Central America, "there is" quote on 21.

45. *NYT*, 21 December 1927, 21, 8 January 1928, 2, 2 May 1928, 1, 3; *LAT*, 12 April 1928, 1.

46. Newton, *Perilous Sky*, 151; *NYT*, 12 January 1928, 1, 5 January 1928, 3, 28 March 1928, "confiscatory" quote on 1–2; Melzer, "Dwight Morrow's Role in the Mexican Revolution," "safeguard" quote on 1:223, "producers" quote on 225; Richard Melzer, "The Lone Eagle in Mexico: Charles A. Lindbergh's Less Famous Record-Setting Flight of 1927," *Journal of the West* 30, no. 1 (1991): 34. In 1929 when Calles faced an uprising among his troops the United States sent him support and Lindbergh personally flew down to train pilots for the Mexican Army to put down the Escobar mutiny (Melzer, "Lone Eagle in Mexico," 35).

47. *NYT*, 17 December 1927, 3, 10 December 1927, 1, 11 December 1927, 1; CAL to R. H. Fredette, 28 December 1973, box 450, folder 9, p. 6, CALP; Fredette, ms. on Lindbergh flight to Mexico and Central America, 27; Newton, *Perilous Sky*, 144.

48. Newton, *Perilous Sky*, 128, 130–31, 371 n. 13.

49. CAL, *Autobiography of Values*, "Tropical" and "native" quotes on 88, "I was told" quote on 91; *NYT*, 29 December 1927, 1.

50. Fredette, ms. on Lindbergh flight to Mexico and Central America, "the roughest" quote on 34; CAL, "To Bogota and Back," 546, 551; *NYT*, 29 December 1927, 1, 8 January 1928, 1; Owen, "Lindbergh Adds a New Chapter," 133; CAL, *Autobiography of Values*, 89.

51. *NYT*, 29 December 1927, 1, 30 December 1927, 1, 4 February 1928, "un muchacho" quote on 1; Owen, "Lindbergh Adds a New Chapter," 133; Fredette, ms. on Lindbergh flight to Mexico and Central America, 17, "prophet" quote on 57.

52. Owen, "Lindbergh Adds a New Chapter," 133.

53. *NYT*, 21 February 1928, "prodigious" quote on 1, 30 January 1928, "semi-mythical" quote on 1, 31 January 1928, 1; Newton, *Perilous Sky*, 132; Fredette, ms. on Lindbergh flight to Mexico and Central America, "one of the" quote on 37.

54. W. E. Carson, *Mexico: The Wonderland of the South* (New York: Macmillan, 1914), "with schemes" quote on 173; *NYT*, 9 February 1928, 1; Davis, *Hero*, 262–63; CAL, "Comments on Davis," 44; CAL, "Lindbergh Charmed by Dancing and Costumes of Mexican Girls," *NYT*, 18 December 1927, 1; "Lindbergh Tells of Flight over Jungles, Past Volcanoes," *NYT*, 29 December 1927, "an attractive" quote on 1; "Lindbergh Writes for the Times While He Is Flying to Mexico City," 1; "Lindbergh Calls for Airways to Link Capitals of Continent," *NYT*, 16 December 1927, 1; "Belize Fetes Lindbergh; He Shows Flying Perils; Off for Salvador Today," *NYT*, 1 January 1928, 1; "Lindbergh Describes Day of Fetes in Which Hondurans Lionize Him," *NYT*, 5 January 1928, 3; "Lindbergh Tells of Enjoying Costa Rican Sporting Events," *NYT*, 9 January 1928, 1; "Friendship for the United States in Nicaragua Impresses Lindbergh," *NYT*, 7 January 1928, "[a] large" quote on 1; "Lindbergh Tells of High Swift Hop over Caribbean in Rain Squalls," *NYT*, 1 February 1928, 1.

55. *NYT*, 1 January 1928, 1, 25 January 1928, 9; CAL, "To Bogota and Back," 558; CAL, *Autobiography of Values*, all quotes on 91–92.

56. CAL, "Lindbergh Praises Skill of Riders and Ropers Who Perform for Him," *NYT*, 19 December 1927, "a gratifying" quote on 1; CAL, "Lindbergh Studies Ruins in Haiti While on His Flight to Its Capital," 7 February 1928, "fields thick" quote on 1; CAL, "Lindbergh Confesses Two Difficulties, How to Thank Hosts and Stay Longer," *NYT*, 8 February 1928, 3; CAL, "Lindbergh Tells of Warm Welcome and Desire to Linger in Guatemala," *NYT*, 30 December 1927, "great number" quote on 1; CAL, "Lindbergh Pictures West Indies as Stepping-Stones of Air Route," *NYT*, 3 February 1928, 1.

57. William R. Shepherd, "All The Americas Meet in Conference," *NYT*, 8 January 1928, "the sunny" quote on 123; Newton, *Perilous Sky*, "practically" quote on 145, 151; CAL to Newton, reprinted in Newton, *Perilous Sky*, 374, n. 47.

58. Newton, *Perilous Sky*, 148, "cavalier" quote on 149; CAL, "Comments on Davis," 43–44.

59. *NYT*, 9 February 1928, all quotes on 1, 14 February 1928, 1, 12 February 1928, 3; Newton, *Perilous Sky*, 149.

60. CAL, "Lindbergh on Flying," *NYT*, 21 October 1928, "probably means" and "open up" quotes on 152; "Lindbergh Calls for Airways to Link Capitals of Continent," *NYT*, 16 December 1927, 1; "Lindbergh Writes for the Times While He Is Flying to Mexico City," 1; "Lindbergh Tells of Panama Hop as Fulfilling Long-Held Desire," *NYT*, 10 January 1928, "compliment" quote on 1, 2; ; "Lindbergh Pictures West Indies as Stepping Stones of Air Route," 1; *NYT*, 15 January 1928, 1, 26 February 1928, 51, 18 December 1927, E7; Smith, *Airways*, 9–10.

61. CAL, "Lindbergh Urges Business to Give Aid for Airlines," *NYT*, 25 December 1927, 1; "Lindbergh Pictures West Indies as Stepping Stones of Air Route," 1; CAL, "To Bogota and Back," 529; Juan T. Trippe, "Charles Lindbergh and World Travel," Fourteenth Wing's Club Sight lecture, 20 May 1977, New York; Newton, *Perilous Sky*, 148–49, 160; *LAT*, 13 February 1928, 2; Fredette, ms. on Lindbergh flight to Mexico and Central America, 60, 62. Trippe would soon augment his connections by marrying the daughter of Edward R. Stettinus, the late Morgan partner and father of the future secretary of state (Newton, *Perilous Sky*, 150).

62. Newton, *Perilous Sky*, "coincided" quote on 129; CAL, "Lindbergh Looks on His Cuban Hop as Forerunner of Air Mail Service," *NYT*, 9 February 1928, "transoceanic" quote on 1.

63. Newton, *Perilous Sky*, 150–51; *NYT*, 13 January 1928, "the greatest" quote on 1, 26 August 1928, 122, 5 February 1928, 49; Fredette, ms. on Lindbergh flight to Mexico and Central America, 46; Freudenthal, *Aviation Business*, 136.

64. Fredette, ms. on Lindbergh flight to Mexico and Central America, "a great traveling" quote on 59, "Even if" quote on 55; *NYT*, 30 December 1928, 22; Newton, *Perilous Sky*, "from hard" quote on 133–34, 333. For a range of interpretations on Lindbergh's effect, see the references in Newton, *Perilous Sky*, 377, n. 87.

65. CAL, *Autobiography of Values*, "abominable" quote on 95; *NYT*, 17 February 1928, 24.

66. *NYT*, 1 January 1928, XX6.

67. CAL, "Lindbergh on Flying," "stir[s]" quote on 152; Owen, "Lindbergh Adds a New Chapter," 133; *CSM*, 10 November 1928, "internationalism" quote on 6.

68. *NYT*, 9 June 1928, "loftier" quote on 6, 20 March 1928, "greatest ambassador" quote on 1.

69. "Why the World Makes Lindbergh Its Hero," 6.

70. William James, "The Moral Equivalent of War," lecture, Stanford University, 1906, www.constitution.org/wj/meow.htm or www.des.emory.edu/mfp/moral.html.

71. For tributes describing Lindbergh in this vein, see Sir Philip Gibbs, "Europe Ten Years after Armageddon," *NYT*, 11 November 1928, 89; *NYT*, 26 June 1927, 7, 13 October 1928, 6, 30 December 1927, 2; Owen, "Lindbergh Adds a New Chapter," 133; "Why the World Makes

Lindbergh Its Hero," 6; John Erskine, "Flight," *Century* 114, no. 513–18 (1927): 518; Guggenheim, *Seven Skies*, 68–69; Berg, 6.

72. Corn, *Winged Gospel*, 56.

Chapter 9

1. Augustus Post, "Columbus of the Air," *North American Review*, September–October 1927, 353–64; *NYT*, 19 August 1927, 16; Corn, *Winged Gospel*, 74–75; Russell Owen, "Lindbergh Leading, Aviation Sweeps On," *NYT*, 20 May 1928, 123; Freudenthal, *Aviation Business*, 91.

2. Hinton, "What Lindbergh Is Doing for Aviation," "Every" quote on 248, "long" quote on 249; *NYT*, 5 May 1929, 31; *WSJ*, 4 June 1928, 3, 12 October 1928, 7.

3. Hinton, "What Lindbergh Is Doing for Aviation," "Within" quote on 248; *WP*, 20 September 1931, M8, 27 June 1928, 6, 11 February 1929, 4; *CSM*, 21 May 1929, 22, 2, 6 February 1929, 2; *NYT*, 14 October 1928, N9, 22 July 1928, 117; *WSJ*, 25 July 1927, 2; Freudenthal, *Aviation Business*, "money" quote on 91.

4. *NYT*, 15 October 1927, 28, 15 December 1927, 41, 23 December 1928, "had been" quote on 114, editorial, 25 July 1928, 20, 22 July 1928, 117; *WSJ*, 27 August 1927, 10, 25 May 1927, 3; *WP*, 20 August 1927, 4; *LAT*, 7 October 1927, A4, 21 December 1927, A4; Freudenthal, *Aviation Business*, 92. Lindbergh and others liked to say that American aviation operated in a free market without subsidies; see CAL, "Lindbergh on Flying: Guggenheim Does Work Others Might Neglect," *NYT*, 23 December 1928, 114. Nonetheless the federal government provided important assistance. The Army Air Corps at Wright Field, the Naval Aircraft Factory in Philadelphia, the Air Station at Lakehurst, the Belleview Laboratory, Bureau of Standards, and the National Advisory Committee at Langley Field all provided research, development, and material assistance to advance American aviation. Moreover the Post Office and Agriculture Departments poured more than $30,000,000 in indirect aid to the industry (Reginald Cleveland, "Aviation Reaches Era of Taking Account of Stock," *NYT*, 13 October 1929, XX14). Under Hoover the government committed more than $120 million to commercial aviation and opened up public lands for airports. See *LAT*, 17 August 1930, 1; *CSM*, 31 August 1928, 125, 9 January 1930, 16.

5. *NYT*, 1 January 1928, "Lindbergh effect" quote on XX6; *WSJ*, 13 December 1927, 3, 25 January 1928, 11; *WP*, 25 August 1930, 1; Bilstein, *Flight Patterns*, 42, 52; Simonson, "Demand for Aircraft," 366, 368; Freudenthal, *Aviation Business*, 123–24.

6. *NYT*, 20 March 1930, 50, 20 May 1928, 47; *WSJ*, 4 February 1929, 1; *LAT*, 5 May 1928, 3, 8 February 1929, "the man" quote on 1.

7. Freudenthal, *Aviation Business*, 123–34; *NYT*, 12 August 1928, "dates" quote on 1.

8. *NYT*, 22 March 1928, 3, 1 March 1928, "Colonel" quote on 1.

9. *LAT*, 22 March 1928, 1, 27 March 1928, 18; *NYT*, 25 March 1928, "simply thrilling" quote on 27, editorial, 27 March 1928, "Who" quote on 26; *WP*, 21 March 1928, 1; *CSM*, 26 March 1928, 8.

10. Fredette, ms. on Lindbergh flight to Mexico and Central America, "having" quote on 21; *NYT*, 21 December 1927, 1, 4 March 1928, 21.

11. *NYT*, 2 May 1928, 1, 17 March 1928, 13, 3 May 1928, 22, 21 November 1928, 20; CAL, *Autobiography of Values*, 96; CAL letter to R. H. Fredette, 15 July 1971, box 450, folder 7, pp. 1–2, CALP; Peter M. Bowers, "The Many Splendid Spirits of St. Louis," *Air Progress* 20, no. 6 (1967): 71. *Spirit*'s last flight was to Bolling Field in Washington on April 30, 1928. There it was disassembled and taken to the Smithsonian.

12. CAL, "Lindbergh on Aviation," *NYT*, 26 August 1928, "It will" quote on 34; *LAT*, 26 August 1928, 1; CAL, "Lindbergh Finds King Democratic," *NYT*, 1 June 1927, "I shall" quote

on 1. In his *New York Times* articles Lindbergh wrote about how planes developed and their various types and components, about airmail's role in changing business, about developing commercial aviation and its continued importance in weaving together the hemisphere, how to fly and navigate, the need to cut down on stunt flying and enforce uniform regulations, and the future of transcontinental flying.

13. "Suggested draft of a Speech for Col. Lindbergh at Boston Meeting of Superintendents of Schools," 15 February 1928, in H. Guggenheim letter to CAL, box 13, folder 366, CALP. He had voiced such strong opposition to having his material ghostwritten, but the press of time sometimes pushed him to sign on to others' work. Thus he accepted *National Geographic*'s offer of $3,000 for an article on his Central America tour that was drafted by a ghostwriter (H. Breckinridge letter to CAL, 24 February 1928, box 5, folder 135, CALP). The famous publicist Ivy Lee, working for Harry Guggenheim, sometimes provided him with quotes to run as his own; see Burnham Ca? [rest is illegible] for Ivy Lee to H. Breckinridge, 7 June 1928, box 13, folder 366, CALP; Earl Reeves, "The Fog Fighter," *Youth's Companion* 103, no. 7 (1929): 379. Scrupulously avoiding any criticism of Lindbergh, Quebec officials nonetheless took offense at the notion that they could not treat Bennett without Lindbergh's heroics in delivering serum; see *NYT*, 30 April 1938, 24; "Lindbergh Flies On," *Youth's Companion* 103, no. 1 (1929), "dropping" quote on 10.

14. *WP*, 13 May 1928, quotes on 1; *NYT*, 4 March 1928, 21. In his own recollections Lindbergh claims that he and his St. Louis supporters were the ones to interest Ford in the project (CAL, *Autobiography of Values*, 97–100).

15. Lindbergh claims that it was he and his St. Louis backers who pitched the idea to Keys, who let on that he had been thinking similarly. Keys of course expanded the scale beyond anything the Lindbergh team had considered: "He thought capital of ten million dollars would be raised. This was beyond anything we had considered" (CAL, *Autobiography of Values*, 101). But the contemporaneous account, including articles by Lindbergh's confidante Lauren D. Lyman in the *Times*, reports that it was Keys who first offered the opportunity to Lindbergh and that until late May 1928 he had repeatedly turned down any connection with the Keys and Coffin project. Only at the last minute did he change his mind and inform Keys that he was willing to accept the offer of the chairmanship of the Technical Committee. Harold Bixby seems to support Lindbergh's version; see "Reminiscences of Harold M. Bixby," Oral History Collection, Columbia University, 9 April 1960, 40; CAL, *Autobiography of Values*, 96–97. My version is based on the correspondence record: Howard E. Coffin letter to CAL, 14 June 1927, box 102, folder 251, CALP; *NYT*, 23 May 1927, 1; Lauren D. Lyman, "Lindbergh Will Aid Aviation in Air and on Ground," *NYT*, 27 May 1928, 137; F. Robert van der Linden, *Airlines and Air Mail: The Post Office and the Birth of the Commercial Aviation Industry* (Lexington: University Press of Kentucky, 2002), 22; Pattillo, *Pushing the Envelope*, 81.

16. *NYT*, 23 June 1927, 3, 24 June 1927, "more useful" quote on 3, 25 June 1927, 3; L. C. Speers, "In Commercial Aviation . . . ," *NYT*, 26 June 1927, XX1; *WP*, 22 June 1927, 1–3, 24 June 1927, 1, 25 June 1927, "future" quote on 1, 26 June 1927, "Rockefeller" quote on 1. A competing group claimed that it too had Washington's support and announced a new airline company capitalized at $50,000,000, expecting to offer its presidency to Lindbergh.

17. "if they" quote in Chester Cuthell letter to CAL c/o Henry Breckinridge, 25 July 1927, box 102, folder 251, CALP; *WP*, 25 June 1927, 1, 24 June 1927, 1–3; *CSM*, 24 June 1927, 3; *LAT*, 24 June 1927, 3.

18. *NYT*, 24 June 1927, 3, 25 June 1927, 1, 3, 26 June 1927, 3; quote in CAL letter to H. Breckinridge, 24 August 1927, box 34, folder 1016, CALP; H. Breckinridge letter to CAL, 29 August 1927, box 5, folder 135, CALP.

19. In August 1927 Breckinridge was in touch with both MGM and Universal Studios. "I enclose a letter from Universal Pictures which has been considered by Mr. Harry Guggenheim and Mr. Dwight Morrow as well as myself," he wrote Lindbergh (H. Breckinridge letter to CAL, 29 August 1927, box 5, folder 135, CALP). Lindbergh wrote back that although he was not interested in a lecture tour he wanted information about the "picture" that would promote aviation (CAL letter to H. Breckinridge, 24 August 1927, box 34, folder 1016, CALP). Subsequently he added, "I would like to take up the motion picture propositions in detail after returning to New York" (CAL letter to H. Breckinridge, 18 September 1927, box 34, folder 1016, CALP). Movies kept coming up. When the army requested permission to use Lindbergh footage for a recruiting film, Breckinridge held them off, explaining that he and Lindbergh were considering another film to promote aviation "out of which also he should receive a financial return" and he did not want to undermine that possibility (H. Breckinridge letter to CAL, 3 October 1927, box 5, folder 135, CALP). Fredette, ms. on Lindbergh and Air Force, box 450, folder 9, pp. 31–32, CALP; *WP,* 24 October 1927, 3; CAL, *Autobiography of Values,* 103; *NYT,* 15 May 1928; van der Linden, *Airlines and Air Mail,* 39–41.

20. *NYT,* 23 May 1928,1, 16; *WP,* 13 May 1928, 1.

21. *NYT,* 24 May 1928, "part time" quote on 8. Under pressure from TAT he amended this to explain that although he was still going to be involved in many other aviation matters, in the beginning he would give the formation of the TAT system his full attention (C. M. Keys letter to CAL, 23 May 1928, box 124, folder 504, CALP); CAL, "Comments on Bruno," 5. CAL, "Comments on Ross," "These warrants" quote on 45. CAL, "Comments on Davis," 55, mentions only the annual salary, ignoring the huge retainer fee and the options. Davis, *Hero,* 294; van der Linden, *Airlines and Air Mail,* 41–43; *LAT,* 24 May 1928, 1; *CSM,* 24 May 1928, 1; Lauren D. Lyman, "Lindbergh Will Aid Aviation in Air and on Ground," *NYT,* 27 May 1928, 137; CAL, "Comments on Bruno," 5 CALP; CAL, Memorandum, 22 August 1929, box 5, folder 135, CALP.

22. H. Breckinridge letters to CAL, 23 January 1930, 6 July 1929, box 5, folder 135, CALP; *NYT,* 23 May 1928, 1, 16, 24 May 1928, 8; *LAT,* 24 May 1928, 1; *CSM,* 24 May 1928, 1; Lyman, "Lindbergh Will Aid Aviation in Air and on Ground," 137; CAL, "Comments on Bruno," 5; CAL, Memorandum, 22 August 1929, box 5, folder 135, CALP.

23. Davis, *Hero,* 243; Milton, *Loss of Eden,* 132–38; Hallion, *Legacy of Flight;* Guggenheim, *Seven Skies,* 73–91.

24. Davis, *Hero,* 292–93; CAL, "Comments on Davis," quotes on 55.

25. *NYT,* 7 November 1928, 15; CAL letter to H. Hoover, 2 October 1928, and note expressing Hoover's "deep appreciation" in H. Hoover letter to CAL, 10 October 1928, quoted in *LAT,* 3 November 1928, 8.

26. Joan Hoff Wilson, *Herbert Hoover: Forgotten Progressive* (Boston: Little Brown, 1975), "I felt" quote on 113; Bilstein, *Flight Patterns,* 171–73; Solberg, *Conquest of the Skies,* 75–80; *CSM,* 6 February 1929, 16; Virginia Pope, "Guggenheim Combines Flying and Diplomacy," *NYT,* 22 September 1929, XX9; Clark, "Two Americas Tied by Bonds of Gold," 123.

27. David Lee, "Herbert Hoover and the Development of Commercial Aviation," *Business History Review* 58 (Spring 1984): 1921–26; Wilson, *Herbert Hoover,* 120; Ellis Hawley, "Three Faces of Hooverian Associationalism: Lumber, Aviation and Movies, 1921–1930," in Thomas K. McCraw, ed. *Regulation in Perspective* (Cambridge, MA: Harvard University Press, 1982), 95–97, 113–14. F. Robert van der Linden's *Airlines and Air Mail* and Douglas B. Craig, *Fireside Politics: Radio and Political Culture in the United States, 1920–1940* (Baltimore: Johns Hopkins University Press, 2000) expand on Hawley's approach.

28. *NYT,* 12 December 1927, 20, 16 December 1928, 1, 13 May 1929, 42, 27 June 1929, 1, 29 June 1929, 33; Pattillo, *Pushing the Envelope,* 76, 80–81; van der Linden, *Airlines and Air Mail,* 50–52; Solberg, *Conquest of the Skies,* 73; Freudenthal, *Aviation Business,* 105–6.

29. Freudenthal, *Aviation Business*, "The sudden" quote on 99; van der Linden, *Airlines and Air Mail*, "We are" quote on 44–45.

30. Freudenthal, *Aviation Business*, 107, quoting Crane Report, U.S. House of Representatives, Committee on Post Offices and Post Roads, House Report 2087, Seventy-second Congress, 2nd session, 1933, pp. 11, 20; *NYT*, 17 April 1929, 9.

31. *WP*, editorial, 23 February 1928, "Ultimately" quote on 6.

32. CAL, "Memphis Makes Record," *NYT*, 10 June 1927, "capitalists" quote on 2; CAL, "Behind Europe in Flying Matters, Lindbergh's View of Our Status," *NYT*, 2 June 1927, 1.

33. Simonson, "Demand for Aircraft," 368. Between 1928 and 1933 the two leading manufacturers were United Aircraft and Curtiss Wright. They had about 75 percent of the military business; the rest went to five leading independents, with almost nothing going to the remaining 279 firms.

34. Solberg, *Conquest of the Skies*, 57–61; Freudenthal, *Aviation Business*, 96, 104; *NYT*, 20 March 1930, "pyramiding" quote on 50; Davis, *Hero*, "big men" quote on 243.

35. A few lone voices criticized him for "representing Guggenheim interests" and for becoming too close with "big men." See Davis, *Hero*, 241–42, 292–93; CAL, *Autobiography of Values*, 97.

36. Davis, *Hero*, "refused" quote on 268–69; CAL, "Comments on Davis," "I supported" quote on 55, 46; *NYT*, 27 May, 1927, IX 17, 1–6; "Charlie Lindbergh Gets a Job," *Literary Digest*, 9 June 1928, 34–36; CAL to Bruce Larson, "Comments for his biography of Charles Lindbergh, Sr.," "If he" quote on 2–3, "to which" quote on 14, "men of" quote on 5.

37. CAL, *Spirit of St. Louis*, 261–62.

38. Casey Jones, "Lindbergh Flies On," *Youth's Companion* 103, no. 1 (1929): 11.

39. CAL letter to Daniel Sheaffer, 16 April 1931, box 34, folder 1026, CALP; CAL, "Comments on Ross," 45; *NYT*, 5 December 1928, 13; CAL, *Autobiography of Values*, 105; CAL, Report for TAT, Winter 1928–29, box 124, folder 509, CALP. "No pilot will be employed who has been known to use intoxicants to excess," and those reporting for duty under the influence will be immediately discharged (CAL letter to Colonel Paul Henderson, 26 May 1929, box 124, folder 505, CALP).

40. TAT, *Plane Talk* 1, no. 7 (1929), box 124, folder 509, p. 1, CALP; CAL, *Autobiography of Values*, 104–5; *NYT*, 16 June 1929, XX14.

41. CAL letter to Donald Hall, 12 January 1930, box 34, folder 1023, CALP; CAL, Report for TAT, Winter 1928–29, box 124, folder 509, CALP; Trippe, "Charles Lindbergh and World Travel," 17.

42. CAL, *Autobiography of Values*, "so large" quote on 103–4.

43. C. M. Keys letter to CAL, 4 February 1929, box 124, folder 525, CALP; CAL letter to C. M. Keys, 12 November 1929, box 124, folder 506, CALP; CAL to Keys, draft of report/letter [1929], box 124, folder 505, CALP; Report on Curtiss Condor, [1929], box 124, folder 512, CALP; CAL, Report on Airline routes, [1928–29], box 124, folder 508, CALP; CAL letter to C. M. Keys, 12 November 1929, box 124, folder 506, CALP; Fragment of CAL Report on TAT services, [1928–29], box 124, folder 508, CALP (this file contains handwritten reports, some only fragments, but reflecting the range of his work as technical adviser); CAL to D. M. Sheaffer, untitled report on inauguration of TAT operations, 1930, box 124, folder 511, CALP; *NYT*, 16 June 1929, XX14.

44. *NYT*, 6 July 1929, 3, 16 June 1929, XX14; Bilstein, *Flight in America*, 19.

45. *NYT*, 9 July 1929, 3, 11 July 1929, 3, 20 August 1929, 3, 11 September 1929, 16; TAT, *Plane Talk* 1, no. 7 (1929): 1; CAL, *Autobiography of Values*, 106.

46. *NYT*, 8 September 1929, 1–2, 9 September 1929, 1; CAL letter to Dan Sheaffer, 19 September 29, box 123, folder 494, CALP; CAL letter to Colonel Paul Henderson, 26 May 1929, box 124, folder 505, CALP; "Report of TAT-Maddux Plane Wreck," box 124, folder 510, CALP.

47. J. T. Trippe letter to CAL, 7 January 1929, box 103, folder 257, CALP; Newton, *Perilous Sky*, 115–23, 133–34, 140–41, 148–49, 160; "Fifteen Businessmen," *Fortune*, 17 March 1938,

"man" quote on 72, quoted in Newton, *Perilous Sky,* 157–58; Trippe, "Charles Lindbergh and World Travel," 1; *LAT,* 13 February 1928, 2; R. H. Fredette, ms. on Lindbergh flight to Mexico and Central America, 60, 62; *NYT,* 8 October 1928, 12; Burden, *Struggle for Airways in Latin America,* 23; Henry Ladd Smith, *Airways Abroad: The Story of American World Air Routes* (Madison: University of Wisconsin Press, 1950), 5–7, 9–11. Another reviewer referred to Trippe as "one of the most cunning business strategists of the twentieth century" (quoted in Newton, *Perilous Sky,* 159).

48. Freudenthal, *Aviation Business,* 168, 170; *NYT,* 21 January 1928, 3, 8 October 1928, 12 *LAT,* 13 February 1928, 2; Burden, *Struggle for Airways in Latin America,* 23; Smith, *Airways Abroad,* 5–10; Newton, *Perilous Sky,* "certain" quote on 139, 140–41. Pan Am's board ultimately included a Harriman (Averell), a Lehman (Robert), a Vanderbilt (William H.), a Whitney (C. V.), and leading representatives from the airline industry. There was also a strong Morgan interest (Freudenthal, *Aviation Business,* 170, 178).

49. Freudenthal, *Aviation Business,* 176–77; U.S. Senate Special Committee on Investigation of Air Mail and Ocean Mail Contracts, Hearings, Seventy-third Congress, 1933–34, "it did not" quote on 2459; *NYT,* 26 April 1929, 2, 4 May 1929, 15, 22 January 1928, 29. "The most impartial review of the awards [of the airmail contracts] indicates that it was Postmaster General Brown's intention that the Pan Am group be granted all foreign air mail contracts" (Burden, *Struggle for Airways in Latin America,* 25).

50. Hal Elliott Wert, *Herbert Hoover, the Fishing President* (Mechanicsburg, PA: Stackpole Books, 2005) 180; *CSM,* 3 December 1929, 6; *NYT,* 15 August 1930, 17 August 1930, 1; *WP,* 17 August 1930, M1; *LAT,* 22 February 1929, 1.

51. *NYT,* 4 February 1929, 18, 7 February 1929, 1, 5 February 1929, 1; *CSM,* 31 January 1929, "fresh" quote on 1, 6 February 1929, 16.

52. CAL letters to J. T. Trippe, 9 December 1929, 12 November 1929, box 103, folder 257, CALP; draft of release by CAL for Pan Am re: Central and South American services, [no date], box 109, folder 380, CALP; Trippe, "Charles Lindbergh and World Travel," "We had" quote on 15, "almost" quote on 15–16; CAL, *Autobiography of Values,* 113.

53. Trippe, "Charles Lindbergh and World Travel," "the American" quote on 10, 15–16; E. E. Wyman letter to J. T. Trippe, 26 June 1930, box 103, folder 258, CALP; C. C. Martin letter to J. M. Eaton, 11 November 1929, box 103, folder 257, CALP; J. T. Trippe letter to CAL, [1928?], box 103, folder 257, CALP; CAL letter to Clyde Kelly, 8 February 1929, box 34, folder 1024, CALP; CAL, *Autobiography of Values,* 108; *LAT,* 19 February 1929, 1; AML, *Hour of Gold, Hour of Lead: Diaries and Letters of Anne Morrow Lindbergh, 1929–1932* (New York: Harcourt Brace Jovanovich, 1973), 96–97.

54. *NYT,* 16 December 1929, 20, 22 August 1930, 1, 2, 11 March 1929, 1; *CSM,* 4 December 1930, 5; Davis, *Hero,* "unless" quote on 262.

55. *NYT,* 14 February 1929, 2.

Chapter 10

1. CAL, *Charles A. Lindbergh: Autobiography of Values* (New York: Harcourt, Brace & Company, 1977), 327. His papers reflect this same quirk; despite his expressed disinterest in possessions he found it necessary to account for everything. Letters, clippings, even odd scraps of paper, all were collected and catalogued. Later in life he would have his poor wife prepare periodic inventories. Every purchase had to be listed with its cost, whether a few pennies or thousands of dollars. And all household items—every article of clothing and furniture, every book and blanket down to the tea strainers and cottage cheese containers—were scrupulously recorded (Berg, 480). The lists made his goals and his achievements tangible, so that when he described his flight to Paris it was not so much in terms of its importance as in the numbers: the

plane's wingspan, how many miles flown, how much gasoline used, the average speed, the revolutions per minute for the motor, and so forth. Later, when he published his Pulitzer Prize–winning account of the flight, he overruled his editor, insisting that all the engineering data, the flight stats, and the lists of his awards, honors, and mementoes all be published with the book (489).

2. CAL, *Autobiography of Values*, 123, "to learn their" quote on 117, "evolutionary," quote on 120–21. He actually goes on for six pages in his *Autobiography of Values* to describe his thinking—not all of it very impressive—largely laying out why the common reasons for dating women did not appeal to him.

3. Ibid., 117, "could stay" quote on 118.

4. Ibid., "breeding" quote on 121, "good health" quote on 118, "Caucasian" quote on 119.

5. CAL, *Autobiography of Values*, 123.

6. AML, *Bring Me a Unicorn: Diaries and Letters of Anne Morrow Lindbergh, 1922–1928* (New York: Harcourt Brace Jovanovich, 1972), "baseball" quote on 89, "amazing" quote on 90, "personal" quote on 91, "adored" quote on 100.

7. Ibid., "too moved" quote on 88, "complete," quote on 93, 104–5; Berg, 186.

8. AML, *Bring Me a Unicorn*, 109.

9. Davis, *Hero*, 273–74; Berg, 184; Susan Hertog, *Anne Morrow Lindbergh: Her Life* (New York: Doubleday, 1999), 29; AML, *Bring Me a Unicorn*, 90.

10. AML, *Bring Me a Unicorn*, "waste," quote on 74, "It won't" quote on 124–25; "the youngest," Berg, 186.

11. AML, *Bring Me a Unicorn*, "I don't" quote on 127, "utterly" quote on 129, "Fool, fool" quote in Berg, 193–94.

12. CAL, "Comments on Davis," "I was" quote on 47; CAL, *Autobiography of Values*, 123; AML, *Bring Me a Unicorn*, "beautiful boy" quote on 100, "Charles" and "Lindbergh himself" quotes on 191.

13. AML, *Bring Me a Unicorn*, 199–202.

14. Ibid., "He *really*" quote on 204, 210–13, "just kick" quote on 213, *"beyond"* and "Oh, I do" quotes on 214; Berg, 195, 215; Hertog, *Anne Morrow Lindbergh*, 78–79; CAL to R. Fredette, 15 April 1974, box 45, folder 10, CALP; Davis, *Hero*, 275.

15. AML, *Bring Me a Unicorn*, 200–232.

16. Ibid., 235, 238–44; Berg, 195; AML, *Hour of Gold*, quote on 232.

17. Davis, *Hero*, 275; Berg, all quotes on 196–97.

18. Davis, *Hero*, 275; CAL, *Autobiography of Values*, 124–25; Berg, 196–97; AML, *Bring Me a Unicorn*, 235, 238–44; *NYT*, 13 February 1929, "he'd have" quote on 1, 3, 6 November 1928, 39: "Deny Lindbergh will wed Miss Anne Morrow; people in the position to know deny not only an engagement but any romantic attachment, saying it was primarily to rest"; *NYT*, 11 November 1928, 15; AML, *Hour of Gold*, 5–6, "smothering" quote on 5.

19. *NYT*, 25 November 1928, 1, 26 November 1928, 1, 27 November 1928, 14, 29 November 1928, 21; AML, *Bring Me a Unicorn*, all quotes on 248–49.

20. *NYT*, 13 February 1929, 1, 3, 14 February 1929, 1, 3; Hertog, *Anne Morrow Lindbergh*, 87, 88; Berg, 198; CAL, *Autobiography of Values*, 127.

21. CAL, "Comments on Davis," 47; *NYT*, 13 February 1929, 1, 28 February 1929, 1, 1 March 1929, 1; AML, *Hour of Gold*, 19; Melzer, "Lone Eagle in Mexico," 35; Davis, *Hero*, 276; *WP*, 1 March 1929, 1.

22. Berg, "a beautiful" quote on 200; CAL, *Autobiography of Values*, 127; AML, *Hour of Gold*, 23.

23. Davis, *Hero*, 277; Berg, 201, 202; CAL, *Autobiography of Values*, 126 (twenty-two, including the bridal couple); CAL to R. Fredette, 15 April 1974, box 45, folder 10, CALP.

24. *NYT*, 4 March 1929, 16, 11 March 1929, 1, 12 March 1929, 3; AML, *Hour of Gold*, "I seem" quote on 47. Decades after the event he retells it with evident pleasure at having outsmarted the press, going on about the detailed plans, while the wedding itself is dismissed in

one sentence. He was especially pleased that one of the New York tabloids, the *Daily News*, appeared on newsstands that afternoon with an article reporting plans for a 1,500-guest wedding "to be held soon." CAL, *Autobiography of Values*, 127; Berg, 202.

25. *NYT*, 28 May 1929, 1; AML, *Hour of Gold*, 6.

26. AML, *Hour of Gold*, 7; CAL, "Comments on Davis," 49.

27. Berg, 198.

28. AML, *Hour of Gold*, "on another's" quote on 4, 7; *NYT*, 11 March 1929, 1; Corn, *Winged Gospel*, 82–83.

29. *LAT*, 2 February 1930, "devoted page" quote on A3; Russell Owen, "The Lindberghs: Bold Flying Partners," *NYT*, 9 July 1933, "Women" quote on SM7; AML, *Hour of Gold*, "infinitely relieved" quote on 11, "flying every" quote on 162, similar letter to Constance on 132; *NYT*, 25 August 1929, 2; CAL, "Comments on Davis," 51; Berg, 208.

30. CAL, "Comments on Davis," 53; Berg, 216; AML, *Hour of Gold*, 96–97; Milton, *Loss of Eden*, 182–83.

31. CAL, "Comments on Davis," 50.

32. Edward Weyer Jr., "Exploring Cliff Dwellings with the Lindberghs," *World's Work* 56 (December 1929): 52–54; Berg, 208–9. See also AML, *Hour of Gold*, 47–62, 72–73, 97–99, 120–21, 157–58.

33. AML, *Hour of Gold*, 96–97; *NYT* 7 October 1929, 1, 10 October 1929, 5, 13 October 1929, 3, 19 November 1929, 24, 5 October 1929, 12, 5 October 1929, 1, 11 October 1929, 29; Davis, *Hero*, 280–82; CAL, "Comments on Davis," 51.

34. *NYT* 12 October 1929, quotes on 10; *NYT* 6 May 1930, 9.

35. Berg, 207; *NYT*, 6 December 1929, 28, 7 December 1929, 2; AML, *Hour of Gold*, "Another" quote on 122, "C" quote on 123.

36. *NYT*, 23 June 1930, 1, 21 April 1930, 1; Lauren D. Lyman, "Again Lindbergh Shows His Air Genius," *NYT*, 27 April 1930, 81; Berg, 214; AML, *Hour of Gold*, "When am" quote to sister Constance on 112.

37. *NYT*, 21 April 1930, 1, 23 June 1930, 1; AML, *Hour of Gold*, "All this" quote on 4, 8, "frightened to" quote on 10, 120.

38. AML, *Hour of Gold*, 142; W. S. Ross, *Last Hero* (1968), 347.

39. AML, *Hour of Gold*, "She is" quote on 121; Davis, *Hero*, 499; Dorothy Hermann, *Anne Morrow Lindbergh: A Gift of Life* (New York: Ticknor and Fields, 1992), 61–62; CAL, "Comments on Ross," 64. "It is true that Anne doused me . . . but my recollection is that it was water" (CAL, "Comments on Davis," 78).

40. AML, *Hour of Gold*, "I suppose" quote on 28, 114, "delight" quote on 143.

41. Ibid., 9, 10; *NYT*, 21 April 1930, 1; Lyman, "Again Lindbergh Shows His Air Genius," 81.

42. Berg, 216–17; AML, *Hour of Gold*, "That's been" quote on 137.

43. AML, *Hour of Gold*, 155, italics added.

44. Ibid., 7, 109, 156, 159; Hermann, *Anne Morrow Lindbergh*, 70, 71; Berg, 219; Hertog, *Anne Morrow Lindbergh*, 138.

45. AML, *Hour of Gold*, "I jumped" quote on 142, "My how" quote on 156.

46. AML, *North to the Orient* (New York: Harcourt, Brace, 1935), 5.

47. CAL, *Autobiography of Values*, 109–10; AML, *North to the Orient*, 10, 140–45; *NYT*, 14 June 1931, SM4.

48. *NYT*, 14 June 1931, SM4; *WP*, 5 June 1931, 6.

49. *NYT*, 13 June 1931, 8, 5 August 1931, 3; AML, *Hour of Gold*, 10–11; AML, *North to the Orient*, 44.

50. *NYT* 25 August 1931, 1, 3, 24 August 1931, 1, 6 June 1931, 3; AML, *Hour of Gold*, 191; Hermann, *Anne Morrow Lindbergh*, 81; Berg, 229.

51. *NYT*, 19 September 1931, 1, 21 September 1931, 8; AML, *North to the Orient*, 117–19, "One dared " quote on 117; AML, *Hour of Gold*, 197.

52. AML, *North to the Orient*, 120, 122–23; *NYT*, 27 September 1931, 1; *WP*, 27 September 1931, M1.

53. *NYT*, 28 September 1931, 8, 3 October 1931, 1; AML, *Hour of Gold*, 199–203; Berg, 231.

54. CAL, *Autobiography of Values*, 129.

55. Berg, 210–12, 348; Robert Rosenbaum, *Aviators: American Profiles* (New York: Facts on File: 1992), 54; CAL, *Autobiography of Values*, 335.

56. David M. Friedman, *The Immortalists: Charles Lindbergh, Dr. Alexis Carrel and the Daring Quest to Live Forever* (New York: Ecco/HarperCollins, 2007), "scientific" quote on 17; CAL, *Autobiography of Values*, 129.

57. CAL, *Autobiography of Values*, quote on 129–30; Milton, *Loss of Eden*, 199.

58. CAL, *Autobiography of Values*, 129–31, "to reduce," quote on 131; Milton, *Loss of Eden*, 199–200.

59. CAL, *Autobiography of Values*, "mysteries" quote on 129, 131–32; Hermann, *Anne Morrow Lindbergh*, 86; Friedman, *Immortalists*, "second only" quote on 4, 6.

60. Friedman, *Immortalists*, 5.

61. Ibid., 7; CAL, *Autobiography of Values*, 131–32, "infection" quote on 133; Berg, 221; Hermann, *Anne Morrow Lindbergh*, 87.

62. CAL, *Autobiography of Values*, "life's limits" quote on 134; other quotes: Friedman, *Immortalists*, 14.

63. Friedman, *Immortalists*, 7.

64. CAL, *Autobiography of Values*, "experiment" quote on 131, "more than" quote on 133.

65. Friedman, *Immortalists*, 25; CAL, *Autobiography of Values*, "a man" quote on 133.

66. Friedman, *Immortalists*, 48; CAL, *Autobiography of Values*, "every detail" quote on 134, 136–37.

67. Friedman, *Immortalists*, 28; CAL, *Autobiography of Values*, 136, 392–93; AML, *Hour of Gold*, "I'm sitting" quote on 158; Milton, *Loss of Eden*, 201–2.

68. Friedman, *Immortalists*, 15, 28.

69. Ibid., 30–40, "What" quote on 39.

70. Berg, 337.

71. Friedman, *Immortalists*, 7.

72. Hermann, *Anne Morrow Lindbergh*, "terrific" quote on 182; Milton, *Loss of Eden*, "decline," and "unassuaged" quotes on 201; Friedman, *Immortalists*, "an error" quote on 30–31, 45, 47.

73. Friedman, *Immortalists*, 9; Alexis Carrel, *Man the Unknown* (New York: Harper, 1935), "Philosophical" quote on 318–19, quoted in Hermann, *Anne Morrow Lindbergh*, 181.

74. CAL, *Autobiography of Values*, "reached" quote on 129, "I felt" quote on 134.

75. Friedman, *Immortalists*, 32–33.

76. CAL, *Autobiography of Values*, "overlapping" quote on 136, 367, "bridges" quote on 373, 396, "After my" quote on 400.

77. Friedman, *Immortalists*, 35, 51.

Chapter 11

1. CAL, *Autobiography of Values* (1998), 320; F. Scott Fitzgerald, *The Crack-Up: With Other Uncollected Pieces, Note-Books and Unpublished Letters, Together with Letters to*

Fitzgerald from Gertrude Stein, Edith Wharton, T. S. Eliot, Thomas Wolfe and John Dos Passos, and Essays and Poems by Paul Rosenfeld, Glenway Westcott, John Dos Passos, John Peale Bishop and Edmund Wilson, ed. Edmund Wilson (New York: New Directions, 1964), 20.

2. Allen, *Only Yesterday,* "idolization" quote on 183; Walter Isaacson, *Einstein: His Life and Universe* (New York: Simon & Schuster, 2007); Delmore Schwartz, "Survey of Our National Phenomena," *New York Times Magazine,* 15 April 1956, "the greatest" quote on 237.

3. Allen, *Only Yesterday,* 183.

4. Thomas Carlyle, *On Heroes, Hero-Worship and the Heroic in History* (London: Chapman and Hall, 1897); Amy Henderson, "Media and the Rise of Celebrity Culture," *OAH Magazine of History,* no. 6 (Spring 1992): 3; Charles L. Ponce De Leon, *Self Exposure: Human Interest Journalism and the Emergence of Celebrity Culture in America, 1890–1940* (Chapel Hill: University of North Carolina Press, 2002); Leo Lowenthal, *Literature, Popular Culture and Society* (Englewood Cliffs, NJ: Prentice-Hall, 1961), 111–16.

5. Richard Schickel, *Intimate Strangers: The Culture of Celebrity* (Garden City, NY: Doubleday, 1985), and *His Picture in the Papers: A Speculation on Celebrity in America Based on the Life of Douglas Fairbanks, Sr.* (New York: Charterhouse, 1974); De Leon, *Self Exposure,* "Please" quote on 36; Daniel J. Boorstin, *The Image: A Guide to Pseudo-Events in America* (New York: Atheneum, 1982), 57–58.

6. De Leon, *Self Exposure,* 39–41, 55–57; De Leon, "The Man Nobody Knows: Charles A. Lindbergh and the Culture of Celebrity," *Prospects* 21 (1996), 369.

7. Maury Klein, *Rainbow's End: The Crash of 1929.* (New York: Oxford University Press, 2001), 8.

8. Wohl, *Spectacle of Flight,* 49; "Why the World Makes Lindbergh Its Hero," "In Lindbergh's" quote on 8.

9. *WP,* 25 June 1927, 5.

10. "Why the World Makes Lindbergh Its Hero," 5.

11. De Leon, "Man Nobody Knows," 357. The concept of the "moral investment" is from Davis, *Hero,* 220.

12. De Leon, *Prospects,* 37; Leo Braudy, *The Frenzy of Renown: Fame and Its History* (New York: Oxford University Press, 1986), 19.

13 F. Scott Fitzgerald, "Echoes of the Jazz Age," in *The Crack-Up,* 20; *NYT,* 11 February 1928, "[A]bove" quote on 31.

14. The phrase is from Braudy, *Frenzy of Renown,* 19. He uses it in a different context.

15. *NYT,* 10 June 1927, "no parent" quote on 22, 30 May 1927, "necking" quote on 18.

16. *NYT,* 12 June 1927, 7.

17. John W. Ward, "The Meaning of Lindbergh's Flight," *American Quarterly* 10 (Spring 1958), 6.

18. CAL, *Autobiography of Values,* "personal" quote on 75; Pisano and van der Linden, *Charles Lindbergh,* 94; Donald E. Keyhoe, *Flying with Lindbergh* (New York: G. P. Putnam's Sons, 1928), 188.

19. *Cincinnati Commercial Tribune,* 7 August 1927, 3; De Leon, "Man Nobody Knows," 350, 351; Marlon Pew, "Shop Talk at Thirty," *Editor and Publisher,* 26 July 1930, 60; "Fame and Privacy," *The Nation* 20 (August 1930): 196.

20. De Leon, "Man Nobody Knows," 353–55, "middle-brow" quote 353, 356; *Cincinnati Enquirer,* 7 August 1927, "have experienced" quote on 16.

21. *Cincinnati Commercial Tribune,* 7 August 1927, 3; 7 August 1927, 1.

22. *CSM,* 2 March 1928,1; *NYT,* 20 June 1927, 1–2, "Once in" quote on 1, 20 June 1927, 1–2, "Lindy's smiling" quote on 1; *LAT,* 17 August 1927, 5, 21 September 1927, A9; *WP,* editorial, 12 August 1927.

23. *NYT*, 25 June 1927, "No shaking" quote on 1, 3; Hermann, *Anne Morrow Lindbergh,* "Silly" quote on 139.

24. Michael Parfit, "Retracing Lindy's Victorious Trip across the Country," *Smithsonian Magazine* 18 (October 1987): "Is it" quote on 208; *LAT,* 25 March 1928, "I can't" quote on 1; CAL letter to H. Breckinridge, 18 September 1927, box 34, folder 1016, CALP; CAL, *Autobiography of Values,* "I felt" quote on 75; Davis, *Hero,* 264.

25. Russell Owen letter to CAL, 1928?, Series 325 I, box 23, folder 647, CALP. Breckinridge wrote that both Col Adler of the *Times* and Guggenheim thought a "gift" to Owen would be appropriate. Indeed Guggenheim thought $1,000 was not enough: "HARRY THOUGHT A LITTLE MORE WOULD BE APPROPRIATE *BECAUSE OF SOUTH AMERICAN ARTICLES* STOP OWEN HAS THIRTEEN ARTICLES PREPARED STOP" (Henry Breckinridge telegram to CAL, 25 September 1928, box 15, folder 116, CALP). In October he sent Owen a check for $1,500 and Owen responded, "I enjoyed doing them with you anyway." But the money was welcome. Russell Owen letter to CAL, 6 October 1928, box 23, folder 647, CALP; CAL letter to Mason, 13 August 1929, box 34, folder 1022, CALP; Davis, *Hero,* 262–63.

26. Luckett, *Charles A. Lindbergh,* 53; Morris Markey, "The Young Man of Affairs, I," *New Yorker,* 20 September 1930, 28; Davis, *Hero,* 265–71.

27. *WP,* 9 August 1927, 1; *Cincinnati Commercial Tribune* 7 August 1927, 3; Gregory, "What's Wrong with Lindbergh?" 32–34, 533, 556.

28. De Leon, *Self Exposure,* 107–29; Berg, "violent" quote on 218; De Leon, *Prospects,* 359.

29. Hermann, *Anne Morrow Lindbergh,* "Is it" quote on 55.

30. AML, *Hour of Gold,* "blaze" quote on 5, "at least" and "we never" quotes on 108, 113; Berg, 200; *NYT,* 26 July 1930, 14; Pew, "Shop Talk at Thirty," 60; Marlon Pew, "Fame and Privacy," *Nation,* 20 August 1930, 195. In CAL, "Comments on Davis," 52, Lindbergh writes of a Morrow servant being offered $5,000 to filch a photo of him, Anne, and the baby.

31. *NYT,* 24 October 1931, 19; Friedman, *Immortalists,* 51.

32. Pew, "Shop Talk at Thirty," 60; Berg, 217–19.

33. Davis, *Hero,* 266; CAL, "Comments on Davis," 45; De Leon, *Self Exposure,* 104, 131; Isaacson, *Einstein,* "If you" quote on 268–69; Braudy, *Frenzy of Renown,* "In nothing" quote on 25.

34. Morris Markey, "Young Man of Affairs, II," *New Yorker,* 27 September 1930, 30–33, "astonishingly" quote on 30.

35. De Leon, "Man Nobody Knows," 359; Markey, "Young Man of Affairs, II," 33.

36. Markey, "Young Man of Affairs, I," 26–29; Markey, "Young Man of Affairs, II," "he spends" quote on 32, 30–33.

37. Wohl, *Spectacle of Flight,* "staggering" quote on 41.

38. Luckett, *Charles A. Lindbergh,* "admired" quote on 18; Berg, "little bit" and "ducking" quotes on 230, "fend" and "There is" quotes on 234; Hermann, *Anne Morrow Lindbergh,* 194.

39. AML, *Hour of Gold,* 231; Berg, "Anne" quote on 240; CAL, *Autobiography of Values,* "I looked" quote on 139.

40. Berg, 246–47.

41. Boorstin, *Image,* "this" quote on 71–72; AML, *Hour of Gold,* 235, 239, 245. Anne wrote to Evangeline on March 6, "We have come to an understanding with two of the biggest men of the underworld" (AML, *Hour of Gold,* 231).

42. Milton, *Loss of Eden,* 237; AML, *Hour of Gold,* 231, "The baby's" quote on 248.

43. AML, *Hour of Gold,* 231.

44. Hermann, *Anne Morrow Lindbergh,* quoting Reeve Lindbergh, 125.

45. *NYT,* 31 September 1934, 4; Berg, 204; AML, *Hour of Gold,* "A long" quote on 250, "like war" quote on 254; Harold Nicolson, *Diaries and Letters, 1930–1939,* ed. Nigel Nicolson (New York: Atheneum, 1966), "real dignity" quote on 184.

46. Berg, quotes on 276, 204, 281.

47. Neal Gabler, *Winchell: Gossip Power and the Culture of Celebrity* (New York: Knopf, 1994), 208–9.

48. AML, *Hour of Gold*, 284; Hermann, *Anne Morrow Lindbergh*, "This morning" quote on 139; Nicolson, *Diaries and Letters, 1930–1939*, 184.

49. *NYT*, 5 January 1935, 1, 14 February 1935, 1.

50. Berg, 330.

51. *NYT*, 3 April 1936, 1.

52. Berg, 275.

53. AML, *Hour of Gold*, "an intense" quote on 303, 313; Berg, 278; CAL, *Autobiography of Values*, 142; CAL letter to editor of United Press International, "Obviously" quote on 16 August 1932, box 34, folder 1028, CALP. "We had not kept Charles Jr. under armed guard. We kept Jon almost constantly under armed guard" (CAL, "Comments, Davis," 58).

54. Hermann, *Anne Morrow Lindbergh*, "not disappoint" quote on 145; Milton, *Loss of Eden*, "the Invincible" quote on 278.

55. Friedman, *Immortalists*, 57.

56. Ibid.

57. Isaacson, *Einstein*, "I am truly," quote on 274, "no gift" quote on 279.

58. Berg, 226, 288.

59. Hermann, *Anne Morrow Lindbergh*, 127; *NYT*, 26 June 1933, 1, 17 December 1933, 1, 2 July 1933, XX7; *WP*, 21 September 1934, 3; AML, *North to the Orient*, 5; Milton, *Loss of Eden*, "As usual" quote on 277; AML, "Flying Around the North Atlantic," *National Geographic* 66 (1934): 259; CAL, *Autobiography of Values*, 140.

60. *NYT*, 9 December 1933, 14, 17 December 1933, 1, 26 September 1933, 23, 24 September 1933, "bourgeois," quote on N1, 25 June 1933, XX7, 23 July 1933, 1, 6 August 1933, 1, 16 August 1933, 9; *WP*, 21 September 1934, 3; Hermann, *Anne Morrow Lindbergh*, 131; Milton, *Loss of Eden*, 279; CAL letter to Juan T. Trippe, 10 December 1931, box 103, folder 263, CALP; CAL letter to Richard W. Robbins, 12 October 1932, box 124, folder 515, CALP; CAL telegram to Richard W. Robbins, 30 November 1932, box 124, folder 515, CALP; draft of report to Trippe, August 1933, box 99, folder 201, CALP; draft of report to Trippe, 15 September 1933, box 103, folder 268, CALP; CAL letters to Juan Trippe, 15 September 1933, 16 October 1933, box 99, folder 201, CALP; CAL letter to Harry Knight, 12 April 1934, box 34, folder 1031, CALP; CAL letter to Pan-American Airlines, 29 May 1934, box 103, folder 271, CALP; Milton, *Loss of Eden*, 281.

61. Milton, *Loss of Eden*, 280; *NYT*, 25 October 1933, "terribly anxious," quote on 21; Berg, "My time" quote on 288.

62. *NYT*, 7 December 1933, 1, 9 December 1933, 14, 13 December 1933, 1, 17 December 17 1933, XX7; Milton, *Loss of Eden*, 281; *WP*, 21 September 1934, 3.

63. Freudenthal, *Aviation Business*, 88, 92–93, 120, 132; *NYT*, 19 July 1932, XX, 13 March 1932, 19, 23 September 1933, 9. See especially *NYT*, 10 September 1933, E1, 26 August 1934, E3, 21 September 1934, 9.

64. C. C. Mosely, "What's Next in Aviation," *LAT*, 14 June 1931, K12.

65. Pecora Report, 110, quoted in Freudenthal, *Aviation Business*, 95, 132; van der Linden, *Airlines and Air Mail*, 106.

66. van der Linden, *Airlines and Air Mail*, 105–6, 108, 132.

67. That is not to say that he was threatened by poverty. His securities portfolio in 1935 stood at $568,000. Memorandum for Mr. H. P. Davison, "Securities of Charles A. Lindbergh, Morgan Bank," 27 March 1935, box 303, folder 13. See CAL, invoice for services, Pennsylvania Railroad, December 1932, box 23, folder 495, CALP; Daniel Sheaffer letter to CAL, 31 December 1932, box 123, folder 495, CALP; Penna. Railroad Co. Statement of Account, December

1932, box 23, folder 495, CALP; *NYT,* 19 February 1934, 1; U.S. Congress, Senate Committee on Post Office and Post Roads Hearings, 73rd Congress, 2nd Session, 1934, p. 142, quoted in Freudenthal, *Aviation Business,* 178; A. H. Geringer letter to AML, 1 February 1932, box 303, folder 10, CALP; *LAT,* 17 October 1934, 9.

68. CAL letter to H. Hoover, October 1932?, box 34, folder 1029, CALP.

69. Walter F. Brown, "Commercial Aviation and the Air Mail," address before the Cleveland Chamber of Commerce, 14 January 1930, quoted in van der Linden, *Airlines and Air Mail,* 114; ibid., 111–13.

70. Ibid., "I do not" quote on 114, 114–16, 125, 208.

71. Ibid., 114–15, 151–57, 165; Hawley, "Three Faces of Hooverian Associationalism," 114; Freudenthal, *Aviation Business,* "I am" quote on 111; Lauren Lyman, "Air Mail Act Spurs the Aviation Industry," *NYT,* 11 May 30, 143; *WSJ,* 26 August 1930, 14.

72. van der Linden, *Airlines and Air Mail,* 114–15, 167, 172–76, 182, 219–25; Freudenthal, *Aviation Business,* 113.

73. Freudenthal, *Aviation Business,* 110; van der Linden, *Airlines and Air Mail,* 169, 185.

74. Freudenthal, *Aviation Business,* 96; van der Linden, *Airlines and Air Mail,* 213–14.

75. Freudenthal, *Aviation Business,* 195.

76. van der Linden, *Airlines and Air Mail,* 260, 261; Arthur M. Schlesinger Jr., *The Coming of the New Deal: The Age of Roosevelt* (Boston: Houghton Mifflin, 1958), 448–50.

77. van der Linden, *Airlines and Air Mail,* 270; *NYT,* 12 January 1934, 3, 17 January 1934, 3, 19 February 1934, 1. The exchange of warrants actually took place in January 1933; C. P. Almeld letter to CAL, 6 January 1933, box 303, folder 11, CALP.

78. In one instance he bought five hundred shares of the Alleghany Corporation, a railroad-related holding company, at $20 per share when it was selling for between $31 and $35 (*NYT,* 25 May 1933, 1). Davis, *Hero,* 294, 496; Schlesinger, *The Coming of the New Deal,* 433–35. Lindbergh's explanation: "I gave the officers of JP Morgan & Co. a completely free hand in administering my account" (CAL, "Comments on Davis," 56). This is doubtful; he generally monitored everything.

79. *NYT,* 11 January 1934, "suddenly" quote on 1, 12 January 1934, 3, 13 January 1934, 3; *LAT,* 12 January 1934, 3; *WP,* 13 January 1934, 22, 19 January 1934, 3.

80. Davis, *Hero,* 332; van der Linden, *Airlines and Air Mail,* 273; *NYT,* 17 February 1934, 7.

81. CAL, *Autobiography of Values,* 141; *NYT,* 12 February 1934, "Your action" quote on 1; *CSM,* 12 February 1934, 1; *WP,* 12 February 1934, 11.

82. *NYT,* 13 February 1934, 1, 15 February 1934, 1, 14 February 1934, "the greatest" quote on 15; Davis, *Hero,* 334; *WP* ,14 February 1934, 8; "wanted to" quote in William Randolph Hearst, "Stuff and Nonsense," 20 February 1934, n.p., clipping in letter from Guy W. Vaughan to CAL, 23 February 1934, box 991, folder 201, CALP.

83. *NYT,* 12 March 1934, 1; van der Linden, *Airlines and Air Mail,* "legalized murder" quote on 277; Davis, *Hero,* 335.

84. van der Linden, *Airlines and Air Mail,* 278–80, 284–85; CAL, *Autobiography of Values,* 142; Berg, 295.

85. *CSM,* 16 March 1934, "one of" quote on 1; *WP,* 17 March 1934, "un-American," quote on 1; *NYT,* 17 March 1934, 1; *LAT,* 15 March 1934, 1; Schlesinger, *Coming of New Deal,* 453.

86. *CSM,* 19 March 1934, 1; Freudenthal, *Aviation Business,* 199; van der Linden, *Airlines and Air Mail,* 290. To his credit, Lindbergh would insist, "It is impossible to over-emphasize the importance of using the best equipment *regardless of by whom it is manufactured*" (CAL letter to Richard W. Robbins, 6 July 1933, box 124, folder 516, CALP, emphasis added).

87. Schlesinger, *Coming of New Deal,* "dented" quote on 455; *NYT,* 15 February 1934, 18; 18 February 1934, E1.

88. Schlesinger, *Coming of New Deal*, all quotes on 454–55. John B. Rae, *Climb to Greatness: The American Aircraft Industry 1920–1960* (Cambridge: MIT Press, 1968), 56–57.

Epilogue

1. *NYT*, 23 December 1935, 1.

2. *Newsweek*, 4 January 1936, 30.

3. Robert A. Rosenbaum, *Aviators* (New York: Facts on File, 1992), "personally distasteful" quote on 56; John Lardner, "The Lindbergh Legends," *The Aspirin Age, 1919–1941* (New York: Simon and Schuster, 1949), "immoral" quote on 306; Roger Butterfield, "Lindbergh: A Stubborn Man of Strange Ideas Becomes a Leader of the Wartime Opposition," *Life*, 11 August 1941, 64; Milton, *Loss of Eden*, 342, 503 n. 14.

4. AML, *Hour of Gold*, 105–6, "Terrible argument" quote on 273, 212.

5. *WP*, 24 December 1935, 8; AML, *Hour of Gold*, 212; Berg, 310, "Well Lindy" quote on 339, "between" quote on 340.

6. *CSM*, 23 December 1935, "Yuletide" quote on 1, 3; *NYT*, 24 December 1935, 1–2, 23 December 1935, 1–3.

7. Meyer Berger, *The Story of the New York Times, 1851–1951* (New York: Simon & Schuster, 1951), 414–19; "A Family Seeks Safety," *Literary Digest*, 4 January 1936, 27; *NYT* 12, December 1935, "and so" quote on 1.

8. *NYT*, 24 December 1935, 1–2; *WP*, 24 December 1935, 8.

9. *New York Daily Mirror*, quoted in *NYT*, 24 December 1935, 2; *New York Herald Tribune* quoted in *NYT*, 24 December 1935, "Barbarism" quote on 2; *NYT*, 23 December 1935, "as though" quote on 1; *WP*, 24 December 1935, 8; *CSM*, 27 December 1935, "press" quote on 18, 24 December 1935, "tumbling Atlantic" quote on 1; *LAT*, 29 December 1935, "refugees" quote on A4.

10. *LAT*, 9 January 1936, A4

11. Quoted in *NYT*, 24 December 1935, 2.

12. *LAT*, 29 December 1935, A4.

13. Berg, 340.

14. Braudy, *Frenzy of Renown*, 21.

15. Wohl, *Spectacle of Flight*, 49–108, quotes on 51.

16. Ibid., "How quickly" quote on 277, 320.

17. *NYT*, 24 July 1936, 1.

18. Hermann, *Anne Morrow Lindbergh*, 187.

19. Hertog, *Anne Morrow Lindbergh*, 297, "magnificent" quote on 299; Berg, "I am beginning" quote on 362.

20. CAL, *Autobiography of Values*, 147; Hertog, *Anne Morrow Lindbergh*, 295–97; Butterfield, "Lindbergh," 67; Lardner, "Lindbergh Legends," 21.

21. Nicolson, *Diaries and Letters*, "the Nazi" quote on 343; "German air strength" quote in J. P. Kennedy letter to Secretary of State, 22 September 1938, box 450, folder 7, CALP; Berg, 375.

22. Berg, 378; Lardner, "Lindbergh Legends," 211; Hermann, *Anne Morrow Lindbergh*, "How" quote on 210.

23. Berg, 381; Davis, *Hero*, 382; L. Mosely, *Lindbergh*, 299–317.

24. CAL, "Aviation, Geography, and Race," *Reader's Digest*, November 1939, 64–65.

25. Ibid., 66–68.

26. Hermann, *Anne Morrow Lindbergh*, "deepest best" quote on 221, "good on" quote on 250, "I shall" quote on 235; De Leon, "Man Nobody Knows," 365–66.

27. Milton, *Loss of Eden*, 387, 409; Davis, *Hero*, 406–7; S. R. Ross, "Dwight Morrow," 318; AML, *Hour of Gold*, 233; Russell Owen, "In the Early Days of Flight," review of Harry Bruno's

Wings Over America, New York Times Book Review, 13 December 1942, "caused" quote on 6; Hermann, *Anne Morrow Lindbergh*, 223, "Nazi lover" quote on 224, 287; Butterfield, "Lindbergh," 75; Lardner, "Lindbergh Legends," 192. Lindbergh denied breaking with Guggenheim and attributed the split with Breckinridge as being in part over the war, adding that Breckinridge himself was not "untouched by anti-semitism" (CAL, "Comments on Davis," 58). Berg, 240, suggests that the break may have been exacerbated by an unpaid loan.

28. Lardner, "Lindbergh Legends," "almost with ferocity" quote on 192; other quotes in *NYT*, 22 October 1939, 29.

29. *WP*, 11 September 1937, 1; Butterfield, "Lindbergh," "evokes a fervor" quote on 67.

30. Davis, *Hero*, 400; Butterfield, "Lindbergh," 23, 69–70; Wayne S. Cole, "Charles Lindbergh and the Battle against Intervention," in *Charles Lindbergh: An American Life*, ed. Tom D. Crouch (Washington, D.C.: Smithsonian National Air and Space Museum, 1977), "the interests" and "subterfuge" quotes on 51–52.

31. Butterfield, "Lindbergh," "sulking" quote on 69–70; Davis, *Hero*, "Lindbergh Line" quote on 382; Boorstin, *Image*, "Palmolive" quote on 73.

32. Cole, "Charles Lindbergh and the Battle against Intervention," 54–55; Boorstin, *Image*, 73; Berg, "lone Ostrich" quote on 409, "somber cretin" quote on 399, 400–402.

33. Berg, 423–24.

34. Ibid., "neither" quote on 414, "ranks" quote on 428, "fifteen" quote on 433.

35. Ibid., "ruthless" quote on 426, 438.

36. Ibid., 449–51; AML, "Changing Concept of Heroes," 309.

37. Hermann, *Anne Morrow Lindbergh*, 286; CAL, *Autobiography of Values*, 361.

38. Michael Collins, foreword in Crouch, *Charles A. Lindbergh*, ix.

39. Hermann, *Anne Morrow Lindbergh*, 282; Berg, 478–80.

40. Berg, 485–87; *NYT*, 29 August 2003, A4, 11 January, 2005, F1, 17 April 2008, F7; Reuters, 29 November 2003.

41. Berg, "The destruction" quote on 470, 487–88.

42. Ibid., 488, 490; Pisano and van der Linden, *Charles Lindbergh*, x–xi; Hermann, *Anne Morrow Lindbergh*, 289.

43. CAL, *Autobiography of Values*, xiii.

44. CAL, *Of Flight and Life* (New York: Charles Scribner's Sons, 1948), quote on 51–52; CAL, *Autobiography of Values*, 282.

45. Judith Schiff, "Values of Flight and Life: The Postwar Activities," in Crouch, *Charles A. Lindbergh*, 71.

46. Ibid., "almost" and "technological" quotes on 79; CAL, *Autobiography of Values*, 377.

47. CAL, *Autobiography of Values*, 272–83, "black men" quote on 284, 285, 354–55, 377, "born" quote on 286.

48. The CAL quotes are from ibid., 385, 390; Hermann, *Anne Morrow Lindbergh*, "large sugary" quote on 204.

49. CAL, *Autobiography of Values*, "lying naked" quote on 396, "beyond" quote on 357.

50. Louis Berg, "The Lone Eagle," review of CAL, *Wartime Journals of Charles A. Lindbergh*, *Commentary* 51 (February 1971), "genuine feeling" quote on 96.

51. CAL, *Autobiography of Values*, "the sensate" quote on 381; Schiff, "Values of Flight and Life," 74.

52. Schiff, "Values of Flight and Life," 74.

53. Ibid., 76.

54. Geoffrey C. Ward, "Fallen Eagle," *New York Times Book Review*, "chronic" quote on 27 September 1998, 14.

55. Carter, *Twenties in America*, 68–69.

SELECTED BIBLIOGRAPHY

Allen, Frederick Lewis. *Only Yesterday: An Informal History of the 1920s.* New York: Harper & Bros., 1931.

Berg, A. Scott. *Lindbergh.* New York: G. P. Putnam, 1998.

Bilstein, Roger E. *Flight in America 1900–1983: From the Wrights to the Astronauts.* Baltimore: Johns Hopkins University Press, 1984.

———. *Flight Patterns: Trends of Aeronautical Development in the United States, 1918–1929.* Athens: University of Georgia Press, 1983.

Boorstin, Daniel J. *The Image: A Guide to Pseudo-Events in America.* New York: Atheneum, 1982.

Braudy, Leo. *The Frenzy of Renown: Fame and Its History.* New York: Oxford University Press, 1986.

Bruno, Harry. *Wings over America: The Inside Story of American Aviation.* Garden City, NY: Halcyon House, 1944.

Burden, William A. M. *Struggle for Airways in Latin America.* New York: Council on Foreign Relations, 1943.

Carter, Paul Allen. *The Twenties in America.* 2nd ed. New York: Thomas Y. Crowell, 1975.

Cassagneres, Ev. *The Spirit of Ryan.* New York: McGraw-Hill, 1982.

Chernow, Ron. *The House of Morgan.* New York: Simon & Schuster, 1970.

Claxon, William J. *Mastery of the Air.* London: Blackie and Sons, Ltd., 1915.

Cole, Wayne S. *Charles A. Lindbergh and the Battle against American Intervention in World War II.* New York: Harcourt Brace Jovanovich, 1974.

Corn, Joseph J. *The Winged Gospel: America's Romance with Aviation, 1900–1950.* New York: Oxford University Press, 1983.

Courtwright, David. *Sky as Frontier: Adventure, Aviation, and Empire.* College Station: Texas A&M University Press, 2005.

Craig, Douglas B. *Fireside Politics: Radio and Political Culture in the United States, 1920–1940.* Baltimore: Johns Hopkins University Press, 2000.

Cronon, William. *Nature's Metropolis: Chicago and the Great West.* New York: W. W. Norton, 1991.

Crouch, Tom D., and Wayne S. Cole, eds. *Charles A. Lindbergh: An American Life.* Washington: National Air and Space Museum, Smithsonian Institution, 1977.

Davis, Kenneth Sydney. *The Hero: Charles A. Lindbergh and the American Dream*. Garden City, NY: Doubleday, 1959.

De Leon, Charles L. Ponce. *Self Exposure: Human Interest Journalism and the Emergence of Celebrity Culture in America, 1890–1940*. Chapel Hill: University of North Carolina Press, 2002.

Eksteins, Modris. *Rites of Spring: The Great War and the Birth of the Modern Age*. New York: Anchor Books, 1990.

Friedman, David M. *The Immortalists, Charles Lindbergh, Dr. Alexis Carrel and the Daring Quest to Live Forever*. New York: Ecco/HarperCollins, 2007.

Freudenthal, Elsbeth. *The Aviation Business: From Kitty Hawk to Wall Street*. New York: Vanguard Press, 1940.

Gabler, Neal. *Winchell: Gossip, Power, and the Culture of Celebrity*. New York: Knopf, 1994.

Gill, Brendan. *Lindbergh Alone*. New York: Harcourt Brace Jovanovich, 1977.

Guggenheim, Harry. *The Seven Skies*. New York: G. P. Putnam's Sons, 1930.

Hallion, Richard P. *Legacy of Flight: The Guggenheim Contribution to American Aviation*. Seattle: University of Washington Press, 1977.

Hardesty, Von. *Lindbergh, Flight's Enigmatic Hero*. New York: Harcourt, 2002.

Hertog, Susan. *Anne Morrow Lindbergh: Her Life*. New York: Doubleday, 1999.

Hixson, Walter L. *Charles A. Lindbergh, Lone Eagle*. New York: HarperCollins, 1996.

Howland, Hewitt H. *Dwight Whitney Morrow: A Sketch in Admiration*. New York: Century, 1930.

Ingells, Douglas J. *Tin Goose: The Fabulous Ford Trimotor*. Fallbrook, CA: Aero Publishers, 1968.

Jablonski, Edward. *Atlantic Fever*. New York: Macmillan, 1972.

Keyhoe, Donald E. *Flying with Lindbergh*. New York: G.P. Putnam's Sons, 1928.

Larson, Bruce L. *Lindbergh of Minnesota: A Political Biography*. New York: Harcourt Brace Jovanovich, 1973.

Lindbergh, Anne Morrow. *Bring Me a Unicorn: Diaries and Letters of Anne Morrow Lindbergh, 1922–1928*. New York: Harcourt Brace Jovanovich, 1972.

———. *Hour of Gold, Hour of Lead: Diaries and Letters of Anne Morrow Lindbergh, 1929–1932*. New York: Harcourt Brace Jovanovich, 1973.

———. *North to the Orient*. New York: Harcourt, Brace, 1935.

Lindbergh, Charles A. *Autobiography of Values*, ed. William Jovanovich and Judith A. Schiff. New York: Harcourt Brace Jovanovich, 1978.

———. *The Spirit of St. Louis*. New York: Scribner, 1953.

———. *The Wartime Journals of Charles A. Lindbergh*. New York: Harcourt Brace Jovanovich, 1970.

———. *We: The Famous Flier's Own Story of His Life and His Transatlantic Flight*. New York: G. P. Putnam's Sons, 1928.

Lomask, Milton. *Seed Money: The Guggenheim Story*. New York: Farrar Straus, 1964.

Lowenthal, Leo. *Literature, Popular Culture and Society*. Englewood Cliffs, NJ: Prentice-Hall, 1961.

Luckett, Perry D. *Charles A. Lindbergh, A Bio-Bibliography*. Westport, CT: Greenwood Press, 1986.

Milton, Joyce. *Loss of Eden: A Biography of Charles and Anne Morrow Lindbergh*. New York: HarperCollins, 1993.

Mosley, Leonard. *Lindbergh: A Biography*. Garden City, NY: Doubleday, 1976.

Mott, T. Bentley. *Myron Herrick, Friend of France: An Autobiographical Biography*. New York: Doubleday, 1929.

Newton, Wesley Phillips. *The Perilous Sky: U.S. Aviation Diplomacy and Latin America, 1919–1931*. Coral Gables, FL: University of Miami Press, 1978.

Nicolson, Harold. *Diaries & Letters, 1930–1939*, ed. Nigel Nicolson. New York: Atheneum, 1966.

———. *Dwight Morrow*. New York: Harcourt Brace, 1935.

Pattillo, Donald M. *Pushing the Envelope: The American Aircraft Industry*. Ann Arbor: University of Michigan Press, 1998.

Pisano, Dominick A., and F. Robert van der Linden. *Charles Lindbergh and the Spirit of St. Louis*. New York: Harry N. Abrams, 2002.

Rae, John B. *Climb to Greatness: The American Aircraft Industry 1920–1960*. Cambridge: MIT Press, 1968.

Rosenbaum, Robert A. *Aviators: American Profiles*. New York: Facts on File, 1992.

Ross, Walter S. *The Last Hero: Charles A. Lindbergh*. New York: Harper & Row, 1968.

Root, Waverly. *The Paris Edition: The Autobiography of Waverly Root*. San Francisco: North Point Press, 1987.

Schickel, Richard. *His Picture in the Papers: A Speculation on Celebrity in America Based on the Life of Douglas Fairbanks, Sr*. New York: Charterhouse, 1974.

———. *Intimate Strangers: The Culture of Celebrity*. Garden City, NY: Doubleday, 1985.

Schlesinger Jr., Arthur M. *The Coming of the New Deal: The Age of Roosevelt*. Boston: Houghton Mifflin, 1958.

Smith, Henry Ladd. *Airways: The History of Commercial Aviation in the United States*. New York: Knopf, 1942.

Solberg, Carl. *Conquest of the Skies: A History of Commercial Aviation in America*. Boston: Little, Brown, 1979.

Tate, James P. *The Army and Its Air Corps: Army Policy Toward Aviation, 1919–1941*. Maxwell Air Force Base, AL: Air University Press, 1998.

van der Linden, F. Robert. *Airlines and Air Mail: The Post Office and the Birth of the Commercial Aviation Industry*. Lexington: University Press of Kentucky, 2003.

Wohl, Robert. *A Passion for Wings: Aviation and the Western Imagination, 1908–1918*. New Haven: Yale University Press, 1994.

———. *The Spectacle of Flight: Aviation and the Western Imagination, 1920–1950*. New Haven: Yale University Press, 2005.

Wilson, Joan Hoff. *Herbert Hoover: Forgotten Progressive*. Boston: Little, Brown, 1975.

INDEX

and CAL's mother, 33
and CAL's pilot training, 31–33, 35–38,
   60, 71, 100, 116
   origin of term, 249n34
   and parachute jumping, 30–31
   and surplus military aircraft, 27
barometers, 85
the Battery (New York City), 126
Battle of Champagne, 101
beacon lighting, 39, 42, 129, 142, 232
Beal, Wellwood, 123
Beech (aircraft manufacturer), 64–65
Belgium, 112
Belize, 157, 158
Bellanca, Giuseppe M., 47, 61–64
Bellanca aircraft, 65–67, 69, 72, 74, 76
Belle Isle, Florida, 177
Bennett, Floyd, 65–66, 167–68, 276n13
Benton, Thomas Hart, 46
Bertraud, Lloyd, 69, 78
B. F. Mahoney Aircraft Company, 167, 168
biographies of Lindbergh, See also *The
   Spirit of St. Louis* (Lindbergh); *We*
   (Lindbergh)
   Buckley on, xvi
   and CAL's finances, 146
   and CAL's late years, 239–40
   and CAL's parenting, 210
   and Fredette, 261n7
   and ghost writers, 135–38, 262–63n39,
      268n57, 268nn60–61
   and patronage of CAL, 140
biomedical research, 194–98, 200, 227, 239
biplanes, 10, 21–22, 40, 66, 126, 189
Bixby, Harold, 37, 60, 63–64, 131–34, 169
Black, Hugo, 219–20
Black Ball Line, 140
Black Hills of South Dakota, 142
Blériot, Louis, 22, 98, 110
blitzkrieg warfare, 228
Blythe, Richard, 80, 81–82, 132, 133, 203,
   265n10
bodyguards, 214
Boeing, William, 171, 172
Boeing Air and Transport Corporation, 166,
   171
Bolling Field, 126, 153, 154
book deals, 134, 135–37
Borah, William, 205
Borden, Mary, 119

Brandewiede, Gregory, 118
Braudy, Leo, 204, 209, 227
Braun, Werner von, 234
Breckinridge, Henry
   as advisor, 180
   alienation from CAL, 231
   and the aviation agenda, xviii
   background, 135
   and CAL biography, 136
   and CAL's business opportunities, 145,
      169
   and CAL's finances, 147
   and CAL's pranks, 190
   and CAL's scientific research, 195
   and CAL's wedding, 187
   and film proposals, 145, 277n19
   and ghost writers, 276n13, 284n25
   and kidnapping, 212
   and promotion of commercial aviation, 146
   relationship with CAL, 287–88n27
Briand, Aristide, 107
Britain. *See* England and Great Britain
Brooklyn Chamber of Commerce, 67
Brooks Field, 33–34, 70
Broun, Heywood, 123, 161
Brown, Arthur Whitten, 53, 114
Brown, Elmer Ellsworth, 162
Brown, Walter Folger, 177, 217–20, 278n49
Brown, William Adams, 186
Bruno, Harold, 80, 132, 133, 203, 265n10
Brussels, Belgium, 112
Bryan, William Jennings, 16
B-24 Liberator bombers, 233
Buckley, William F., Jr., xvi
Buckman, Clarence B., 6–7
Bureau of Aeronautics, 77
Bureau of Air Navigation, 50
Burwell, Harvey S., 153, 154
Butterfield, Roger, 229
Byrd, Richard E.
   America accident, 65–66
   and aviation tours, 140
   and CAL's flight, 84, 98, 123
   and the Orteig competition, 63, 74, 76, 81,
      86, 101–2
   polar flight, 36, 51, 54
   and support for aviation, 60
   transatlantic flight, 65, 114–15
   and Washington celebrations, 124
   and Wright engines, 72

congratulatory note to CAL, 106
and consolidation of aviation industry, 219
and Dwight Morrow, 148
and Fonck flight, 55
Hemingway on, xvii
and Latin America relations, 151–52, 155–56
and military commission for CAL, 130
and Morrow, 133
and promotion of commercial aviation, 50
response to CAL's flight, 117
State of the Union address, 152
Coolidge, Grace, 122, 125
Corn, J. J., 28, 77–78
Corrigan, Douglas, 75
Costa Rica, 157, 178
Coughlin, Charles, 231
Crane Commission, 219
crashes. *See* accidents and crashes
Cronon, William, 59
Crosby, Harry, xvi, 96
Cross of the Legion of Honor, 109
Croydon Airport, 113
Cuba, 157, 159–60, 171, 178
Curtin, Lawrence, 55, 56
Curtiss, Glenn, 23, 47–48
Curtiss Aeroplane. *See also* Curtiss-Wright Corporation
and amphibious aircraft, 52
and CAL's role in commercial aviation, 168–71
Falcon biplane, 189
hawk pursuit planes, 126
JN-4 aircraft, 27, 31–32, 33, 37, 252n9
and legal battles, 249n25
NC-4 aircraft, 123
P-1 pursuit biplane, 126
and status of American aviation, 46
and stock prices, 154, 165, 168, 170
and support for Orteig competitors, 80
and TAT, 169
and transatlantic designs, 47–48
Curtiss Airfield, 77
Curtiss-Wright Corporation, 171, 277n33, 278n33

Daedalus, 20
Daily Mail (London), 52

Daily News (tabloid), 227, 280–81n24
Damien Agricultural College, 159
dangers of flying. *See also* accidents and crashes; weather
and airmail service, 37, 40–43, 189, 221, 258–59n101
and barnstorming, 27, 31–33, 36, 38, 57, 136
and CAL's Latin America tour, 159
and entertainment aviation, 24, 27
European vs. U.S. aviation, 45–46
fatigue, xv, 91–94, 138, 258–59n101
and Latin America tour, 156–57
and military training, 35
and night flying, 39, 41–42, 72, 76, 81, 153, 221
and parachutes, 30–31, 35–36, 38, 57–58, 70, 175, 192, 251–52n94
Daniel and Florence Guggenheim Foundation, 50, 147
Davies, Marion, 145
Davis, Dwight F., 116
Davis, Kenneth S., 146
Davis, Noel, 65, 66
Davison, F. Trubee, 119
Davison, Harry, 173
Davison, Henry, 48
Death Valley, 142
de Havilland aircraft, 25, 35
Delage (French pilot), 103–4, 105
democracy, xix, 119, 198, 225, 227, 229–33
Dempsey, Jack, xvii
dentistry, 10
Denver Rocky Mountain News, 162
Department of Aviation (proposed), 144
Department of Civil Aviation (Britain), 50
Department of Civil Aviation (Mexico), 155
Depression (economic), 209–10, 220, 224–25, 238
der Arbeitsmann, 231
Detroit Free Press, 87
Detroyat (French pilot), 103–4, 105
Deutsch de la Meurthe, Rana, 109
DH-4 aircraft, 40, 41–42, 70–75
Diaz, Adolfo, 151
Dingle Bay, Ireland, 93
diplomacy and foreign relations
and CAL biography, 261n7
CAL's impact on, 161–62
and CAL's political views, 232

flying boats. *See* amphibious aircraft
flying circuses, 24, 26–29, 38
Foch, Ferdinand, 109–10
Fokker, Anthony
    and the *America* accident, 65–66
    and American aviation, 47
    and amphibious aircraft, 267n39
    and consolidation of aviation industry, 172
    and multiple-engine aircraft, 49
    and the Orteig competition, 76, 86
Fokker Company, 51, 61, 177
Fonck, René, 25, 54–56, 57, 61, 63
Food for Victory Program, 15
Ford, Edsel, 48–49
Ford, Henry
    and airline conglomerates, 168
    and airmail service, 48
    and aviation reliability tours, 49
    and CAL's father, 15
    and CAL's Mexico trip, 154
    and flight with CAL, 142
    and mechanical engineering, 17
    and military aircraft, 233
    and support for aviation, 59
Ford Motor Company, 169, 233
foreign relations. *See* diplomacy and foreign
    relations
Fortune, 177
41st Squadron, 42
Foulois, Benjamin D., 220
France
    awards given CAL, 107
    and CAL's flight, xvi, 89, 95–97, 98–100
    and CAL's politics, 230
    CAL's reception in, 96–97, 98–101, 103–5,
        106–12
    and commercial aviation, 166
    and English Channel flights, 22
    and European aviation, 45
    Foreign Office, 107
    French Air Force, 53
    and German rearmament, 229
    and military aircraft, 45
    relations with the U.S., 100–101, 103, 105,
        107–9, 111
    and route surveys, 216
    and support for aviation, 23, 25, 44, 50
    and transatlantic attempts, 53–54, 65–69,
        76, 82, 99, 106
    and World War I, 25, 53

Franklin, Benjamin, 109
Fredette, Raymond H., 261n7
Friedman, David M., 195
fuel consumption, 71–72, 82, 255n12
Fund for the Promotion of Aeronautics,
    50–51

Garbo, Greta, 227
Gatty, Harold, 188
Gehrig, Lou, 128
gender equity, 187–88
General Aviation Manufacturing
    Corporation, 172
General Motors, 172
genocide, 238, 239
George V, King of England, 113
Germany
    and all-metal aircraft, 48
    and American aviation, 47
    and American diplomacy, 100–101, 117,
        119
    and CAL's flight, xvii
    and CAL's politics, 15, 228–32, 234
    captured warships, 27
    and commercial aviation, 45, 49, 151, 166
    and government support for aviation, 25
    and rearmament, 45, 216, 228–29
    and South American aviation, 151
    and transatlantic flights, 49, 114–15
    and World War I, 25
Gibson, Hoot, 46
gifts given to Lindbergh, 145, 167, 267n38
Gill, Brendan, xvi
Gilman, Charlotte Perkins, 28
Gimbel, Ellis A., 115
gliders, 189
Goddard, Robert H., 194
Goldwater, Barry, 243n1
Gómez, Juan Vicente, 158, 159
Good Neighbor policy, 161
Göring, Hermann, 229
government support for aviation.
        See also World War I; World War II
    and airmail service, 57, 177, 218, 219,
        221–22
    and airports, 27, 45, 51, 120, 171, 275n4
    in Europe, 24–25
    France, 23, 44, 50
    and German rearmament, 45, 216,
        228–29

marriages, 2–3, 3–4, 5–6, 6–7
and monopolies, 173
and politics, 6–7, 13–14, 32, 223
and race issues, 12
Lindbergh, Charles Augustus
affairs, 234
awards and honors (*see main entry*)
birth of, 4
childhood, 1, 4–13, 180
dating and courtship, 183–84
discipline and work ethic (*see main entry*)
education, 4, 10–13, 14–16, 16–18
engagement, 185–86, 208
family background, 1–16
first flight, 30
first plane, 31–32
homes of, 1, 5, 191
military service (*see main entry*)
and parachute jumps, 35–36, 42, 57–58, 70, 251–52n94
and parenting, 210, 234, 239
perfectionism, 88
political ideology, xix, 225, 227–29, 230–33, 237, 239–40
race issues (*see main entry*)
spiritual beliefs, 236–37
wedding, 186–87
Lindbergh, Eva (half sister), 3, 13–14
Lindbergh, Evangeline (mother)
and the aviation reliability tour, 143
and birth of CAL's child, 191
and CAL's marriage, 185, 214
and CAL's move to England, 225
and CAL's return to the U.S., 122
and childhood of CAL, 1, 5, 12–14
correspondence with CAL, 34
and discipline of CAL, 204–5
and education of CAL, 11, 18, 19
and flight exhibitions, 10, 29
and home fire, 6
marital problems, 7–8
and mental issues, 12
and Mexico City trip, 154–55
notification of flight success, 106
and the Orteig competition, 67, 79, 89
and Paris phone call, 107
and personality of CAL, 180
on piloting as career, 32
and Washington celebrations, 124
Lindbergh, Jon (son), 214, 225, 227

Lindbergh, Lillian (half sister), 3, 13
Lindbergh, Mary (father's first wife), 2–3
Lindbergh, Reeve (daughter), 212, 234
Lindbergh Alone (Gill), xvi
"Lindbergh on Flying" (column), 144, 167
Linde, Harm von, 72–73
Lindholm Manor, 1
Lippmann, Walter, 149, 227, 231
Little Falls, Minnesota, 2, 3–4, 6–7
Littlefield, B. H., 42
Lloyds of London, 84, 89–90
Lockheed Company, 188
Locklear, Ormer, 46
Lodge, Edwin Albert, 3, 4
l'Oiseau Blanc (the *White Bird*), 67–69, 76–77, 102
London Daily Mail, 23
London Times, 23
Long, Huey, 231
long-distance flying
and airmail, 37
and the aviation reliability tour, 143–44
and British aviators, 108
and CAL's flight, 51–52, 86–97, 201
and *Columbia* flight, 114
and early records, 24
and endurance records, 74
and fuel consumption, 72
and multiple-engine aircraft, 54, 70
longitude, 248n13
Longworth, Nicholas, 147
Los Angeles, California, 142
Los Angeles Chamber of Commerce, 142
Los Angeles Times
aviation columns in, 144
on the aviation reliability tour, 143
on CAL's celebrity, 122
on CAL's flight, 89
on CAL's move to England, 226
on New York celebrations, 128
Love, Philip, 142
Luft Hansa, 45, 49
Lutfwaffe, 228
Lyman, Lauren "Deak," 207, 224, 226, 276n15
Lynch, Harold, 30–32, 33

Maben, Georgia, 32
MacCracken, William P., Jr., 81, 159, 162, 218

death, 193–94
on engagement of CAL, 185
and film proposals, 277n19
and finances of CAL, 134–35
and Mexico ambassadorship, 147–52, 154, 160–61, 181
and the Morrow Committee, 49–50
and promotion of aviation, 140, 146, 147
Morrow, Dwight, Jr., 181
Morrow, Elizabeth, 181, 182, 195
Morrow Committee, 49–50
Morrow Report, 50
Moscow, Russia, 216
Mount Taylor, 176
Mulligan, Ed, 80
multiple-engine aircraft, 54, 70. *See also* trimotor planes
Musser family, 4
Mussolini, Benito, 45–46, 118, 212, 227–28
mythological figures in aviation, 20

Nagasaki, Japan, 228
Nanking, China, 193
The Nation, 161
National Aeronautic Association, 65, 73, 82
National Air Races, 255n12
National Air Transport Corporation, 48, 168, 169, 171–72, 217
National Aviation Program, 146
National Flood Relief Commission (China), 193
National Geographic, 276n13
National Geographic Society, 147
nationalism, 68, 99, 119, 123
National Press Club, 125
National Research Council, 131
nature preserves, 238
Navaho Indians, 188
naval aviation, 67
navigation
and Anne Lindbergh, 190, 191–92
and beacon lighting, 39, 142
and CAL's studies, 73–74
and compasses, 54, 85, 91, 115, 138, 258n88
courses over the Atlantic, xv, 55, 74, 87–89
and dead reckoning, 108
and design of *Spirit of St. Louis,* 71–72
and government regulations, 81

and the great circle path, 51–52, 55, 66, 69, 74, 257n66
and Latin America tour, 153, 154
and longitude, 248n13
and passenger service, 174
and railroads, 40
Navy High Hat Acrobatic Team, 188
Nazism and CAL, xix, 228–33
NC-1 aircraft, 52
NC-3 aircraft, 52
NC-4 aircraft, 52–53, 65, 123, 174
Nebraska Aircraft Corporation, 29
Nelson, Thomas, 189
neutrality movement, 230, 231, 233
New, Harry S., 46, 48, 125, 156, 165
New Deal, 220
New Republic, 205
newspapers and news media. *See also* publicity and public relations; tabloid press; *specific publications*
and advertising, 132
attention to aviation, 59
aviation columns, 144
and the aviation reliability tour, 141–43
and birth of Lindbergh child, 191
on CAL's awards, 166–67
and CAL's columns, 167
CAL's distaste for, 206–7, 224, 262–63n39
and CAL's engagement, 185–86
on CAL's flight, 89–90, 99–100, 102–3, 106–7
and CAL's Mexico visit, 153, 158
and CAL's move to England, 224–27
and CAL's return to the U.S., 123–24
and CAL's time in Paris, 107, 110, 111–12
and CAL's wedding, 186–87
and celebrity of CAL, 129–30, 205
depiction of CAL, 207–8
and flying contests, 23
and interviews with CAL, 107–8, 117, 146
and kidnapping trial, 213
and Latin America tour, 152–53
newsreel films, 130, 208
and the Orteig competition, 79–80
and promotion of aviation, 60
and Wayles, 261n18
and the *White Bird* flight, 69
Newton, Wesley Phillips, 161
New York American, 23, 56
New York City, 22, 94, 125–29, 146

Russia, 216, 228, 229, 234–35. *See also*
    Soviet Union
Ruth, Babe, xvii, 128
Ryan, Claude, 28
Ryan Aeronautical
    and CAL's flight, 81, 85, 89, 94
    CAL's negotiation with, 63–65
    and CAL's return to the U.S., 131
    and construction of *Spirit of St. Louis,*
        70–76
    and replacement for *Spirit of St. Louis,*
        167

Sacco, Niccola, 101
Sackville-West, Vita, 210, 213
Sandinista guerrillas, 157
Sandino, Augusto César, 151
San Jose Rotary Club, 158
Santa Fe Railroad, 176
Santo Domingo, 157
Saturday Evening Post, 235
Scadta (Sociedad Colombo Alemana de
        Transporte Aéreo), 151, 156, 177
Schiff, Jacob, 148
Schiff, Mortimer, 148
Schlesinger, Arthur M., Jr., 222
Schwab, Charles, 128
Science, 200
sciences and scientific research, 11, 194–97,
        199, 200, 235
Scientific American, 23, 24, 51, 67
seadromes, 130
sea power, 27
Senate Banking Committee, 219
Service Cross of the Order of the German
        Eagle with Star, 229
The Seven Skies (Guggenheim), 134
Sharkey, Jack, 89
shipping by air, 141
shortages, 25
Siegfried, André, 101
Sikorsky, Igor, 47, 54–56, 58, 65
Sikorsky aircraft, 54–56, 58, 65–66, 171, 178
Sirius aircraft, 188–93, 215
skydiving, 41
The Skyman (film), 46
Smith, Al, 127, 170
Smith, Dean, 41
Smithsonian Institution, 7–8, 147
Snow, C. P., 209

social Darwinism, 198
social impact of aviation, 28
Sociedad Colombo Alemana de Transporte
        Aéreo (Scadta), 151, 156, 177
South America, 49, 156, 160, 177, 178.
        See also Latin America
Soviet Union, 228, 234–35. *See also* Russia
space program, 236
speed records, 190–91
Spirit of St. Louis (aircraft)
    and autobiography title, 268n61
    and aviation promotional tour, 134,
        140–41
    construction of, 70–75
    cost of, 71
    design considerations, xv, 71–73, 75, 82,
        86–87, 119, 279–80n1
    financing for, 133
    given to the Smithsonian, 167
    Goldwater on, 243n1
    instrumentation in, 85, 90–91, 114–15,
        138
    and Latin America tour, 153, 154
    naming of, 63
    NX prefix, 75
    press photography, 203
    reassembled in the U.S., 126
    return to Mitchell Field, 129
    swastika symbol on, 74
    weight of aircraft, 71–72, 74, 85, 243n1
    words of tribute, 94
Spirit of St. Louis Corporation, 133
The Spirit of St. Louis (Lindbergh), 235,
        268nn60, 61
Spoils Conference, 218, 221–22
sponsorships for the Lindbergh flight, 59,
        62–63
Square du Havre, 99
St. John's, Newfoundland, 89
St. Louis, Missouri
    and airline corporations, 169, 175
    and airmail routes, 37, 39–40, 57, 69
    and air races, 33
    and beacon lighting, 39
    CAL's return to, 144
    and celebrations of CAL's flight, 129–30
    and early aviation, 37
    and museum collection, 167
    and passenger service, 175
    and politics of CAL, 232